I0867681

THE WISDOM OF YOUTH

Essays Inspired by the Early Work of Jacques and Raïssa Maritain

THE WISDOM OF YOUTH

Essays Inspired by the Early Work of Jacques and Raïssa Maritain

EDITED BY TRAVIS DUMSDAY

AMERICAN MARITAIN ASSOCIATION

Distributed by
THE CATHOLIC UNIVERSITY
OF AMERICA PRESS
Washington, D.C.

Copyright © 2016 American Maritain Association
All rights reserved
Manufactured in the United States of America

Distributed by the Catholic Univesity of America Press
620 Michigan Avenue, N.E., 240 Leahy Hall
Washington, D.C. 20064

Library of Congress Cataloging-in-Publication Data
The wisdom of youth : essays inspired by the early work of Jacques
and Raïssa Maritain : / edited by Travis Dumsday.
pages cm
Includes bibliographical references and index.
ISBN 978-0-9827119-8-9
1. Maritain, Jacques, 1882–1973. 2. Maritain, Raïssa, 1883–1960.
3. Catholic Church and philosophy. 4. Catholic philosophers.
I. Dumsday, Travis, editor.
B2430.M34W57 2016
194—dc23 2015022684

This volume is dedicated to the memory of one of its contributors, Matthew S. Pugh (1955–2015), who passed away towards the end of the publication process. His death is a loss not only to his family, friends, and Providence College, but also to the broader community of Thomistic scholars.

Contents

Acknowledgments

I would like to extend my sincere thanks to Michael Torre and Giuseppe Butera for their kind offer to edit this latest contribution to the AMA book series, and for the unfailing support shown me throughout the effort. Each individual contributing author is also owed great thanks; as the reader will quickly discern, these are quality works that could have found a home in many a prominent venue, and we are so pleased that they chose to publish with us. Much is owed too to the committee of anonymous referees who evaluated the many submissions to this volume (many more than could be accepted). Though I cannot of course thank the committee's members publicly here, they know who they are and can rest assured that their work is very much appreciated. Gratitude is also due to Peter Koritansky and James M. Jacobs, both editors of previous AMA volumes, for helpful advice. I would also like to thank Anne Kachergis for the beautiful job she did with the cover art. Finally, my work on this volume was completed thanks in part to funding from the Canada Research Chairs program.

TRAVIS DUMSDAY

Introduction

The Wisdom of Youth

Jacques and Raïssa Maritain are unquestionably among the most important Catholic public intellectuals of the twentieth century. Jacques' stature within contemporary Thomistic philosophy remains unparalleled. His staggering output encompasses original contributions to metaphysics, the philosophy of nature, natural theology, aesthetics, ethics, political theory, and epistemology. Raïssa's own literary output similarly places her in the highest ranks of contemporary Catholic poets and memoirists; moreover her contributions to Thomistic thought are by no means negligible. In addition to her vital role as a discussant in the Maritains' Thomistic Circle from 1914 onwards, and her own theological publications (especially with respect to Christian thinking on Judaism), it was of course she who first turned Jacques onto St. Thomas.

Over and above their published works, the Maritains contributed to Catholic intellectual and spiritual life by way of their unique witness. In their earliest years together as undergraduates at the Sorbonne, they displayed a passionate commitment to discovering truth. That commitment served to carry them step by step from their initial metaphysical naturalism to a spiritual view of reality (under the influence of Henri Bergson), and finally to the Christian faith. Upon their reception into the Catholic Church they entered into a joint apostolate of friendship, opening themselves and their home to a truly diverse array of philosophers, painters, poets, scientists, students—really anyone with an interest in truth, whether believers or non-believers. The fruitfulness of their continued commitment to this activity over the course of decades (and through harrowing trials of severe illness and wartime dislocation) is evident in the sheer number of conversions that flowed from it. These conversions were not the product merely of the Maritains' facility with sophisticated arguments for the truth of the faith (though that facility remains of perennial importance), but of their genuine love for others. Their many personal friends—and many more correspondents, who often formed deep attachments to the Maritains—attest clearly to this. As the cause of their canonization progresses (however slowly and haltingly), the amassing of documents pertaining to their heroic virtue will likewise continue, no doubt resulting in a still more complete picture of the impact of their joint witness, both within their own lifetimes and since.

Given that this witness began so early in their married life, it is particularly fitting to consider the lives and works of the *young* Maritains: hence the overarching theme of the present volume. Some of the contributing authors connect with this theme very explicitly, focusing on aspects of their early life together and their early writings (and those of important interlocutors like Bergson and Garrigou-Lagrange). In other chapters the connection is less explicit, but throughout the link remains, insofar as each piece engages in some way with the Thomistic tradition that the Maritains came to devote themselves to so early in their intellectual careers.

The volume is divided into six sections. In what remains of this introduction I will provide a short précis of each contribution, in order of their appearance. Information about the authors themselves can be found in the "Notes on Contributors" section toward the end of the book.

The first section begins with Florian Michel's "Jacques and Raïssa Maritain: Reputation for Holiness and Spiritual Fruitfulness." Michel uses the tools of historical scholarship to explore the heroic virtues of the Maritains and the astonishing breadth and depth of the impact they had on their contemporaries. He also takes the opportunity to makes some important methodological points concerning the ways in which academic historians can contribute to the relevant work preceding a cause for canonization.

In "A Life Shared: The Complementarity of Jacques and Raïssa Maritain," Prudence Allen begins by providing some conceptual analysis of the notion of complementarity, and the history of the term's usage (especially in modern Catholic thought). She then proceeds to examine the myriad ways in which, through both their writings and their lived witness, the Maritains exhibited the genuine complementarity between man and woman. In the course of doing so she provides fascinating insights on their married life and on the impact that life had on their work as scholars and public intellectuals.

Brenna Moore explores the neglected political dimensions of Raïssa's literary output in "Out of the Shadows: Raïssa Maritain on Poetry and Making Violence Visible." Focusing in particular on Raïssa's wartime poetry, Moore argues that this work carries profound political implications by constituting clarion calls for justice and for the protection of the Jewish people during the Holocaust. Far from being apolitical or divorced from the traumas of the day, this poetry is intended to supply a human face to the sufferers, and to evoke empathy on the part of the Catholic reading public for their Jewish brothers and sisters. These works remain some of the only French Catholic art of the period designed for this purpose. Moving beyond that particular historical circumstance, Moore proceeds to consider the broader, continuing lessons to be drawn from Raïssa's strategy of employing art in the pursuit of social justice.

In "Simone Weil: Love of God, Affliction, and a New Saintliness," E. Jane Doering delves into Weil's writings on evil and the human response to severe affliction. According to Doering, Weil's claim is that the demands of genuine compassion call for a new kind of sanctity, one that truly engages with the suffering of the afflicted (where that affliction encompasses both physical and psychological torments). Relatedly, Christians must learn a new attitude towards their own suffering, such that they can interpret it not merely as useful for other ends, but as something that can carry with it intrinsic meaning and even a kind of beauty. Along the way they must remain ever mindful of the fact that severe affliction, while a testing ground for some, often serves to rob others of all traces of faith.

In "The 'Annex' to Maritain's 1914 Lectures on 'The Spirit of Modern Philosophy': The Role of Germany in Modern Philosophy," Michael Torre turns to a neglected portion of Jacques' early published work. The 'annex' on German thought was written during the early days of World War I, at a time when the French had already suffered staggering battlefield losses. They were seen by Jacques as his own unique contribution to the war effort (his attempt to join the army, having been foiled by a health issue). He did not revisit this material in his own later work, and the secondary literature has said almost nothing about it. Nevertheless it remains of considerable biographical interest and sheds light on aspects of Jacques' early thinking. Torre here explores it in detail, both in its own right and in relation to the larger set of lectures on the history of modern philosophy, of which it is a part.

Matthew Pugh, in "Maritain, Critical Realism, and the Intuition of Being," begins by summarizing some common Thomistic critiques of Jacques Maritain's view concerning the metaphysical intuition of being. He then proceeds to address some of these by laying out what exactly that intuition is for Maritain, and likewise what role it plays in his epistemology. According to Pugh, for Maritain the metaphysical intuition of being is at the foundation of all our knowledge, and especially of our knowledge of metaphysics. The intuition is in fact implicit in all our acts of knowing. As such it has a crucial role to play in Thomistic epistemology.

Very much in contrast to Pugh's chapter, John Wippel argues in "Maritain and Aquinas on Our Discovery of Being" that Maritain is incorrect in his contention that an intuition of being is a part of Thomistic epistemology (let alone a foundational part). Wippel argues that the metaphysical intuition of being is absent from Aquinas' own texts; moreover, this absence is not a consequence of some oversight on the part of St. Thomas, but rather results from the fact that the existence of such an intuition would be incompatible with Thomistic epistemology properly construed.

"Maritain and Dewan on the Intuition of Being and the Birth of Metaphysics" sees Jason West defend Maritain's claim that the intuition of being is the appropriate place of departure for the science of metaphysics. Specifically, that claim is defended against an objection formulated by Lawrence Dewan, O.P. Dewan argues that by assigning the mind's encounter with being to the act of judgement, Maritain makes too sharp a divide between ordinary experience and metaphysical knowledge. West replies that Maritain offers a much more dynamic and interactive presentation of the roles of abstraction and judgment than this objection seems to admit.

Doug Flippen, in "The Non-Abstractive and Non-Conceptual Character of Poetic Intuition in Maritain," explores a different aspect of Maritain's broader perspective on intuition. Specifically, Flippen discusses Jacques Maritain's longstanding interest in the question of how the human intellect is involved in the appreciation of, and creation of, fine art. Attempting to explain the role of the intellect in this, Maritain posits a twofold operational life for the intellect: in the first, the intellect is informed by an intelligible likeness abstracted from a phantasm. In its second life, the intellect is informed by a spiritualized, but not abstracted, sensible emotion. As informed in this latter fashion, the intellect is obscurely pointed, not to common aspects of reality, but to that singular thing which caused the emotion. In this second life, the intellect is able to enjoy, but especially to create, some *singular thing*. To understand the intellect's second life, one that is non-abstractive and non-conceptual, Maritain unites sense and intellect as closely as possible while striving to preserve their differences. Flippen argues that this unitive attempt fails for lack of clarity, and suggests a strategy for improving the account while still preserving some of Jacques' central insights on poetic intuition.

Mark Moes draws connections between Jacques Maritain's critique of Bergsonism and Socrates' critique of Heracliteanism in "Metaphysics, Epistemology, and Theology in Plato's *Theaetetus* 151d–187e and in Maritain's *Bergsonian Philosophy and Thomism.*" Moes further explores how Maritain's discussion of Bergson's philosophy of intuition links in with Maritain's later writings on eastern mysticism; along the way he summarizes Maritain's attempt to reconcile the reality of Buddhist and Hindu mystical experience (with its often *prima facie* pantheistic content) with Christian orthodoxy.

Heather Erb, in "Springs of Abundant Life in the Philosophical and Theological Orders: Maritain, Bergson, and Aquinas," contrasts the concept of "life" in Henri Bergson and Thomas Aquinas. Specifically, she examines the various critiques of Bergson's philosophy of religion based on his final work, *The Two Sources of Morality and Religion* (1932), and traces the concept of *vita* (in relation to *ordo* and *visio spiritualis*) in Aquinas's philosophical and theological works. Aquinas's use of the analogous concept of *vita* illumines the correlation he envisions between the natural and supernatural orders, and between natural, ascetic, and mystical theologies. Bergson, in contrast, gives limited scope to natural and revealed theology in his philosophy of religion, and diminishes the nature of moral obligation as understood by scholastics. Both Jacques Maritain and his Dominican mentor, Reginald Garrigou-Lagrange, critique systems such as Bergson's that divide experience from reason and mysticism from natural theology. Erb explores this critique in depth, along the way illuminating various facets of the Thomistic perspective on mystical experience and its relation to both natural and revealed theology.

"Maritain's *Aufhebung* of Bergsonian Intuition" sees Bernadette O'Connor clarifying the relationship between the understanding of intuition in Jacques Maritain and Henri Bergson. O'Connor argues that Maritain's critique of Bergson on intuition is only partial, insofar as Maritain seeks not to overturn wholly Bergson's account, but instead to preserve the best of it. He does so specifically by reconceiving Bergsonian intuition as poetic inspiration rather than a source or instrument of metaphysics.

John Deely's "Gilson, Poinsot, Maritain, and the Future of Thomism" is a clarion call for two things: greater recognition of the vitally important role that John Poinsot (John of St. Thomas) played in Jacques Maritain's understanding of Thomism, and a corresponding increased engagement with Poinsot's ontology of signs, and indeed of relations more broadly. That ontology carries significant implications for the Thomistic view of persons, categories of being (in particular the need to move beyond a fixation on the substance/accident distinction as the principle division of being), and even trinitarian theology.

In "Christian Philosophy: Reconciling the Temporal and the Eternal," James Jacobs looks at three examples of prominent apologetic strategies (two historical and one recent), evaluating them in light of Thomistic philosophical principles, in particular the analogy of being. He argues that the underlying apologetic methods employed by Descartes and Alvin Plantinga, while very different from each other, both incorporate serious philosophical errors. These errors both diminish their ultimate utility as challenges to secularism, and, more importantly, carry certain risks of misconstruing theological doctrines. Jacobs contrasts these with what he sees as the more salutary efforts of Cardinal Newman, who, though not an explicit exponent of Scholastic philosophy, manages not to deviate from orthodoxy in his method of challenging atheism.

"Why are there Minds in the Universe?" This is the question taken up by James Schall, S.J., in his chapter. What is the purpose of conscious, finite beings inhabiting this universe? Could God have made a universe physically identical to our own, with the one exception that no intelligent life ever arises in it? Schall argues that such a universe, devoid of finite intellects, would be incomplete in a manner genuinely defective; hence God would not create such a universe. The universe is made to be known and admired not only by its creator but by free finite intellects, whose own good is bound up with that task of knowing (and loving each other and their Maker).

"Scale, Anonymity, and Political *Akrasia* in Aristotle's *Politics* 7.4," by Joshua Schulz, articulates and defends Aristotle's argument in *Politics* 7.4 that there is a rational limit to the size of the political community. Aristotle argues that size can negatively affect the ability of an organized being (*any* organized being, natural or artificial) to attain its proper end. After examining the metaphysical grounds for this principle, Schulz proceeds to defend Aristotle's extension of it to the political realm. He takes up the idea that the state is in the relevant sense an organism, one with a proper end and hence a proper function. The size of a *polis* can affect its ability to perform this function, whether negatively or positively. Here Schulz argues that excessive growth promotes anonymity among citizens, such that individual voting citizens come to lack personal knowledge of public figures, especially politicians. That lack of knowledge inhibits voters' ability properly to evaluate the characters of those seeking public office. More broadly, excessive state size frustrates the personal familiarity between citizens required for the exercise of distributive and restorative justice, since it is more difficult to discern who is owed what. Schulz suggests several ways in which Aristotle's argument, if sound, is important for contemporary issues in moral psychology, Rawlsian political philosophy, and big data analytics.

Heidi Giebel and Benjamin Huff contribute to the understanding of Thomistic virtue theory in "Justice, Benevolence, and Friendship: A Confucian Revision to Thomistic Ethics?" There they discuss a potential challenge to Aquinas' categorical scheme of the virtues, one arising out of the ethics of Mencius. Specifically, Mencius posits benevolence as a cardinal virtue, whereas Aquinas does not. Yet there seem plausible reasons for going with Mencius on this, even reasons arising from aspects of Aquinas' own moral system. After considering several potential strategies for reconciling Aquinas and Mencius on this point, Giebel and Huff settle on the idea that justice/fairness and benevolence both be categorized as two principal species of what they term a "super-cardinal" virtue, that of justice-fellowship. They argue that this new categorization supplies a more plausible location for benevolence within Thomistic ethical theory, and further serves to resolve certain existing puzzles within it.

In the final chapter, "St. Bonaventure, St. Thomas, and Eudaimonism," Daniel Shields examines the objection that Aristotelian eudaimonism is fundamentally flawed because fundamentally egoistic, as it posits one's own happiness (conceived as the fulfillment of one's nature) as the ultimate end of the moral life. This objection might *prima facie* be thought to carry over to the axiologies of prominent Scholastics. However, Shields argues that both Bonaventure and Aquinas sidestep it (though in somewhat different ways). Neither St. Bonaventure nor St. Thomas Aquinas are, strictly speaking, eudaimonists, insofar as neither holds that one's own happiness is the ultimate end of the moral life. The ultimate end is rather a common good, namely God Himself as He is in Himself. Happiness is the activity by which one attains God, and so it is the *penultimate* end of the moral life, an "end under an end (*finis sub fine*)." St. Bonaventure indentifies this penultimate end as charity, for he who loves God has God. Loving God unites one to Him, and is thus what happiness principally consists in. St. Thomas, on the other hand, identifies the penultimate end as knowing God, not loving Him. Nevertheless, because God Himself, and not one's activity of knowing Him, is one's ultimate end, it is better to love God than to know Him, for love draws one away from oneself and towards God. St. Bonaventure and St. Thomas thus put forward an ethics of humility, in which one's own perfection is radically subordinated to God.

These essays collectively form a powerful demonstration of the ongoing influence of the Maritains on Christian scholarship, and, more broadly, of the vitality of contemporary Thomistic thought.

I

JACQUES AND RAÏSSA

Models of Sanctity

FLORIAN MICHEL[1]

Jacques and Raïssa Maritain

Reputation for Holiness and Spiritual Fruitfulness

I. Introduction

This study seeks to connect two elements, distinct in themselves and yet closely tied together in the life of the Maritains, to answer the following question: how are the links made between the "reputation for holiness" and the "spiritual fruitfulness" of the Maritains? When Jacques Maritain died at Toulouse on April 11, 1973, there was a strong feeling, according to the witnesses, that "it is a saint that we are burying." The same one who wrote to Jean Cocteau in 1926 that God had "turned him inside out like a glove" upon his conversion had become, on the ecclesial level, in the words of Paul VI in 1973, "a master in the art of thinking, living, and praying,"[2] and on the academic and historiographical level the model par excellence of the Catholic intellectual in the twentieth century.[3]

1. This essay was translated from the original French by Fr. Gerald Twadell.

2. Pope Paul VI, Angelus message of 29 April 1973, published in *Osservatore Romano, Documentation Catholique,* and *Cahiers Jacques Maritain* [*CJM*], Kolbsheim, nos. 4–5 (1982): 59. John Paul II, who in a message of 15 August 1982 considered Maritain "one of the most significant heralds of reason," wrote similarly: "Maritain was truly a master. It is for that reason that his thought agrees in an exemplary way with the great project of the Magisterium of the Church for the contemporary era." *CJM,* Kolbsheim, nos. 4–5 (1982): 60–62.

3. See Claude Langlois, "La naissance de l'intellectuel catholique," in *Intellectuels chrétiens et Esprit dans les années 20,* edited by Pierre Colin (Paris: Cerf, 1997), 213–33; Ralph McInerny, *The Very Rich Hours of Jacques Maritain. A Spiritual Life* (South Bend, Indiana: University of Notre Dame Press, 2003).

The reputation for holiness, which in canonical terms has a very strict definition,[4] is situated for the historian at the intersection between the individual history of a man and the communal understanding of the demands of Christian living at a given moment. The intellectual and spiritual fruitfulness of the Maritains is very closely connected to their reputation for holiness. These are two mutually supporting elements, both cause and effect. If the wake of the Maritains is rich in conversions and baptisms, it is precisely because of their reputation for holiness, which acted like a magnet. It was a holiness verified and strengthened by these conversions. One converted and/or sought baptism in order to enter the Church with the Maritains in the genealogy of the "great friendships" because one had a sense that theirs was a "new style" of being Christian, which opened up a horizon. While the press sometimes whispers rumors of the opening of the process of canonization of the Maritains—such as the French and Roman newspapers in February 2011—it is important to define the position that the historian, without resorting to hagiography, could assume on the question of the circular causality between the "fruitfulness" of the Maritains and the "reputation for holiness" which surrounds them. There cannot be a question of yielding to a gilded legend, nor of denouncing a blackened legend. The road is narrow,

4. We might begin with *Dictionnaire de droit canonique*, edited by Raoul Naz (Paris: Letouzey et Ané, 1942), s.v. "Causes de béatification et de canonisation." This article summarizes clearly the provisions of the code of canon law of 1917: the informational process has for its object to establish the reputation for holiness of the servant of God, supported by the "spontaneous report," "originating with serious and honest persons" (c. 2050, § 2); at least eight witnesses are required to establish the reputation for holiness; but extra-judiciary testimony, including funeral eulogies, have no probative force. The 1983 reform of canon law envisages (c. 1403) that the causes of canonization of the Servants of God are governed by a particular pontifical law, published under John Paul II, in the Apostolic Constitution *Divinus perfectionis magister* of 25 January 1983 and in the norms of 7 February 1983. The definition of the "reputation for holiness" does not change: see the letter of Benedict XVI to the members of the plenary assembly of the Congregation for the Causes of Saints, 24 April 2006: "This reputation which the Code of Canon Law of 1917 wanted to be *'spontanea, non arte aut diligentia procurata, orta ab honestis et gravibus personis, continua, in dies aucta et vigens in praesenti apud majorem partem populi'* (c. 2050, §2), is a sign from God which indicates to the Church those who merit being placed 'on the pedestal' and to shine 'for all those who are in the house' (Matt. 5:15)." The principal characteristics of the reputation for holiness are therefore both the spontaneity of the witnesses, "honest and serious persons," and a continuous and widespread diffusion among a significant part of the people of God. See also and especially the instruction *Sanctorum Mater* (2007), which in article 4 defines the reputation for holiness as "the wide opinion among the faithful concerning the purity and integrity of life of the Servant of God and the heroic degree of his virtues," and which in article 7 repeats the formal characteristics of the reputation for holiness as they had already been defined in the 1917 Code of Canon Law.

but it has been followed successfully for other historical periods and it raises the hope that the question of contemporary holiness can legitimately become an object of study for the academic historian.

This proposal is built around three principal points, each of which deserves to be studied in depth for its own sake. These are only avenues and suggestions for future work. The first part will take up methodological and biographical matters. The second will attempt to establish the chronology and some of what is at stake in the reputation for holiness of the Maritains. The third section will examine the conversions and baptisms which marked the life of the Maritains. Jacques Maritain himself wrote in the preface to *Raïssa's Journal*: "I also see why the struggle was so brutal and so rapid, baptisms were raining down, blows also." The "blows" have been studied by historians—multiple crises of Catholicism, the crisis of the *Action française*, the crisis of collaboration, and neo-modernist crisis, the fall of France, betrayals, weaknesses and hardenings of friends, and so forth. But the conversions, the baptisms, the "gifts from heaven," as Raïssa pointed out in *We Have been Friends Together*, were not lacking, and the godchildren, not unlike divine grace, belong to the many.

II. Methodological and Biographical Remarks.

In terms of historical writing it must be recognized that it is not easy to treat this *fama sanctitatis* as an historian. To simplify the matter, there are two distinct issues. A first series of problems, which will not be considered here since they belong to the area of juridical and canonical expertise, arise from the "reputation for holiness" considered in view of a process for canonization. From this point of view it is necessary to establish objectively, with official criteria, the virtuous and exemplary life, the orthodoxy of the writings, and posthumous miracles, all to be considered by the competent Roman congregation. The reputation for holiness is but one aspect of the canonization process. The second series of problems concerns the *vox populi.* These take into account the "reputation for holiness" without the finality of official approbation, and consequently remain on the level of "holy rumor." The letters, testimonies, or articles written and published by witnesses, whose probative force can be quite weak on the judicial level, offer items that can be mobilized and analyzed by the historian. It is principally a question of the "reception" of the personage and work of Maritain. To be complete, it would also be necessary to consider as well those elements that are both contrary and corollary to this reputation for holiness. The "black legend," that of the "intransigent Maritain," the anti-modern philosopher, who had acquaintances with *Action française*, or who was lacking in charity because of his "too brutal" intellectual or apostolic "vehemence," contradicts, without neutralizing it, the "red legend," that of the "liberal Maritain," the Thomist prodigal son, unfaithful to his first masters, who became a "traitor" in 1926 by following the papacy, in 1938 by denouncing the Spanish nationalists, in 1944 by becoming an ambassador of the Christian-Democrat French Republic, and so on. Some integrist religious do not hesitate to denounce the "unworthy" end of Maritain and to send him to hell.[5] In terms of hagiographical writing, these elements could nevertheless be cited in support of that which they attempt to deny. What could be more common than that the "saint" suffers not only "calumny" but calumny spread by a certain number of clerics? The line of Joan of Arc always passes through an episcopal burning at the stake. The historian ought to bring necessary clarifications to those different levels. The efforts of Maritain historiography over the past fifteen years in Italy and France has tried to serve this purpose.

The second, more biographical, remark is about the theme of fruitfulness of the Maritains that their contemporaries were the first to underline. Thus François Mauriac in *Le Figaro* of 11–12 July 1948 noted: "The fidelity [of the Maritains for their vocation] has made of their modest home [in Meudon] one of perhaps the most fruitful centers of spiritual life in France and even Europe. In their home, knowledge turns to love: the order of the spirit rejoins the order of charity, therein lies the whole secret; for whoever says fidelity is saying charity." Charity alone is fruitful, and the question, paradoxical only in appearance for a couple who since 1912 had sought "to renounce the flesh in order to give themselves more exclusively to Jesus,"[6] and who had "renounced the hope of surviving in sons or daughters,"[7]

5. See in this regard Jean-Dominique Fabre, *Le Père Roger-Thomas Calmel (1914–1975), un fils de saint Dominique au XXe siècle* (Suresnes: Clovis, 2012), 594–95. Close to the Lefevrist movement, Fr. Calmel, O.P., in an article entitled "Extravagances maritainiennes," published in the review *Itinéraires* (March 1974): 193, wrote thus: "We had wished for Maritain an end so much more worthy of his first friends, his first masters: Psichari, Fr. Clérissac, Fr. Garrigou-Lagrange, men eminent by their faith, holiness, attachment to the Tradition."

6. Jacques Maritain, "Amour et amitié," in *Œuvres complètes* [*OC*] (Paris: Éditions Saint Paul, 1992) 13:744. See Jacques Maritain, *Carnet de notes* (Paris, DDB, 1965); *Approches sans entraves* (Paris: DDB, 1973).

7. The phrase of Jacques Maritain is found in the unpublished version of *Raïssa's Journal*, 1962, but is suppressed in the published edition, *OC*, 15:175.

takes on a great significance: it permits Jacques and Raïssa Maritain to be understood in the human and existential perspective that they held most dear, that of "great friendships," of "adventures in grace," of conversion, of filiation by adoption, and in a certain number of cases by baptism. The Catholic intellectual intends, like a midwife, to take up the pen to "deliver" minds and hearts, so that the Kingdom might arise in the domain of culture by a fermentation or an extraction. The theme, classic with the Maritains, is that of the "apostolate of the pen."[8] For Maritain it is a question of "attacking the devil on his own ground" and of "pulling down from their places" "the principalities, powers and rulers of this world of darkness"[9] by injecting Christian values into the heart of the world of secular culture: the arts, literature, and poetry.

Testimonials regarding the success of the Maritains are not lacking. Among dozens of others, one can take that of Étienne Gilson who, in a lovely letter of January 1953, sought to console Maritain who was suffering doubts: "What is marvelous is that in spite of everything your word has found so many echoes in so many hearts and minds freely won over to these permanent truths. From the time that they have once more become themselves in you, they have again begun to germinate and flower.... I am the ideal witness to assure you that your work is great, true, salutary, fruitful."[10] Or again there is this letter written to Raïssa Maritain by one of their friends, after the publication of the second volume of *We Have been Friends Together* in November 1944: "Even more than the earlier volume, I surprised myself by sobbing in reading the story of the death of your father. Every part of it is equally beautiful. Everything goes straight to the heart, everything is true, pure, strong, dazzling. Bless you for the good that you have done me and that you will do to many other souls. You could not offer more perfect thanks for so many beautiful adventures in grace."[11] The book of philosophy, the autobiography, the article or the poem, which are so many testimonials to grace received, extend, share, and carry on the same grace throughout the community of readers.

In his note on "Love and Friendship," first published in *Nova et Vetera* in 1963, then once more in the *Carnet des notes* in 1965, Jacques Maritain

8. Jacques Maritain, "L'apostolat de la plume", *OC*, 6:97–101.

9. Jacques Maritain, "Avertissement", *Journal de Raïssa* (Paris: DDB, 1963), 13; Jacques Maritain, "Foreword," *Raïssa's Journal* (Albany, New York: Magi Books, 1974), 13–14.

10. See *Correspondance Maritain-Gilson* (Paris: Vrin, 1991), 182–84.

11. See *Correspondance Maritain-Simon. Les Années américaines*, vol. 2 (Tours: CLD, 2012), 169.

wrote thus: "The spiritual companionship between spouses to aid each other mutually in moving towards God found itself strengthened and realized in a superior fashion in a wild love for God. As for the other essential end, procreation, it was not refused but transferred to another level, it was a spiritual progeny that these spouses awaited from God, and it was to that that they devoted themselves. *Centuplum accipietis* [You will receive a hundredfold]."[12] There should be no doubt that in writing these lines Maritain simply gave thanks for the "hundredfold" that Raïssa and he had been able to receive and for which the historian can, in some slight degree, give an account.

III. "Fama sanctitatis"

The most direct way to evoke the reputation for holiness of Jacques Maritain is to begin at the end, Easter Saturday 1973, at Toulouse among the Little Brothers of Jesus. Contemporary testimonies provide evidence that those who surrounded "Brother Jacques" had the intimate conviction of burying a saint. At present there are at least four published testimonials about the final days of Maritain—three from Dominicans, the fourth published by a Little Brother of Jesus. Sr. Marie-Pascal, the Dominican who served as secretary to Maritain, and who was the last to speak with him, in June 1973 composed for Cardinal Journet a brief account of Jacques' last day. Jean-Yves LeLoup, a defrocked Dominican, pays homage, to hear him tell it, a bit like that which shadow pays to light, in his autobiography, published in 1991 under the title *L'Absurde et la Grâce. Fragments d'un itinérance*. Fr. Jean-Miguel Garrigues, O.P., presents a fuller and more substantial testimony in his autobiography, published in 2007 under the title *Par des sentiers resserrés. Itinéraire d'un religieux en des temps incertains*. Lastly, Maurice Maurin published in 2012 several pages on the death of Jacques Maritain in his work *Vivre la fraternité au coeur du monde*—that testimony can be prolonged by some fragments from the Little Brothers published in the *Cahiers Jacques Maritain* no. 66. All the testimonials converge in evoking

12. Jacques Maritain, *Carnet des notes* (Paris: DDB, 1965), 348; Jacques Maritain, *Approches sans entraves* (Paris: DDB, 1973), 235. The full passage in the Gospel of Matthew (19:29) is as follows: "And everyone who has given up houses, or brothers or sisters or father or mother or children or lands for the sake of my name will receive a hundred times more, and will inherit eternal life."

the *ultima verba* and indicating with adequate precision the ecclesial circumstances of the philosopher's death.

The difference between the great age of the one who was departing and the youth of the Dominican monastery of Rangueil, marked by the charismatic renewal and the Paschal feasts celebrated with a bit of "holy folly" that year, is striking. In the uncertain ecclesiastical times at the threshold of the 1970s, Maritain saw a deep consolation. He received the Sacrament of the Sick on Holy Thursday, was able to assist at the Easter Mass, and expired the following Saturday. Sr. Marie-Pascale wrote: "I saw Jacques for a long time on the eve of his death. He had asked me to come to give me his mail, but then he kept me and we spoke as two friends. He was in his easy chair, full of light and sweetness, and lucidity as well. I particularly shared with him the celebration of Easter such as we had just experienced it with our brother Dominicans: the liturgy, the presence of groups of young charismatics, the encounters, the prayer meetings, the visit of Bishop Guyot.... Jacques was enthusiastic and saw there an authentic sign, a hope for God's action in his Church."[13] From the testimony of Br. Maurice Maurin one will remember the charity that Jacques displayed toward all those around him, and especially his scruples regarding the Dominican sister, reproaching himself for exploiting her labours.

According to the witness of Fr. Garrigues, at Easter 1973 eight hundred guests from the charismatic movement were at the monastery of Rangueil: "In the lodge opposite the Repository, Maritain was suffering from angina and all those who knew him were praying for him. From time to time, a Little Brother would whisper in our ear news of his state. He did not die, even seemed to improve all the while saying that he was going to die and, after an Easter week spent in putting his affairs in order and saying his goodbyes, he suddenly expired without agony on the Saturday of Easter."[14]

In 1991, Jean-Yves Leloup bore witness to his encounter with Maritain: "Anyone who allowed himself to be gazed upon by Jacques Maritain came away washed as by a fountain and scrubbed as with a massage glove. That happened to me several times. So much love and so little complacency! I remember one of his remarks: My little one, have the heart hot, but keep

13. Letter published in *Correspondance Maritain-Journet*, vol. 6 (Paris: Saint Augustin, 2008), 753–54.

14. Jean-Miguel Garrigues, *Par des sentiers resserrés. Itinéraire d'un religieux en des temps incertains* (Paris: Presses de la Renaissance, 2007), 219.

the mind cold.... I will not forget the time of meditation that was given me to live near him. Teilhard de Chardin speaks about prayer as a considerable energy. This energy, I have felt almost palpably in the chapel of the Little Brothers when Jacques Maritain was praying. For me, it was almost unbearable, I am happy to believe in God and remain in the light of faith; I have a hard time bearing the moments when I am not able to deny his evidence. Jacques Maritain made God 'evident.' One understands then that while he fascinated some, he made others flee."[15]

From the hand of Fr. Garrigues one finds similar elements:

> I arrived at Toulouse at Christmas 1972 and Maritain died at Easter 1973. I therefore saw him for only a few months. He was 90 years old but he had maintained an astonishing intellectual vitality. He no longer gave to the Little Brothers of Jesus more than 'seminars,' in the course of which he spoke very freely of his research in one or another area of philosophy or faith. But the acuity of his mind had remained intact.... I was able to see him very often at Mass at the monastery where he willingly came, because he especially liked the liturgical music that Brother André Gouzes composed. I also liked to catch a stealthy glimpse of Brother Jacques during the hours of exposition of the Blessed Sacrament, recollected in adoration at the back of the chapel of the Little Brothers. His thin and wrinkled face, translucent as an icon, haloed in hair white and luminous as snow, was animated by forget-me-not blue eyes of incredible intensity. His youthful spirit made him interested in the charismatic renewal which was unfolding at Rangueil under his very eyes, and it was to question us about this that he received us, Brother Albert-Marie [de Monléon] and me, in the lodge where he lived with two other brothers. He told us on that occasion that he would like to be young, to take a guitar and go sing about Jesus in the cafés. Whoever encountered him could not help being struck by his attentive listening, as well as by his wisdom and interiority. At the same time, everything in him expressed a true humility.... Each day he spent several hours in adoration or in silent meditation.[16]

A detailed description of the burial and celebrations at Toulouse and Kolbsheim would be valuable but we will only mention two points: the remarks delivered, and one of the readings chosen by Cardinal Journet for the Mass at Kolbsheim. The Cardinal, his old friend, himself in his eighty-third year, read on this occasion a fragment taken from Maritain's *De l'Église du ciel* from 1964, where there was a discussion of the "unnoticed saints"

15. Jean-Yves Leloup, *L'Absurde et la Grâce. Fragments d'un itinérance* (Paris: Albin Michel, 1991), 161–62.

16. Garrigues, *Par des sentiers resserrés*, 215.

and the "uncanonizable elect." In an obvious way the Cardinal referred this page of Maritain back to Maritain himself, including him among the blessed, who "are at one and the same time our contemporaries and who form a kind of fringe by which the Church of Heaven is at every generation in contact with the time that passes and in so to say, physical, or if you prefer, psychological, continuity with the Church militant."[17] Maurice Maurin also reports the private and public comments of Cardinal Journet: "Many people heard him say: 'Jacques: that is holiness; that is a saint!' Shortly after, he declared on the radio: 'Jacques Maritain, how many sufferings he endured! What tenderness of heart he had! What pity for sinners! How many souls did he lead to the Church, to the truth of the Gospel, to the love of Jesus! It was an immense train of light.'"[18] Sr. Marie-Pascale also wrote to Cardinal Journet in June 1973 that Maritain had lived with "two saints," to which the Cardinal replied that he could not "think of the three except to pray to them."[19]

Beyond the testimonials of spring 1973 and the circle of close friends, the question needs to be asked about the "reputation for holiness" of Jacques Maritain over a longer timeframe. It is not a matter of anticipating the judgment of the Church, but of recognizing this "reputation" as a fact to be historically situated, and to follow it as well in the press, the autobiographies published, and the private correspondence. As early as August 1937, in a letter, Charles du Bos developed the theme and made an attempt to clarify the nature of the Maritainian holiness:

> I read while still in Switzerland your admirable text: *De la guerre sainte....* When *Religion et culture* appeared, I said to myself that the study that I would hope so much that life and strength might permit me one day to write about you would be entitled: *Jacques Maritain et de la sainteté de l'intelligence*. More and more, to the very extent that events never cease to become more complicated and to develop their atrocious cacophony, this holiness becomes in you a sort of martyrdom, for it *is* one for the intelligence to have to make and remake the point daily, and the luminous, unshakable patience, with which, in the face of any event at all, and no less before any audience whatsoever, you reestablish the truth in its purity.[20]

17. See *Correspondance Maritain-Journet*, 6:751.

18. Maurice Maurin, *Vivre la fraternité au cœur du monde* (Paris: L'Harmattan, 2012), 250.

19. See *Correspondance Maritain-Journet*, 6:755–56. The third member of this trio was Raissa's sister, Véra.

20. Letter of Charles Du Bos to Jacques Maritain, August 1937, Maritain Archives (MA), Bibliothèque Nationale et Universitaire de Strasbourg.

In December 1938 in Chicago, then in March 1939 at the University of Notre Dame, Charles du Bos delivered the promised conference talk entitled "Jacques Maritain and the holiness of intelligence."[21] In 1954, the Dominican Jean de Menasce wrote in the New York review *Commonweal*: "While I do not belong to the Congregation of Rites, I hold Maritain to be a saint. But his holiness is not that of a monk, nor of a priest, and I cannot imagine him in those states of life."[22] On 18 November 1972 under the pen of Carlo Bo, the Italian newspaper *Corriere della Sera* published an article entitled "Maritain, il Santo dell'Intelligenza." A friend of Maritain wrote in 1973 in a Canadian paper that an authentic American altar would soon contain the burnt relics of the Canadian Jesuit martyrs, and a piece of chalk held by Maritain. Maurice Zundel testified to the extreme spiritual importance of his encounter with Maritain in the review *Nova et Vetera* in 1974:

> I cannot think of Jacques Maritain without experiencing the radiance of a serene and diaphanous virginity. Eminent philosopher by profession, mystic by vocation, his entire person spoke of God who was the Life of his life. The rock-solid rigor of his thought is an aspect of his genius, but it cannot reveal what his presence by itself was capable of communicating. Never did grace appear to me more gracious than through his visage which it imbued with its beauty. The supernatural seemed in him so natural that one could not see his body itself except in the light with which he was clothed.... No one was more fraternal, more apt to understand the difficulties which mark out our journey toward God.... That is why I call upon him spontaneously as the most harmoniously holy being that I have ever encountered.[23]

In the autobiographies of those who knew Maritain and in the correspondence exchanged, one picks up again converging elements. Hélène Iswolsky reported in *Light before Dusk*: "From his books I knew only a severe philosopher and an ardent polemicist; he was, however, sweetness itself. It shone from his gray and luminous eyes, on the delicate forehead, in the pensive smile.... It was a kind of radiance."[24] Elizabeth de Miribel in *La liberté souffre violence* is more explicit still: "In Maritain's house, all is at peace. One goes into his living room as into a sanctuary. Maritain impressed me

21. Charles du Bos, "Jacques Maritain and the holiness of intelligence," published in translation as "Jacques Maritain ou la sainteté de l'intelligence," *Cahier Charles du Bos*, no. 23 (June 1979): 7–16.

22. Jean De Menasce, "Not the philosopher, but the man," *Commonweal*, New York, June 11 1954, p. 243.

23. Maurice Zundel, "Jacques Maritain, un homme vierge," *Nova et Vetera* 1 (1974): 1–2.

24. Hélène Iswolsky, *Au temps de la lumière* (Montréal: L'Arbre, 1945), 86.

deeply. Of average height, rather frail, he had just enough body to retain his soul. He seems to have stepped down from the entrance of a cathedral."[25] According to Anne Fremantle, a friend of the Maritains at Princeton, Maritain was palpably a saint.[26] Maurice Sachs wrote: "When the door opened, I saw entering a man who resembled all the images of Christ."[27] The same theme is developed bringing forward the metaphor no longer of a saint but of "spice": "The Maritains threw pepper in the eyes and nose. A healthy sneeze shook a whole Catholic clan. One began to live again, for one always lived intensely with the Maritains; they were the spice of the modern French Church."[28] Thomas Merton was struck at his first meeting with Maritain, described in *Seven Storey Mountain*, as an impression of "tremendous kindness and simplicity and godliness."[29] Writing for the *Figaro littéraire* in November 1963, Mauriac seems to accord healing powers to the Maritains: "The wounded and the dead, one saw falling about them, and they gathered them up, and they healed many, and resuscitated some.... He and Raïssa were contemplatives, but in full battle. They possessed God, they overflowed with Him, but it was to the addicts of literature that they gave their life.... I believe now that Maurice Sachs is saved, that certain failures at Meudon will only have been in appearance, and that Raïssa and Jacques will be joined together before the Father with all their flock. Not one will be lost."[30]

Testimonials in personal writings are not lacking either. Ernest Psichari on 7 October 1913 thus wrote: "The good God loves you much, beloved brother, and He does not protect you from trials, as He is accustomed to do with those He has truly chosen. For my part, I see nothing else in the tribulations that are sent to you than a new proof of the election that so obviously has marked the two of you." He likewise wrote in a letter of 25 February 1913: "For you, my great brother, you are so much a child of God that I consider all the evils that befall you as necessary stages towards holiness."[31] Julien Green, after one of his last meetings with Maritain, entered

25. Elizabeth de Miribel, *La liberté souffre violence* (Paris: Plon, 1981), 58–59.

26. Anne Fremantle, *Pilgrimage to People* (New York: David McKay, 1968), 135.

27. Maurice Sachs, *Le Sabbat* (Paris: Corréa, 1946), 146, cited in *CJM*, 4–5 (1982): 45.

28. Ibid.

29. Thomas Merton, *The Seven Storey Mountain* (New York: Harcourt, Brace and Company, 1948), 219.

30. François Mauriac, *Bloc-notes, Figaro Litteraire*, Paris, November 1963.

31. Letter cited in *CJM*, 4–5 (1982): 38.

in his notebook on 5 October 1970: "His face maintains that angelic expression that I have seen in him since 1925 and which makes him so dear to me."[32] Certain tributes are touching. From a slightly naïve student at Chicago in 1939: "Doing a study on contemporary French thought I would like to include that of Jacques Maritain. Could you help me by telling me what place he holds in the University? Is he a philosopher, a man of science, or a saint? I attended his conferences at the University during his visit to Chicago; and I admire his absolute faith. Is that typical today?"[33] A goddaughter from New York wrote: "I have tried to be like Jacques, that is, like Jesus. I have managed to be nothing but Emily."[34] After reading *Raïssa's Journal* she further wrote: "The result will be the canonization of Raïssa. It cannot be otherwise. She is one of the greatest saints and mystics of all time. From her youth, God has prepared her for Himself."[35] A friend organized a collection for the health of Maritain whose halo seemed just as large as that of St. Thérèse in the eyes of the young students of a high school seminary in the southern United States.[36] Another, whose marriage was threatened, asked nothing less than a miracle. From the depths of her distress she wrote: "Then I thought of you who are so good and who at the same time, as an intelligent saint, know the problems of the world and the cares of men who are not so good."[37] And a month later she continued: "I am afraid that a miracle will be needed. Could you not do one, dear Jacques?"[38] Maritain's reply was both humble and charitable: "If I could accomplish a miracle, never would I be more desirous of showing healing powers. But I am a poor, weak man, with just a deep affection for the two of you."[39] And an-

32. Julien Green, *Journal*, 5 October 1970, *O.C.*, vol. 5 (Paris: Gallimard, coll. Pléiade, 1976), 576.

33. Letter of Laura Dodd to John Nef, 15 February 1939, Maritain Archives, Bibliothèque Nationale Universitaire de Strasbourg, [MA].

34. Letter of Emily Coleman to Jacques Maritain, 24 November 1951, MA.

35. Letter of Emily Coleman to Jacques Maritain, 4 May 1962, published in Claire Coleman, *Une amitié américaine, Jacques et Raïssa Maritain–Emily Holmes Coleman, 1942–1971* (Paris: DDB, 2013), 262.

36. Letter of John Griffin to Jacques Maritain, 18 July 1959, MA: "I read a part of your letter to our young seminarians at Mount Carmel—they put their pennies back in their pockets with disappointment. They are mostly Mexican and Louisiana-French youngsters. You would have been touched. They have never read you—too young yet—but your name is a legend with them, of course. Helping you would have thrilled them only slightly less than if they had been called on to help the Holy Father or Saint Thérèse."

37. Letter of Maude Hutchins to Jacques Maritain, 21 April 1947, MA.

38. Letter of Maude Hutchins to Jacques Maritain, 20 may 1947, MA.

39. Reply of Jacques Maritain to Maude Hutchins, to June 1947, MA.

other wrote to thank him and ask for a relic: "I am human and have a body, I want something personal of yours, for instance your signature. I am sure it sounds childish but let us think of it as a type of relic, a relic of the saint of the intellect.... The major purpose of this letter is to thank you for giving order to my life."[40] A letter of Julien Green to Maritain speaks with all the purple force of the poet: "I know you well enough to know that you do not care for any admiration. Allow me to say at least that I admire God in you. You offer us the wide avenues of your soul and I see there only the light."[41]

Neither Raïssa nor Véra are forgotten in the canonization process of the Maritains. From a friend suffering from cancer who felt the pause in his pain one can read from the spring of 1960: "I turned toward Véra. I said to her: 'Was it you who did this, dear Véra?' And it seemed to me that she replied: 'No, my dear Yves, it is the Lord,' an answer that seems so much like her, don't you think? But tell me: is this the first miracle of Véra, or has she done some others? Really, it is not a miracle in the proper sense, but it is the equivalent in many respects."[42] Yves Simon, Jacques Maritain, and Charles Journet were personally convinced that Véra had "passed to the side of those to whom one prays."[43] Likewise Jean Cocteau upon reading *Raïssa's Journal* remarked: "She is a secret saint, a queen of the invisibility of true poetry."[44]

An American friend, Marshall Suther, another student of Maritain, offers another testimony: he is not Catholic, but he was opened to hope and to the transcendence of life thanks to the Maritains. He writes: "You and Raïssa have given me twenty years of—of what? Twenty years of hoping for the possibility of not being completely lost. During this whole time I even had the impression of being the instrument of something good, and I had confidence because without exception in those cases I had the impression of acting in a way that you had taught me. I believe I am saying this without any sentimental exaggeration—you have made me exist. I believe that you will understand, and I do not want to be writing you a book.... It is to you and to Raïssa that in a very real sense, I owe this hope."[45] In the course of his correspondence with Maritain one can sense that he is making his way little by little towards the faith: "I am beginning almost to believe that I

40. Letter of Stephen Weglian to Jacques Maritain, 6 September 1961, MA.
41. Letter of Julien Green to Jacques Maritain, 27 March 1965, MA.
42. Letter of 27 February 1960, *Correspondance Maritain-Simon*, 2:511.
43. Ibid., 509–10.
44. Letter of Jean Cocteau to Jacques Maritain, Christmas 1962, MA.
45. Letter of Marshall Suther to Jacques Maritain, 20 December 1960, MA.

have a little bit of faith," he wrote in 1965.[46] "There is not much news. No, that is not true; there is the fact that the persons for whom I asked prayers from you and Raïssa in moments of crisis are doing admirably well at the moment.... Raïssa and I are having quite a few conversations."[47]

The public or private testimonies do not all present the same sharpness of analysis. Certain ones are no more than the evocation of the "light" or the "angelic face" of Maritain. Others are more developed. Placed side by side they complement each other. The holiness here is original: it is that of a married couple who have passed through the fire of the despairs of the modern world, who are united in a wild love for God, attached immovably to the life of prayer, to the sacramental life, to the life of wisdom and the life of grace, all the while being plunged into the heart of the world—by their intellectual and professional situation, by the circulation of their writings, by their real and intellectual sense of hospitality, by a sense of friendship and of "existing with."

IV. The Baptisms: "Centuplum accipietis"

Broadly speaking, there often seem to be "converts" and "godchildren" in the Maritainian universe. We would like to identify the godchildren in the strict sense of the three Maritains. We will not refer to all the names, far more numerous, known or unknown, of those that the Maritains set on, or put back on, the path toward God and who continued to have a lively gratitude towards them: people like Ernest Psichari, Erik Satie, Julien Green, Pierre Reverdy, Jean Cocteau—"I was hesitating on the brink of heaven like an imbecile.... It was then that you pushed me. Pushed me in the back by a blow from your soul.... [P]ushed me headfirst."[48] Nor will the names of all those Jews or Christians be recalled who were able to grow in intimacy with God thanks to the Maritains: Renée Neher-Bernheim wrote to Maritain of her admiration for his work, "which permitted me, a believing Jew, to better understand Christianity and which in my own faith opened me equally to many perspectives that your so profound richness of thought necessarily arouses in the conscience of all your readers."[49] We want to or-

46. Letter of Marshall Suther to Jacques Maritain, 21 September 1965, MA.

47. Letter of Marshall Suther to Jacques Maritain, 30 January 1968, MA.

48. Words of Jean Cocteau, cited by Raïssa Maritain in "Gifts from Heaven," chap. 7 in *Adventures in Grace* (New York: The Catholic Book Club, 1945), 191.

49. Renée Neher-Bernheim, *Éclats d'une amitié. Avsholom Feingberg et Jacques Maritain* (Paris: Parole et Silence, 2005), 155.

ganize, as much as possible, the list of the seventy-five godchildren of the three Maritains identified as of this date thanks to the patience of Dominique Mougel. This database, gathered from archival discoveries, was created because the Maritains never kept a list of all their godchildren.

The Maritains themselves were baptized on 11 June 1906, on the feast of Saint Barnabas the Apostle. Following a traditional pattern, the two young converts in turn became "converters."[50] The following year their niece, Eveline Garnier, the daughter of Jeanne Maritain-Garnier, herself a convert, received baptism: she was the first godchild mentioned in *We Have been Friends Together*. It must be underscored how much the Maritains experienced each baptism not just as a work of grace, but also as a spiritual conquest, as an uprooting from the profane world, from familial or social values, in contrast with the turbulent baptism of the children of Péguy. As far as we know, the last godchildren were from the American harvest. The last voyage of Maritain to the United States in 1966 was the occasion for three baptisms: that of Doris Dana, 29 October 1966, who had been Maritain's secretary during the war; that of Amanda Griffin, the youngest daughter of John Griffin, the anti-racist journalist from Texas who authored *Black Like Me*; and that of Edwyn Tiryakian, son of Edward Tiryakian, a former student of Maritain at Princeton.

Between 1906 and 1966, Jacques, Raïssa, and Véra were godparents to seventy-five persons baptized in Belgium, in France, in Canada, and in the United States. One can notice certain thresholds: between 1906 and 1926, a dozen baptisms took place. The publication in 1926 of the correspondence with Jean Cocteau, and that in 1944 of *We Have been Friends Together* were moments of acceleration. Jacques gave his first name to Jacques Levaux, Jacques Grunelius, Jérôme-Odon-Jacques Lemaître, Jean-Marie-Jacques Tichy, the son of Véronique Bloy. In just one case "Maritain" became a given name when John and Claire Coleman named their son "Thomas Maritain Coleman." Raïssa was the given name for a little girl born among the circle of the Maritains: Jacques made reference to the birth of a goddaughter baptized "Raïssa-Marie" in a letter to Abbé Journet of 20 April 1963.[51]

50. Frédéric Gugelot, *La conversion des intellectuels au catholicisme en France 1885–1935* (Paris: CNRS, 1998).

51. *Correspondance Maritain-Journet*, 20 April 1963, vol. 5 (Paris: Saint Augustin, 2006), 589: "Charles, very mysterious things are happening. A dozen years ago a child of 17 years [Josette Arrazola de Onate] wrote from France to Raïssa after having read *We Have Been Friends Together*. She soon became deeply attached to her, wishing for her salvation with all her heart. This young girl experienced terrible times. And then, after Raïssa's departure for the other life, she has been,

Among the godchildren is found the grandson of Léon Bloy. There were children born to Catholic friends such as Claude Bourdet, Yves Simon, Jacques de Monléon, and Roland Dalbiez. There were those such as Jean and Suzanne Marx, who both were friends from highschool. There were couples such as the parents of Raïssa: Mr. Oumançoff, who died in February 1912 and was baptized with water from Lasalette, *in articulo mortis*, with his daughter as godmother and the attending doctor as godfather, and Mrs. Oumançoff who was baptized in 1925. There were also the Grunelius, Alexandre and Antoinette, and their son Jacques. There were families such as that of Allen Tate and Caroline Gordon. On 22 December 1950 Jacques entered in his notebook: "A baptism like that one in America has a strangely heartrending feeling." Maritain described the event for Journet: "The good God gave us a great gift for Christmas: Raïssa and I were the godparents of Allen Tate, a poet and critic of great value (the best American critic, I believe) was baptized the Friday before Christmas. His wife had converted several years ago. His daughter is taking instructions and expects to receive baptism in a few months. Pray for this family whose uprightness and generosity move us deeply."[52] Following Tate it is his whole family that enters the Church: on 16 March 1951, the baptism of Nancy Wood, daughter of the Tates, and her husband Percy, took place.[53] For its part, over three generations of the Coleman family entered the Church: Emily, John, and Dunstan, all godchildren of the Maritains. There were the families of painters, like Jean Hugo or Eugénie Rappoport from the Chagall family, musicians (Dom Clément Jacob, Peter Nabokoff, son of Nicolas Nabokoff, Roland Manuel), academics (Gustave Cohen, Raphaël Pividal), diplomats (Jean Marx), writers, students like Willard Hill (who spent some time in France at the Dominican *Eau Vive* school of philosophy), and Eleanor Walker, baptized on Broadway in March 1943. She was at that time a student at Columbia; Jacques was her godfather at baptism, Raïssa her godmother at confirmation. There was the daughter of the Protestant socialist deputy

in two years, totally transformed; it is like a spiritual miracle, due entirely to the unseen action of Raïssa. She married a year ago, and a little girl was just born, called Raïssa-Marie of whom I will be the Godfather."

52. *Correspondance Maritain-Journet*, vol. 4 (Paris: Saint Augustin, 2005), 117–18.

53. See the correspondence of Allen Tate, Caroline Gordon, and Jacques Maritain, published in *Exiles and Fugitives: The Letters of Jacques and Raïssa Maritain, Alan Tate, and Caroline Gordon*, edited by John M. Dunaway (Baton Rouge, Louisiana: Louisiana State University Press, 1992), 30–31.

André Philip. From the Protestant world came the Grunelius and several American friends. There were several "sheep of Israel" as Jacques put it: the daughter of Emmanuel Chapman, himself a convert; Gustave Cohen, who "hoped to be counted among the great friendships," those which are "silent, secret and deep"[54]; Jean and Suzanne Marx, friends from the Lycée Henri IV; Ruth Nanda Anshen; Dorothy Rotschild; Achsa Belkind from a family of the Zionist pioneers; Roland Manuel; Emmanuel "Manu" Jacob, who died in a concentration camp, remembered in the *Carnet des notes*; Eugénie Rappoport, saved thanks to the intervention of Msgr. Fontenelle and Jacques Maritain. There were also some precarious baptisms such as that of Maurice Sachs, whose godmother was Raïssa and whose godfather was Jean Cocteau. There is a tempered, yet sharp, plea in *We Have been Friends Together* concerning this godson, who did not stay firm, but whom Raïssa always loved, as the pages in the *Raïssa's Journal* show on 16 November 1947: "he calls evil, evil; and good, if he had not the strength really to seek it, he has at least aspired to it, and he certainly suffered from not being able to attain to it."

V. Conclusions

Since the preceding has had as its sole object to open up a field for reflection, it is not possible at this point to close off all the questions. It would be necessary to expand the dossier in multiple directions and to pursue with greater precision this *fama sanctitatis* of the Maritains, including Véra, since among the three there was, as Jacques said, "as it were, just one breath."[55] It would be necessary to go back to the beginnings, to recapture the stories and settings, to analyze the spreading of their reputation for holiness, the variances, the commonplaces, the disputes—whether hidden from sight or out in the open—in Paris, Québec, and Rome.

It would also be necessary to reflect on the modest acceptance of the Maritain spouses *post mortem*, and to deepen the question of the communion of the "living saints."[56] The philosopher continued to be read, and

54. Letter of Gustave Cohen to Jacques Maritain, 22 October 1941, MA.

55. Jacques Maritain, *Carnet des notes, O.C.*, 12:219: "I do not think that there has ever been among three human beings a union as close and deep as that which existed amongst us. . . . There was, as it were, just one breath that kept us alive."

56. See the letters exchanged between Maritains and Blessed Pope Paul VI, and between Maritain and Blessed Msgr. Vladimir Ghika. See, for instance, the letter of Ghika to Maritain, 22

the great friendships went on. "He continues to exercise a considerable influence on philosophy and the culture of our time," wrote John Paul II in 1982.[57] But certain elements usually found in the canonical stories of the lives of saints are missing: no pilgrimage has been organized to their tombs, no miracle has been reported, no "Maritainian school" has flourished since 1973. Neither the historian, nor Maritain himself (faithful to the "poor means" and convinced that "Thomism has never succeeded in the world and will never succeed there"[58]), have a need of such "signs" in any case. There is such a contrast between the veneration of Maritain during his lifetime and the present situation that it seems as though obstacles were set up on the path to a calm reception of the work of the Maritains in the last quarter of this century. Even if the Church has sometimes canonized saints "against the tide," it has to be recognized that their intellectual and elitist profile is hardly appreciated in an age of mass culture. The stakes for Thomistic philosophy are such—and very legitimately so—as to arouse debates, even controversies, in keeping with the less than flexible "Thomist manners" described by Étienne Gilson in his memoirs. The Maritains' vow of chastity offends many in a time of "hypersexuality." The "deterritorialization" of their tombs at Kolbsheim, a tiny Alsatian village far from Meudon, far from the high places—Paris, Rome, New York, Princeton, where the Maritains had lived—is also perhaps a factor. The post-conciliar ecclesial crises also played their part since, according to some, the author of *The Peasant of the Garonne* was too conservative, whereas for others the Council itself was a distant outcome of *Integral Humanism*. Maritain's acceptance on the ecclesial, and even the ecclesiastical, level is at the least uncertain. One might take this ambivalence as evidence that Maritain could not speak to every "party" within the Church. But as the ideological waters recede, it will become increasingly apparent to all that Maritain's thought transcends the barriers isolating the different camps from each other.

It would also be important to reflect on the reasons the one who was buried as a saint by his friends has never seen his process opened, even though the Church under John Paul II sought out lay people for canonization, and Thomism never fell out of favor in Rome. John Paul II, at the

October 1925: "I look forward to seeing you again and leaning on your good friendship. Waiting for that moment, I do it, from afar, within the communion of the saints."

57. *CJM*, 4–5 (1982): 60.

58. *Correspondance Maritain-Gilson*, 192. On this point see Étienne Fouilloux, *Une Église en quête de liberté* (Paris: DDB, 1998), 118–19.

end of the 1980s in an interview with Ramon Sugranyes de Franch, president of the International Institute Jacques Maritain at the time, even clarified, without putting aside the question, that the moment for the beatification of the Maritains had not yet arrived. Of course, the reflex of the members of the Maritain Circle (unlike the friends of Thérèse of Lisieux or Charles de Foucauld) was to produce not a hagiography but, skipping this step, proceeded instead to an "examination of the writings." One might consider, *a posteriori,* the publication of the seventeen volumes of the complete works, and the six volumes of the Maritain-Journet correspondence, to be included in this project, the touchstone for obtaining a *nihil obstat.* Canon 2042 of the Code of 1917 included the obligation to proceed to such an examination of the unpublished writings of the one who was a candidate for beatification. The same Code of 1917 (c. 2049) required, however, that one undertake as soon as possible the process of the one that was considered worthy of canonization: "The legislator is wary of a lengthy delay beyond thirty years and wishes that in this case, before going ahead, it be well-established that this delay is not hiding some fraud, some deception, some maneuver, and that it is not a consequence of culpable negligence."[59] The instruction *Sanctorum Mater* (2007) does not renounce the delay of thirty years (articles 26 and 27).[60] If the cause is launched more than thirty years after the death of the servant of God, it is necessary to examine the motives at the origin of this delay to see if there was not dishonesty or deception. Is the delay, or at least the slowness, in the opening in the case of the Maritains the expression of some doubt, not about their holiness, but about the usefulness of promoting *this* kind of holiness in the postconciliar Church of the last quarter of the twentieth century? Is it more simply the avowal of a continuing urgency about the dissemination of the philosophical work, in the very manner followed by Maritain? Has not the "Maritain Circle," an Association created by Jacques in 1962 with limited resources, been frightened by the administrative and juridical question of a process which naturally did not form part of the objectives that Maritain had assigned it? Maritain had even formally forbidden the Circle "to undertake anything at all that would resemble propaganda or publicity, a systematic effort at dissemination, or the idea of promoting a school, or worst of all, to honor a name" (Charter of the Circle).

59. *Dictionnaire de droit canonique,* s.v. "Causes de béatification et de canonisation."

60. Accessible online at http://www.vatican.va/roman_curia/congregations/csaints/documents/ rc_con_csaints_ doc_20070517_sanctorum-mater_en.html

Did not the Little Brothers of Jesus, since Jacques was one of them, feel too weak to bear the weight of a long procedure? After all, it took ninety years (1916–2005) for the beatification of Blessed Charles de Foucauld.

Another issue calling for further analysis is the emergence of this "new style of holiness" such as *Integral Humanism* had sought to define it in 1934–36, that is to say, according to the very terms set out by Maritain. This holiness "descends from the heaven of the sacred toward the things of the secular world and its culture"; it is a holiness "turned towards the temporal, the secular, the profane," and which corresponds to the passage from one political and spiritual style of Christianity, a "Baroque" Christianity, Tridentine, Continental, sometimes with totalitarian pretensions, to another contemporary, insular, Christianity in diaspora,[61] where the freedom of the act of faith is the surest guarantee of its purity. At the moment when Maritain wrote the pages of *Integral Humanism*, pages which have all the clarity of a roadmap, he intended both to suggest a pathway to his contemporaries and to define the demands of his own itinerary. Was Maritain—antimodern *and* ultramodern—opening the paths to the Council and criticizing certain postconciliar excesses, the saint of the movement and continuity between two models of Christianity? It will be necessary to prolong this reflection within the work of Maritain itself, the works on ecclesiology and the autobiographical texts particularly, since like Augustine of Hippo or Thérèse of Lisieux, Jacques, "the ungainly deep-sea diver, advancing as best he might in the midst of the underwater fauna of captive truths,"[62] "the beggar of heaven disguised as a man of the times," "the secret agent of the King of Kings in the territories of the Prince of this world," made use of the genre to declare his faith and the graces received, and to try to define also, in poetic metaphors, the path of holiness that he intended to traverse.

61. Jacques Maritain, *Les Îles*, 1932, in *O.C.*, 5:1069–80: "There over the isles passes the wind from the sea, and you do not know whence it comes nor whither it goes. And these isles are of little account, like a bit of dust on the water—*ecce insulae quasi pulvis exiguus* [see, the islands are like fine dust] (Isaiah 40:15)—and this very weakness and this very smallness are the proper means of the spirit, and one can believe that a time is coming where the great mountains will be less asked to celebrate God in showing his glory, than the tiny isles [to do so] by accepting his sufferings. The islands signify again discovery and voyage, and not escape, but conquest. The evil also that spiritual Diaspora, that powder of fire, dispersed across the world where one can see with probability enough one of the future forms of Christianity."

62. Jacques Maritain, *Carnet de notes*, *O.C.*, 12:220.

PRUDENCE ALLEN, R.S.M.

A Life Shared

The Complementarity of Jacques and Raïssa Maritain

I. Introduction

In this lecture, I will attempt to describe what could be called "The Maritain Model of Complementarity," especially as it was lived out in the early years of Jacques and Raïssa's lives together. Drawing upon Raïssa's *Journals* and *Memoirs* and Jacques' *Notebooks,* we are offered glimpses into certain moments in their lives together. From these recorded glimpses, it is possible to construct a model for how they lived and to identify essential components in their multi-dimensional complementarity as it developed over time with the qualification: the deep relational dynamic within a marriage can ultimately be grasped only by the man and woman who live it out together.

In order to assess the "Maritain Model of Complementarity," I will also place their lives and writings in the historical context of the meaning of complementarity in the history of philosophy. At first view it seems odd to make this claim, because in their early lives together they hardly used the word "complementarity," and they also rarely wrote about woman's identity in relation to man *per se.* However, seven years after Raïssa's death and five years before Jacques' death, in an informal talk given at Kolbshein in 1967, an extraordinarily rich text about the genuine complementarity between man and woman is evident.[1] In my view, Jacques and Raïssa's lived experi-

1. Jacques Maritain, "Let us make for him a helpmate like to himself," chapter 8 in *Untrammeled Approaches,* vol. 20 of *The Collected Works of Jacques Maritain,* translated and edited by

ence together contributed something essential towards defending integral sex and gender complementarity. Since a core theme of this volume is on the early Raïssa and Jacques, this paper will consider the lived experience of integral complementarity before returning to Jacques' text towards the conclusion.

II. The Meaning of Complementarity

When the complementarity of a woman and man is being considered, it is important to distinguish between the historical development of the *concept* of complementarity and the historical development of the use of the *word* "complementarity."

The concept of complementarity as applied to human beings has three essential components which can be categorized as equal dignity, significant difference, and synergetic relations. Perpetual tensions between the first two essential components have existed in the history of philosophy. Sometimes, as in Plato, significant difference is missing; other times, as in Aristotle, equal dignity is missing. When both essential components of equal dignity and significant difference are held in tension, a synergetic effect often occurs.

In Medieval philosophy the first two essential components of man/woman complementarity began to be recognized. St. Augustine defended the *equal dignity* and *significant difference* of woman and man in respect to the communion of saints in heaven, but he had elements of lack of equality and of lack of differentiation for women and men in the temporal world. St. Hildegard offered arguments in defense of *both the equal dignity and significant differentiation* of women and men in the world.[2] In Modern Philosophy, however, the essential component of *significant difference* disappeared in Cartesianism, and the essential component of *equal dignity* disappeared in various new theories of either male natural superiority or female natural

Bernard Doering (Notre Dame, Indiana: University of Notre Dame Press, 1997), 151–64. The editor's footnote adds. "Cf. *Nova et Vetera,* 1967, no. 4, pp. 241–254. (Translations of this text have appeared in Spanish, Italian, and Czech)". I am very grateful to Brooke Deely for bringing this extraordinary text to my attention. The talk was given to the Little Brothers of Jesus. See Brooke W. Smith (Deely), *Jacques Maritain: Antimodern or Ultramodern? An Historical Analysis of His Critics, His Thought, and His Life* (New York: Elsevier, 1976), especially chapter 4, for her analysis of Jacques' life with Raïssa, especially pp. 139–58.

2. Evidence supporting these claims can be found in Sr. Prudence Allen, R.S.M., *The Concept of Woman: The Aristotelian Reformation, 750B.C.-A.D. 1250* (Grand Rapids, Michigan: Eerdmans, 1985–97), 218–35 and 292–314.

superiority. The need for a solid Neothomist metaphysics, which would be able to maintain simultaneously both equal dignity and significant difference, kept increasing until the twentieth century when the significant work of the Thomist Circles of the Maritain's occurred as the word "complementarity" began to be used by others.

1. *Historical Development of the Word "Complementarity"*

The word seems to have been used first by Niels Bohr in Italy in 1927 in application to the wave and particle theories of light.[3] At the level of physics there can be no synergetic effect from relation of these two operations as they mutually exclude each other. Niels Bohr extended his use of the word "complementarity" to many other fields, but not to woman and man's related identities.

In 1929, Dietrich von Hildebrand described the "metaphysical complementarity" of husband and wife in marriage.[4] Bernard Lonergan reviewed in 1943 an English translation of Hildebrand's book (1942) of the previous lecture on marriage, and he applied "complementarity" directly to woman and man at the levels of biology, psychology, philosophy, and theology.[5] In 1967, Jacques Maritain described the "complementarity" of qualities of femininity and masculinity, the "mutual complementarity" at the heart of humanity, Eve "as being a person whose *being-woman* is complementary to the *being-man* of Adam [and] Adam is a person whose *being-man* is complementary to the *being-woman* of Eve"; and the ontological fullness of human nature is evident in the mutual complementarity of woman and man in "the activity of the blessed."[6] In 1969, Karol Wojtyla used the word "complementarity" in the Polish edition of *The Acting Person* to describe relations of solidarity. In 1975, R. Buckminster Fuller used the term to refer to male and female in *Synergetics*.[7]

3. For references to the following examples of the use of the word "complementarity" see Sr. Prudence Allen, R.S.M., "Man-Woman Complementarity: the Catholic Inspiration," *Logos: A Journal of Catholic Thought and Culture* 9, no. 3 (2006): 1–22.

4. See Dietrich von Hildebrand, *Marriage the Mystery of Faithful Love*, published in 1929 in German as *Die Ehe* based on the same theme of his lecture in 1923 (Manchester, New Hampshire: Sophia Institute Press, 1991), especially pp. 14–15.

5. See Prudence Allen, R.S.M., "Metaphysics of Form, Matter, and Gender," *Lonergan Workshop* 12 (1996): 1–26.

6. Maritain, "Let us make for him a helpmate like to himself," in *Untrammeled Approaches*, 160.

7. Prudence Allen, R.S.M., "Fuller's Synergetics and Sex Complementarity," *International Philosophical Quarterly* 32 (1992): 3–16.

Then in 1979, Pope John Paul II employed "complementarity" extensively in his audiences on the Theology of the Body to describe the creation of woman and man from the beginning and the way that their union leads to synergetic effects in the generation of families and the vocations through which females discover the meaning of their femininity in motherhood and males discover the meaning of their masculinity in fatherhood.[8] In 1995, Pope John Paul II elaborated multiple dimensions of the *ontological complementarity* of women and men in the context of the UN World Conference on Women (1995): *biological complementarity* (including *physical complementarity* and *psychological complementarity*); *individual complementarity*; personal *complementarity*; and *spiritual complementarity.*[9] Pope John Paul also drew upon a theology of the Holy Trinity as a Divine Communion of Three Persons, equal in their Divinity, significantly different in their Relations, and eternally generative in their union. He suggested that human communion of persons could grow in likeness to this Divine Communion through the action of the Holy Spirit.[10]

With this general introduction to the history of the concept of complementarity and of the word "complementarity" in hand, we can now turn to consider directly the lived complementarity of Jacques and Raïssa Maritain and their friends.

III. Lived Complementarity of Raïssa and Jacques in the Early Years (1900–1917)

1. Complementarity in Student Friendship (1900–1901)

Of the two students in the year 1900 in Paris, Raïssa immigrated to France with a Russian and Jewish background and Jacques was French with a liberal Reform background. Both had lost any commitment to religious faith; both were studying science at the Sorbonne. Raïssa described her isolation as a new student: "I went by myself through the courts and corridors filled with noisy and talkative young people. All alone, knowing no one, I

8. See John Paul II, *Man and Woman He Created Them: A Theology of the Body,* translated by Michael Waldstein (Boston: Pauline Books and Media, 2006), 166ff.

9. See Prudence Allen, R.S.M., "Philosophy of Relation in John Paul II's New Feminism," in *Women in Christ: Toward a New Feminism,* edited by Michele Schumacher (Grand Rapids, Michigan: Eerdmans, 2003), 67–104.

10. See Prudence Allen, "Integral Sex Complementarity and the Theology of Communion," *Communio: International Catholic Review* 17 (1990): 523–44.

spoke to no one; I did not try to know anyone, I was concerned only with the professors."[11] Bursting into Raïssa's introverted and self-focused world came Jacques:

> I was leaving M. Matruchot's plant physiology class one day in a rather downcast frame of mind, when I saw coming toward me a young man with a gentle face, a heavy shock of blond hair, a light beard and a slightly stoop-shouldered carriage. He introduced himself and said he was forming a committee of students to start a movement of protest among French writers and university people against the ill-treatment to which Russian Socialist students had been subject in their own country. (At that time in Russia there were student riots which were severely repressed by the Czarist police.) And he asked me to join this committee. Such was my first meeting with Jacques Maritain.[12]

Raïssa describes how these two students "soon became inseparable," building up a friendship in long walks home, in "endless conversations" about the meaning of life, the desire for truth, and sharing the same "profound concerns."[13]

Looking back at these early days from a much later perspective of her Catholic faith, Raïssa summarizes beautifully her experience of the initial discovery of their equal dignity, significant difference, and synergetic relations:

> For the first time I could really talk to someone about myself, emerge from my silent reflections in order to share them, put my torment into words. For the first time I had met someone who at the outset inspired me with absolute confidence, someone who from that moment I knew would never disappoint me; someone with whom I could so readily come to an understanding on all things. Another Someone had pre-established between us, and in despite of such great differences of temperament and of origin, a sovereign harmony.[14]

As students, Jacques and Raïssa introduced one another to art and music, thereby further enriching their growing friendship. The very next year, in 1901, as is well known, they also entered into a suicide pact. Raïssa described how she believed she had become an atheist. Jacques and Raïssa both were beginning to despair of finding deeper answers to their questions about the meaning of life. Consequently, they "reached a solemn decision"

11. Raïssa Maritain, *We Have Been Friends Together,* translated by Julie Kernan (Garden City, New York: Image Books, 1961), 40.

12. Ibid., 41.

13. Ibid., 42.

14. Ibid.

to face "the nightmare of a sinister and useless world"; if they did not find a meaning and value of life "the solution would be suicide ... before our youthful strength was spent. We wanted to die by a free act if it were impossible to live according to the truth."[15] At this dangerous point, the seed of complementarity among the two friends was in great risk of vanishing.

2. *Bergson on the Free Act and the Beginning of Spousal Love for the Maritains (1901–1904)*

Jacques's *Notebooks* recorded the following terse entry: "First course of Bergson, followed by us, school year 1901–1902."[16] Bergson opened up for both of the students a world of metaphysics and confidence in being able to learn truth about reality. It was a deep love for the truth that welled up from the depths the souls of Raïssa and Jacques, and it saved them from the despair of their confrontation with relativism. Later on in her third notebook of 1919, Raïssa wrote: "I give thanks to God who put in my heart such an ardent love of truth when, ignorant of the divine Truth, I lived among sceptics and atheists."[17]

Bergson taught the two young students that the human being has two spiritual faculties—intellect and will; and the human soul has the great potential to make a free act. Raïssa summarized the student notes she made of Bergson's lectures on this theme:

> For Bergson, to say that the whole soul is engaged in one of its acts is to say that it is free. The whole personality may be "in a single one of them, provided that we know how to choose it. And the outward manifestation of this inner state will be just what is called a free act, since the self alone will have been the author of it, and since it will express the whole of the self."[18]

Raïssa was fascinated by Bergson's philosophy of the human person. She continued to summarize his words: "It is the whole soul, in fact, which gives rise to the free decision: and the act will be so much the freer the more the dynamic series with which it is connected tends to be the fundamen-

15. Ibid., 67–68.

16. *Notebooks*, 75.

17. *Raïssa's Journal Presented by Jacques Maritain*, translated by Magi Books (Albany, New York: Magi Books, 1974), 113. The quotation continues: "That desire which the physical sciences could not satisfy because they are partial, and which modern philosophies completely frustrated by their relativism, was fulfilled by the revelation of Catholic doctrine and of Thomist philosophy."

18. Raïssa Maritain, *We Have Been Friends Together*, 76.

tal self."[19] She realized that growing in inner freedom unfolds over time, that "our acts spring from our whole personality" and that "the very feeling of duration comes from this continued process of our free activity in the depths of consciousness."[20]

Before long, Jacques and Raïssa began to make free acts in relation to one another. The first example is their decision in 1902 to become engaged. Raïssa took the initiative in the moment and later described her response as flowing from God into herself and irrevocably binding her to Jacques:

> Our engagement took place in the simplest way, without any proposal. We were alone in my parents' living room. Jacques was sitting on the rug, close to my chair; it suddenly seemed to me that we had always been near each other, and that we would always be so. Without thinking, I put out my hand and stroked his hair; he looked at me and all was clear to us. The feeling flowed through me that always—for my happiness and my salvation (I thought precisely, although then the word "salvation" meant nothing to me)—that always my life would be bound up with Jacques'. It was one of those tender and peaceful feelings which are like a gift flowing from a region higher than ourselves, illuminating the future and deepening the present. From that moment our understanding was perfect and unchangeable.[21]

Jacques in turn described his response to this new the bond with Raïssa as flowing outwards from them into the world beyond:

> [W]hen we had returned into the room, and were resting on the window ... we both felt—our souls happy—our truth, our definitive truth. I write this in order to fix in my memory the congenial setting and the external situation; but what took place on the inside of our souls filled us with an inexhaustible happiness. Life appeared to us, our life, such as it should be, and in silence we promised each other irrevocable promises. Fortitude, the luminous and clear School, the School of life, or sincerity, the School in which we will animate souls, in which we will cause by appeals, songs and rays, the soul and real life to come to the surface of existence. The School from which men and women of truth and of harmony will emerge.[22]

This school of harmony, which Jacques envisioned, had already brought a new harmony into their inherited differences of nationality, religious backgrounds, and temperaments. In addition to their Russian/French and Jewish/liberal Reform traditions, their different temperaments could be generalized at this point as Raïssa's introverted temperament and Jacques'

19. Ibid., 77.
20. Ibid., 78–79.
21. Ibid., 84–85.
22. Jacques Maritain, *Notebooks,* 15. See also ibid., 75.

extroverted temperament. Both Raïssa and Jacques received joy and peace in their mutual recognition of their life-long bond of love and friendship and the call into a school of truth and harmony; but living out this bond would now require much labor and suffering.

In the summer of 1904, a new complementary difference of sickness and health revealed itself to the young couple. On a summer vacation with her parents, her sister Vera, and Jacques, Raïssa became deathly ill with retropharyngeal abscess. Her throat became so swollen that she could hardly breathe. In her words: "I recall that one night when it was Jacques' turn to watch beside me, he repeated over and over again, 'Breathe, breathe!' And I would feebly draw a breath."[23] Vera went to Paris to bring back a surgeon, who operated immediately. According to Raïssa: "Vera held the lamp while Jacques held my head. It was just in time, the abscess was enormous and I might have strangled completely. But I was saved at the last minute."[24] Raïssa was literally carried back to Paris for a "long and interminable and painful convalescence."[25]

The events surrounding the curing of the severe illness marked the beginning of the collaborative work of the threesome: Jacques, Raïssa, and Vera. Out of this suffering, Jacques and Raïssa made together a further mutually free human act. In Jacques' journal: "26th of November 1904. Marriage of Jacques and Raïssa."[26] This marriage was a civil marriage.

3. *Complementary Suffering and Discovery of Jesus Christ (1906–1909)*

Visitations of illness on Raïssa became a recurrent pattern over the next years. In the context of this suffering, Jacques and Raïssa made the life-transforming free acts of deciding to be received into the Catholic Church and to have their civil marriage be sacramentally confirmed by the Church. Again Jacques' terse description recorded the events:

> Illness of Raïssa during the whole month of February 1906.—From mid-April, at Bures. Relapse of Raïssa. Monday, the 11th of June, 1906 (St. Barnabas), baptism of the three of us by Abbé Durantel and the sacramental marriage of Jacques and Raïssa, in the Church of St. John the Evangelist.[27]

23. Raïssa Maritain, *We Have Been Friends Together*, 85.
24. Ibid., 86.
25. Ibid.
26. Jacques Maritain, *Notebooks*, 19. See also ibid., 75.
27. Ibid., 76. Also, *Raïssa's Journal*, 22.

After Jacques passed his *aggrégation* in 1906, he and Raïssa moved to Heidelberg, Germany in August.[28] Jacques recorded on October 9th something Raïssa shared with him: "In the middle of the night she was awakened by these words which she heard: "You are always looking for what must be done. There is only to love God and to serve Him with all your heart."[29] Jacques described his love for Raïssa's character in a lengthy and beautiful reflection of October 28:

> Goodness. Purity. Raïssa always goes to the bitter end, with a direct intention and an upright will. Her courage is without calculation and her pity without defense.... She has always lived for truth; she has never resisted truth. She has never bent her mind, nor lied to her suffering. She always gives without retaining anything.... Her thought, her genius, tends always to intuition. As she is wholly interior, she is wholly free. Her reason can be content only with the real, her soul only with the absolute.[30]

Jacques continued a loving pondering of his wife's character in a reflection on the deep meaning of her Jewish inheritance:

> In her passion for concrete certitude, in her respect for Wisdom and her love for Justice, in her indomitable humor and her vigilance in dispute, as also in the ardor of her blood and the precision of her instinct, everywhere she bears with her the nobility and the privilege of the race from which she is born, of the elder Race ... *Puella Hebraeorum!*[31]

After further reflection on the meaning of Raïssa's Jewish identity, Jacques shared a new significant difference of woman/man that she revealed to him:

> In her there is not only beauty, but that living spiritual light which is like a glance of God above beauty, and which we call grace.... Awe-inspiring and magnificent gift, in which the primitive splendor of Eve is reflected, and which descends as a trial on a few women of this fallen world. And for her, as for all those women on whom grace was conferred, grace is not an exception which sets them apart from other women, but rather the very excellence and the mystical characteristic of their sex.[32]

To conclude his testimony of love, Jacques described Raïssa's love of God and how he understood her vocation in this light:

28. Raïssa Maritain, *We Have Been Friends Together*, 142.
29. Jacques Maritain, *Notebooks*, 20.
30. Ibid., 31–32.
31. Ibid., 32.
32. Ibid., 32–33.

Finally, she loves God, she has always loved God, even before knowing Him.... And because she loves God, she can rest only in Him! This vocation is that of humanity itself, I know; but those who are marked for the glory of God are not outside humanity, they are the very characteristic and the essence of humanity. When you are afflicted, Raïssa, remember my testimony. And You, my God, Father of the poor, without Whom nothing exists, and with Whom the humblest can do everything, in Whom all Grandeur resides, support her with Your strength, spread Your grace over her, *give her what you command, and command her what you will!*[33]

From these selected extracts of Jacques Maritain's writing about his wife at this early time in their marriage, we can see that he understood and loved her complementary relation with him. He did not consider accidental characteristics of her identity, but rather those which penetrate her whole being, as a Jewish now Christian contemplative woman. He prayed for her, and freely gave her to God, to follow completely the Christian vocation the Lord had given her without holding her back.

In mid-December, Vera came to visit the Maritains.[34] She took care of Raïssa who again became deathly ill with amoebic enteritis in January, 1907. Raïssa wrote: "My condition grew still worse and, without knowing whether I wished to live or die, I asked for Extreme Unction and received it on January 17."[35] Jacques recorded his own agony at the severity of her illness and later his joy at her recovery:

13th January, 1907. Raïssa is ill.... Began novena in common to Our Lady of La Salette.... 15th of January, Raïssa is very ill. She wishes to receive the anointing of the Sick.... 16th of January. Extreme weakness. The doctor sees no hope except in an operation. No, not that! I go to see Chaplain Keck. He will hear Raïssa's confession this evening at six o'clock, and will bring her Holy Communion and the Anointing of the Sick tomorrow.... 17th of January, 1907. The Anointing of the Sick is experienced by Raïssa as a new baptism, she is suffused with grace and with peace. Ineffable grace of total abandonment to God and the joy of suffering. Vera and I feel its victorious gushing forth.... As for the body, the improvement is sudden and undeniable. The doctor is amazed.[36]

By March, Jacques, Raïssa, and Vera made their de Montfort Consecration to Mary; at the end of June to early July, they took a pilgrimage to La

33. Ibid., 34.

34. For Jacques' extensive reflections on the different temperaments and character of Vera and Raïssa, see *Notebooks*, 189–218.

35. Raïssa Maritain, *We Have Been Friends Together*, 143.

36. Jacques Maritain, *Notebooks*, 36.

Salette.[37] The conjunction of beatitude and suffering in the weeping Mary of La Salette helped the Maritains overcome their previous understanding of the limits of Aristotelian metaphysics, which saw perfection in pure act only. Raïssa wrote:

> This conjunction of suffering and Beatitude is allowed neither by theology nor by Aristotle. Beatitude means absolute fullness, and suffering is the cry of that which is wounded. But our God is a crucified God: the Beatitude of which He cannot be deprived did not prevent Him from fearing or mourning ... or from passing through the throes of death on the Cross, or from feeling abandoned.... For a created being, to be capable of suffering is a real perfection; it is the lot of life and of the spirit, it is the greatness of man.[38]

On July 6, Jacques, Raïssa, and Vera received the Sacrament of Confirmation.[39] A few months later, Raïssa wrote to Jacques and described herself as "the guardian of a Kingdom" that she cannot see, but which she must defend.[40] Jacques also wrote out the horarium or "ora et labora" that the threesome were now following together.

At the beginning of Lent (March 6, 1908) suffering struck again when Raïssa fell ill with an angina. In Jacques words, "It is grave, a kind of diphtheria."[41] Then Jacques also became ill with diphtheria. Fortunately, Vera was spared, and she was able to bring them back to health with the help of a nurse. During the time of suffering, however, on March 19, Jacques gave a testimony of his gratitude to Raïssa:

> My beloved Raïssa! I will know only in Paradise all I owe to her. Every good comes from God. But as earthly intermediary, *everything* has come to me through her, from her heart, from her reason, from her prayers, from her counsels, from her example, from her sufferings, from her virtues, from her love for God, and from her tender love for miserable me.[42]

37. Ibid., 39–41.

38. Raïssa Maritain, *We Have Been Friends Together,* 148–49. See also Prudence Allen, R.S.M., "Mary and the Vocation of Philosophers," *New Blackfriars* 90 (2009): 50–71, appearing also in *The Vocation of the Catholic Philosopher: From Maritain to John Paul II,* edited by John Hittinger (Washington, D.C.: American Maritain Association, 2011), 51–76.

39. Raïssa Maritain, *We Have Been Friends Together,* 22 and 144–150; and Jacques Maritain, *Notebooks,* 41.

40. Ibid., 42.

41. Ibid., 47, and Raïssa Maritain, *We Have Been Friends Together,* 172.

42. Jacques Maritain, *Notebooks,* 48. He copied this passage on June 10 and again 36 years later in Princeton.

While Jacques recovered and returned to his scholarly work, Raïssa had a relapse. In Jacques' words: "Towards the end of August ... Raïssa's health becoming very bad."[43] Raïssa described an unexpected gift of her illness: "While Jacques was working and meditating on his own problems, I made the acquaintance of the Angelic Doctor. This privilege was due to two causes: the return of illness in my life, and the entry into our lives of Father Humbert Clérissac."[44]

4. *Aquinas, Complementarity of Faith/Reason, and Communion of Persons (1909–1912)*

In this next section on the lived complementarity of Raïssa and Jacques, we discover once again Raïssa initiating an important new advancement for their married vocation. According to Jacques, before March 1909, Raïssa, when bedridden again for a month, "plunged in the *Summa*."[45] Jacques described her discovery of Thomas this way: "In the first months of 1909, Raïssa falls in love with the *Summa theologiae*."[46] A year later, in his entry of April 10, 1910, Jacques still described Raïssa's experience of this discovery like an observer looking in from the outside: "Raïssa continues to read St. Thomas with the same winged joy."[47] Yet, Jacques himself did not undertake to read Thomas for another half-year. Finally, he wrote on September 15, 1910: "*at the urging of Raïssa,* I begin to read the *Summa theologiae,* with which in my turn I fall in love."[48] At this point the vocations of Jacques and Raïssa begin to move along another vector.

Raïssa observed that "We ... became attached to Saint Thomas as to a real friend, by sympathy, by admiration and by gratitude."[49] She and Jacques soon pondered the relation of faith and reason in his work: "A theologian par excellence, it is nevertheless as the *metaphysician* of the intellect and of reason, in which he defends the value of the authentic faculties of real knowledge, that Saint Thomas first impressed us. Because of these things he is also dear to the Church, which is the guardian of human integrity as well as of revealed truth."[50] Raïssa also admired the integral complementarity of faith and reason in the Angelic Doctor: "Saint Thomas *by his life, his*

43. Ibid., 49.
44. Raïssa Maritain, *We Have Been Friends Together*, 172–73.
45. Jacques Maritain, *Notebooks*, 51.
46. Ibid., 77.
47. Ibid., 62.
48. Ibid., 77; my emphasis.
49. Raïssa Maritain, *We Have Been Friends Together*, 184.
50. Ibid., 185; my emphasis.

spirit and his teaching offers us an example of the most harmonious and efficacious union of the light of reason, or faith and of mystical experience."[51]

At the same time as this new opening to the thought of Thomas Aquinas occurred, Raïssa and Vera worked professionally on Jacques' other publishing projects. In 1910, Jacques wrote that "Raïssa does an entire work on Bergson for me ([from which I greatly profited in my articles, and later in my book. If I had been less *grob* [coarse], this book should have appeared under our two names. And Raïssa would doubtless have deterred me from many of those violences which I was to regret afterwards.])"[52] Raïssa and Vera also helped with writing and then in 1911 proofing his Lexicon.[53]

The pattern of immersion into suffering continued for the threesome. Raïssa suffered greatly from the physical pain of sciatica.[54] Vera became so ill that she had "to renounce her hope of becoming a nurse."[55] And Jacques underwent what he called "violent temptations against the faith."[56] Coming courageously through these sufferings, all three then made significant free acts: on September 29, 1912 they became Benedictine Oblates. Vera "made ... a very clear choice, which was to live with her sister and me [Jacques] by religious vocation."[57] On October 2, 1912 Jacques and Raïssa took a vow to live as brother and sister.[58] While Raïssa's continued severe illnesses would be a practical impediment to normal marital relations, a vow to live a celibate marriage would have been an exceptional spiritual act of deep intensity confirmed by the Church. Raïssa also came to understand later that, while the sacramental marriage bond between husband and wife ends with the death of one or the other spouse who is free to marry again, their Christian friendship endures eternally.[59]

After the three became Benedictine Oblates, in 1924, Raïssa entered in her Fourth Notebook an insight about essential characteristics of Divine Communion and its relation to human beings: "Love ... demands not only *union* of wills, but also *distinction* of persons. Trinity of divine Persons."[60]

51. Ibid., 186; my emphasis. See also Prudence Allen, R.S.M., "Person and Complementarity in *Fides et Ratio*," in *The Two Wings of Catholic Thought: Essays on Fides et Ratio*, edited by David Foster (Washington, D.C.: The Catholic University of America Press, 2003), 36–68.

52. Jacques Maritain, *Notebooks*, 62–63.

53. Ibid., 52 and 79.

54. Ibid., 70.

55. Ibid., 73

56. Ibid.

57. Ibid.

58. Ibid., 77.

59. See Prudence Allen, R.S.M., "Friendship, Gender, and Vocation," *Josephinum: Journal of Theololgy* 15 (2008): 102–39.

60. *Raïssa's Journal*, 164.

Jacques, in 1961, nearly fifty years after becoming an oblate, wrote about ways that this combination of "union of wills" with distinction of persons worked in their lives together. He offered an extraordinary insight into the meaning of integral complementarity in their small community of three persons:

> I do not think that there ever was a closer and more profound union between three human beings than that which existed between us. Each was open to the other two with an entire sincerity. Each was extraordinarily sensitized to the other two, and ready to give everything for them. It was, so to speak, a single act of breathing which held us in life.
>
> And yet, not only did the personality of each differ a great deal from that of the other two, and not only did each have a sacred respect for the liberty of the other two; but in the bosom of this marvelous union of love which the grace of God had made, each kept his solitude intact. What a mystery! The more we were united, the more each proceeded alone; the more each bore the burdens of the other two, the more each was alone in bearing his own burden. Thus the unity of the little flock only grew with the years, but the solitude of each of us only deepened at the same time, sometimes cruelly, to tell the truth. It was God's hand.[61]

The solitude of each person referred to by Jacques likely included the acute aloneness that their mutual vocations imposed on one another especially through Jacques' long periods away from the community for lecturing and Raïssa's times of severe pain and illness.

The insight of Jacques Maritain about the nature of the communion the three shared anticipated developments of the Second Vatican Council, specifically elaborations of *communio* in the work of Cardinal Ratzinger and elaborations about the likeness of human communities of persons to the Divine Communion of Persons in the Holy Trinity by Karol Wojtyla/Pope John Paul II. The principles of integral complementarity (equal dignity, significant difference and synergetic union) were clearly evident in Jacques' description of the lived experience of their community of three.

IV. Raïssa and Jacques' Lived and Articulated Principles of Complementarity in Later Years

One question that naturally comes to mind when writing about the lived complementarity of Jacques and Raïssa was what they wrote about woman's

61. Jacques Maritain, *Notebooks*, 73–74.

identity or man's identity *per se.* There are occasional reflections that they made separately and in conversation together about woman's identity and by comparison about man's identity as well. In my view, these descriptions seem to be very ordinary for the times (early twentieth-century) and nations (France and Germany) where they lived.

1. *Raïssa and Jacques' Writings about Differentiation of Woman and Man Per Se*

In her second Notebook of 1919 Raïssa described ways in which human beings experience shame (*pudeur*) when confronted with a conflict between their spiritual nature and their lower animal or vegetative nature. Then she added:

> *Pudeur* is commonly more accentuated in woman because woman is to some extent above and below animal nature: above, by the greater purity of her life—I am speaking in general;—below, because her maternal functions are vegetative rather than animal. For these two reasons it is more repugnant to her to be recalled to her carnal functions.
>
> A true and total love, a Christian marriage, idealize even the flesh because they unite not only two bodies, but two humanities.[62]

In two important ways, Raïssa was careful here to avoid stereotyped resolutions; she began with the qualification "I am speaking in general." Then she also avoided a Cartesian mind/body dualism in the conclusion she drew about Christian marriage as the union of two humanities.

In editing the journal, Jacques added his personal footnote to this passage: "Raïssa wrote these lines in 1919—After the second world war she might have added (it is something she often said to me) that when a woman thinks she has emancipated herself by rejecting what is characteristic of her nature 'in general', her immodesty becomes worse than that of man. (J.)"[63] It is difficult to interpret the comparison in engendered "worseness" of immodesty in women or men which resulted from the rejection of one's nature. Contemporary evidence seems to suggest that the rejection of one's nature as female or as male has disastrous results for both. Consider the relative immodesty of the fifty "so-called" genders recently listed in Facebook.

In another example, Raïssa wrote her thoughts in response to a 1919

62. *Raïssa's Journal*, 94.
63. Ibid., 94n4.

questionnaire about philosophical studies for girls because, as Jacques commented in his editorial note, "At that period girls were the best philosophical pupils at the Institut Catholique in Paris."[64]

> Among all the sciences it is metaphysics which, after all, seems to me the best suited to a feminine mind with a gift for abstraction. I am not saying that women are gifted for cutting a figure as great philosophers—but only for understanding and assimilating the philosophy of great philosophers.... Women possess keenness of intellectual vision. But not *active* power of mind: they make excellent pupils but as a rule they do not create, either in the arts or the sciences. They lack the self-control, the patience, the wisdom (in the speculative order where wisdom and power are synonymous) to order and co-ordinate, draw all the conclusions. But they assimilate the great abstract truths extremely well.[65]

As Raïssa continued to think through the questionnaire, we actually see her own example contradicting what she says a woman usually does because she, in fact, demonstrates self-control, patience, wisdom and creativity. Raïssa argued that when metaphysics "governs theodicy and ethics, a woman who is philosophically minded is drawn to it by preference, in order to examine in this supreme light what her whole life ought to be."[66] She observed that women love metaphysics and ethics because a "[w]oman's realism delights in the knowledge of ultimate realities"; furthermore, "Her great capacity for loving attaches her more strongly to the Truth and induces her to dedicate herself to it."[67]

Raïssa introduced a theme that will be picked up and elaborated in great depth in John Paul II's *Fides et Ratio*: "Faith has been attacked in the name of the Intellect. It is in the name of the Intellect that it must be defended nowadays."[68] She concluded this section by referring to passages on this theme written by previous philosophers, such as Aquinas: "Truth is the rule of the intellect and of the will; it has an absolute and legitimate power over the whole man. Not to follow the truth which the intellect shows us is to disobey God; for the intellect is, in us, a certain similitude of the uncreated light (St. Thomas)."[69]

64. Ibid., 111n1.
65. Ibid., 111.
66. Ibid., 112.
67. Ibid.
68. Ibid.
69. Ibid., 113.

2. *Thomist Circles and Integral Complementarity of Woman and Man (1914–1937)*

We turn now to consider the most important contribution of the Maritains to the history of complementarity, namely, their collaboration in providing a school within which and from which the metaphysical foundations of Thomism would be updated and made applicable to contemporary problems in philosophical anthropology, especially the problem of overcoming the unisex momentum of Cartesianism. A Neothomistic metaphysics open to contemporary science makes it possible to defend significant differences among women and men without losing their equal dignity or sliding into superficial generalizations.

On February 8, 1914 the first meeting of Thomist studies occurred at the Maritain home.[70] In the context of the eruption of World War I, Jacques tried to serve in the war, but he failed to be assigned to fighting. Instead he began to work in the barracks on a book on Descartes. In Raïssa's words: "Shortly afterward, he was discharged and returned home, restored to his vocation as a philosopher.... He resumed his courses at the Institut Catholique."[71]

Raïssa further described the new orientation of Jacques towards Thomistic philosophy—an orientation that would become pivotal for the defense of integral complementarity by Catholic philosophers:

> [Jacques'] freedom has grown greater, and he has better understood his vocation as a philosopher engaged in the drama of the profane world and temporal civilization. He has become more and more convinced that the philosophy of Saint Thomas, with its incomparably powerful structure, has remained for centuries bound up in the forms of theology, without expanding for its own sake, according to its essence; and that the time has come for it to take its proper form, its internal organization and its autonomous development as a philosophy. He has embarked upon this task, and it will be, he believes, the great task of the philosophers of the future, if the future does not betray itself, and if workers are not lacking.[72]

Neothomism provides the key components desperately needed after Descartes' philosophy rejected forms and with them a metaphysics of *hy-*

70. Jacques Maritain, *Notebooks*, 133.

71. Raïssa Maritain, *We Have Been Friends Together*, 350. See also Jacques Maritain, *Notebooks*, 78.

72. Raïssa Maritain, *Adventures in Grace*, 353. Raïssa summarized this attitude about Jacques's vocation as "woe to me if I do not Thomistize"; ibid., 352.

lomorphism. Cartesianism led to an approach of metaphysical dualism towards the human being, by trying to join a sexless mind to a mechanical body. While Descartes retained the equal dignity of women and men, he lost all possibility for a philosophy of significant difference. Post-Cartesian philosophy degenerated into either unisex or accidental differences in human beings. To recover the fundamental truth about the human being, embodied, as a man or as a woman, the Neothomist metaphysics includes the following: first, the soul/body composite identity of each substantial human being; second, the same human soul being simultaneously the form of a specific organic body and a spirit in communion with other spirits; and third, relation with others as essential, not accidental to a human person.

The metaphysical foundations for a new Thomistic foundation of philosophical anthropology was laid by Jacques Maritain in the Thomistic circles and in his own research and writing in these middle years. Raïssa observed: "At the time dealt with in this book [1909–1917], and for several years more, Jacques, as I have already said, concerned himself wholly with metaphysics and pure ideas."[73] Jacques Maritain in "Art and Beauty" suggested an aesthetic recovery of the meaning of form through a renewed Thomistic approach to beauty: "Finally, and above all, this radiance itself of the form, which is the main thing in beauty, has an infinity of diverse ways of shining on matter"; and he immediately adds in a note: "By *'radiance of the form'* must be understood an *ontological* splendor which is in one way or another revealed to our mind, not a *conceptual* clarity.... It is a Cartesian misconception to reduce clarity *in itself* to clarity *for us*."[74] If the radiance of form is ontological, then it demands a *hylomorphic* meaning of the form/matter distinction. Maritain's recovery of form observed that: "to say with the Schoolmen that beauty is the splendor of the form on the proportioned parts of matter, is to say that it is a flashing of intelligence on a matter intelligibly arranged."[75]

In "The Majesty and Poverty of Metaphysics," Jacques Maritain argued that a metaphysics which closes in on itself reveals its poverty which needs

73. Ibid., 353.

74. Jacques Maritain, "Art and Beauty," in *Art and Scholasticism and The Frontiers of Poetry*, translated by Joseph W. Evans (New York: Charles Scribner's Sons, 1962), 28; my emphasis. See also Jacques Maritain, *A Preface to Metaphysics: Seven Lectures on Being*, translated by Lewis Galantiere and G. B. Phelan (New York: Sheed and Ward, 1948).

75. Maritain, "Art and Beauty," 25; my emphasis. Maritain refers to *Summa theologiae* I, q. 39, a. 8 and q. 5, a. 4, ad 1.

to open to "a truth we may serve. For that truth is the food of the spirit. And, by the better part of ourselves, we are spirit."[76] Maritain repeated his *hylomorphic* understanding of the human being: "Yet, man is flesh and spirit, not held together by a thread, but *substantially united*."[77] A metaphysics which is not closed off on itself, but which rather opens up to the transcendent, was Maritain's goal: "That, then, is the poverty of metaphysics (and yet its majesty, too). It awakens a desire for supreme union, for spiritual possession completed in the order of reality itself and not only in the concept. It cannot satisfy that desire."[78]

Jacques described the extraordinary goal of the Thomist Study Circles which met monthly in the Maritain's home from 1919–1939 as "to examine a little more closely, in free discussions, the doctrine of St. Thomas, and to bring it face to face with the problems of our time."[79] The composition and background of those attending over the years was very rich and varied: "There were young persons and old persons, male students and female students, and professors—laymen (in the majority), but also unbelievers, Jews, Orthodox, Protestants."[80] In August of 1921 Raïssa initiated another development into the dynamic of their marriage. She had again been seriously ill and wrote in her Journal: "A month of illness. A month of convalescence. Jacques saves me by taking me out in an invalid chair."[81] Jacques then added the following footnote to this passage in his edited version of her journals:

> Dear Père Garrigou-Lagrange, who visited us several times ..., sometimes took my place in pushing the invalid's wheel-chair along the roads. It was during one of these promenades that Raïssa had the idea of asking him if he would consent to come every year to preach a retreat to the friends we would gather together to hear him. He immediately agreed. That was the origin of the annual retreats of the 'Thomist Circles'.[82]

The first retreat was held September 30 to October 4, 1922.[83] Jacques described the atmosphere of these retreats and why, in his view, they were so successful:

76. Jacques Maritain, *Distinguish to Unite or The Degrees of Knowledge*, translated by G. Bles (Notre Dame, Indiana: University of Notre Dame Press, 1995), 4.

77. Ibid., 16; my emphasis.

78. Ibid., 7.

79. Jacques Maritain, *Notebooks*, 133.

80. Ibid., 134.

81. *Raïssa's Journal*, 126.

82. Ibid., 126n3.

83. Ibid., 132.

They were received in the hearth of a family, they were guests of Raïssa Maritain. Such meetings and such a work in common are inconceivable without a feminine atmosphere. There were three women in the house: there was Raïssa's mother—she attended the meetings, more often than not, without understanding much of them, but too good a Jew, and of too serious a mind, not to take pleasure in intellectual debates. And she busied herself with the samovar, and with the dinner to be prepared for the evening. There was Vera, silent and diligent, who took care of everyone, and listened passionately to the discussions, not without secretly praying that everything would go well. And above all there was Raïssa, who received everyone in her fraternal charity, and who did not cease for many days to carry all of this work in her prayers. She was the ardent flame of these meetings, in which she took an active part, always discreetly, but with the mad, boundless love of truth which burned in her. It was very evident that without her—and without her little sister—there would have been no Thomist circles, any more than there would have been a Meudon (any more than there would have been a Jacques Maritain).[84]

In this beautiful description, Jacques anticipated perfectly the principle that John Paul II will call "the genius of women," rooted in her propensity to receive and foster the development of new life in persons within her sphere of activity. This principle will become a key element in the contemporary articulation of a significant difference in the contribution of women and of men to their relations of complementarity.[85]

In 1923 the Maritains moved their home to Meudon. Soon Raïssa took another initiative: she composed a Rule of Life for herself, Jacques, and Vera.[86]

Since Edith Stein is the person who first identified what could be called "the root of woman's genius" as later developed by John Paul II, it is interesting to ponder the fact that she had visited the Maritains and participated in their times of study and retreat. In a letter of 1932, Edith Stein wrote to Jacques Maritain: "My heartfelt thanks for your kindness in sending me your important new work [*The Degrees of Knowledge*]. To study it will be a great gain for me.... I recall with great pleasure the wonderful day in Juvisy and the hours spent in your home. With grateful and most cordial greetings to your dear wife (Raïssa) ..."[87] In 1933, Edith Stein wrote a second letter to Jacques and Raïssa Maritain, in which she thanked them for the gift:

84. Jacques Maritain, *Notebooks*, 134–35.

85. See Sr. Prudence Allen, R.S.M., *Mulieris Dignitatem*: Twenty Years Later: An Overview of the Document and Challenges," *Ave Maria Law Review* 8 (2009): 13–47.

86. Ibid., 151–55. Jacques inserts this Rule of Life into her Third Notebook when published.

87. Edith Stein, *Self-Portrait in Letters*, translated by Josephine Koeppel, O.C.D. (Washington, D.C.: ICS Publications, 1993), 124–25.

> You have given me great joy with your beautiful book.... I, too, cherish a grateful memory of the beautiful hours in Juvisy and Meudon. All during the past month I have been greatly consoled by the thought of having such good friends united to us by the bond of faith. I no longer have my position with the Pedagogical Institute and I will be leaving Münster in a few weeks. But do not be concerned about me: ... ('All things work together for the good of those who love God.').[88]

Just before this letter was written, Hitler denied the opportunity of those Christians with Jewish inheritance to teach, and so Edith Stein had to leave her position at the Pedagogical Institute. She was then free to request entrance into the Carmelite Monastery in Cologne, and later was martyred at Auschwitz in 1942.

A direct connection between Edith Stein and John Paul II came through her classmate and good friend Roman Ingarden. In *Memory and Identity* John Paul II revealed that he had learned about Stein through Ingarden, who was a professor in Cracow after WWII.[89] It is interesting to ponder the fact that Garigou-LaGrange, who was so closely connected with the Maritains over several years of directing the Meudon retreats, became the director at the Angelicum of Karol Wojtyla's doctoral dissertation, "Faith According to St. John of the Cross."[90]

Jacques Maritain's presence at the beginnings of French Personalism adds another important contribution to the defense for integral complementarity. Beginning in 1928, Emmanuel Mounier "becomes [a] regular participant at Meudon,"[91] French Personalism officially began in 1932 when Emmanuel Mounier and Jacques Maritain founded in Paris the journal *Esprit*. Within the next two years they met regularly with Gabriel Marcel and Nicholae Berdjaev and together wrote a "Personalist Manifesto."[92] In 1936 Mounier defended the equal dignity of women and men when he published in *Esprit* an article entitled "La femme aussi est une personne" (Woman is also a person).[93] Catholic personalists distinguished the individual from a person. Maritain elaborated on the importance of Thomis-

88. Ibid., 146–47.

89. John Paul II, *Memory and Identity: Conversations at the Dawn of a Millenium* (New York: Rizzolli, 2005).

90. John Paul II, *Faith According to St. John of the Cross* (San Francisco: Ignatius Press, 1981).

91. Jacques Maritain, "Maritain Chronology," in *Untrammeled Approaches* (Notre Dame, Indiana: University of Notre Dame Press, 1997), xxvi.

92. See Emmanual Mounier, *A Personalist Manifesto,* translated by Monks of St. John's Abbey (New York: Longmans, Green and Company, 1938).

93. Emmanuel Mounier, "La femme aussi est une person," *Esprit* (1936): 291–97.

tic foundations for the human person. He also developed in lectures from 1939–1945 the distinction between the individual who is more focused on self-determination and a person whose open ego and capacity for self-gift to others has a greater value.[94]

French personalism was communicated to the Polish underground during WWII. It provided an intellectual foundation for the development of Lublin Thomistic Existential Personalism through the collaboration of Karol Wojtyla and M. A. Krapiec.[95] Principles of a Thomist metaphysical foundation for philosophical anthropology flourished more when John Paul II articulated them for the universal Church in his audiences on the Theology of the Body (1979), in *Mulieris Dignitatem* (1988), and in documents related to the 1995 Beijing conference on women.[96]

3. *Thomist Circles and Integral Complementarity of Vocations (1940–1969)*

When Raïssa, Jacques, and Vera began their little community, at first they thought they should model it upon religious life (but in the world).[97]

Reviewing these early years while looking back in 1965, almost fifty years later, Jacques wrote:

> It is true that at the outset we regarded ourselves a little as lay monks and lay cloistered nuns, and that not without some bravado and much naiveté.... But these illusions soon vanished. *We were laymen, engaged unreservedly in the state of lay life*; and the more the years passed, the more we felt ourselves simple laymen, laymen of the common run of the people. But this little flock of three belonged to Jesus Christ.[98]

Jacques' affirmation in writing that the vocation of the lay state is important for the complementarity of vocations that they had lived during and following the years of the Thomist circles. From the beginning, the three collaborated with members of the clerical state, the religious state, and the

94. See Jacques Maritain, *The Person and the Common Good,* translated by John J. Fitzgerald (Notre Dame, Indiana: University of Notre Dame Press, 1966).

95. See Sr. Prudence Allen, R.S.M., "Analogy and Human Community in Lublin Existential Personalism," *The Toronto Journal of Theology* 5, no. 2 (1989): 236–46; and "A Woman and a Man as Prime Analogical Beings," *American Catholic Philosophical Quarterly*, 66 (1992): 456–82.

96. These are collected in Pope John Paul II on *The Genius of Women* (Washington, D.C.: United States Conference of Catholic Bishops, 1997).

97. Jacques Maritain, *Notebooks,* 202.

98. Ibid., 204; my emphasis.

lay state. Their collaboration was extraordinary and synergetic. Many men and women were converted to the Catholic Faith and found their own vocations among the three primordial vocations or derived variations. In short, the Maritains lived the *communio* of the Church's complementary vocations long before the principles were articulated during and following the Second Vatican Council.

In one interesting passage written in 1964, Jacques Maritain described how a characteristic of complementarity among members within the same vocation is to protect the vocation of others. He wrote how Vera protected Raïssa, and in this one case he actually used the word "complementarity":

> Well, nothing had more need of being protected than this strength [of Raïssa], because, even already as mere gift of nature, it was not of this world, in the sense in which poetry is not of this world either. It was enough to enable her to triumph, at any cost, over fear and over anguish; it was not enough to spare her from them. *Through the blessing of a complementarity which love alone can produce,* the admirable courage of Vera ... protected the strength which made oaks kneel by protecting the lily of the valley, the too vulnerable envelope, the heart of Raïssa open to all suffering as well as to all beauty.[99]

There are many examples of Raïssa and Jacques protecting one another's vocation. I will briefly describe two. In the first one, when Raïssa was undergoing much suffering physically and spiritually, Jacques came to protect her. In Raïssa's words: "Afterwards the flood of nameless misery returned, but then God sent me my dear Jacques who set to making the sign of the *Cross* all over me, as they do for Extreme Unction, and I was calmed."[100] Lest this description of Raïssa seem to suggest that she had a melancholy disposition, Jacques described her love of dancing, games, and the fact that "we laughed a great deal in our house."[101]

In the second example, Raïssa protected Jacques' vocation of teaching, lecturing, and writing. Before, during, and after World War II, he traveled to Canada, the United States, and Rome. While he was in Chicago in 1944,

99. Ibid., 197. In another passage of the same notebook entry, Jacques also reflected on two of the three essential components of complementarity: "Striking at first, all these differences between the two sisters were only differences of temperament, which covered a fundamntal likeness of a much greater importance"; ibid., 191.

100. *Raïssa's Journal,* 203. The passage continues: "Contrary to all hope, I was able to go downstairs at 3 o'clock for the talk Père Garrigou-Lagrange always gives in our house during the retreat."

101. Jacques Maritain, *Notebooks,* 200.

Raïssa wrote the following correction to him, when he appeared to be thinking that his travels were causing her more suffering:

> If there is one thing in the world I cannot bear, it is that you should be unhappy. I hope with all my heart that this "moment of sadness" which made you write that letter on Saturday morning was only a moment. *You have been suffering from an oppressive delusion,* for there is nothing in the instability and insecurity of our life for which you are responsible.... What I *am* sure of is that you will always do what God will most want you to do—and that is the greatest security and stability of all—and that we will always find ourselves where God will prefer us to be. Besides all this, I do well know, my dear beloved, that the burden of decisions rests entirely on your shoulders, like the burden of excessive work that never ceases to weigh you down.... But for all that is peculiar to our life, to my life with you, I give thanks to God with my whole soul. He has given me a marvelous lot!—the best that could have been destined for me. In you, I have found all the sweetness and light I needed, and still do need. Of that light ... I have had the first fruits and the sweetest part. And your so dear love which has always surrounded me, helped me, given me courage to live. So do be happy too, my beloved Jacques, as much as it is possible to be in this world. Be of good heart, my beloved. We belong to him who has conquered the world.[102]

V. Conclusion

There is no doubt that the lived experience of complementarity by Raïssa, Jacques, and Vera passed from an initial focus on characteristics like nationality, religious heritage, male and female, appearance and temperament, sickness and health, to a deeper level of the personal being of each person in communion with the others. Thus, we could say that their bond of complementarity moved from experiences to ontology, or from sentiment and attraction to metaphysical truth. This metaphysical truth was permeated by a vital spirituality given to them through their Baptism, Confirmation, Eucharistic communions, and their repeated acts of total self-gift to God and to one another according to their respective vocations. Their Christian lives and community together integrated in each one of them and in all together the multifarious elements of their complementary.

Jacques and Raïssa provided three major original contributions to the developing philosophical defense for the integral complementarity of woman

102. *Raïssa's Journal,* 298–99. The italics in the passage on "oppressive delusion" is my emphasis; the italiczed *am* is Raïssa's emphasis.

and man. The first original contribution of their collaboration came through their Thomist Circles and Retreats. By their initiation of and support for the renewal of the philosophical study of the works of St. Thomas Aquinas, and more specifically by recovering the metaphysical foundations of his thought from within his theology and then applying these foundations to contemporary problems in the world, they opened up a wide pathway for the recovery of form in its dual operations in soul and spirit and of *hylomorphism* as the true metaphysical foundation for the individual human being, for the most part differentiated as a woman or as a man. *Hylomorphism* is essential for holding the significant difference of woman and man in tension with their equal dignity and for releasing genuinely synergetic effects of their relations.

Jacques provided the second original contribution to the developing history of the complementarity of woman and man by his reflections on the passage from the Book of Genesis, "Let us make for Adam a helpmate like to himself." Although this talk was written after Raïssa's death, it is no doubt the fruit of their many conversations with one another over the course of their lives together.[103] Its text, printed in French in 1967 (in *Nova et Vetera*) serves as a very important transition into the path-breaking work of John Paul II's Theology of the Body.[104] In addition to the references to complementarity of woman and man summarized early in this paper, Jacques Maritain also brings his intelligence and faith to bear on the history of woman and man's relations with one another. Specifically, he argues against Aristotle's view "that woman is a man that nature accidentally botched up" and forcefully concludes that "[t]he conception of woman as a botched-up man, and of masculinity as the peak of human nature, is contrary to philosophical reason ... [and] is contrary as well to the text of Genesis. . . ."[105]

Against Thomas Aquinas, Maritain argues that the reduction of a woman's help to man to be simply to generate the species is "flabbergasting ... [and] [t]here is not a single word in Genesis to support such an assertion, which totally ignores the evident complementarity of the feminine and

103. The talk was given to the Little Brothers of Jesus, a community he went to teach in Toulouse shortly after Raïssa's death. For a description of his years with the Little Brothers of Jesus, including taking vows as a member of the community two years before his death, see Brooke Smith (Deely), *Jacques Maritain*, 155–58.

104. See *Nova et Vetera* 4 (1967): 241–54. (Translations of this text have appeared in Spanish, Italian, and Czech.) See note 1 above for reference to the 1997 English translation in Jacques Maritain, *Untrammeled Approaches.*

105. Jacques Maritain, "Let us make for him a helpmate like to himself," 154.

masculine types, as well as the fact that their differential qualities are those of the spiritual soul itself which informs the body according as it is individualized in one direction or the other."[106] Finally, in this remarkable set of reflections, Jacques Maritain began the hard work of articulating how women and men have equal dignity of persons; significant differences in their respective identities, before and after the Fall; and most significantly how their ontological complementarity works in their vocations without sliding into overvaluation of woman or of man and into loss of differentiation in a move towards androgyny.

The third original contribution of the Maritains' collaboration is found in the actual lived experience of Raïssa, Jacques, and Vera. Long before the principles of integral gender complementarity were articulated, these three Christian friends discovered by trial and error, through suffering and elation, the meaning of their interwoven lives as a *communio* of persons in likeness to the Communion of the Three Divine Persons. We Catholic philosophers and theologians should be very grateful to this "Maritain Model of Complementarity."[107]

106. Ibid., 162. In the passage referred to (*Summa theologiae* I, q. 92, a. 1, c.) Thomas was arguing that God needed to create woman to help man in the work of generation because more perfect animals require generation to occur by the union of two different kinds of powers, the active power in the male and the passive power in the female.

107. I am very grateful to Sr. Mary Judith O'Brien, R.S.M., J.D., J.C.D. for her editing suggestions for this paper.

II

THE MARITAINS AND THEIR CONTEMPORARIES

War, Theodicy, and Justice

BRENNA MOORE

Out of the Shadows

Raïssa Maritain on Poetry and Making Violence Visible

For scholars who may know something about Raïssa Maritain, it is inevitably through her beloved two-volume memoir, *Les grandes amitiés* (1941 and 1944), published in English as *We Have Been Friends Together.*[1] There she richly details the early life she and Jacques shared, and set in motion the circulation of stories now standard for our understanding of the couple: the suicide pact, the conversion, the discovery of Aquinas, the vast network of friendships. But each chapter of the memoir relates in complex ways to temporality: moving forward slowly through actually only a small sliver of time, her chapters mainly lead inward. They track the development of Raïssa's own spiritual and intellectual journey, hovering mostly in the 1910s, when the Maritains were young adults. The second volume does not move chronologically much beyond the first, and both volumes end with her reflections on the ravishing intensity that Léon Bloy's life and thought exerted on her own. Volume Two closes with a meditation on Bloy's death

1. The first volume of the memoir was published as *Les grandes amitiés* (New York: Éditions de la Maison Française, 1941), and then translated into English by Julie Kernan as *We Have Been Friends Together* (New York: Longmans Press, 1942). The second volume was published along with the first in the French edition, *Les grandes amitiés, Les aventures de la grâce* (New York: Éditions de la Maison Française, 1944), but was issued separately in an English translation by Julie Kernan as *Adventures in Grace* (*Sequel to We Have Been Friends Together*) (New York: Longmans Press, 1945). Both volumes are currently reprinted in Raïssa Maritain, "Les grandes amitiés," in *Œuvres completes Jacques et Raïssa Maritain*, vol. 14, edited by Jacques Maritain and Raïssa Maritain (Paris: Éditions Universitaires, 1993). Hereafter, *Œuvres completes Jacques et Raïssa Maritain* [*OC*].

in 1917, when Raïssa was 34. She never completed the third volume she planned to write while in Italy in the postwar period.

The stories we then have of Raïssa's life and thought cover only the first three-and-a-half decades of her life; she had not even published her first scholarly, sole-authored piece of writing until she was 48, and she lived until the age of 77. Hence, none of her scholarly life, as a writer, an *intellectual*, appear in the memoir—they were outside the purview of the deeper, more youthful memories she called up to tell her life story. So what happened in all those years not covered in *Les grandes amitiés*?

In this essay, I aim to fill in this gap and see Raïssa as a mature intellectual, which serves as a backdrop to my central argument: I want to push back on readings of Raïssa Maritain as the apolitical, silent partner of the more publically-oriented Jacques, immune from the political crises of the twentieth century. Raïssa, I want to argue, presents what E. Jane Doering and I have called "a new kind of sanctity," a sanctity rooted in (1) spiritual practice; (2) the creation of art (mainly poetry); and (3) an abiding commitment that both prayer and art must situate themselves in "the storm of life [*l'orage de la vie*]," and be able to speak from and to the traumas and aspirations of the contemporary, political present.[2] In particular, Raïssa's art aimed to inculcate awareness and compassion among the vast majority of Catholics in the 1940s and 1950s who were indifferent to the suffering of Europe's Jews during the Shoah. The "politics" of her spirituality and her art were not the judiciary politics of the state, but worked in the terrain of shaping attitudes and sensibilities of those who read her poetry and memoirs and those who knew her. Bringing to light the political dimensions of Raïssa Maritain's life and writings helps us not only re-assess her legacy beyond the material in *Les grandes amitiés*, but also rethink the assumption that views the realms of aesthetics, poetry, and spirituality as separate from the political. [3]

2. Raïssa Maritain, *Journal de Raïssa*, in *OC*, 15:150.

3. Resources that have been helpful in my thinking on this topic include Carolyn Forché, *Twentieth Century Poetry of Witness* (New York: Norton Press, 1993); Maureen O'Connell, "Sacramental Imaginary: New Directions in Catholic Humanism," in *The Catholic Studies Reader*, edited by James Fisher and Margaret McGuinness (New York: Fordham University Press, 2013), 372–94.

I. Raïssa Maritain (1883–1960): Biographical Introduction

But first, the biographical that requires some archeological digging: Raïssa, particularly in her early career, tended to publish furtively, anonymously or under initials. For example, her first book, *Le prince de ce monde*, a reflection on the demonic in modernity, was published in 1929, and appeared only under "RM."[4] Not until she was 48 years old in 1931 did Raïssa publish her first sole-authored piece under her full name, a poem entitled the "La couronne d'épines [Crown of Thorns]."[5] The poem appeared in *Vigile*, a short-lived Catholic literary journal founded by Charles du Bos, Paul Claudel, and others.[6] In this issue, the name Raïssa Maritain appeared alongside Henri Bremond, Étienne Gilson, François Mauriac, and Jacques. Here she came out of the shadows a bit, and her scholarly life began to flourish. Her reputation in the literary community grew shortly after, when her first two books of poetry, *La vie donnée* and *Lettre de nuit*, appeared in 1935 and 1939. She went on to publish ninety poems in four volumes before her death in 1960, and published related essays on poetry and aesthetics, presenting widely and internationally on these themes. During the war years from 1940–1945, Raïssa wrote a handful of chilling theological poems about the violence unfolding in Europe that remain among the very few artistic Catholic voices of lamentation and protest at the destruction of European Jewry as it was occurring, not after. I engage a close reading of three of these poems in the next section.[7]

In the same period when she was launching her career as a poet, Raïssa's prose occupied itself increasingly with the theme of Judaism, the theme that

4. Raïssa Maritain, *Le Prince de ce monde* (Paris: Desclée de Brouwer, 1929); translated by Gerald B. Phelan as *The Prince of this World* (Toronto: Pontifical Institute of Medieval Studies, 1933). For more on the life of Raïssa Maritain, see Judith D. Suther, *Raïssa Maritain: Pilgrim, Poet, Exile* (New York: Fordham University Press, 1990); Brenna Moore, *Sacred Dread: Raïssa Maritain, the Allure of Suffering, and the French Catholic Revival, 1905–1944* (Notre Dame, Indiana: University of Notre Dame Press, 2013).

5. Raïssa Maritain, "La couronne d'épines," 1*Vigile* (1931): 97–101

6. See Denis Pelletier, *Vingtième Siècle: Revue d'histoire* 63 (July 1999): 167–69.

7. Raïssa's complete poems, along with all of her other published prose, are found in *OC*, 14 and 15. The majority of her poems have not yet been translated into English, but the English-speaking world is indebted to Judith Suther for her beautiful book, the first book on Maritain in English, *Raïssa Maritain: Pilgrim, Poet, Exile*, in which she translates selections of Raïssa's poetry, and offers excellent literary analysis.

would become one of the central concerns of her scholarly life. Although Raïssa never fully severed ties with the Judaism of her family, her thinking on the Jewish question underwent significant developments throughout her adult life.[8] Shortly after she converted to Catholicism, her earliest writings relied on the classic binary opposition between the true Israelite (as actual or incipient Christian) and the false, carnal Jew.[9] But by the early 1930s, her understanding had evolved considerably, and Raïssa came to be seen by some members of their intellectual circuit as a "pioneer of Jewish-Christian relations."[10] Her writing on the Jewish question stemmed from the Meudon years, when their home was a salon to many other Russian Jewish émigrés who had moved to France and settled in Meudon after the Russian revolution. Raïssa and Vera spoke Russian at home, considered themselves (increasingly) Jews in the Christian religion, and their home was known in this community a welcome place for Russian-Jewish exiles, including their friends Marc and Bella Chagall. In 1935, she published *Histoire d'Abraham,* an exegetical reading of Genesis to explore the inner life of Abraham.[11] In this work, Raïssa dismantled the classic accusation of Jewish legalism by showing how Abraham's fidelity to the law is grounded in love, and Abraham consequently becomes the figure who "unites the two testaments to one another."[12] Raïssa's essay was republished in the postwar period, expanding the conversation which had been initiated by her friend John Oesterreicher, later one of the drafters of *Nostra Aetate.* When Oesterreicher set up an institute of Judeo-Christian studies at Seton Hall University in 1953, he launched a series, *The Bridge,* dedicated to exploring the theme "Spiritually we are all Semites"—the famous words of Pope Pius XI spoken in 1938. The inaugural 1955 volume of *The Bridge* included a revised version of Raïssa's *Histoire d'Abraham,* published in English under the title "Abraham and the Ascent of Conscience."[13]

8. For more on this theme see Richard F. Crane and Brenna Moore, "Cracks in the Theology of Contempt: The French Roots of Nostra Aetate," *Studies in Christian-Jewish Relations* 8 (2013): 1–28; Brenna Moore, *Sacred Dread,* 98–133.

9. Raïssa Maritain, "Récit de ma conversion," in *OC,* 15:827–37.

10. Helene Iswolski, *Light before Dusk: A Russian Catholic in France* (New York: Longmans, Greene, 1942), 179.

11. Raïssa Maritain, *Histoire d'Abraham ou La sainteté dans l'état de nature* (Geneva: Nova et Vetera, 1935). Reprinted in *OC,* 14:568–617.

12. Raïssa Maritain, *Histoire d'Abraham,* 591.

13. Raïssa Maritain, "Abraham and the Ascent of Conscience," in *The Bridge: A Yearbook of Judaeo-Christian Studies,* edited by John M. Oesterreicher (New York: Pantheon Books, 1955), 23–53.

During the war years, however, from 1940 through 1944, Raïssa spent most of her energy in her New York apartment waiting out the exile from France that would become permanent.[14] She spoke no English, and in addition to her wartime poems, Raïssa primarily dedicated her scholarly energies to turning to the earlier years of her life. In this period, she introduced to her readers her early mentors and friends that played a role in the renaissance of Catholic thought and culture in interwar Paris—a culture that had, by the war, nearly crumbled. This is the setting of her memoir *Les grandes amitiés,* but during that time she also edited and translated Léon Bloy for a new generation, and penned important pieces on Bergson and Péguy as well. After Raïssa's death in 1960, new editions of *Les grandes amitiés* appeared in 1962, 1963, 1966, and 1974, published in French English, Spanish, Italian, Polish, and Hungarian.[15]

As for Jacques, he lived thirteen years as a widower and never fully recovered from the loss of Raïssa. But he felt her spiritual presence acutely in his mourning: "I am a man in pieces," Jacques wrote to Charles Journet seven years after Raïssa's death, "held up entirely by the hands of Raïssa. I no longer am in control of anything, there remains nothing of of *me* in my agency [*il n'y a plus de moi agent*] [sic]; if anything good remains in the work for which people want me to survive, it is owed, every time, to what I receive from her, and it passes through me as water through a sieve, I remain empty [*je rest vide*]."[16] This was Jacques' existential and spiritual state when he set to work in establishing Raïssa's legacy. Most significantly, he initiated and oversaw the publication of her spiritual journal [*Journal de Raïssa*] that had left him "bewildered" in its intensity, detailing her vivid experiences with God over a forty year period.[17] Later, Harper-Collins listed this *Journal* one of the top one hundred spiritual books of the twentieth century.

Beyond her writings, Raïssa Maritain as a person influenced not only Jacques but also artists, poets, intellectuals: the poets Catherine Pozzi and Emily Snow; theater critic Jan Kott, scholar of Jewish-Christian relations,

14. Julie Kernan, *Our Friend Jacques Maritain: A Personal Memoir* (Garden City, New York: Doubleday), 1975.

15. René Mougel, "Relire *Les grandes amitiés,*" *Cahiers Jacques Maritain* 48 (June 2004): 27–37.

16. Charles Journet and Jacques Maritain, *Correspondance Journet-Maritain,* edited by René Mougel (Fribourg: Éditions Universitaires, 2006), 6:478.

17. Jacques Maritain, "Avertissement," in *OC,* 15:159.

Osterreicher, along with Marc Chagall, Thomas Merton, and Dorothy Day, all attested to Raïssa's influence and friendship in their writing and correspondence.[18] Most recently, in the winter of 2013–2014, the New York Jewish History Museum presented a work on Marc Chagall's wartime paintings while he was exile in New York (together with the Maritains), and the museum book featured Raïssa's own scholarship on the Jewish roots of Chagall's paintings.[19]

This brief intellectual-biography has been a mere sampling of Raïssa Maritain's intellectual accomplishments. Even so, we can see the topics and genres that were the center of gravity in her intellectual life: poetry and memoir, spirituality, Judaism, friendship. What could be more classically "apolitical," in topic and style of writing, particularly compared with Jacques' work in the international arena, in political philosophy, human rights, and public policy?

II. Poetry and Politics for Raïssa Maritain

The themes of Raïssa Maritain's writings, particularly mysticism and aesthetics, and the genres in which she wrote them, poetry and memoir, are often indicted for their evasion of reality and their tendency to withdraw from the political present. This is what partly drives the tendency to see her as the "silent" or "apolitical" partner in her marriage. One *Commonweal* article from several years ago, viewed her as "astonishingly sheltered from what was happening socially and politically in Europe." For this reviewer, there was an accusation: she cannot "be a model to emulate" because she "never involved herself with Jacques' political work nor addressed, at least in conventional terms, social problems."[20] For others, Raïssa's supposed immunity from history and politics inspired abiding admiration. For Thomas Merton, Raïssa was "immersed in the supernatural" and stood "in

18. See Thomas Merton, *The Seven Storey Mountain* (New York: Doubleday, 1989), 60; Sarah Gordon, "Flannery O'Connor and the French Catholic Renaissance," in *Flannery O'Connor's Radical Reality*, edited by J. Gretlund (Columbia, South Carolina: University of South Carolina Press, 2006), 68–84; Mark Bosco, S.J., *Graham Greene's Catholic Imagination* (New York: Oxford University Press, 2005); William Bush, *Georges Bernanos* (New York: Twayne, 1969), 55; Dorothy Day, "There Is No Time with God," *Catholic Worker* 1, no. 7 (November 1953): 1, 7.

19. Susan Tumarkin Goodman, *Chagall: Love, War, and Exile* (Yale University Press, 2013), 33 and 114.

20. Madeline Marget, "Too Much Ado about Raïssa," *Commonweal* 117, no. 17 (October 12, 1991): 586–87.

sharp relief to this century of torment, duplicity, and confusion."[21] Through a close analysis of three of Raïssa's poems, all of which are focused intensely on human suffering, I want to complicate this reading. Admittedly, the poetry that emerged from her spiritual experiences is rarely political or even religious in the overt sense of its content. Often she presents realistic snapshots of singular events and people: a mother holding her son's lifeless body, coffins beneath the sunshine, the sound of a bird's wing.

Consider "Pietà," a 1938 poem Raïssa wrote for her friend Christine van der Meer de Walcheren, whose second son had died suddenly as an adult. (Twenty years earlier, during WWI, her two year old had also died. The boy had been Raïssa's godson.)

> Come wails lamentations and tears
> Come sobs and cries rise up like the sea
> Wash away with your waves our bitter refusal
> Flow abundantly from the source of the soul
> Death has touched the docile Victim
> God gathers all around the night of the Cross
> And he placed his Son into your arms . . .
> And Your tears will wash his bloodied face.
> . . .
> Stunned silence keeps you company
> In your exile, Queen of Compassion.[22]

Here Raïssa captures something of the unbearable pain of a mother in mourning, and gives it universal meaning through the theological symbol of the Pietà. The poem was an invitation to grieve ("Come wails lamentations tears"), to tap into and generate feelings of affliction in a moment of a mother's unthinkable loss. By writing poetry to and for her friend's bereavement, Maritain gave words to the brutal singularity of another's pain that would have otherwise gone unarticulated, accompanied only by the "stunned silence" she describes chillingly in the final two lines.

I think we might tend to see a poem like this as merely "personal" writing, in the stereotypically feminized realm of the private sphere, where emotion and love preside. Although she recast the loss theologically, in terms of Christian symbolism, it remains nonetheless in the domain of emotional

21. Thomas Merton, *Literary Essays of Thomas Merton,* edited by Patrick Hart (New York: New Directions, 1984), 308. I also discuss this in more detail in *Sacred Dread,* 16–20.

22. Raïssa Maritain, "Pietà," in *OC,* 15:542. This translation is my own; cf. Judith D. Suther, *Raïssa Maritain,* 83.

love and familial–friend relations. As Carolyn Forché has argued, we tend to distinguish this from political writing, which we associate instead with public relationships and the juridical politics centered on state political action and intervention.[23] Yet Raïssa's work breaks down the division we use to think about personal and political writing. All of her poems *were* personal in a sense—like "Pietà" they were concrete snapshots of individuals, often snapshots of experiences of suffering, like this woman (her friend/Mary) in mourning, the gritty specificity of a mother's tears washing a son's face. Yet for Raïssa, this has profound social-political meaning and import; it was even, one could argue, a political strategy. Let me explain.

During WWII, Raïssa often reflected that the most shocking of the atrocities of the *Shoah* was the fact that "human madness and human cruelty have been given permission to go to all lengths, unchecked," and of the "six million massacred" ... "*so little is said.*"[24] Jacques too described, vividly and painfully, a pervasive inability or unwillingness to name suffering and death in 1940–1944 for what it was. Jacques was appalled that so many could "witness such a spectacle," he wrote, "*without seeing it.*"[25] In 1944, in *Les grandes amitiés*, Raïssa quoted a lengthy passage from a book her godfather Léon Bloy had written in the midst of the First World War, *Au seuil de l'Apocalypse* (1916). Towards the end of her book, she pulled from Bloy's words about the human refusal to see the pain of others, particularly during war: "I see people going about their business as if nothing were happening," Bloy wrote in 1917 (and Raïssa quoted in 1941), "entertaining themselves as much as they can, while each day thousands of men are being massacred. There's a total indifference among all those whom the war does not threaten. Supernatural blindness [*Aveuglement surnaturel*]."[26]

Throughout the war, Raïssa Maritain suggested that a way to combat this indifference—Bloy's notion of "supernatural blindness"—is to give a name "to those who died in Auschwitz, and call up a *face* among them." In her experience, she continued in a letter to a friend, the sadness for the millions can coalesce around the image of a single human being: "the vast sorrow one feels for all other victims itself assumes a face which haunts you with

23. See Carolyn Forché, *Twentieth Century Poetry of Witness* (New York: Norton Press, 1993), 31.

24. Letter reprinted in Raïssa Maritain, *Journal de Raïssa*, in *OC*, 15:436.

25. Jacques Maritain, "On Anti-Semitism," *Christianity and Crisis* 1, no. 17 (October 6, 1941): 2–5.

26. Raïssa Maritain, *Les aventures de la grâce*, in *OC*, 14:1070.

unspeakable horror and compassion."[27] It is precisely such "faces" that occupy most of Raïssa's wartime poetry, as it was in "Pietà," a mother stunned in her misfortune, wiping dry the blood-stained face of her child. This way of communicating the concrete experiences of particular people, through poetry, was a way to render real and vivid political violence that could be at best seen as abstract, distant, and at worst covered over, occluded, denied. Consider, for example, "Le Prisonnier" (1943), where the issue of wartime imprisonment in Europe is made visible through a "face behind bars":

> Thy servant is in irons
> In the Shadow of death
> Lord deliver him
> I see his face behind bars
> Like a saint's face in holy pictures
> His wide face protruding eyes
> Fringe of black hair on his brow
> Streaked with white wool
> He looks like the Christ
> Of Quentin Matsys
> He gazes straight in front
> Stunned at his misfortune
> He sees God's sky
> And that all will go well
> No he is not yet painted
> In the holy pictures
> He sits on his bed
> His head in his arms
> He weeps
> Alone among enemies
> Who hate all he loves
> For whom his kindness his intelligence
> Are objects of contempt
> Prisoner of his innocence
> He keeps patience
> . . .
> He is like the Christ
> Of Quentin Matsys
> He is learning
> The Language of Heaven

27. Raïssa Maritain to Ascha Belkand, December 24, 1945, in *Journal* de Raïssa, in *OC*, 15:436.

Like the "stunned silence" of the Virgin, this prisoner too is "stunned at his misfortune [*étonné*] ... all will not go well." The portrait of black hair streaked with white, head fallen, both personalizes and concretizes unimaginable wartime horror. Like her friend Christine who had lost her son, here the (presumably Jewish) prisoner is depicted through Christological symbolism ("like the Christ") and sacralized ("like a saint's face"), images her largely Catholic readership could comprehend, and empathize with, as her friend Marc Chagall's *White Crucifixion* painting had done five years earlier.[28] Depicted both personally and theologically, the portrait of the Christ-like prisoner is not a safe, apolitical image: it contains universal claims, reminding Maritain's readers that the politics of war are felt most acutely on the level of the concrete individuals who are entangled in its violence, using a Christian idiom with which her readers could connect.

Later that same year (1944), Raïssa penned a poem several pages long that was published in *Commonweal* in French and in English, "Deus excelsus terribilis." This is a long poem that spans several pages, a lamentation about the reality of the war and God's seeming inability or refusal to intervene. Here is a small excerpt:

> France, shattered, fouled, ravaged,
> Famine there, wasting bodies,
> The children who will not grow up,
> Adolescents who are in slavery
> In prison in captivity
> ...
> What cannot be imagined
> What cannot be told
> What the mind refuses to bear
> Four million Jews or more have suffered
> Death without consolation
> ...
> Women with their children they would not give up
> Hurled themselves from windows
> Old men shortened their days
> Because they saw their hope condemned
> ...

28. Ziva Amishai-Maisels, "Chagall's 'White Crucifixion,'" *Art Institute of Chicago Museum Studies* 17, no. 2 (1991): 138–53.

It is because You Yourself, our God,
You have forsaken us.
And the Angel of Truth keeps silent—
The mirror of Your indifference—
Because You have abandoned us to ourselves
. . .
It is time, awaken Lord Jesus, come!"

In 1943 Jacques read this poem over the airwaves of Free France radio encouraging the French resistance. The horrible, vivid specifics here of old men, women, and their children give a kind of "face" to (in 1943) the "four million or more Jews who have suffered death without consolation." While "Le Prisonner" presents the Jewish prisoner as Christ-like, raised to the heights of the sacred to evoke compassion and empathy among Christians, here in "Deus Excelsis Terribilis" the theological tradition Raïssa evokes is darker. God is absent among the victims—God "has forsaken us," she writes here, "abandoned us to ourselves." Jesus is only the imagined recipient of a plea, asleep during her cry: "it is time, awaken Lord Jesus, come!" This theological language evokes the lamentation Psalm 88, a Psalm which Raïssa knew well. Here Raïssa's notion of the "face" surfaces, but here, according to the psalmist, it is God's face, hidden: "But I cry to you for help, Lord; in the morning my prayer comes before you. Why, Lord, do you reject me and hide your face from me?"

The darkness of Psalm 88 and "Deus Excelsis Terribilis" extends its reach into Maritain's prose reflections late in the war, when she showed less and less hope. By 1944, she had very little faith that even the most raw, vivid poetry personalizing the war and the outpouring of lamentation it meant to evoke, could exert any power over the events of her day. She described her day as a "time of hatred, time of sorrow [*la douleur*]. Haggard hope does not know what to cling to.... Our time of blood and death; of tortures, of despair, of chaos, of disconsolation, of misery, of famine, of anguish [*d'angoisse*], of accursed discoveries; time of irremediable and boundless calamity; drowning every heart which cruelty has not yet devoured." She continued:

Then, poetry! let poetry do penance, let her be silent, because she has not words for the reality of our time; let her veil her face; let her stop flirting with our sorrow; let her forget flowers, games, graces, rhetoric and eloquence; let her strip herself and humble herself if she wishes to survive the unimaginable, the indescribable, the moral darkness of our time.[29]

Here the face is *poetry's* face; like God's in Psalm 88, it is in hiding from the horrors of the day. Her earlier wartime poems considered above—"The Prisoner," "Pietà," and "Deus Excelsus Terribilis"—each *attempted* to describe the reality of Europe, however unthinkable ("the unimaginable, the indescribable"). Presumably for Maritain this was a better alternative than that chosen by those who say nothing (supernatural blindness, go about their business as if nothing were happening), yet the voice of poetry was never enough, never fully satisfying to Raïssa.

But her poems were among few Catholic voices in Europe and the United States speaking out about the violence against Jews during the war years, as it was occurring, urging recognition and response. Although she never engaged in policy work like Jacques did, her writings are certainly not apolitical. One priest who wrote to Raïssa after reading her wartime writings, claimed that she knew how to speak to "my heart *and* open my intelligence."[30] Her poems and prose, published in Catholic and literary journals in Europe and the United States, urge us to reconsider the boundaries we draw between personal and political writings. The "poetry of witness," to use Carolyn Forché's term, often occupies a space *between* these two realms. We need to describe the space between institutional religion and the intuitional state, on the one hand, and the supposedly safe, apolitical havens of the personal and spiritual, on the other. In this space grief and loss are recognized for how fiercely singular they are for those who experience them, however directly they map onto larger social and political forces. Furthermore, her poetic voice put into circulation a theological language that had once only belonged to the "sacred enclave" (to use the language of Michel de Certeau) of her own spiritual life.[31] The combination of poetry and theology gave her access to a different kind of language (rich in metaphor and symbolism, a mix of genres, short lines) that could describe the world in a new way, a world that exceeded rational discursive description, even if it was never fully adequate for her.

Perhaps it is for the way in which they drew on the affective and the ra-

29. Raïssa Maritain, "La poésie de notre temps," in *OC*, 15, 717.

30. Maurice Pierquin to Raïssa Maritain, December 13, 1941, Jacques and Raïssa Maritain Archives, Kolbsheim, France.

31. Michel de Certeau, *The Possession at Loudun* (Chicago: University of Chicago Press, 1996), 51.

tional modes that in several of Jacques' most effective speeches, he included excerpts of Raïssa's poems to give his readers a different way of seeing the political reality he aimed to describe. In addition to the 1943 resistance speech reading "Deus Excelsus Terriblis," in his important 1941 English essay "On Antisemitism" he drew from Raïssa's poem on Chagall. Her poem about Israel was an epigraph to his book, *Mystery of Israel.* Jacques and Raïssa give us two different ways of accessing the political—Jacques working more closely with the juridical sphere and the state, Raïssa working in less direct spheres of writing (aesthetic, poetic, memorial), all of which aimed to inculcate recognition of the reality in her midst that was too easily ignored by her Catholic readers.

III. Conclusions: Reading Raïssa Today

What about reading Raïssa today? First, her tactic of personalizing political problems speaks to us in the contemporary present, raising questions about the possibility and even the limitations of evoking empathy for making a more humane world. Although New York is a shared context for both of us, my own present differs radically from Raïssa's wartime context as a Jewish (by blood) woman in exile. Yet the shock she expressed at just how little was said about the suffering in her own time resonates. In New York City, there are currently 22,000 homeless children, more than even during the Great Depression.[32] And as in Maritain's own time, it is shocking how infrequently most New Yorkers discuss this real problem, or even know about it. These vast numbers are overwhelming but easy to dismiss because they are so abstract. Indeed, it is hard even to think about these numbers and their meaning without the kind of "face" Maritain had in mind and tried to visualize in poetry. Others agree: at the end of 2013, a Pulitzer Prize-winning journalist for the *New York Times*, Andrea Elliot, generated an enormous amount of public discussion of New York City's homeless problem with an incredible five-part essay in the *Times* depicting the life of one eleven-year old girl, Disani, entangled in the web of New York City's broken homeless shelter system.[33] This widely-read *New York Times* essay gave a "face" to the

32. Ian Frazer, "Hidden City: New York has more homeless than it has [sic] in decades. What should its next mayor do?" *The New Yorker* (October 28, 2013), 38–44; Coalition for the Homeless of New York City, *State of the Homeless in 2013* (March 2013): 2.

33. Andrea Elliot, "Invisible Child: Girl in the Shadows: Disani's Homeless Life," *New York*

vast problem of homelessness in our city, and even newly elected Mayor Bill DiBlasio evoked Disani's story in a major speech on the state of the city only days after the story was printed.[34] Vivid personal portraits *do* have the power to combat indifference ("supernatural blindness") as Raïssa predicted and hoped. But they cannot alone guarantee social change; perhaps she recognized this, and it explains some of the raw anguish and despair that hovers over her poems and prose written late in the war: "Let poetry be silent!" Works of art like poetry have to be part of a broader politics, not the final world, lest they drift into a sentimentalization or an aestheticization of suffering. Yet the efforts of social activists today to transform New York's problem with skyrocketing income gaps and homelessness, or anything else, cannot succeed without empathy—empathy nurtured through mediums like poetry, film, theater, journalism that put *lives*, faces, back into the stories we tell about our world. When we tell compelling, artistically moving stories about men, women, and children in the present, we can see things we would have otherwise missed, and imagine other possible futures.

Yet it must be noted that when Raïssa Maritain did personalize suffering, she emphasized the pain, graphic suffering, proximity to death in horrendous detail. Just in the poems we have discussed, the images were brutal: blood-streaked faces, people jumping out of windows, a face collapsed in arms. This of course reflected the brutality of her time, but it is also indebted to the huge influence which Léon Bloy and the decadent literary imagination exerted on her life and art. The ethical impetus here was an important one; it aimed to make visible—in bright blazes across the sky—unpleasant aspects of reality everyone wanted, in her time, to cover over. But I remain haunted by the concern that such consistently graphic accounts of suffering could have the potential effect of dehumanizing the people they seek to help. The "faces" in Raïssa's art are so often deeply afflicted, and to render the *humanity* of the suffering victims visible, we might need to show not only how communities and individuals within them struggle as victims, but also the ways in which they thrive.

Times, December 9, 2013, http://www.nytimes.com/projects/2013/invisible-child/?n=Top/News/U.S./U.S.%20States,%20Territories%20and%20Possessions/New%20York%3Fref=newyork#/?chapt=1 (last accessed: November 6, 2014).

34. Jill Colvin, "De Blasio Invokes Dasani in Vow to Change City's Approach to Its Homeless," *New York Observer*, December 12, 2013, http://observer.com/2013/12/de-blasio-invokes-dasani-in-vow-to-change-citys-approach-to-its-homeless/#axzz32H6IIi5A (last accessed: November 6, 2014).

Finally, one last remark about Raïssa's intellectual and artistic output: she was already forthy-eight years old by the time she published her first poem. What took her so long? Shy? Too deferential to Jacques' work and neglectful of her own? Sick? Lazy? For Raïssa, her art, even as it connected so deeply with the political events of her day life, stemmed from religious experiences that were deeply personal, almost totally private. As she would come to explain it it, her poems only flourished after the long hard work of the cultivation of the inner life; she had for almost thirty years been focused on daily silence and contemplative withdrawal, for no other purpose or audience than God. This process of spiritual growth, she claimed, laid the foundations for the creation of her art. In a 1937 letter to her friend Albert Béguin, Emmanuel Mounier's successor at the personalist journal *Esprit,* she wrote: "I know that it was not in the continual clamor of the imagination, but in the heart of silence, when that silence attained a certain degree of depth and purity, that nearly all the poems in *Lettre de nuit* and *La vie donnée* were born."[35] She claimed that the art came to her in the context of silence that then needed to be "expressed" or "exteriorized" as poems.[36]

So a first poem at age forty-eight? This is what the gradual maturation of deep creativity sometimes looks like. When his first book came out, Wallace Stevens was forty-three. Robert Frost was thirty-nine.[37] This model of the slow, gradual cultivation of the inner life and the creation of art stands in sharp relief to that manifested in our own culture, obsessed as it is with multitasking, prolific productive output, constant communication and self-presentation. It seems our culture could use beacons of solitude, patience, and a deep inner life like Raïssa Maritain's, now more than ever. When advising the spiritual seekers that came to her, Raïssa always said that the first job of a Christian is to cultivate that state that people avoid—being alone. "Make a monk's cell in your heart," she wrote to her godson Maurice Sachs as early as 1924, "where you can go, any time, and be alone with God."[38] The making of room for God can take years, decades.

But unlike many contemplatives before her, she insisted that these silences must be cultivated while one is "in the storm of life," in the city, among

35. Raïssa Maritain, *Journal de Raïssa,* in *OC,* 15:410–12.

36. Raïssa Maritain, "Sens et non-sens en poésie," in *OC,* 15:660.

37. Dana Gioia, "Can Poetry Matter?" *The Atlantic,* May 1991, available at http://www.theatlantic.com/past/docs/unbound/poetry/gioia/gioia.htm (last accessed: December 17, 2014).

38. Maurice Sachs, Jacques Maritain, and Raïssa Maritain, *Correspondance Maurice Sachs et Jacques et Raïssa Maritain 1925–1939* (Paris: Gallimard, 2004), 60.

friends, immersed in traumas of one's own culture and day. For Raïssa, contemplative silence is the foundation, but not the final resting place of the poet. She may well have been writing autobiographically when she declared that the "true contemplative" and the "true poet" are "mysteriously connected to the life, work, and hope of men today."[39] Drawing from the inner life to which she so carefully attended in silence, Raïssa also faced the outer world, and put into circulation language to describe it anew. In the end, Raïssa Maritain is so far from the caricature of the apolitical, silent wife of Jacques, isolated and in the background. Gone is the image of the sickly mystic hidden in the shadows.

39. Raïssa Maritain, "Message aux poètes qui sont à la guerre," in *OC*, 14:1137.

E. JANE DOERING

Simone Weil

Love of God, Affliction, and a New Saintliness

"Earthly things are the criterion of spiritual things.

If, on the pretext that only spiritual things are of value, we refuse to take the light thrown on earthly things as a criterion, we are in danger of having a non-existent treasure."[1]

Simone Weil wrote in her last letter to her friend and mentor, the Dominican priest Father Perrin: "Today it is not nearly enough to be a saint; but we must have the saintliness demanded by the present moment, a new saintliness, itself without precedent."[2] She calls such a sanctity: "a fresh spring, an invention, … a new revelation of the universe and of human destiny."[3] Her deep empathy for the most vulnerable in society defined this new type of sanctity, which would be governed by love of the universe, love of God, and compassionate love for those who suffer. She knows, however, that compassion for the afflicted is an impossibility. "When it is really found, it is a more astounding miracle than walking on water, healing the sick, or even raising the dead."[4] In this essay, we will look at how she reconciles her confidence in God's all-encompassing love with the existence of heart-rending human suf-

1. Simone Weil, *First and Last Notebooks*, translated by Richard Rees (New York: Oxford University Press, 1970), 147.

2. Simone Weil, *Waiting for God*, translated by Emma Craufurd (New York: Harper and Row, 1973), 99.

3. Ibid., 51.

4. Simone Weil, *Writings Selected*, edited by Eric O. Springsted (New York: Orbis Books, 1998), 43.

fering. Through a study of her late essay, "The Love of God and Affliction,"[5] we highlight the importance she gives to each person's obligations toward the "anonymous other," the difficulty in giving selfless attention to the marginalized, the positive force of supernatural grace, and the way both joy and affliction can equally lead to a self-emptying love of God.

For Simone Weil joy and suffering are equally precious gifts that must each be fully tasted in its purity, without trying to mix them. Through joy, the beauty of the world penetrates our soul; through suffering, it penetrates our body. Joy can inspire one to overflow with love for the source of that joy. On the contrary, affliction, the extreme form of suffering, leaves one perplexed, questioning unceasingly, "Why?" "Why me?" "What purpose can my suffering possibly serve?" Her philosophical exploration of this apparent contradiction in God's having created through love and for love, yet giving affliction the power to seize the very souls of the innocent, has its foundation in her observations of actual conditions. Her search led to her call for a new kind of sanctity, one that engages a sense of obligation toward others: an obligation to love and an obligation to value the intelligence. Such obligation requires an apprenticeship in the ability to focus one's full attention.

In her 1942 essay on the love of God and affliction, she elaborates the idea, already expressed in her Notebooks and then expressed to her mentor Father Perrin, that "Suffering is a *metaxu*,"[6] [an intermediary, a bridge], a gift which God has sent us through love.[7] Extreme suffering, in the form of affliction, however, is far worse for it attacks the human person on three fronts: physical pain, distress of soul, and social degradation, and leaves a permanent mark on the soul. Simone Weil reminds the reader that Christ's own body kept the marks of the stigmata. No one is protected from affliction, for it can strike at any time. Our human condition leaves us totally exposed, for our flesh is fragile; our soul is vulnerable; our social personality is exposed to every hazard. One only need think of the victims of the Holocaust; the displaced Okies, as portrayed by John Steinbeck; or human beings turned to chattel, such as Frederick Douglas and Solomon Northrop describe.

5. Ibid., 41–71; "*L'amour de Dieu et le Malheur*", Simone Weil, *Oeuvres complètes*, tome 4, vol. 1, edited by André Devaux and Florence de Lussy (Paris: Gallimard, 2008), 346–74.

6. Ibid., 294.

7. Simone Pétrement, *La vie de Simone Weil* vol. 2 (Paris: Fayard, 1973), 405n1.

In Weil's imagery, a person in affliction "quivers like a butterfly pinned alive to a tray." She continues the graphic metaphor by describing affliction as a nail, whose point transfixes "the very center of the soul; its head, the whole of necessity throughout all space and time," applies an "immensity of force, blind, brutal, and cold."[8] The context for these reflections was the shattering of human lives all around her during the Second World War. This suffering and affliction penetrated to the very heart of her being; she grieved for the souls who might not maintain their orientation toward God's love. While supporting Pascal's conviction that man's persevering, despite the realization that the universe could crush him, enhances his nobility,[9] she adds that even with this comprehension, we can and must still love this world here below in all its forms. Our knowledge of affliction can give more piercing sweetness to our joy, just as the frailty of cherry blossoms enhances their beauty.

Her style of probing in this essay reveals her philosophical approach to this most recalcitrant of paradoxes. To fathom the enigma of affliction within a world created by God, who has created nothing but love and the means to love, she draws on the sources she knows intimately, such as writings of the ancient Greeks, the New Testament, selections from the Jewish Bible, and her own experiences. To underpin her argument, she skillfully uses all the rhetorical devices at her command: images, metaphors, comparisons, allusions. She believes that helping her fellow beings understand the manifold ways of God's love, even the most repugnant, is the message of "pure gold" that she has been given to transmit.[10]

Two fundamental aspects of her inquiry plausibly stem from the stoic philosophy of Epictetus. First, everything has a purpose or a goal that fits into a harmonious teleological whole. Second, we can survive, find a use for everything that happens to us, without being degraded, and still be thankful.[11] She believes that if she can penetrate the *raison d'être* of affliction, she can endeavor to be thankful even for extreme suffering in the

8. Weil, *Writings Selected*, 54.

9. Simone Weil, *Oeuvres complètes*, tome 6, vol. 2, edited by André Devaux and Florence de Lussy (Paris: Gallimard, 1997), 577n403.

10. Simone Weil, *Oeuvres complètes*, tome 7, vol. 1, edited by Robert Chenavier (Paris: Gallimard, 2012), 296. In a last letter to her parents, she writes: "*Mais, j'ai moi aussi une espèce de certitude intérieure croissante qu'il se trouve en moi un dépôt d'or pur qui est à transmettre.*"

11. For this juxtaposition of philosophers, I am indebted to Diogenes Allen and Eric O. Springsted in their essay, "Le malheur: une énigme," *Cahiers Simone Weil* 2, no. 4 (December 1979): 184–96.

human condition. That affliction can strike anyone anywhere is only too evident. Her chosen word *malheur* in French conveys this element of contingency or occurring by chance. Despite this factor of randomness, she insists that one's reaction to this devastation of mind and body is, nevertheless, a matter of choice. She cites Epictetus who affirms that no one can appropriate another's free will.[12]

Simone Weil had grown up in a secular Jewish family. In her "Spiritual Autobiography,"[13] written for Father Perrin also in 1942 just before leaving France for the United States, she explains that she had never "sought for God." As a young intellectual, she had considered "the problem of God as a problem the data of which could not be obtained here below." Without reliable data, she believed that one would most likely reach a wrong conclusion, and this would be the "greatest possible evil." In any case, it seemed to her that being in the world, our business was to adopt the best attitude toward the problems of the world, which at this time, she concluded, did not depend on the solution of the problem of God. Nonetheless, in the 1930s, she had three compelling contacts with Christianity, the most profound of which was in 1938, when, in her words, "Christ himself came down and took possession of me."[14] From that spiritual visitation on, her writings reflect a steadfast belief in the Creation, the Passion, and the Trinity, and the invincible love that is the essence of all three.

For our mystic philosopher, creation is a perpetual witness of love. Her unique understanding of Creation and its web of cosmic interactions is that God withdrew, declining to command wherever He had the power. She sees Creation, the Passion, and the Eucharist all as movements of withdrawal, each act a refusal to employ the power within His command. Thus God, in His providence, puts before humankind an archetype of behavior influenced by love. His act of creation initiated the orderly movements within the cosmos, whose components follow inviolable laws of nature, the most powerful of which is the force of gravity. This order of the world Weil calls "blind Necessity"; she declares, "Everything that is real is subject to Necessity,"[15] with all the limitations imposed therein.

12. Simone Weil, *Oeuvres complètes*, tome I, edited by André Devaux and Florence de Lussy (Paris: Gallimard, 1988), 255.

13. Weil, *Waiting for God*, 61–83.

14. Ibid., 69.

15. Weil, *Oeuvres complètes*, tome 6, vol. 2, p. 380.

Simone Weil envisions Necessity as having two faces; the one that God beholds is pure obedience, but the one that confronts humankind in the finite world can bring brutal affliction. In saying, "affliction is some thing that imposes itself upon a man quite against his will," she evokes Hector's sad reflection on the fate of his beloved wife, Andromache, who as a captured war trophy, will be enslaved to the Greeks' slightest whim. He laments: "In spite of yourself you will submit to the pressure of a harsh necessity."[16] In fact, Simone Weil comments, the entire *Iliad* suffers under the constraints of affliction.

Not only is the material universe subject to the force *par excellence* of gravity, but humankind's carnal nature is also imbued with its own downward pull and is similarly subject to laws. Some characterize this baser inclination as "moral gravity." Consequently, Simone Weil proposes that matter is a perfect model for us in its obedience to God's will. She insists: "We must love the world here below"; it is in the beauty of the material world that harsh necessity becomes an object of love. She offers the example of ocean waves, which in perfect obedience to gravitational force rise to a certain height, but then fold in. In keeping with her view of harsh necessity, she states: "The sea is not less beautiful in our eyes because we know that ships are sometimes wrecked."[17] On the contrary, this reality adds to the sea's precarious beauty.

In her last letter to Father Perrin, she describes "moral gravity" in human beings, along with its counter-force: supernatural grace. She writes: "The mechanical necessity [of humankind's animal nature] holds all men in its grip at every moment. They only escape from it is in proportion to the place held in their souls by the authentically supernatural."[18] Escape in this context means amassing a sufficiently strong positive force to resist the destructive power of humankind's downward pull of the ego. For Weil, this positive force is supernatural grace, which is available to every individual who fully consents to God's love, even when it entails intense suffering. She uses the model of a friend who, returning from afar, grasps one's hand so tightly that it hurts. One must be grateful for this, for the pain is a sign of deep affection. She repeats, "Pure joy and pure pain are two aspects of the

16. Simone Weil, "L'amour de Dieu et le malheur," in *Oeuvres complètes*, tome 4, vol. 1, p. 562n48.

17. Weil, *Writings Selected*, 50.

18. Weil, *Waiting for God*, 92.

same infinitely precious truth. Fortunately so, because it is this that gives us the right to wish joy rather than pain to those we love."[19]

There is a universal obligation to see that all individuals might have sufficient strength to withstand the effects of "moral gravity" within themselves and in others. She illustrates our natural bent for mistreating the defenseless by the phenomena of an injured hen whose wound attracts the sharp pecking of the others. Countering this inclination to abuse the vulnerable requires the ability to give genuine unselfish attention to another's basic human needs: physical, social, and psychological, so that each person can freely embrace God's truth. According to Weil, cruelty and negligence not only damage our physical bodies, but far worse, they stifle the soul's aspiration toward the good.

To this end, Simone Weil drafted a statement of human obligations, a credo that she elaborated as a prologue to her last work, *The Need for Roots*. The word "obligation" suited her vision of this human imperative better than "rights" because everyone has inalienable obligations; one's rights, however, only serve if others consent to recognize them. Her credo of obligations has its foundation in her belief that there is a reality outside this world, "that is to say, outside space and time, outside man's mental universe, outside any sphere whatsoever that is accessible to human faculties. Corresponding to the reality, at the center of the human heart is the longing for an absolute good, a longing that is always there and is never appeased by any object in this world."[20] She further claims, "The only thing that is identical in all men is the presence of a link with this reality outside the world."[21] Consequently, whoever recognizes this longing, along with the ability to direct one's attention to the reality beyond this world would, by necessity, hold every human being without exception as something sacred and worthy of respect.

This respect entails inalienable obligations that can only be expressed indirectly to others by compassionately attending to any deprivation of basic needs from which they might be suffering. To each innate human need there is a corresponding obligation; those of the body (food, warmth, sleep, health, rest, exercise, fresh air, etc.) are evident, although insufficiently regarded as sacred.

Our French philosopher then makes a unique contribution by listing

19. Weil, *Writings Selected*, 59.
20. Ibid., 132.
21. Ibid., 134.

the needs of the soul, which are less straightforward, but every bit as necessary. They too are sacred and can be considered in pairs of opposites that balance and complete one another. They are equality and hierarchy; consented obedience and liberty; truth and freedom of expression; personal property and collective property; punishment and honor; security and risk; plus solitude with privacy. Buttressing these needs is having roots in several environments, such as, a country, a language, and a shared cultural and historical past.

In today's environment of rampant inequality in the access to vital necessities, only a new form of sanctity can begin to provide for those who suffer grim deficiency in their basic needs of body and soul. Political and economic priorities are light-years away from applying justice in these terms as a means to elevate the common good either on a local or global level. For Simone Weil, justice requires according full attention to one's neighbor. She understands that giving attention involves an emptying out of oneself to allow space for the other's concerns to fill one's soul, thus restoring a sense of dignity in the afflicted. The void thus created opens space for Christ to do good works through our physical body. In her notebooks, she states, "Attention, taken to its highest degree, is the same thing as prayer. It presupposes faith and love."[22]

In her essay, "The Right Use of School Studies with a View to the Love of God," she evokes the legend of the Holy Grail, which for her symbolizes "the miraculous vessel that satisfies all hunger by virtue of the consecrated Host." The grail will belong to the first comer who asks the guardian of the vessel, a king three-quarters paralyzed by the most painful wound, "What are you going through?"[23] His wound, whether due to harsh natural conditions or criminal actions, has caused grievous suffering to soul and body. But an act of offering selfless attention to the afflicted is so difficult and rare that only a miracle allows it to happen. The Samaritan who stopped to attend to the needs of the anonymous victim of violence lying by the road provided the possibility for an afflicted being to become whole once again.

Even if many more people would recognize their obligation to reduce the causes of others' bodily, mental, and social privations, Simone Weil understood that there would never be a complete elimination of intense

22. Simone Weil, *The Notebooks*, vol. 1, translated by Arthur Wills (New York: Putnams Sons, 1956), 205.

23. Weil, *Writings Selected*, 98–99.

suffering. She confessed to Father Perrin that any encounter with the affliction of other people, those who are indifferent or unknown to her as much as those she knows, including those of the most remote ages of antiquity, causes her atrocious pain. It so "utterly rends my soul that as a result the love of God becomes almost impossible for me for a while."[24] She adds a trusting note in her journal: "The extreme greatness of Christianity lies in the fact that it does not seek a supernatural remedy for suffering but a supernatural use for it,"[25] which is the quest she undertook in the final years of her life.

The essence of her search to resolve the perilous impasse—to love God under conditions of extreme suffering—devolves on the Cross. She contends that only one thing enables us to accept real affliction, and that is the contemplation of Christ on the Cross, considering it as a model. She reminds us: "Affliction constrained Christ to implore that he might be spared, to seek consolation from man, to believe he was forsaken by the Father."[26] "The Cross of Christ is the only source of light that is bright enough to illumine affliction," for she believed that wherever there is affliction there is the Cross—concealed, but present to anyone who chooses truth rather than falsehood, and love rather than hate.

She rejects the trivialization of the idea of carrying one's Cross by applying this expression to life's daily little inconveniences. Instead, she asserts, "to bear one's cross is to bear the knowledge that one is entirely subject to this blind necessity in every part of one's being, except for one point in the soul, which is so secret that it is inaccessible to consciousness."[27] In her philosophy, perfectly happy individuals—if they recognize, truly, concretely, and unfailingly their own frailty and the possibility of affliction—can enjoy happiness in full measure and at the same time endure the Cross.

For her, Christ's affliction, as well as Job's, contains the truth of our condition. Job comes to understand this reality, but first we hear his distraught accusation: "He laughs at the affliction of the innocent!" This cry reveals his despair that he can no longer hear the testimony of his own conscience, and he implores God to be his witness. Despite the crushing force—material, psychological, and social—imposed on him, and his despair that only

24. Weil, *Waiting for God*, 91.
25. Simone Weil, *Gravity and Grace* (New York: Routledge, 1997), 73.
26. Weil, *Writings Selected*, 44.
27. Ibid., 57–58.

meets silence, Job believed and obeyed. According to Simone Weil, this is the epitome of perfection, which merits restitution, and she points out that once the veil of Job's flesh had been rent by affliction and he accepted his fragility, the world's stark beauty was revealed to him. She puts her self on guard, "I should not love my suffering because it is useful. I should love it because it is."[28]

From her earliest writings, one can trace her concern over the destructive effects of force on human psyches and communities. In "The *Iliad*, or the Poem of Force," written in 1940, she pinpoints the most poignant destructive consequence of force in the terse opening statements: "The true hero, the true subject, the center of the *Iliad* is force. Force employed by man, force that enslaves man, force before which man's flesh shrinks away." She continues, "from its first property (the ability to turn a human being into a thing by the simple method of killing him) flows another, quite prodigious too in its own way, the ability to turn a human being into a thing while he is still alive. He is alive; he has a soul; and yet—he is a thing."[29] Simone Weil calls on us to denounce the terrible consequences wreaked by morally reprehensible aggressions, such as physical violence, enslavement, and torture.

Her foreboding is that, if in the darkness of pain, discouragement, and solitude, where there seems to be nothing to love, and the soul ceases to love, God's absence becomes final. She calls those who plunge men into affliction before they are prepared to receive it "killers of souls."[30] Nevertheless, if the soul can go on loving in the void, or at least wanting to love, then one day God will come to show himself and the beauty of the world to this soul, as He did to Job. "The only choice given to [human beings], as intelligent and free creatures, is to desire obedience or not to desire it."[31] If one does choose obedience, a new necessity is added to mechanical necessity, a necessity constituted by the laws pertaining to supernatural things.

Weil's preoccupation with the souls of the afflicted is very pertinent today: humiliation, pain, and distress strike capriciously without warning. Criminal acts like brutality and involuntary servitude hover below the radar of people's consciousness. The UN International Labor Organization statistics show that 20.9 million victims are forced to work by coercion or

28. Weil, *Gravity and Grace*, 72.

29. Weil, "The Iliad, or the Poem of Force," translated by Mary McCarthy, *Chicago Review* 18, no. 2 (1965): 5–30. Accessible online at http://www.jstor.org/stable/25294008?seq=10.

30. Weil, *Writings Selected*, 44.

31. Ibid., 50.

threat, and 1.2 million children are trafficked annually for sexual exploitation.[32] In addition to unconscionable behavior, natural disasters such as floods, storms, and earthquakes also pulverize the innocent. In 2013, earthquakes in the Philippines, typhoons in India, hurricanes, and tornadoes in the United States left thousands of victims writhing in anguished despair. Global problems of food supply and malnutrition daily bring affliction in their wake. Weil writes that human crime, the cause of most affliction, is part of blind necessity because criminals do not know what they are doing.

Simone Weil's deepest concern is that many of those souls who fall into affliction will not have the endurance to maintain their faith in God, and that bystanders, repulsed by the condition of the sufferers, cannot offer them the needed attention to enable their free consent to God's love. She notes that affliction can cause God to appear absent for a time, "more absent than light in the utter darkness of a cell." To make their plight worse, on-lookers despise these victims of hazard, who appear, in her words, like "half-crushed worms." She writes: "One could weep tears of blood to think how many unfortunates are crushed by affliction without knowing how to make use of it."[33]

Some victims do remain steadfast in their faith, but not all can. Testimonies from survivors of the Holocaust attest to the poignant range of attitudes towards affliction. The writings of Victor Frankl, an Austrian neurologist and psychiatrist, forced to do slave labor in the Dachau concentration camp, and of Etti Hillesum, a Jewish woman who kept diaries from 1941 until her death in 1943 in Auschwitz, movingly give evidence to an unshaken faith in the goodness of God, even while undergoing intense suffering. On the contrary, Ellie Wiesel, a Nobel Peace Laureate and witness of many atrocities in Buchenwald, bitterly rejects any idea of God's goodness.[34]

For Weil, only those beings whose whole soul is inhabited by supernatural grace can embody compassion. To be able to confront the depths of affliction with steady attention, one must be prepared by love of the truth to accept the death of one's illusory self. This is the death of which Plato spoke when he said "to philosophize is to learn to die." But sometimes the intensity of the affliction destroys the sufferers' will to endure, especially

32. Colleen Dunne, "Efforts against Trafficking in Game Lead-up," *National Catholic Reporter*, 50, no. 7 (2014): 1.

33. Weil, *Writings Selected*, 70.

34. Robert Arp expands on these examples in "Suffering as Theodicy," *Cahiers Simone Weil* 23, no. 4 (December 2000): 413–23.

if they lack charitable attention from others. Such charity is a sacrament. Affliction, when it is consented to, accepted, and loved, is truly a baptism. But, the peril is, as Weil asserts, that too often the circumstances and ferocity of the affliction destroy the will to believe.

Simone Weil gives a beautiful image of the positive effect of this lacerating baptism by affliction, in which God comes and, without our knowing, places in us a little seed of divine love that grows of itself. Like any viable growth, conditions must be nurtured; pulling the weeds and cutting the grasses is arduous and stinging because they are part of our flesh. Eventually the divine seed becomes a beautiful tree that is ineradicable; only a betrayal could uproot it. The birds of the air come and perch in the branches. It is the most beautiful of trees: "No forest bears its equal."[35] At this point, the soul belongs to God and must traverse the long distance back to God. This space is the great distance between God and His son on the cross, whose supreme union "echoes perpetually across the universe in the depth of the silence ... like a pure and heartrending harmony. This is the Word of God.... Those who persevere in love will hear this note from the very lowest depths into which affliction has thrust them."[36]

To conclude: in Simone Weil's vision of the human condition, the desire for the state of perfection entails a great deal, but what it entails can hardly be imagined until the fearful effects of affliction are experienced. Still, once there, face to face with affliction, a true commitment is possible, through a more secret, more mysterious, more miraculous contact even than a sacrament. Such an implicit sacrament is realized by listening in silence to the vibration of supreme love bound in a supreme union. In her religious acumen, there cannot be a greater good than to share in the distress of the abandoned Christ. She desired to share in the suffering of the Cross and to participate in this union with the supernatural. Compassionate attention to all of God's creation opens the path for such a union. Attention requires a self-denial that allows for a new kind of saintliness, which, to her mind, would be a necessary innovation for humankind. Our contemporary world needs saints with the genius and the enduring quality of love as models of unselfish fulfillment of our human obligations, according to the mystical philosophy of Simone Weil.

35. This is a line from a sixth century Latin hymn sung on Good Friday, referring to the wood of the Cross.

36. Weil, *Writings Selected*, 46.

MICHAEL D. TORRE

The "Annex" to Maritain's 1914 Lectures on "The Spirit of Modern Philosophy"

The Role of Germany in Modern Philosophy

I. The Setting: The First World War

One hundred years ago, shortly after the publication of *La Philosophie Bergsonienne,* Jacques Maritain began to prepare a series of four lectures on the Spirit of Modern Philosophy that he delivered in April and May at the Institut Catholique.[1] The first two were on "The Cartesian Reform."[2] The first was published in the June 1 edition of the *Revue de Philosophie.*[3] Within weeks of its publication, Archduke Ferdinand of Austria, the heir to the throne of the Austrian Empire, was gunned down in Sarajevo. The second was published in the same review.[4] Within one month of its pub-

1. By the urging of Cardinal Lorenzelli, Prefect of the Congregation of Studies, he was appointed to the chair of The History of Modern Philosophy at the Institut Catholique in June, 1914, directly after these lectures. See Raïssa Maritain, *Adventures in Grace* (New York: Longmans, Green and Company, 1945), 210.

2. The articles were in three sections: "Preparations for the Cartesian reform," "Descartes and theology," and "Independence of spirit," with the first article comprising the first two sections.

3. "L'Esprit de la philosophie modern: La réforme cartésienne," *Revue de Philosophie* 24, no. 6 (1914): 601–25. For the text of both articles, see Jacques and Raïssa Maritain, *Oeuvres Complètes,* vol. 1, edition established by Jean-Marie Allion, Maurice Hany, Dominique and René Mougel, Michel Nurdin, and Heinz R. Schmitz (Paris/Fribourg Suisse: Éditions Saint-Paul/Éditions Universitaires, 1986), 823–52 (for the first article) and 853–87 (for the second article).

4. "L'Esprit de la philosophie modern: L'indépendence de l'esprit," *Revue de Philosophie* 25, no. 7 (1 July 1914): 53–82.

lication, all of Europe was going to war. Edward Grey (the British Foreign Secretary) warned Germany in late July that England would enter the war were Belgium's neutrality to be violated, but his warning came too late to halt the momentum of events. Crowds in various European capitals (including London) expressed their jubilation at the start of the conflict, but Lord Grey's own view proved prophetic: "The lamps are going out all over Europe. We shall not see them lit again in our time."

The slaughter was soon underway. In the first two weeks of the war, in the "Battle of the Frontiers" that occurred between August 10 and 24, 1914, the French suffered a quarter million casualties and 77,000 deaths. To give some perspective on the enormity of that number, this is almost 20,000 more men than the United States lost in *all* of the Vietnam War, and it was suffered by a population one-fifth its size. In a galant but absurd tactic, one that would punctuate this most grotesque of human conflicts, on August 22nd some Frenchmen stormed German machine-guns facing them. The French lost 27,000 men killed that day (thereby outdoing the later butchery of the Battle of the Somme, when the British lost close to 20,000 men in its first day). They continued to lose frightful numbers in the First Battle of the Marne, during one week's fighting in early September. After but one month of carnage, France had lost almost as many dead as the United States was to lose in Europe throughout *all* of World War II.[5] By the end of the fighting, almost 75 percent of French military men had been killed, wounded, were missing in action, or captured: a figure of some 6,000,000. To see Verdun today is still to weep: the sea of crosses over its rolling hills disappears from view.

Jacques Maritain, although pronounced unfit for service due to the effects of a childhood bout with pleurisy, was not to be spared the war's devastation. The war caught him by surprise on the Isle of Wight, invited by the Benedictines of Solesmes to vacation there at Quarr Abbey.[6] Within three

5. The "Battle of the Marne" added to the "Battle of the Frontiers" some 80,000 dead (for a total of about 157,000) and the same number wounded (for a total close to half a million). By contrast, throughout World War II, the USA lost some 135,000 men killed in Europe, with some 450,000 wounded; in the entire Atlantic theater (and including the Navy and Airforce), it lost some 187,000 men killed with some 570,000 wounded. The figures (for either Europe or the Atlantic Theater, respectively) are roughly comparable: more French dead relative to the first, less to the second.

6. Raïssa Maritain, *Adventures in Grace*, 212. They arrived there on August 1, 1914 only to learn of the war just beginning, which they had not believed possible. See Raïssa Maritain, *Raïssa's*

weeks time, the dearest friend of his youth, Ernest Psichari, was dead from a bullet to the temple in the disaster of August 22nd, at Rossignol.[7] Two weeks later, his older friend and mentor, Charles Péguy, died from a bullet to the forehead in the first day of fighting in the Battle of the Marne (more precisely, the battle of Ourcq), at Villeroy,[8] some sixty miles east of Paris.

The war brought an end to many things. Not merely "The old Lie: Dulce et docorum est / Pro patria mori,"[9] and not merely the belief in "God, King, and Country." (The war saw the deposition of four emperors—Russian, German, Austrian, and Turk—as well as a call for an international order and authority and an increase in agnosticism and atheism.) It brought a halt not merely to a Western European expansion in the world that had been going on since the beginning of the modern era (one that then began to be "rolled back," with the loss of European colonies), but an end to an entire world-order and epoch. It put an end to an aristocratic standard and way of life and ushered in the age of mass society. Just as the Black Death marked the beginning of the end to the Medieval World, so the Spanish Flu that came at the war's end marked an end to the Modern World. (It carried off perhaps more than 50,000,000 people world-wide and led to six times the number of fatalities in the United States than the number of its men who died in the war.) The lights of the world that Lord Grey had known went out not just for his lifetime, but for ours. A new order, for Europe and for the world, was coming into being.

II. Combat Duty: Warring Against the German Character of Modern Philosophy

If I have begun this way, it is at least in part to provide some needed context. In October, as the "race to the sea" came to an end and the West-

Journal, presented by Jacques Maritain, preface by René Voillaume (Albany, New York: Magi, 1974), 24.

7. Raïssa Maritain citing Adjutant Galgani's account given to Psichari's sister, Henriette, in *Adventures in Grace*, 143. Henriette forwarded it to Henri Massis, who then quoted it in his book *Notre ami Psichari* (Paris: Flammarion, 1936). Raïssa also refers us to Henriette's *Ernest Psichari, mon frère* (Paris: Plon, 1933) and Colonel Alphonse Louis Grasset's *La Surprise de la division. Rossignol-Saint-Vincent* (Paris: Berger Levrault, 1932).

8. Raïssa Maritain citing the evidence of Victor Boudon, *Avec Charles Péguy de la Lorraine à la Marne*, preface by Maurice Barrès (Paris, Hachette, 1916), in *Adventures in Grace*, 76.

9. Wilfred Owen, "Dulce et Decorum Est," *Collected Poems* (London: Catto and Windus, 1963), 55.

ern Front that was to remain virtually unchanged for four years was established, the Maritains left the Isle of Wight and returned to Paris.[10] At that time, the *Revue Thomiste* was preparing its September-December edition, which featured the last of Maritain's spring lectures as its lead article.[11] And it was then that Jacques began his first course as a professor at the Institut Catholique; it went from November through May, and included twenty-two lectures or "conferences."[12] The course continued his previous lectures, on the Spirit of Modern Philosophy, as it had first come to full expression in the thought of Descartes. Now, he intended to reveal the deeper source of the malaise there diagnosed: namely, the "German spirit," as Luther had first articulated it and as it continued to the present moment.[13] As he says at the very start, his "subject was commanded, so to speak, by the circumstances themselves": the war they were presently suffering.[14] Raïssa is entirely right in characterizing these lectures as a "combat duty, a sort of intellectual contribution to the war."[15] If Jacques was barred from taking up a rifle to do battle for his country, he would take up the arm of his intellect,[16] to fight (in Raïssa's words) "against an aggressor who had begun by cutting himself off spiritually from the community of Western nations, and whose Pangermanist metaphysics had finally paved the way for a policy of domination and military conquest."[17]

To the best of my knowledge, no historian or Maritainista has bothered

10. According to Raïssa, they stayed "two months" with the Benedictines, Jacques later beginning his course at the Institut Catholique on November 6, 1914; *Raïssa's Journal*, 24. Jean-Luc Barré says the same, but he may simply be following Raïssa. See Jean-Luc Barré, *Jacques et Raïssa Maritain: Les Mendiants du Ciel* (Paris: Stock, 1995), 184.

11. Jacques Maritain, "L'Esprit de la Philosophie Scolastique: La Liberté Intellectuelle," *Revue Thomiste* 22 (1914): 517–42.

12. The lectures were published in *La Croix* from December through August. See *Oeuvrès Completes*, 1:889, 910n, 1018n, and the editors' comment on 1136. (The editors of the *Oeuvres Completès* refer to these lectures as an "Annex" to "The Spirit of Modern Philosophy," and I have followed this usage.)

13. Jacques and Raïssa Maritain, *Oeuvres Completès*, vol. 1, "Annex," 905.

14. Ibid., 891; my translations throughout, of all material from the *Oeuvres Complètes*.

15. Raïssa Maritain, *Adventures in Grace*, 213.

16. Soldiers at the front, facing soldiers who suffered and died in the same hellish conditions as they did, were often "put off" when returning home on leave to encounter a populace who demonized these soldiers as the "Enemy": an "Other" for whom they had no empathy. There is something, I think, of this character in the "intellectual fight" of Maritain's lectures: Germany is too readily treated as the "Other," the "Enemy."

17. Ibid. If Raïssa's unapologetic words seem extreme and unfair, we should remember that they were penned in the dark days of World War II, when the Nazi occupation of France seemed to render them all too true.

to analyze these lectures on "The Role of Germany in Modern Philosophy."[18] This is perhaps not too surprising, for it would not be easy for many to have gotten ahold of back issues of *La Croix*, the newspaper in which they first appeared.[19] Nor did Maritain ever "make anything" of them in his later work. The articles only became generally available in 1986, with the publication of the first volume of the Maritains' *Oeuvres Complètes*. I am going to treat them in three parts. First, I want to note their first and main thesis. Second, I want to give a summary account of his history's directive line. Finally, I want to ask what light the articles throw upon Maritain "at his beginning" and upon his intellectual project at that time. This will be my principal focus throughout: the "Young Jacques."

I think I should first say, however, what I have already put in a note: except for the first, introductory, lecture that is complete, we only have Maritain's summaries of his lectures, which (judging by the first one) seem to be roughly a third to half the lectures' original length. No doubt his full thought was more subtle and more fully worked out than we have in these summaries. (However, the only critical point I am going to make here is directed at what Maritain says in his first lecture, which was published in its entirety, and was not summarized.)

When I first read Raïssa's description of these lectures as "combat duty," I wondered whether they might have a "journalistic," or even "jingoist" savor, whether they would incline towards over-simplification or even vilification. Unfortunately, this is indeed the case. Since I am going to be sharply critical here, perhaps I should begin with how the one Maritain scholar who has said anything about these lectures describes them. Jean-Luc Barré (surely Maritain's most thorough and most careful biographer) summarizes his lectures in these terms:

> ... he continued his course at the Institut Catholique, analyzing the role of German philosophy in the modern world and the responsibility of Lutheran cul-

18. Jean-Luc Barré devotes two brief paragraphs to them, less than one page, in *Les Mendiants du Ciel*, 185; that is the only reference to these lectures in the literature on Maritain of which I am aware.

19. *La Croix* is a general interest Catholic newspaper, at one time very widely read, and still in print today. It was founded by the Augustinians in 1880 and run by them for its first 20 years. Only the first of Maritain's lectures was published in its entirety ("Le rôle de l'Allemagne dans la philosophie moderne: Introduction," 891–909); thereafter, his lectures were only summarized, usually in some seven pages, or about a half to a third of the length of their conferences (at least judging by the first one).

ture—"violence at the service of the flesh"—in the "universal conflagration." The site of the infection is located in the "monstrous hypertrophy of the German 'me'." Kant, Hegel, but also Descartes, Rousseau, Michelet, Renan are accused pell-mell of having collaborated in the work of destruction, serving the cause of modernism and the "Germanization of thought," which delivered man to himself "without any other God than the God it had made." The present war is the "settling of accounts of at least three centuries of prevarications, in which all the nations have had their part." And Maritain concludes that the [human] race will only be saved if it takes the side of "Saint Thomas against Kant" and restores a civilization that is "purely, integrally, Catholic." From November, 1914, to May, 1915, these lectures of philosophy were set on demonstrating the deep meaning of the war, a "supreme conflict" between two cultures and two conceptions of man.[20]

Barré then goes on to follow Maritain in saying it was hardly surprising—as "death gallops through the world and goes through it at a furious pace"[21]—to recall she who had appeared to two shepherds in tears to warn of just such vast devastation.[22] In the light of the war's horrors, how not see La Salette as Truth and Melanie as Mary's chosen and reliable mouthpiece?[23]

But this distracts us from my present concern. Maritain's own account is in fact far harsher than even Barré's summary lets us see. Maritain begins by distinguishing the France of 1914 from that of 1814: this is not a war of the forces of a French revolution, and world-wide democracy, against the forces of a German champion of European reaction. Rather, Frenchmen are willing to die both simply for France herself and because she is "the eldest daughter of the Church."[24] She is opposed by a Germany that has already profited from French revolutionary ideas, which are now being used to destroy her, by a nation "that itself represents in the world an artificial creation of violence and pride that clearly supposes despotism and a militarism without check," a country that "forms the living antithesis of princi-

20. Barré here quotes from a variety of Maritain's lectures on "Le rôle de l'Allemagne dans la philosophie moderne": from the first (e.g., 893) to the last (e.g., 1025).

21. See Maritain, *Notebooks* (Notre Dame, Indiana: University of Notre Dame Press, 1984), 82 (which Barré quotes on 185).

22. Barré, *Les Mendiants du Ciel*, 185.

23. He later notes that Notre Dame de Reims was burned down by German shells on that September 19, the vigil of the feast of the Seven Sorrows, "that is to say the civil and liturgical anniversary date of the very hour of the apparition of La Salette, where the Holy Virgin, weeping, called people to penitence and to all the requirements of the supernatural life": see "Le rôle de l'Allemagne dans la philosophie moderne," *Oeuvres Complètes*, 1:952. The tears of La Salette were for the horrors to come of World War I.

24. Maritain, *Oeuvres Complètes*, 1:892.

ples of order and tradition."[25] Moreover, Germany "has been the perpetual source of seditions against European order, and its historic role seems to have been almost ever constantly to menace, with an incredible fury, the heart and center of that order, Rome and the Papacy."[26] France, in short, is engaged in a holy war to defend Catholic civilization.

This is but the beginning. Maritain uses an account of the British *Morning Post* (not the most unbiased of sources, especially in this time of war!) to make his point: some German soldiers have attacked, with "an astonishing rage," Catholic churches, cathedrals, and priests in "admirable Belgium."[27] This leads him rhetorically to ask, "[I]s not after all what characterizes German culture above all a prodigious development of technical materials, a use of tools colossally perfected at the service of a 'me' left to its own nature, at the service of a humanity free from all spiritual principle and of all supernatural principle, in brief, at the service of the flesh?"[28] Furthermore, he again rhetorically asks, "[I]s not this despotic and artificial work—where the tense will of the human animal tries to create by its sole

25. It would seem that Maritain would equally have opposed the unification of Italy that had occurred at the same time as that of Germany: it, too, would have been an "artificial work of violence and human will," one that had left the Pope at the time of his writing (and until 1929) still a "prisoner in the Vatican."

26. Ibid; my translations throughout. Maritain's litany of German sedition is lengthy: Caesar's remark (quoted by Aquinas) that Germans saw nothing wrong with "brigandage" (901), their invasion of the Roman empire (901), Clovis urging his troops against those who barbarically tortured children and women (902), Luther's support of the Teutonic order, which led to Prussian apostasy (900), etc. The German character is summarily reduced to a combination of "Gemüth" (i.e. sentimentality) and realism (902–903): of the romanticism and Bismarkian realpolitik that together marked Germany in the nineteenth century. Perhaps such a list can be "justified" in the name of patriotism and "combat duty," but it is hardly better than propaganda.

27. Ibid., 893. He continues with this kind of journalistic, anecdotal, reference. He later quotes from a letter to the *Figaro* in support of the view that Germany in the twelfth to thirteenth century, and again in the seventeethn to eighteenth century, was entirely under the influence of French culture (899). Thus Alexander of Hales, Albert the Great, Bonaventure, and Aquinas—despite being English, German, and Italian—turn out all to be representatives of specifically French culture! He later will defend such a position, arguing that Albert, for one, was the result of the "admirable expansion of Cluny," and that Germany had thus been "penetrated by the intellectual influence of France." See "L'etat actuel de la philosophie allemande," originally published in *La Revue Universelle* 4, no. 24 (15 March 1921): 705–20, and reprinted in *Oeuvres Complètes*, 2:1143–57. All of scholasticism, with Paris as its center, manifests "the hegemony of the French genius on the world" (912). He quotes a Berlin professor's claim that Germans are superior in Christian virtue as "obviously pathological" (904). He even informs us that Beethoven cannot be used as an example of German culture, since his grandparents were Belgian (901)! It is hard to be patient before such arguments. (Notably, he has nothing to say about J. S. Bach, a quintessentially German composer of Lutheran music.)

28. Ibid.

forces alone an organization, a nation, a civilization—anything other than the natural outcome of the individualism and the naturalism of the Reformation?"[29] And here we then arrive at his thesis baldly stated:

> We are watching a supreme conflict, not only of barbarity, but between German culture and French culture, between that in the German culture that is most specifically German and that in the French culture that is most intimately French, that is to say, in two words, between a Lutheran culture and a Catholic civilization.[30]

Nor does he shrink from stating his thesis plainly:

> This war puts us in front of the deepest historical and moral realities abruptly brought to view: it is not about what appears on the surface; it is about what it truly is; it is about what will come to be; in a word, it is about these people in the divine intention. And, from the point of view of the states allied against Germany, these seem to possess a clear providential significance.[31]

Holy war indeed! Catholic France (and Catholic Belgium), England and its Established Church, and Orthodox Russia are all in a "holy alliance" against Protestant, Lutheran, Germany.

Maritain feels sure of his ground. Given the deep causes and differences now "abruptly brought to view," an account of modern German philosophy will lay bear what is essential in the present conflict. For, he argues, "German philosophy is, in effect, the intellectual fulfillment of Lutheranism and it is one of the factors—I believe one could say the most important factor—of German culture."[32] And now we come to what I take to be Maritain's deepest personal concern. What is demanded of the French is a "severe examination of conscience."[33] For this alien German thought and culture has "infiltrated" its own. One of the liberating possibilities of this war, then, is that France can "return to herself," to her true, and deeper, traditions, to the full embrace of her Catholic faith and also of the philosophy closest to it. Maritain's entire vision builds to a crescendo and is worth quoting in full:

> Is it not a rigorous duty—for those who do not bear arms, and whose parents or dearest friends have been killed or may be killed by the enemy—to dedicate themselves, to the utmost measure of their forces, so that the victory acquired by French blood will produce all its fruits, and to ensure the definitive extirpation, in all of its domains, of the causes of the abominable evil that today menaces France and the universe, and which will menace it tomorrow, if this radical purification is

29. Ibid.

30. Ibid.

31. Ibid., 893–94.

32. Ibid., 894.

33. Ibid.

not seriously carried out. It is the honor of Catholic philosophy, of Thomist philosophy—I will not say, alas, always of Catholics themselves!—to be, and to show itself essentially to be, rebellious towards the spirit of German philosophy and to have constantly denounced German individualism and subjectivism, and in particular that of Kantianism, all of which have introduced into the world the most tyrannical, the most desperate, the most merciless barbarity.[34]

He ends this argument in the first article with these words:

It depends upon French intelligence to achieve the victory of French arms and to annihilate at the same time the principle with its fruit: Lutheran and modernist individualism, naturalism, and subjectivism along with pangermanism. No better opportunity will ever be offered it. Should God give it this victory, then one will be able to say that the present war marks for the world, at least for a time, the end of a sickness of at least three or four centuries.[35]

And, in May, 1915, he ends his entire series of twenty-two conferences with these words:

... in order to save our race and our intellect, it is to a civilization purely, integrally, Catholic that we must return; and, as regards what concerns philosophy in particular, it is neither Victor Cousin nor Auguste Comte nor Descartes that we ought to take for our masters, but Saint Thomas. Saint Thomas against Kant![36]

This holy war, then, pits Thomism against Kantianism: a people inspired by the crown of medieval philosophy against one inspired by the chief voice of a modern philosophy set against it. To fight against German philosophy is to fight against Modernism and the spirit of a modern philosophy rooted in Luther and in German culture. To defend France is to defend her against *that* enemy.

I think we must recognize just how foreign Maritain's vision of the war's deepest issue is from that of any historian. He or she would likely note first the decline of Turkish power in the Balkans, and the rise of

34. Ibid. He came to believe that the war had indeed succeeded in the "extirpation" of which he speaks here: "It seems that the terrible awakening of the war has delivered French thought—alas, at what price!—from the influence of German philosophy that had weighed on it like a nightmare throughout all of the 19th century and especially since 1870." "L'etat actuel de la philosophie allemande," originally published in *La Revue Universelle* 4, no. 24 (15 March 1921): 705–20, and reprinted in *Oeuvres Complètes*, 2:1141, 1143–57. He came to believe that—excepting academics—German philosophy was likely no longer to "infuse in our [French] veins the various poisons distilled from the spirit of Kant."

35. Ibid., 907.

36. Ibid., 1025.

late nineteenth-century nationalism. This had led to independent Balkan states, who fought amongst themselves for territory, and created a conflict between declining Austrian power and growing Serbian ambitions, in relation to Bosnia in particular. This fueled the tension between Germany—supporting its weaker ally, Austria—and Russia, defender of the Serbs. This tense situation was set off by a bunch of disaffected youths, who were manipulated by Black Hand Serbian nationalists. It seems the plot against the Hapsburg heir had come to the attention of the Serbian government, but it merely issued a bland warning to Austria. Even without knowing of Serbian knowledge of this plot, Austria seemed intent on war, as indicated by its ultimatum to Serbia, which it presumed the latter could not accept, and its decision to go to war despite the latter's willingness to "eat crow." But Serbia did not expect to placate Austria by its response, and, knowing it had support from Russia, began to prepare for war even before its reply was sent. Meanwhile, German thinking remained ambivalent. The Kaiser only wanted Austria to be strong against Serbia and to assert itself (a limited aim of "stopping in Belgrade" that the English tried to further), but the German war ministry wanted the war to extend to Russia, because it feared the latter's swiftly growing industrial and military might. Germany, having won Alsace and Lorraine in the war of 1870, had no further territorial ambitions in France and only felt the need to attack it to obtain a swift victory (as in 1870) and avoid a two-front war. It had even less interest in Belgium, save as a needed means of reaching France, and it certainly did not want to find itself at war with Great Britain. The latter chose to fight because it, like France, was worried about the ascendency of German power. At the start, Italy stayed apart from the fight, later to join against Austria.

If we now bother to reference the religious backgrounds of these increasingly secular states, we find an initial conflict between Muslim and Orthodox power in the Balkans, coupled by a war between *Orthodox* states (the second Balkan war pitting Bulgaria against Serbia and Greece). The next tension that came into play was between Catholic Austria and Orthodox Serbia and Russia. The conflict that truly widened it was between Germany, led by Protestant Prussia, and Orthodox Russia. Finally, and as a side effect of that conflict, due to treaties, came the conflict between "*Protestant* Germany"[37] and the secular, if "historically *Catholic*," Third French Repub-

37. The quotation marks are meant to recall that Germany was composed of Catholic Bavaria, as well as Baden and Württemberg ... not to mention its Catholic ally in the war: the Austro-

lic and Great Britain and its Protestant Church of England. Catholic Italy later attacked Catholic Austria. From an historian's point of view, to cast this entire conflict as a holy war of Catholic France (the Church's "eldest daughter") against Protestant Germany is, in a word, preposterous.

I would be the last to deny the power and efficacy of ideas in relation to political events. Nevertheless, the willingness to see contingent events and the blood of men as "pawns" in a deeper intellectual struggle of ideas, as Maritain does, seems too close to an unconscious Hegelianism.

Perhaps that is unfair. Nevertheless, it is fair to ask what controls an account such as Maritain's. What *method* is there behind this "intuiting" of divine intentions and the discerning of deepest causes? What protects this account from being anecdotal and arbitrary? It seems not much.

I think we must admit that this history is not our dear Jacques at his best.[38] In fact, whatever the elegant intellectual dress it may wear, his historical account is little more than thinly disguised patriotic propaganda. Let us allow that a man's thought is influenced by his time. Patriotic talk was the natural air that most breathed in 1914. And now you can understand why I began as I did. When the first battles of the war had left your country with some half million wounded and some 150,000 dead, including two of one's dearest friends shot in the head, it is both easy to understand and to forgive (but not to be edified by) this patriotic account of the war's supposed nature and deepest causes.

Hungarian Empire! Maritain dismisses all of this: German Catholics are under the "impulsion" of Protestant Prussia; ibid., 1023. The Battle of Sadowa gave a "definitive blow" to the power of Austria and Catholic Germany (955).

38. It should be noted, I think, that Maritain has a less negative view of the Protestant Reformation in the few pages he gives to it in *Integral Humanism* (whose very limited attention to it reveals a different account of Western civilization, one that underlines far more the pernicious effect of Renaissance anthropocentrism): see *Integral Humanism* (New York: Charles Scribner's Sons, 1968), 16–17 and 25 (a work from 1936). By the time of the *Philosophy of History* (New York: Charles Scribner's Sons, 1957), he has become even more careful, confining the "vectoral laws" to be discerned within history to a very high level of generality. It would also be instructive to compare what he has to say of various German philosophers in his work on ethics from the 1950s with this earlier account. Indeed, if this first account (which, as noted, he then "let lie") is quite flawed, it also indicates Maritain's later willingness to let go of any false or unfair caricature. Perhaps (in some contrast to what is later suggested in IV), Maritain's thought can best be seen to develop from a tendency towards a "sweeping overview" (that has some affinity with Augustine's spirit in *The City of God* and that no doubt was attractive to his deeply "Augustinian" godfather) to a more careful tendency and a more sober "narrative" (one that has a closer affinity to the "schooled" mind of Thomas).

III. The Spirit of Modern Philosophy: Some Key Ideas Summarized

That said, I want to move on from Maritain's dubious history to his more interesting analysis of modern philosophical ideas. This began with his articles on Descartes, in the spring of 1914, and continued with his 1914–1915 articles on German philosophy: an annex to, or a continuation of, his analysis of the Spirit of Modern Philosophy. Let me give you a brief overview of his entire history, from Descartes through German philosophy up to his present moment.

Maritain's first two published articles are a solid achievement: some sixty-four pages devoted to an analysis of Descartes. His introductory article on German philosophy is then followed by five conferences on Luther and his time: some forty-two pages. Having connected Luther back to Descartes and modern philosophy, he then turns to Rousseau, in only one conference. (However, one would be justified in seeing all of these articles taken together as the first version of the book he published a dozen years later: *Luther, Descartes, Rousseau.*) He then turns to three conferences on Kant and four on the post-Kantian philosophy of Fichte, Schelling, Hegel, nineteenth-century German science, Schopenhauer, and Nietzsche. These total some forty-seven pages, being briefer summaries. He finally concludes by indicating the influence of this German philosophy upon such nineteenth-century French thinkers as Mme de Staël, Victor Cousin, Michelet, and Quinet (as well as the academic scientism of the Sorbonne). His conclusion, as I have already noted, is that a French "examination of conscience" needs to purify French thought of its "contamination" by ideas rooted in the soil of Germany and needs to return French philosophy to the purity and truth of Saint Thomas.

It is striking to encounter many of the ideas of his later works already in this first general work on modern philosophy. He has already read Pierre Duhem[39] and is under no doubt that Thomism is perfectly compatible with empirical science. This latter became entangled in a mechanistic and materialistic philosophy, but is separable from it. Although he has not worked out the details of how to relate empirical science to a realist philosophy of nature and metaphysics, he is confident that one can succeed in this task.

39. See Maritain, "L'Esprit de la philosophie moderne," *Oeuvres Complètes,* 1:826n3. Duhem's *Système du monde* (Paris: Hermann, 1913) had only appeared in the previous year.

Again, we already find here his description of Descartes' "mathematization" of human cognition and his "angelism."[40] Likewise, we find here its central mistake (one shared by other moderns), namely of confusing the immaterial idea with a material image and making it the term of human intellection, rather than the means by which an object is made present within the intellect: treating the idea as a *quod*, rather than as a *quo*.[41]

He attacks Descartes on a number of different grounds,[42] but his first error (and the one that most deeply vitiates his entire philosophical enterprise), is the most important, namely his desire to have philosophy be *independent* from faith and theology: "the spirit of Cartesian philosophy, and here is the first character essential to modern philosophy, is its *antitheological* spirit."[43] Descartes accomplishes this by making theological truth *so* transcendent to human reason that it has nothing to do with the latter, with the work of science and philosophy: "If it requires an extraordinary assistance of heaven, if one must be *more than human* to study revealed truth rationally, theology becomes a domain reserved to prophets and the inspired and the ordinary theologian understands only unwarranted presumptions, and is chattering about the inscrutable."[44] Philosophy, by contrast, will be grounded in clear and distinct ideas, ones proper to the human measure. Our idea of God, despite being asserted to be clear and distinct, in truth becomes entirely impenetrable, an unknown "x": "God is so great and so high that it would be entirely vain (and even impious) to try to understand Him: such is, in brief, the agnosticism to which, perhaps despite himself, Descartes condemns himself."[45] Yet this is entirely in keeping with his whole project; for Descartes's fundamental aim was to establish his physics upon a ground that could not be assailed either by theology or by any metaphysics previously allied with it. Descartes—and with him all of modern philosophy—insists on its *independence* from faith and theology. Any philosophy that recognized its incompleteness, its openness to a higher truth, and its need to be instructed by such a truth would be a false philosophy. This is the fundament of *modernism*.

40. Maritain, "L'Esprit de la philosophie moderne," 861.

41. Ibid., 873.

42. He accuses Descartes of three great denials: of the reality of the revealed truth found in faith and theology; of the reality of the created beings by which our mind is measured; and of the unity between individual knowers that is established through adherence to a tradition of learning. See ibid., 856–87.

43. Ibid., 837; emphasis in original.

44. Ibid., 839.

45. Ibid., 846.

What Maritain aimed to show in his lectures on German philosophy was that this crucial character of Cartesianism and modern philosophy was in fact *derivative*, that it was only the French way of appropriating a doctrine traceable to Luther, its first and most vigorous proponent. His analysis of Luther is based upon the recent study of Fr. Denifle.[46] Luther's theology is explained by his psychology. He begins with a "practical Pelagianism," trying to become virtuous by his own forces; but this proves impossible: his concupiscence is invincible. This then leads him to his "liberating insight": it does not matter that we are radically corrupt, incapable of not sinning, for Christ has thrown His mantle of justice over us and we need only have faith in Him to be freed from this impossible inner struggle. Whence his "motto": to sin strongly but believe even more strongly.[47] And thus Maritain describes his position as an "inverted Pharisism."[48] The *center* of his thought is not God but himself: "the intimate satisfaction and consolation of this 'me' … there is the goal."[49] And it is in the name of this "inner me" that he stands against the Pope and the Church.

The consequence of his "breakthrough" and his stand against his own tradition is to create a religion freed from all authority and a modern subjectivism of which he is the true founder.[50] In the name of his "inner sentiment," he will then stand against reason and the intellectual discipline of scholastic theology, calling reason the devil's whore. Nevertheless, Luther ought rightly to be understood as the ancestor of modern rationalism; for

> the true foundation of modern rationalism, the only principle that counts in its eyes, is that the spirit of man and of his science is fully and absolutely independent and recognizes no authority above itself, neither that of God nor that of objective reality. In this sense Luther, by his revolt against the spiritual authority of the Church and by his contempt for objective truth, is truly the ancestor of modern rationalism.[51]

And just as he arrives at this in an inverted way (by rejecting the value of reason), in a similar way he becomes the father of modern *naturalism*. For his doctrine creates "a split, an unbridgeable gulf, between the order of nature and of grace."[52] His "élan of sentiment" leaves man still "enclosed with-

46. Henri Denifle, *Luthertum in der ersten Entwicklung* (Mainz: Kirchheim, 1904).
47. Maritain, "Le rôle de l'Allemagne," *Oeuvres Complètes*, 1:928–29.
48. Ibid., 929.
49. Ibid., 930.
50. Ibid., 932.
51. Ibid., 933–34.
52. Ibid., 938.

in his own nature," one that cannot be vivifed and transfigured by God's grace; and thus, "with Luther, naturalism is introduced into the world."[53] Likewise, he is the author of modern individualism, of the rupture between the individual and tradition and the holy Church. Each person is left to the absolute liberty of his freedom of conscience, divorced from any spiritual authority to which he is answerable. And so Maritain reaches the following "summation":

> From the egocentric principle posed by Luther derives the subjectivism, the naturalism and the individualism that at bottom designate three aspects of one and the same thing, namely the independence and sovereignty of "me": subjectivism is the rupture of me, the knowing subject, with objective being; naturalism is the rupture of me, the principle of natural action, with the supernatural order and God; individualism is the rupture of me, the individual, with the whole of which I am a part.[54]

Luther, in short, is the true father of a modernism that "tends essentially to protestantize the Catholic faith ... to Germanize the Catholic faith."[55]

Maritain has little difficulty in showing how, according to its own mode, Descartes's philosophy possesses the same characteristics as Luther introduced. And, not surprisingly, he goes on to show that Kant is really the apotheosis of the false ideas of his German forebearer. Finally, he shows how—through the nationalism of Fichte and the dialectic of Hegel—these same characteristics continue to live on in the German soil that produced them, but now as a goal to be achieved in history and through the will of men. In this way, these ideas are connected to a pangermanism that gave rise to a united Germany, that "artificial creation of violence and pride": to a country "that clearly supposes despotism and a militarism without check" and that France is now set upon checking in her present life-and-death struggle. Reading his account, one could be in no doubt of what Maritain would think of "Transcendental Thomism": it could be nothing less that "consorting with the enemy" and failing to recognize the degree to which Kant and Thomas were implacable adversaries, representatives of opposing Protestant and Catholic cultures.

53. Ibid., 939.

54. Ibid., 945–46.

55. Ibid., 949.

IV. The Two Maritains: The Soul of France and the Dream of America

I come now to my final interest: what light these lectures shed on "The Young Jacques."

I think, in the first place, they clarify what likely led Pierre Villard to divide his legacy between Maurras and Maritian. Villard, in his own words, wanted his gift to "safeguard what subsists of the intellectual and moral patrimony of our country"[56] or the deepest commitments of the France for which he was willing to die, a France older than its revolution. Maurras' monarchism defended this older France politically and Maritain's Thomism defended the same spiritually and intellectually. We should remember that it was in *these* conferences that Villard had first encountered, and became captivated by, Maritain. Now, as patriotic as they may be, nothing in them is connected to politics or monarchism *per se*; they are devoted entirely to the intellectual and spiritual order. There is, then, no reason to hold that Villard's bequest required that he saw a deep commitment of Maritain to Maurras' own politics. I have argued against this interpretation of the bequest in the past;[57] I would do so even more strongly from a reading of these lectures. No one disputes that Maritain was disaffected with the religious stance of the Third Republic and that he was thus willing to be a "fellow traveler" with Maurras's monarchism; but there is no reason to argue his commitment to *Action Française* went much deeper than that. What Villard would have seen in these lectures was not such a commitment, but Maritain's own intellectual and spiritual commitments. Thus, the twin goals—political and intellectual—that Maurras and Maritain gave to *La Revue Universelle* were likely faithful to Villard's own intentions; they likely captured the different commitments that he himself had encountered in these two men.

As a second point, these lectures should alert us to just how *French* Maritain is at the beginning of his career. From these, we cannot but ask how well he knew Germany. If one reads his description of their time in Hei-

56. Quoted from Barré, *Les Mendiants du Ciel,* 215, citing Maritain's *Notebooks.*

57. See my "To Philosophize *for* the Faith: Jacques Maritain's Intellectual Vocation," in *The Vocation of the Catholic Philosopher,* edited by John P. Hittinger (Washington, D.C.: American Maritain Association, 2010), 110–31, 114n7. I am there taking issue with Ralph McInerny: see his *The Very Rich Hours of Jacques Maritain: A Spiritual Life* (Notre Dame, Indiana: University of Notre Dame Press, 2003), 60–65.

delberg, for example,[58] one gets the impression that it was devoted to establishing the spiritual foundations of the extraordinary "cenacle of three" that he, his wife, and her sister were to live for fifty years. They are closed in upon themselves and their spiritual life. Apart from his meetings with Driesch, it seems he had little interaction with any other Germans. Certainly, we never hear of trips in Germany or of German acquaintances, much less friends. (The only Protestant friend that, to my knowledge, he ever refers us to is Swiss.[59]) Driesch appears to be the only German intellectual Maritain really knew. When we turn to his work, it is again rather striking who is not even mentioned: people such as Wilhelm Dilthey, Max Weber, Ernst Troellesch, Romano Guardini, and Thomas Mann.[60] Husserl is mentioned in passing, in one paragraph; Max Scheler is merely mentioned.[61] Maritain's intellectual appetite was voracious and truly catholic, and his later works include many references to those not French.[62] But, as a young person—and, after all, not surprisingly!—the thinkers he "takes on" are quintessentially French: Bergson, Descartes, the academics of the Sorbonne. Again, while "Meudon" seems to take in all that is then intellectually alive, its conversations were centered on the intellectual world of *Paris*.[63]

This helps me now make sense of a remark of Raïssa's that had puzzled

58. See Maritain, *Notebooks*, 43.

59. See ibid., 189. (Vergara was a friend Vera and then Raïssa had made in their youth.)

60. Maritain mentions Mann at one point, from a magazine article, to ally him with the Nietzchean sentiment that bloodshed is sometimes justified; ibid., 1017. Neither here nor in the next dozen years does he ever refer to any of his literary works (*Buddenbrooks*, *Magic Mountain*, etc.).

61. See "L'etat actuel de la philosophie allemande," *Oeuvres Complètes*, 2: 1153. Maritain notes the evident influence of Catholics upon Husserl's thought (Bolzano, Brentano), but thinks he is still trapped in idealism. He is largely dismissive, just as he continues to be of all German thought. (He speaks of him more positively two years later in "Le Realisme Thomiste," first published in *La Revue Universelle* 13, no. 3 [1 May 1923]: 378–90 and then as chapter 9 of *Reflexions Sur L'Intelligence et sur sa vie proper* [1924], grouping him with Driesch as ones who reconnect with Aristotle; but the reference is again in passing, one line. See his *Oeuvres Complètes*, 3:364.) He recognizes there are Neo-scholastics in Germany, but he holds out much less hope for Thomism in Germany than in France, for the former must confront an ingrained Kantianism and the even deeper anti-Catholic and anti-Latin sentiments of Lutheranism ("L'etat actuel," 1156–57). This essay of 1921 on German philosophy evinces exactly the same perspective as his 1914–1915 lectures.

62. Nevertheless, it is striking how little true "engagement" there is with non-French thought. One could contrast this, I think, with what one finds in another French Catholic convert, Gabriel Marcel, who obviously felt he could learn something from men such as Heideggar and Jaspers. See, for example *Entretiens: Paul Ricoeur Gabriel Marcel* (Mayenne, France: Floch, 1968).

63. This also comes across strongly in Barré's biography: it is almost entirely centered on France and Paris.

me. On the very first page of *Les Grandes Amitiés,* she speaks of the desolation she is now experiencing at the Fall of France (in World War II) and the loss "of the hope that sustained us in our work: the hope that the love of Christ could penetrate and transform this world."[64] Now, of course, such hope is natural to any Christian. But Raïssa's aim seemed more particular, and more bound up with France herself. In fact, it seems to me that it is *that* world, indeed the intellectual world of *Paris,* that she and Jacques had hoped could be "penetrated and transformed by the love of Christ." It could be so if the Church and her "sanctioned philosophy," that of Thomas, could penetrate and transform *that* intellectual world. *This* was the great hope and ambition that informed all of their "work" between the wars: they would, in the words of his 1914 lecture, "dedicate themselves to the utmost measure of their forces" to liberate French thought from three centuries of error and help ensure that a truer philosophy might reign again within it. They were animated by this, more particular and limited, hope, and it is this hope that they felt had "almost been lost" with the fall of France.

And this leads me to my concluding reflections. Jacques wrote for over sixty years. I think it is fair to see his writing as breaking into two parts. The first is centered on, and almost entirely dedicated to, Paris and its intellectual life. It is his commitment to his *country* and to its intellectual struggle that is made clear by these lectures. With but very few exceptions, the first thirty years of their lives as Catholics were lived entirely in Paris. They were given over to one central cause: the nourishing and the flourishing of Thomism within Parisian intellectual life. That their life was so focussed on this goal in part explains, I think, why they did not return to Paris after World War II. For, while the First World War seemed to make the achievement of that goal possible, and focused all of their hope and energy upon it, the Second World War ended the world in which that project had any real hope of success. Neither Raïssa nor Jacques could seriously envision being able to re-dedicate themselves to such a narrow goal or believe in its success after the Second World War.

The late thirties saw their lives move—at first tentatively, but finally decisively—away from their "Parisian center" and to the larger world: to concerns such as the Spanish Civil War and—even further afield—to the New World of Argentina, Canada, and the United States. Perhaps it would be

64. Raïssa Maritain, *Les grandes amitiés* (Paris: Desclée de Brouwer, 1949), 11; my translation.

fair to see *Integral Humanism* as the harbinger of this "shift of center." It was to prove decisive for them. After the war, they are first in Rome (not Paris), and then return to the New World. When Jacques finally returns to France, he repairs to Toulouse or Kolbsheim (not Paris); for the whole life project of "the Young Jacques" was a thing of his past. He had "moved on."[65]

Many have remarked that there is ever a "dialectic" to Maritain's thought when it comes to the modern world: both a "no" and a "yes." In one sense, this is just the common fare of any Christian intellect, saying "no" to sin and "yes" to the possibilities opened up by grace. But we are here speaking of something more particular, of the "spirit of modern philosophy." And here I think it is fair to say that, while his thought is never unequivocally one or the other, what one hears "loud and clear" from the Young Jacques is a "no": whereas, from the Elder Jacques, the "yes" can be heard more strongly. This is particularly true in relation to his views on democracy and it is easy to see why. For the Young Jacques, French democracy is an enemy of French Catholic civilization, and is a vehicle for the false coin of modernism that is undermining it; for the Elder Jacques, American democracy is a friend of French Catholic civilization, a force that liberated it from Nazi totalitarianism. It is hardly surprising—given what he had experienced of American hospitality during and after the war—that his *Reflections on America* should end up being unduly optimistic, just as his earlier reflections on democratic France should have been unduly pessimistic. But there is more to it than that. Jacques's center of gravity has shifted. I think this can be captured by this one rhetorical question: Is it even remotely conceivable, within the bounds of anything believable or practically possible, that the Young Jacques could have identified with Saul Alinsky?

But it is, after all, "small beer" to say that Maritain goes from being an

65. Indeed, it is perhaps not too far amiss to see his thought as shifting between two centuries. Historians are wont to speak of the "19th century" as being between 1789 and 1914. When Jacques begins to write, as evidenced in these lectures on German Philosophy, he is fighting battles of the 19th century: of the artificial creation of the German Empire, of the false infiltration of Germanic science and philosophy within 19th century French thought, of the need to make Leo XIII's call for a renewal of Thomism become a reality. He continues to have this "mind-set" after the First World War and it is perhaps not too far wrong to see 1926 and his break with *Action Française* as beginning to turn him away from that "19th century project" and to the "new Christendom" he begins to envision in *Integral Humanism*. His decision to return to Princeton after Rome is a part of his "new center" and new project. And the American Maritian Association, and its some 24 volumes of essays, bears witness to the "fertile field" for Thomism that Maritain believed he had caught sight of in the United States and the wisdom of devoting his energy to help secure its future.

"anti-democrat" to a "Christian democrat," a change already foreseen in the events of 1926 and his turning decisively away from *Action Française*. Nor is it surprising that he, like the Catholic Church, moves away from Vatican I and the fight with Modernism towards Vatican II and "letting in some fresh air." Nevertheless, these lectures should also alert us to the degree to which Maritain "remains himself" throughout his career, the degree to which his central ideas and commitments are present "from the beginning." For, along with his "disengaging" from Bergson in his first book, these lectures on Modern Philosophy, and their annex on German philosophy, are his first true work. And, because they are, they deserve more attention from Maritainistas than they have thus far received.

Perhaps their greatest surprise is the intellectual conflict that Maritain clearly signals as most crucial. It is not the fight with scientism, or how rightly to relate metaphysics and the philosophy of nature with modern and contemporary science. Neither is it the false epistemology or theory of knowledge at work in Descartes and so many moderns. Rather, it is the right relation that should obtain between nature and grace, philosophy and theology. The modern malaise is more spiritual than intellectual: it is the "spiritual independence" that contemporary man desires for himself. And thus he signals that the single most important intellectual challenge for a Catholic philosophy is to articulate correctly and well the relation between itself and theology, between human reason and divine faith, between nature and grace. No task could be more urgent.

In the end, what these lectures most strikingly convey is the degree to which Maritain was a convert, was someone who, like a glove, had been "turned inside out." He had "come in from the cold." He recognized there was a true and very serious difference between being within the ambit of faith and being without; between being with the Church and her holy Tradition and being without; between being willing to depend on her truth and insisting on remaining independent. Although Maritain "mellows" with age, and even regards his youthful zeal as unduly harsh (against Bergson in particular, for example), nevertheless (and as the *Peasant of the Garonne* bore eloquent witness) there was ever a severe strain to all of his thought, one born of the recognition that, in this life—and especially for a Catholic philosopher in the contemporary West—one was ever in a "culture war" in which there were true foes. His first thought was decisively forged in the crucible of the Battles of the Frontiers, of the Marne, of Verdun, and of all the horrific slaughter of World War I, before which (he believed) Our Lady wept bitterly. Maritain was a gentle man, one who loved many, who had a "tender heart," who was congenitally "of the Left." But these first lectures should remind us of his steel within, of his tough-mindedness and intransigence: he could not bear arms in World War I, but he never ceased to do battle and be vigilant for that Catholic truth and that Catholic tradition of philosophy that he had discovered and with which he had fallen in love.

≈ III ≈

JACQUES MARITAIN ON INTUITION

MATTHEW S. PUGH

Maritain, Critical Realism, and the Intuition of Being

Anyone familiar with the writings of Jacques Maritain knows that Maritain steadfastly maintained that metaphysics must be grounded in what he called the metaphysical intuition of being (hereafter referred to as the MIB). As such, the MIB is absolutely central to Maritain's metaphysics, and Maritain made numerous attempts to clarify what the MIB is, and why it is necessary for metaphysics. The notion was nevertheless not well received by his Thomist colleagues. Indeed most of them, including the equally famous Gilson, rejected the idea. They did so for many reasons, some broad and some more technically specific. Among the former were: the MIB carries with it exclusionist and/or elitist implications; the MIB is obscure, even mystical, and thus makes metaphysics dependent on some kind of natural mysticism; the intuition of being is an inverted vestige of Bergson's notion of intuition; the MIB is not genuinely Thomistic, since it is apparently not found in Thomas's writings. Among the philosophically more technical were: the MIB is superfluous—it is simply not needed for beginning metaphysics, since there are other less problematic and Thomistically authentic ways of starting metaphysics; the MIB is by its very nature an impossibility—there can be no such thing; or the MIB demands too much from the data on which it draws, and hence cannot give us a knowledge of immaterial *ens*, the true subject of metaphysics, and so forth.

Now certainly the notion of the MIB is not an easy notion to grasp. Indeed, it may be the most difficult in Maritain's philosophy. This in part accounts for the confusion surrounding it, as well as the criticisms it has faced. Nevertheless, the real problem is a more fundamental one: we cannot understand what the MIB is, let alone see the necessity for it, until the crucially important role it plays in grounding knowledge is explained. My contention is that this has never really been done, not even by Maritain himself. Heretofore the criticisms of the MIB have focused on what the intuition is said to evoke, namely the concept of being (*ens*) itself, and how it could possibly do so, while neglecting to examine the MIB from the standpoint of its function in the abstractive theory of knowledge.

My task in this paper, then, is to elucidate what Maritain means by the MIB by showing how it is central to Maritain's epistemology, why it is inseparable from it, and how the MIB is implicitly and necessarily contained in the condition for the very possibility of knowing. I intend to show, in other words, that the MIB is implicitly contained in every act of knowing, since it is really nothing more than the intuition of the intelligibility of being itself.

In order to accomplish my task, I shall employ what Maritain calls the confirmatory rational analysis or critique of knowledge, as this bears on the MIB. Though the confirmatory rational analysis or critique of knowledge cannot produce the MIB, it can show the necessity for it by showing how it is implicitly, but not explicitly, contained in every act of knowing insofar as it is grounded in the very condition for intelligibility itself. And in this respect it must never be forgotten that, though the method of analysis or critique uses what Aquinas calls the way of resolution (rather than the way of composition), wherein the intellect seeks to resolve many particular truths into one self-evident principle by moving from effects to causes, the starting point and terminus for all reasoning is intuition.[1] In other words, by showing how every act of knowing as such is resolved in the principle of intelligibility, the confirmatory rational analysis or critique of knowledge simultaneously shows how the intuition of the intelligibility of being is the condition that is presupposed by every act of knowing.

In order to indicate, then, how knowing is resolved in the principle of the intelligibility of being and hence how the MIB is the condition presupposed by and implicitly contained in every act of knowing, the paper is accordingly divided into two parts. Part I begins with a brief examination

1. Thomas Aquinas, *Expositio super Boetium de Trinitate*, q. 6, a. 1, c., translated by Armand Maurer as *The Division and Methods of the Sciences* (Toronto: Pontifical Institute of Medieval Studies, 1986), 70–73.

of the starting point of critique in Maritain's critical realist epistemology, namely, the given-ness of knowledge and its inseparability from being. That examination reveals that the key to understanding their unity is the principle of identity, and that the whole knowing process, beginning with sense perception and proceeding through to simple apprehension and judgment, is subsumed under or governed by the principle of identity. Hence in the rest of Part I each of these is considered in turn—sense perception, simple apprehension, and judgment—from the standpoint that the principle of identity plays in them in the critique of knowledge. Part II, section 1 of the paper establishes that the principle of identity operative in and governing the knowing process (and presupposed by the intelligibility of being) is resolved in the fundamental immateriality of being. It establishes that embedded within every act of knowing is an implicit intuition of the non-materiality of being, the MIB that is then made explicit when the intellect turns to an examination of its own contents in the critique of knowledge. There the MIB is made explicit in the form of a special positive judgment which sees that *esse* actuates more than material being, which sees that the same 'what' exists simultaneously in both a material and non-material mode; that judgment in turn gives rise to the concept of metaphysical being (*ens*)—a concept that of course incorporates the co-metaphysical components of essence and existence. Part II, section 2 then examines the nature of the concept of metaphysical being (*ens*), and shows that that concept (made possible by the MIB and affirmed in judgment in both positive and negative form) is an adequate starting point for metaphysics, and that it perfectly coheres with Aquinas's definition of metaphysical being (*ens*). Finally, I conclude that not only is the concept of metaphysical being evoked by the MIB adequate or sufficient for beginning metaphysics, it is also necessary for beginning metaphysics, since it is at least implicitly the foundation for every act of knowing.

I. Maritain's Critical Realism

Now for Maritain, "critique" in a critical realist epistemology is a purely reflexive activity. In this regard, both its procedure and its starting point are radically different from the procedure and starting point in idealism. In critical realism, the task of critique is not to see that we can or do know, for as Maritain said, "It would be absurd to demand that philosophical thought begin, even before it knows anything validly, by proving that it can know (for it could only do so if it did know)."[2] Rather, the task of critique in critical realism is to know what knowledge is, to penetrate to its very nature by using the intellect to turn reflexively toward itself and examine its own contents, and the acts which give rise to knowledge. What Maritain's critical realist epistemology takes as its starting point, then, is the existence in the world of knowledge itself. For critical reflection reveals that knowledge is immersed in existence, is immersed in the world; that knowledge and existence are inseparable; and that being is by its very nature intelligible. This is clear in that if the existence of knowledge in the world is taken as the starting point of critique (which is simply the knowing of knowledge), then *what* is known when knowledge is known is *being* in the *form* of intelligibility. That is, insofar as knowledge exists, every act of knowing must contain, at least implicitly, a reference to being. In effect, by showing that the proper starting point for critique in critical realism is the given-ness in the world of knowledge itself, the critique of knowledge brings to light the condition that makes knowledge possible, namely, the intelligibility of existence.

So, the starting point for a critical realist critique of knowledge is not the self-enclosed *cogito* as in idealism,[3] but the intellect reflexively contemplating its own knowing activity made possible by the given-ness of being's intelligibility. This means that critique reveals first and foremost that existence is given in and with every act of knowing. That is, knowledge *actually* and not merely possibly exists. Put differently, the starting point of critique is not, as Maritain says, "I am aware," but rather "I am aware, or know, that something exists."[4] But in knowing that something exists, we are aware that what is "is," that a thing is the same as, or "is" one with, itself. We are aware, in other words, of the first principle of being, namely, the principle of identity. And because the principle of identity is the first principle of being, and because critique reveals that the first act of the intellect seizes intelligible

2. Jacques Maritain, *The Degrees of Knowledge*, 4th edition, translated by Gerald B. Phelan (New York: Charles Scribner's Sons, 1959), 74.

3. It should be noted here that for Maritain, the problem of knowledge is not to be understood in the context of Cartesian skepticism or doubt. That is, for Maritain, "to know" means to have access to the extra-mentally existing thing. That we do in fact have this access is a given and is the starting point for critique, since any attempt to begin critique with Cartesian doubt is self-defeating.

4. Maritain, *The Degrees of Knowledge*, 76.

being, the intellect seizes intelligible being under the principle of identity. Furthermore, since the intelligibility of being is only made known through knowledge, the principle of identity, as the grounding principle for the intelligibility of being, must govern or subsume every step of the knowing process, from sense perception, to simple apprehension, to judgment, which in the latter case becomes the foundation for the MIB.

1. Sense Perception

The critique of knowledge reveals that sense perception takes place under, or is subsumed by, the principle of identity in the following way. Though sensation is an entirely immanent action that terminates in the senses themselves, the senses are nevertheless able to grasp the sensible thing just as it exists outside the mind and become intentionally one with it, precisely because the extra-mentally existing thing acts in a transient manner on the senses. That is, when the senses receive from the thing acting on them through the thing's material qualities an impressed likeness of the thing which determines the sense organs in a specific way, the senses become intentionally one with the thing in first act insofar as they are one in the same operation. The impressed senses then produce in a second immanent and terminal act an expressed likeness of the thing in imagination and memory. Hence the same thing that exists outside the perceiver with an extra-mental existence exists intentionally in the perceiver as an object of perception having sensory unity in the form of impressed and expressed sensory species. In effect, the immanent act of sensation terminates in an object (the object of perception) which implies, as Maritain says, "the actual existence of the thing within its very objectivity."[5] It is in this way, then, that the senses receive (under the principle of identity in the form of intentional sensory unities) existence into themselves so as to become the foundation for knowing, first in simple apprehension, and then in judgment.

2. Simple Apprehension

The principle of identity also subsumes the abstractive process of concept formation in simple apprehension, insofar as the intuition of essences in and through concepts presupposes a unity of thing and formal object effected in the mind. "Thing" here simply refers to what exists extra-mentally,

5. Ibid., 115–18.

or can exist for itself. "Object" refers to the thing as it exists under its changed conditions or mode in the intellect. Thing becomes formal object in the mind when the agent or active component of the intellect reduces to actuation what is potentially intelligible in the sensory image, by abstracting the intelligible element of the sensory form away from all of the individuating or material characteristics of the sensible form. The potentially intelligible form is here made actually intelligible. This form, or *species impressa*, is the presentative likeness of the thing existing immaterially in the mind. At this stage the intellect intentionally becomes the abstracted formal object in first or initial act. But at this point, the intentional formation of the object takes place at a purely pre-conscious level—it does not become fully conscious until the intellect intentionally becomes the object in second act through the production of the *species expressa*, or "uttered" presentative form—a form which is presented to the intellect via the concept or formal sign.

Now the function of the formal sign is to make something other than itself known before becoming first known itself. That is, the essence of the formal sign is to bear the mind to something other than itself. (Formal signs become known in themselves only when the mind reflexively turns to examine its own contents.) And what the formal sign or concept makes known in this case is the formal object—wherein the intellect and thing have become fully or intentionally one—as *species expressa*, or "uttered" presentative likeness. Thus the formal sign or concept plays a dual role in knowing: entitative in that it modifies the knowing subject, and functional in that it fully becomes the formal object as *species expressa*, or presentative likeness, in a non-material way. In essence, *what* is intuited or known in the concept (formal sign) or *species expressa* is the thing as formal object, which though singular in the thing of nature and purely abstract and universal in the concept, is neither singular nor universal in itself.[6]

It is the principle of identity, then, as the first principle of being, that accounts for both the unity of the thing as thing with the unity of the object of perception (determined as presentative likenesses in external sense and imagination), and the unity of the thing as thing with the unity of the thing as formal intelligible object revealed in the presentative likeness of the formal sign or concept. That is to say, the unity or identity of the formal intelligible object (thing as object) is grounded in the thing as thing through the unity or identity of the object of perception with the thing as thing.

6. See ibid., 119–28. See especially Maritain's helpful chart on ibid., 122; also ibid., 123n.

3. *Judgment*

Something of the extra-mentally existing thing, then, is given through sense perception and under the principle of identity to the intellect in the abstractive formation of the intentional object intuited in simple apprehension and made known in a concept or formal sign. And, since being means what exists or can exist, and since (as the critique of knowledge shows) what is first presented to the mind is what exists under sensory/material conditions, the first concept that the intellect forms is the concept of material being. But though simple apprehension knows something of being (*ens*), namely material being (*ens*), it does not know existence (*esse*) as such, for the emphasis in simple apprehension is on knowing the "something" or "what" in "I know that something exists." Rather, it is judgment, the act of the intellect, that completes the act of knowing by returning the intellect to the thing as thing initially grasped by the senses; judgment that knows, or intuits, existence. Of course simple apprehension presupposes what is apprehended in judgment, namely, a thing's act of existing. For every essence abstracted by simple apprehension signifies an intelligible determination *and* something which has that determination. The object of the concept "hexagon," for example, also signifies that something (at least possible) exists with that determination. Nevertheless, only judgment apprehends existence as such, since it is the act by which the intellect sees and asserts that a predicate and a subject which differ in notion are identical or are one in the thing. It sees and asserts that X is Y, or as the case may be, that X is not Y. Judgment thus returns the mind from the level of abstracted formal object or essence, to the level of thing possessing existence. In other words, the unity of thing which simple apprehension tears asunder in the abstractive formation of the intentional object is restored by judgment. As Maritain puts it, the task or function of judgment is to effect a reconciliation after a struggle. Judgment restores in the mind the unity which the thing has preceding simple apprehension. Yet the unity which judgment restores lies outside the entire order of simple apprehension, since the judgment relives in an act proper to the intellect the act of the thing as it exists *prior* to simple apprehension. More specifically, judgment affirms the unity of the thing in existence through the intentional reliving of the act of existing in the mind that the thing exercises outside the mind. It is the seeing and the asserting of the conformity or identity of two unities or identities:

the unity formed in the intellect between subject and predicate, and the unity of these in the extra-mentally existing thing.[7]

Judgment, then, is both existential and intuitive. And here we must be careful to observe an important distinction that supports the claim, but one that is often overlooked. Judgment is defined as the act of the mind by which it unites by affirming or separates by denying. Uniting or composing, and separating or dividing, however, are not the same as affirming or denying. In uniting or composing, the intellect compares two concepts in the mind and "sees" or intuits their identity with the things that they stand for; in separating or dividing the intellect compares two concepts and "sees" or intuits that the things they stand for are different. Affirming or denying, however, bear on the notion of assent, which in turn bears on what is. As such, the act of affirming or denying is added to the act of composing or dividing. Assent, or judgment proper, then, must be preceded by the formation of a mental enunciation, what Maritain calls the "proposition to be judged," that has for its matter the concepts that it uses, and for its form the union or separation of composing and dividing via the copula in positive "is," or negative "is not," mode.[8]

In the proposition to be judged, however, "is" functions in a merely copulative way. That is, "is" merely expresses composition or division without thinking the "is" as an *act of being*. "Is" only becomes truly judicative when the mind thinks "formally the act of being as an act."[9] Thinking *the act of being as an act* constitutes assent; it is an assertive act which affirms or negates the predicate of the subject. In effect, the mental enunciation or proposition to be judged simply links in the mind two concepts via the copula in an existence "which is not yet thought as being an existence in act, as existence effectively held."[10] The mental act does not in other words think them in relation to *what really exists*, and must be completed by an assertive act (affirmation or negation) which "completes their composition formally in *the act of* existence itself," and "declares the concepts joined to be identified with one another in extra-mental *existence*."[11] It is an assertive act which "sees" that what is formed in the mind conforms to what exists, or can exist, outside the mind.

7. See ibid., 88.

8. See Jacques Maritain, *An Introduction to Logic* (London: Sheed and Ward, 1973), 82–93.

9. Ibid., 83.

10. Ibid., 86.

11. Ibid., 88.

Here a number of key points about judgment come to light. First, judgment proper, or assent, is necessarily grounded in immanent enunciations wherein "is" functions in a merely copulative way. This means that the "is" of judgment proper is necessarily grounded in the copulative "is." As Maritain avers, the verb "to be" always signifies actual or possible existence, even when it is used as a copula. Both the proposition to be judged, and judgment itself, bear on being, on what is, and indeed are so intimately linked that one could say that the former makes possible the latter, and the latter demands the former. Secondly, both the proposition to be judged, and judgment proper, are intuitive in nature. Both involve eidetic "seeing"; the first involves the "seeing" of simple apprehension which supplies the materials (concepts) for the formation of the immanent mental enunciation, which it composes or divides in various ways by comparing, or once again, "seeing" how they fit in relation to each other; the second involves the "seeing" or intuiting of the conformity of what has been formed in the mind with what exists extra-mentally. In judgment proper the intellect "sees" or intuits that what it has formed within itself, what it has intentionally become, is really conformed to what exists outside the mind.

Now it is precisely when judgment proper intuits that the unity or identity expressed in a proposition like "X is Y" corresponds to, or is really conformed to, the unity or identity in the thing that exists outside the mind that the judgment possesses truth. Truth, of course, is defined as the adequation of thing and thought. But adequation is grounded in the principle of identity, and it is here that the critique of knowledge reveals the vitally important, unique, and indeed peculiar role that the principle of identity operative in judgment proper plays in justifying the MIB.

The unity or conformity that the judgment proper intuits is based on a conformity of being under two existential aspects: the *esse* or mode of existing that things have when they are outside the mind, and the *esse* or mode of existing that things have when they are known in the mind. That is, things exist differently in our thought than they do in extra-mental reality. When the intellect and intelligible become one in act, a unity is effected between thing and thought in such a way that a change occurs in the thing's condition, in the way that it exists—not entitatively or in itself as such, but simply as known to the mind. So, the mode of being (*esse*) of the thing, but not its essence or "what," changes. Because we are talking about two modes of existing for the same "what," insofar as the thing as thing and thing as formal object have one and the same term of knowledge, and insofar as the formal object known in a concept affects a real modification of the knowing subject, there is an underlying unity between thing as thing, and thing as formal object known in thought. Since knowing's mode of existing is that of the intellect, the intellect in act becomes the intelligible in act. Hence it is the unity of being under the principle of identity that enables judgment to "see" or intuit an "identification in the mind that corresponds with an identity in the thing," and likewise to intuit "the conformity of an identification with an identity."[12] Judgment, then, is resolved in the principle of identity, the grounding principle or condition for the intelligibility of being.

It should be noted here that the identity or unity that is the basis for judgment's intuition of the conformity between the two identities or unities being spoken of here is not numerical identity, nor strict/isomorphic identity, nor even the identity of formal equivalence.[13] It is rather a metaphysical unity grounded in the intelligibility or essence itself. Yet the sameness that has two modes of *esse*—one extra-mental and the other mental—is not a third thing or entity that stands over and above the two instances of *esse*; it is not itself a being. Maritain is clear about this, for he basically agrees with what Aquinas has to say in *De Ente et Essentia*[14] about natures considered absolutely, and joins him in his rejection of Avicenna's attempt to give being to essences so considered. For Maritain, the essence or nature considered in abstraction from its two existential modes of being constitutes one and the same "thing," though only in the line of knowing, not in the line of entity, since both existential modes of the thing as thing, and thing as known, terminate in the same object of knowledge. As presented before the mind as a formal object known by the intellect in first act, the absolute essence is properly neither universal nor concrete, neither one nor many. Yet though the essence absolutely considered abstracts from every

12. Maritain, *The Degrees of Knowledge*, 88.

13. Numerical identity refers to a thing's self-sameness. Numerically identical entities share *all* of their properties, including the same place and time. Strict identity (also called isomorphic identity) refers to two spatio-temporally distinct things, like two balls, that otherwise share a relation of complete sameness. The identity of formal equivalence refers to the identity of meanings between words related by the copula "is," as in "a triangle is three points in a plane joined by straight lines."

14. See Thomas Aquinas, *On Being and Essence*, translated by Armand Maurer (Toronto: Pontifical Institute of Medieval Studies, 1949), 39–42.

being, it prescinds from no one of them. Hence it only actually exists either in things, or in the mind. For the knowing subject, this means that the nature absolutely considered—Maritain's formal object existing in the mind as neither universal nor concrete—must reveal itself to the intellect in and through a formal sign, concept, or *species expressa,* wherein it then takes on the characteristics of universality and community. The unity or identity that Maritain is talking about, then, is a unity grounded in the intelligibility of being, insofar as that is a unity grounded in the potential intelligibility of the thing as it exists outside the mind.

In regard to judgment proper, this unity in the line of knowing means that when the intellect intuits the conformity of an identification with an identity, the unity or conformity referenced is a unity understood not in relation to the mode of existing of the thing as thing, nor of the mode of existing of the intellect in its knowing activity through formal signs, "but in reference to the existing of the thing taken in its pure value of intelligible object." It is a correspondence "lived in the mind by the mind, as it is realized (or may be realized) outside the mind."[15]

II. The Metaphysical Intuition of Being

1. *The Immateriality of Being* (Ens)

The adequation of thing and thought that is the foundation for knowledge (that judgment affirms) is made possible by the essence's ability to exist under two modes: a material mode and a non-material mode. At the same time, implicit in every judgment is an intuition of the non-materiality of being (*ens*), in both its essential (*essentia*) and existential (*esse*) aspects. Here we must recall to mind exactly what it is that makes being intelligible. The critique of knowledge reveals that being is intelligible precisely to the extent to which it is non-material. That is, a being is intelligible just to the extent to which it is separated from matter, for matter masks the intelligibility of being insofar as matter is the principle of the individuation of things. A being's degree of separation from matter is indicated by its conceptual definition. Therefore being (*ens*), as the condition for the possibility of knowing, must be essentially non-material, for the condition for a being's intelligibility cannot be of the same nature as that which masks its intelligibility. The condi-

15. Maritain, *The Degrees of Knowledge,* 88.

tion for the possibility of intelligibility, then, is non-materiality. In seeing that being is fundamentally intelligible, the intellect implicitly understands that being is fundamentally non-material, for it implicitly sees within itself, in the intuitive acts of simple apprehension and judgment, the non-materiality of intentional or mental being. Knowing as judging presupposes mental being, it "sees" that propositions formed within itself in mental, immaterial being are conformed under the principle of identity to the being of the extra-mentally existing thing. It sees, in other words, that the same thing (at least in the line of knowing) exists with two different modes of *esse*, one material, the other immaterial. Hence in the immaterial act of knowing, the intellect, as a non-material power of the soul, lays hold of what is non-material and potentially intelligible in the thing in terms of both "what" the thing is (through the intuitive and abstractive formation of the intentional object made known in a concept in simple apprehension), and its existence (*esse*). The latter is intuited in the judgment in either basic attributive, two-concept propositions, or in existential judgments, wherein a subject is joined with existence.

However, the implicit intuition of the non-materiality of being (*ens*) imbedded in every act of knowing only becomes explicit in the MIB. The MIB is an intuition that simply releases what is implicitly given in every act of knowing. In seeing that it is the same thing that exists with two distinct modes of *esse*, the intellect sees that *esse* is not confined to material being, that *esse* also actuates non-material being: namely, the first order intentions constituting mental being. We should remind ourselves here that the realm of mental being—meaning in this case the intellect and its first order intentions (as opposed to *entia rationis*, or beings of reason)—does not constitute a lesser mode of being. The intelligibility of being that is actuated in knowing is an essential aspect of real being (*ens*) and inseparable from it. Indeed first order intentions (Maritain's formal objects known in and through formal signs) are just the actuations of what is potentially intelligible in the non-material component of the extra-mentally existing thing. Of course, these first order intentions are not to be confused with second order intentions (the aforementioned *entia rationis*), the logically classificatory concepts that are formed in the intellect when the latter turns toward itself and examines them as known and from the standpoint of the ideal relations that obtain between its first order intentions. The former cannot exist as such outside the mind, but first order intentions or formal objects can exist outside the mind (as many) in individual things. However, precisely *as* formal objects or *possibilia* proper they exist only in the mind where they have neither universality nor particularity, which is why Maritain calls them possible beings and why he says that possible beings fall, along with extra-mentally existing beings, under the category of real being.[16] And they have real being because they represent, under the mode of non-material, mental existence the same thing (the essence) which exists outside the mind as many. So, the potential intelligibility of being, grounded as it is in the non-material component of being, can only be actuated or make itself known to us, become present to us, in the non-material intellect and through its non-material operations.

Now as we have seen, being is indeed known under the principle of identity operative in simple apprehension and judgment. And since being (*ens*) is composed of both essence and existence, this means that both essence and existence reveal their intelligibility to the intellect: essence in abstraction and existence (*esse*) in judging. Thus both essence *and* existence are intelligible, and though each is intelligible in its own way, their intelligibilities are inseparably linked insofar as judgment restores what simple apprehension tears asunder, and insofar as when the intellect says "I know that something exists" (which is the starting point for critique) it combines within itself two acts—one which says "I know that *something* exists," and the other which says "I know that something *exists*." In other words, the MIB is an intuition of being that is presented to the intellect in and through a concept of being (*ens*). That is, the MIB is an intuition of the existence (*esse*) of an essence, as these are thought together in the concept of *ens*—a concept grasped at what Maritain calls the third degree of formal abstraction.[17]

Nevertheless, the MIB bears primarily on *esse*, and it bears on *esse* when the intellect takes hold of itself at the same time that it makes a fundamental judgment of existence prefaced by an experience (not to be confused with the MIB itself—which is not an experience)[18] that jolts the intellect so profoundly that what is implicitly contained in every act of knowing

16. Ibid., 130–35.

17. For Maritain's most thorough exposition of this all important notion, see his *A Preface to Metaphysics: Seven Lectures on Being*, translated by Imelda Choquette (New York: Sheed and Ward, 1948), 75–89.

18. Maritain refers to these experiences as the concrete approaches to the MIB. See ibid., 49–54. Also see Jacques Maritain, *Existence and the Existent*, translated by Lewis Galantiere and Gerald B. Phelan (New York: Pantheon Press, 1948), 19–22.

becomes explicitly revealed to the knower in a judgmental intuition that at one stroke makes known both the being of the extra-mentally existing thing and the non-material or intentional being of the knower. It is the intuition occurring in a positive judgment that sees that *esse* actuates more than material being. That intuition holds in a vital cognitive tension an awareness of the conformity of intentional being with extra-mental being. Via that intuition one sees the fact that what makes being intelligible is being's non-materiality, that being is fundamentally immaterial. One sees, in other words, in the conformity lying at the heart of judgment, that intentional being, as the *actuation* of the intelligibility of being, is real. The MIB, then, is a positive, intensive, eidetic visualization in a judgment of the immateriality of being. In effect, the MIB is the intuition that the being of beings, being qua being, or being itself, if you will, is intelligibility or immateriality—an intuition of being that is precisely the intuition needed for metaphysics.

2. *The Metaphysical Concept of Being* (Ens)

So the MIB, as a judgmental intuition that affirms the primacy of existence (*esse*), while at the same time implying and preserving essences,[19] is foundational to the formation of the concept of metaphysical being (*ens*). As we have seen, this simply means that the positive, intensive, visualization/intuition of being is given in an intuition of the essence existing with two modes of *esse*: a fact which not only tells us something vitally important about *esse*, but also clears up a fundamental confusion about the MIB itself and its relationship to the concept of metaphysical being.

As Maritain says, when the MIB proclaims in a judgment "this being is," and frees or releases into full intelligibility the act of being (*actus essendi*) implicitly contained in the initial concept of being (*ens*)—in this case the non-metaphysical concept of vague being—it conceptualizes what it has released into the concept "to-exist" (*esse*) at the same time that it forms the metaphysical concept of *ens* (since each is mutually or reciprocally conditioned by the other). But this is not a releasement in the sense of an abstraction wherein the intellect "pulls out," if you will, the existence of the thing from the thing, in the way that simple apprehension "pulls out" the potentially intelligible component or form from phantasms. Existence

19. See Maritain, *Existence and the Existent*, 4.

is not an essence, and judgment bypasses the whole line of simple apprehension. Yet existence is intelligible, indeed it is ultimately the very source of intelligibility itself. Rather, the MIB is a judgment wherein the intellect intuits, sees, and asserts that the act of existing of the thing which the intellect relives in an act peculiar to itself (when it intentionally joins two concepts together (as in attributive judgments) or a subject with existence (as in existential judgments)) is conformed in an identity with the unity of the thing as an essence/existence composite, that is, as a being (*ens*). In effect, when the MIB lays hold of the intellect in its judging activity, it sees that *esse* actuates non-material as well as material being, and it sees in the same moment that what makes a being, *as* a being, be fundamentally intelligible is just its immateriality.[20]

This, then, is the foundation that is sufficient for the formation of the metaphysical concept of being (*ens*), as well as the starting point for metaphysics. For the positive visualization of *esse* in and through the concept of *ens*—remembering that *esse* and *ens* are given together, though *esse* receives primacy in judgment—in the MIB evokes at the same time a separation in the form of a negative judgment. That is, implicitly contained in the MIB is a knowledge not only of the essence/existence distinction (since judgment sees under the principle of identity that it is the same thing that exists with two modes of *esse*), but also and more importantly a knowledge of the fact that being (*ens*) is not itself material. It is not of being's nature to be in matter (though it can be in matter), because in the purest sense being is fundamentally intelligible and hence fundamentally immaterial. It must be em-

20. On the formation of the concept of existence, see ibid., 22–34. The concept of existence that Maritain has in mind is judicative in origin, and is not to be confused with the concept of existence, which is abstractive in origin. This is a distinction that Maritain consistently made throughout his career, and never abandoned. In *A Preface to Metaphysics*, it is the abstractive concept of existence (and hence being) that gives rise to the many non-metaphysical or falsely metaphysical concepts of being spoken of there, including: vague being; logical being; pseudo-being; and the being of dialectics. All of these false concepts of being result from treating being as a universal gotten at via extensive visualization/abstraction. He returns to the distinction again in *Untrammeled Approaches*, translated by Bernard Doering (Notre Dame, Indiana: University of Notre Dame Press, 1997), 219–36, where he distinguishes the "second" concept of existence from the "first" concept of existence. The "second" concept of existence, which of the two is the genuinely metaphysical one, is formed *after* the intellect's intuition of the act of existing known in a judgment of existence, and is the result, as he also made clear in *Existence and the Existent*, of the reflexive turn of simple apprehension to what is intuitively grasped in basic existential judgments. In the "first" concept of existence, the intellect brings an *already* formed notion of existence, which it has drawn in an abstractive operation from phantasms, to the judgment which predicates or joins existence, now thought after the manner of a universal, to a subject.

phasized though that the separation in question is a separation or negation only in the sense that it says that *esse* need not actuate only material being; it is not to be confused with a separation that leads to the so-called negatively neutral concept of being maintained by some Thomists as the proper starting point for metaphysics.[21] The negation or separation being referred to there says that that which makes a being be, need not be identified with that which makes a being be some given kind of being. This, however, is an inherently empty notion.[22] Rather the separation that the MIB evokes is grounded in a *positive* judgment of the intelligibility, and hence immateriality, of being. So here the being designated by the concept of metaphysical *ens* is separate, just as Aquinas says, in that it depends neither for its *being*,[23] nor its being known, on any kind of matter, though it can be in matter (else we could not say that matter exists). Because the concept of metaphysical being evoked by the MIB recognizes that *esse* actuates both material and non-material being, and that the actuation of the intelligibility of being in mental being is grounded in the immateriality of extra-mental being under the principle of identity—that the "is" or identity of judgmental intuition

21. See John F. Wippel, "Metaphysics and *Separatio* in Thomas Aquinas," in *Metaphysical Themes in Thomas Aquinas* (Washington, D.C.: The Catholic University of America Press, 1984), 69–104.

22. The difference between the two notions of separation at issue here is a very subtle but important one. Fr. Wippel's separation is a separation that recognizes a distinction between that which makes a being be (presumably its *esse* or act of existing), and what makes it be some kind of being. Were there no *esse/essentia* distinction, there could not be different *kinds* of being, since *esse* would be restricted to *a kind* of being, and this consideration is enough to give us a notion of being adequate for beginning metaphysics. However, since Wippel does not recognize the MIB, and since for him all positive judgments of existence initially terminate in material being, the recognition of the *esse/essentia* difference, *in this case,* does not lead us to a recognition of anything other than the fact that *esse* need not be confined to *kinds of material being*. Also, we must ask what the object of such a negatively immaterial, neutral concept of being (*ens*) is. All we can say of it is that it is neither exclusively material, nor exclusively immaterial. As Wippel admits, it does not give us knowledge of positively existing immaterial beings. In effect, since the concept is not grounded in any kind of positive judgment of existence, the concept of negatively immaterial being seems to resemble more the concept of being taken as a super-genus gotten at via abstraction without precision, than anything grasped in a judgment, even a negative one. For this possibility, see Joseph Owens, *An Elementary Christian Metaphysics* (Milwaukee, Wisconsin: Bruce Publishing Company, 1963), 57–67, and Joseph Owens, *An Interpretation of Existence* (Milwaukee, Wisconsin: Bruce Publishing Company, 1968), 14–43.

23. That is, being qua being is separate in the sense that the intelligibility of being, which just *is* its immateriality, is obviously not dependent on any kind of matter; otherwise the potentially intelligible and non-material component of a being would be *reducible to matter,* or pure potency/receptivity—though they can be *in* matter. In other words, both that which makes a being be actually what it is, as well as be or exist flat out, would be reducible to matter.

is the "is" of intelligibility, which in turn is the "is" of immateriality—the metaphysical concept of being is the concept of that which is *separate in the sense of a transcendental.*[24] In other words, it designates that which is separate in being as well as in notion. Hence, insofar as the metaphysical concept of being (*ens*) is grounded in the MIB, what the concept of being designates is neither *a* being that can never exist in matter, like God and the angels, nor a universal like "animal," which though notionally separate (known we should note, through an *abstraction* without precision—not through judgment) from "rational" and the other differences it subsumes, is nevertheless not ontologically separate from them. Yet the being in question is always the being of some being, though it is not, as said, itself a being.[25]

It should be clear that though the MIB is grounded in the immateriality of first order intentions, because the MIB is the intuition of thing and thought presupposed by the intellect's actuation of the thing's potential intelligibility—in both essential and existential mode—the immateriality of the former is sufficient for the formation of the concept of metaphysical being (defined as that which depends neither for its being, nor its being known, on any kind of matter). Of course *it is understood that first order intentions do not themselves satisfy that definition.* But they need not do so in order to be adequate data for the MIB to draw on. It is sufficient that they are nothing more than the actuations (under the principle of identity) of the intelligibility, and hence immateriality, of real being. The MIB is just the intuition that what makes a being be intelligible *as* a being is its fundamental immateriality, and that a fully intelligible being must be fully immaterial. The MIB, then, sees and releases the immateriality of being for intelligibility—an immateriality implicitly given in every act of knowing. And this explains why there is no need in Maritain's metaphysics for

24. As Maritain says in *Untrammeled Approaches*, 235, we must view being as "the king of the transcendentals," otherwise we risk losing sight of the fact that the analogy of being is the key to the analogy of the transcendentals, and will be likewise tempted to treat being in the mode of an essence, as a kind of super-genus—a mistake that even Aristotle made. We must understand, in other words, that the act of being is not the same act as the act of the form. The latter is invariably thought after the manner of an essence, even though it is designated "act."

25. The passage in Thomas's *Expositio super Boetium de Trinitate*, q. 5, a. 1, ad 5, where Aquinas makes a comparison of being (*ens*) with the generic notion "animal," is obviously an analogous one. The concept of being (*ens*) designates what can be in matter, and so in this sense "subsumes" its material differentiae, but being is separate in that being's intelligibility and hence its immateriality is analogously found in every being—an intelligibility that by definition cannot be reduced to matter, and so is not dependent on it, though it can be in it.

an intuition of immaterial, but extra-mentally existing, beings such as God and the angels; it also explains why they are not needed as a starting point for metaphysics. What *is* essential for metaphysics is simply to see in judgmental intuition that the condition for the very existence of knowledge is being's fundamental immateriality, an immateriality given in every act of knowing, but only made explicit in the MIB.

Finally, the concept of being (*ens*) that the MIB evokes as a concept of the intelligibility of being, is necessarily an analogous concept. It must be so, since being is always the being of some being. As stated above, being qua being is neither a being nor a universal. It is only found in beings, but in neither a univocal nor equivocal way. Hence the concept of being (*ens*) is an analogous concept that captures a transcendental. The "is" intuited in judgment is the "is" grounded in a comparison of two existential modes (the material and the non-material); it is the seeing of the conformity of two analogous proportions to each other—that X's *esse* is to X's being (*ens*) as Y's *esse* is to Y's being (*ens*). Here, implicit in the metaphysical concept of *ens* is once again the metaphysical concept of *esse*, a concept of that component of any *ens* that makes it stand, not simply outside mental being (since mental or possible being is *also* a mode of real being), but that makes it exist at all.

III. Conclusion

In conclusion, the critique of knowledge demands the MIB. The confirmatory rational analysis of knowledge, following the way of resolution, demonstrates that every act of knowing when completed by judgment is resolved in the principle of identity, which is resolved in the principle of the intelligibility of being, which in turn is resolved in the immateriality of being. It demonstrates that the MIB is implicitly contained in the intuition of being more broadly construed, an intuition presupposed by, and given in every act of knowing as, the latter's precondition.

Yet, though the confirmatory rational analysis of knowledge demonstrates the necessity for the MIB, and that a concept of being adequate for metaphysics is evoked by it, the critique of knowledge,[26] following the way

26. The intellect must be formally determined by the MIB; otherwise we go round the concept of metaphysical being without actually knowing it. This has been the fate of many a metaphysician, even the greatest, according to Maritain; see *Untrammeled Approaches*, 235. One can

of resolution, is a step-by-step process that cannot give to the intellect the MIB. The MIB is an eidetic visualization experience (though not an empirical experience) given by nature in a judgment that, as such, sidesteps the whole process of analysis. It is rather the immediate and explicit intuition occasioned by nature, of the fundamental immateriality of being, of that in the order of being which precedes analysis, as the latter's necessary and ordinarily contained starting point. In effect, the confirmatory rational analysis or critique of knowledge is able to confirm what it confirms, and reach by way of resolution the concept of *ens commune,* because all rationality is grounded in *intellectus,* intellectual or intuitive thinking; and the intuition in this case is the MIB. The MIB is simply the direct, immediate releasement of what is implicitly contained and presupposed as the starting point for all rationality.

---

talk about metaphysical being, and through critique see the necessity for it in a theoretical fashion, but until one has the MIB, one does not actually know metaphysical being in a formal way.

JOHN F. WIPPEL

Maritain and Aquinas on Our Discovery of Being

As regards the title of my paper, "Maritain and Aquinas on Our Discovery of Being,"[1] I might note that there is some ambiguity in the meaning of the English term "being" when it is applied to the metaphysical thought of Thomas Aquinas. It is all too often used to translate the Latin term *esse* and thus carries with it an ambiguity in that it may refer to the act of existing viewed as an intrinsic ontological principle in every existing entity, a principle that is distinct from its essence; or it may simply refer to being understood as "that which is" or "that which has *esse*." When discussing Aquinas's own position here, therefore, I will restrict my usage of the term "being" to signify the Latin *ens* (which, he writes, signifies "that which is" or "that which has *esse*"),[2] and I will use the expression "act of existing" or "act of being" to signify *esse* taken as the intrinsic principle that actualizes essence in every existing thing and hence is required to account for the fact that an individual entity or being actually exists. Regarding this latter usage some ambiguity may still remain, however, because Thomas at times uses the verb *esse* or *est* simply to signify the fact that something exists ("Socra-

1. An earlier version of this paper was published in a special issue of *Studia Gilsoniana* 3 (2014): 415–44. I thank the editor and publisher of that journal for permission to reprint it, in revised form, in the present volume.

2. See, for instance, Aquinas's *In de Hebdomadibus*, 2 (Leonine ed., vol. 50, 271:57–59): "ens, sive id quod est"; ST I-II, q. 26, a. 4 (Leon. ed., 6:190): "ens simpliciter est quod habet esse"; *In duodecim libros metaphysicorum Aristotelis expositio* IV, n. 535, edited by M.-R. Cathala and R. M. Spiazzi (Turin, 1950), 151: "Dicit ergo primo, quod ens sive quod est, dicitur multipliciter"; *Quaestiones disputatae De potentia*, q. 7, a. 7, edited by Paul Pession (Turin-Rome: Marietti, 1965), 204: "substantia est ens tamquam per se habens esse."

tes is"). At other times he uses it to signify the intrinsic *actus essendi* that he posits to account for that fact. Although this crucial distinction is not clearly recognized by all Thomistic scholars, it should be, and Cornelio Fabro should be given credit for having emphasized its importance very effectively.[3]

For my purposes here I am interested in presenting and comparing both Maritain's and Aquinas's accounts of our discovery of being (*ens*) as existing and of being as being. Because Aquinas (at least on my reading of him) and Maritain both distinguish between a *prephilosophical notion of being*, which for Aquinas and for Maritain in many of his discussions involves our knowledge of being as existing, and our *knowledge of being as being*, I will divide this paper into two major parts: Part I will involve our discovery of being as existing; Part II will discuss our discovery of being as being (*ens inquantum ens* or *ens commune*)—the subject of metaphysics. In each part I will present their respective accounts and will also indicate how Thomistic Maritain's approach really is by noting similarities as well as certain differences between the two. I will also consider Maritain's appeal to an intuition of being in some of his presentations of both the prephilosophical notion of being ("the vague being of common sense," as he styles it) and especially in his explanation of our discovery of being as being. Because in his final discussion of these issues his thought has undergone significant development, I conclude my presentation of Part II with special treatment of this text, and will note that it departs significantly from Maritain's earlier view, and also differs significantly from Aquinas's position concerning our discovery both of a prephilosophical notion of being, and of the notion of being as being.

In bringing out these differences in the conclusion of this paper, I will also turn to Gilson's critical reaction to Maritain's defense in this final paper both of an intellectual intuition of *esse* and of two or even of three concepts of existence. Although I fault both Gilson and the late Maritain for not incorporating Aquinas's doctrine of *separatio* into their respective accounts,

3. See his "Elementi per una dottrina tomistica della partecipazione," in his *Esegesi tomistica* (Rome: Libreria Editrice della Pontificia Università Lateranense, 1969), 435: "Perciò l'autentica nozione tomistica di partecipazione esige di distinguere *l'esse* come atto non solo dall'essenza ch'è la sua potenza, ma anche dall'esistenza ch'è il *fatto* di essere e quindi un 'resultato' e non un principio metafisico." For texts where Thomas uses *esse* or *est* in judgments of existence expressing facticity, see his *Expositio libri peryermenias*, rev. Leonine ed. 1*1, II.2, 88:36–40 and ST II-II, q. 83, a. 1, ob. 3.

I agree with Gilson in not finding support for an intellectual intuition of being or of existence in Thomas's texts.

I. Our Discovery of Being as Existing.

There are important texts in Aquinas where he refers to our discovery of *esse* as occurring not in the intellect's first operation, namely abstraction (taken in the strict sense, whereby we know what something is) but at the level of the intellect's second operation, namely judgment (whereby we recognize intellectually a thing's *esse*). Consider, for instance, *In I Sent.*, dist. 38, q. 1, a. 3, sol:

> Since in a thing there are two [factors], the quiddity of a thing and its *esse*, to these there correspond two operations on the part of the intellect. One which is called by the philosophers *formatio* whereby it apprehends the quiddities of things, which is also called by the Philosopher in *De anima* III the 'understanding of indivisibles.' The other grasps (*comprehendit*) the *esse* of a thing by composing an affirmation because also the *esse* of a thing composed of matter and form, from which it takes its knowledge, consists in a certain composition of form with matter or of an accident with a subject.[4]

It is clear from this text that one discovers *esse* not by means of abstraction and the intellect's first operation, whereby it understands a thing's quiddity, but by means of judgment, the intellect's second operation. And thus one can account for the complexity involved in our understanding of being (*ens*) or "that which is" with its quidditative side being grasped by the intellect's first operation, and the existential aspect grasped by its second operation—judgment. But one may still ask whether *esse* as it is used here refers to a thing's intrinsic *actus essendi* (act of existing), or only to the fact that it exists. At the very least it must refer to grasping a thing's existence in actuality (facticity), but it may well also refer to grasping its act of existing. For earlier on in this same work Thomas has already introduced his view

4. "Cum in re duo sint, quidditas rei, et esse eius, his duobus respondet duplex operatio intellectus. Una quae dicitur a philosophis formatio, qua apprehendit quidditates rerum, quae etiam a Philosopho, in III *De anima*, dicitur indivisibilium intelligentia. Alia autem comprehendit esse rei, componendo affirmationem, quia etiam esse rei ex materia et forma compositae, a qua cognitionem accipit, consistit in quadam compositione formae ad materiam, vel accidentis ad subjectum." *Scriptum super libros Sententiarum*, vol. 1, edited by Pierrre Mandonnet (Paris: Lethielleux, 1929), I, d. 38, q. 1, a. 3, sol., 903. Translations into English are mine unless indicated otherwise. For Aristotle see *De anima* 3.5, 430a26–28.

that there is a composition (and hence distinction) of essence and *esse* in creatures (see dist. 8, q. 1, a. 1; q. 5, a. 1, sol.; and a. 2), and therefore at this point he can take that issue as now given.

In his Commentary on the *De Trinitate,* in q. 5, a. 3, Thomas recalls from Aristotle's *De anima* these same two operations of the intellect. He writes:

> And these two operations correspond to two [factors] that are present in things. The first operation looks to (*respicit*) the very nature of a thing, according to which the thing understood holds a certain grade among beings, whether it be a complete thing, such as some whole, or an incomplete thing, such as a part or accident. The second operation looks to (*respicit*) the very *esse* of the thing, which results from the union of the principles of a thing in composites, or accompanies the simple nature of the thing, as in simple substances.[5]

Here Thomas uses the same Latin verb (*respicit*) to refer to the the intellect's first operation in grasping a thing's essence or nature, and its second operation in grasping its *esse.* And he does the same in another text from his Commentary on *I Sent.,* d. 19, q. 5, a. 1, ad 7: "the first operation looks to (*respicit*) the quiddity of a thing; the second looks to (*respicit*) its *esse.*"[6] In these two texts it seems more likely to me that he is using *esse* as explicitly signifying actual existence taken as facticity. And he is also assigning to judgment some apprehensive function—the ability to grasp *esse.* But if we follow the order of discovery, once Thomas has established the distinction and composition of essence and the act of existing in every finite being, when he uses the term *esse* he may then also have in mind the act of existing.

Another aspect of Aquinas's theory of knowledge must also be taken into account, namely his view that all of our knowledge begins with sense experience.[7] Any Thomistic account of our discovery of being as existing must, therefore, respect this aspect of his theory of knowledge, and presumably will also have to recognize a certain role for some of the internal senses as well, especially of the imagination and its production of phan-

5. "Et hae quidem duae operationes duobus quae sunt in rebus respondent. Prima quidem operatio respicit ipsam naturam rei, secundum quam res intellecta aliquem gradum in entibus obtinet, sive sit res completa, ut totum aliquod, sive res incompleta, ut pars vel accidens. Secunda vero operatio respicit ipsum esse rei; quod quidem resultat ex congregatione principiorum rei in compositis, vel ipsam simplicem naturam rei concomitatur, ut in substantiis simplicibus." *Super Boetium De Trinitate,* q. 5, a. 3 (Leon. ed., vol. 50, 147:96–105).

6. *Scriptum super libros Sententiarum,* Mandonnet ed., 1:489: "prima operatio respicit quidditatem rei; secunda respicit esse ipsius."

7. See *Super Boetium De Trinitate,* q. 6, a. 2 (Leon. ed., vol. 50, 164:71–76).

tasms or sense images in providing potentially intelligible data upon which the abstracting power of the intellect can operate by rendering it actually intelligible and submitting it to the possible intellect. The possible intellect then can understand what something is, and can also form judgments about it. These judgments may simply involve the attribution of a predicate, grasped by the intellect's first operation, to a subject, apprehended by the same operation, or the denial of this. But for Aquinas there is also another kind of judgment in which the intellect affirms explicitly that the subject itself is or exists such as "Socrates is" or "Socrates exists." And it will be incumbent on such a theory to explain how such judgments—existential judgments—can occur.

Finally, I have found it necessary to distinguish within Aquinas's account of our discovery of being as existing and, for that matter, our discovery of the notion of being (*ens*) itself, between an understanding of being that is common to every thinking human being, on the one hand, and on the other hand, the metaphysical notion of being as being which, according to Thomas, is the subject of metaphysics. It is well known that, on a number of occasions, he refers to being (*ens*) as that which is first known to the intellect and, presumably to every thinking human being.[8] At times he indicates that this primacy of being applies to the order of resolution and hence by implication not necessarily to the chronological order.[9] By saying this he means that whatever we may grasp with our intellects, if analyzed carefully, it may be reduced to being taken as "that which is." Hence, whatever is required to account for our knowledge of "that which is" will also be required to account for our discovery of this prephilosophical notion of being, or with what Maritain himself refers to as the "vague being of common sense."[10]

8. For references to a number of such texts see my *The Metaphysical Thought of Thomas Aquinas: From Finite Being to Uncreated Being* (Washington, D.C.: The Catholic University of America Press, 2000), 41nn56–59.

9. See *De veritate*, q. 1, a. 1 (Leon. ed., vol. 22.1, 5:100–104): "illud autem quod primo intellectus concipit quasi notissimum et in quod conceptiones omnes resolvit est ens, ut Avicenna dicit in principio suae Metaphysicae." See also ST I-II, q. 94, a. 2 (Leon. ed., vol. 7, 169–70); *In De Trin.*, q. 6, a. 1 (Leon. ed., vol. 50, esp. 162:374–82). For discussion of these see my *The Metaphysical Thought of Thomas Aquinas*, 42–44.

10. My translation. For a slightly different English translation ("*vague* being known to common sense"), see Jacques Maritain, *Existence and the Existent*, translated by Lewis Galantiere and Gerald Phelan (New York: Pantheon Books, 1948), 26, translated from *Court Traité de l'Existence et de l'Existant* of 1947. For the French I am using *Jacques et Raïssa Maritain: Oeuvres Complètes*, vol. 9 (Fribourg Suisse: Editions Universitaires, 1990), 34: "Plus on médite sur ce sujet, plus il

At the same time it is also important to recall how difficult Thomas thinks it was for philosophers to arrive at a consideration of being as being. Indeed, in ST I, q. 44, a. 2, he finds them passing through three stages: (1) the earliest philosophers, being cruder (*grossiores*) in their thinking, posited only sensible bodies as beings, and proposed only accidental motion and causes of the same; (2) others reached a higher level and distinguished between form and matter and posited more universal causes such as Plato's ideas or Aristotle's ecliptic circle of the sun. But both groups still viewed being only as "this being" (*hoc ens*) or "such being" (*tale ens*); (3) finally some arrived at a knowledge of being as being and hence investigated the causes of beings not only insofar as they are "these" or "such," but insofar as they are beings.[11] This text is surprising in that here Thomas does not place Plato and Aristotle at the highest level—among those who grasped being as being, even though a year or so earlier in his *De potentia*, q. 3, a. 5, he had written: "Still later philosophers such as Plato and Aristotle came to a consideration of universal *esse* itself."[12] If we may set aside that issue, however, the text from ST I, q. 44, a. 2, makes it clear that Thomas does not think that every human being reaches a knowledge of being as being, the subject of metaphysics. Hence one should distinguish between his account of our discovery of being at what I will call the prephilosophical or premetaphysical level, and the discovery of being as being, the subject of metaphysics.

As for Maritain's account, one can find most of the elements I have mentioned in Thomas's own theory in the French philosopher's *Existence and the Existent,* along with supporting references he himself gives from some of his earlier writings. Of course, he also says much about an intuition of *l'être,* especially in his *Existence and the Existent,* and that will require additional attention. Finally, I will compare what he says there with his last treatment of all of this in his "Réflexions sur la nature blessée."

In *Existence and the Existent,* Maritain observes that our knowledge is "immersed in existence" and that "existence—the existence of material things—is given us at first by sense." Hence sense perception attains an object as ex-

apparaît que c'est de cette façon que l'intelligence conceptualise l'existence, et qu'elle se forme idée de l'être—de l'être *vague* du sens commun."

11. See Leon. ed., vol. 4, 457–58.

12. *De potentia,* q. 3, a. 5 (in *Quaestiones disputatae,* vol. 2 [Turin-Rome: Marietti, 1965]), 49: "Posteriores vero philosophi, ut Plato, Aristoteles et eorum sequaces, pervenerunt ad considerationem ipsius esse universalis; et ideo ipsi soli posuerunt aliquam universalem causam rerum, a qua omnia alia in esse prodirent."

isting by reason of the real and existing influence such an object exercises on our sense organs. But, he continues: "Sense attains existence in act without itself knowing that it is existence" and delivers it to the intellect without sense knowing that it is intelligible. And the intellect knows existence and "calls it by its name, which is *being*" (French: *l'être*).[13]

Maritain then notes that the intellect disengages intelligibles from sense experience and through the process of abstraction reaches natures or essences which it grasps apart from their material existence at a given space and time. It does this in order to restore them to existence through judgments asserting that "it is so" (*ita est*) such as "the earth revolves around the sun," meaning thereby that "the earth *exists* in physical existence as characterised by the movement described." Hence even such judgments have an existential function if they are expressing something that is true.[14]

Maritain then discusses the intellect's first operation (simple apprehension) and describes its object as "the intelligible density of an existent subject, rendered transparent in act to the mind and identified with the mind's vital activity by and in the concept." Or, as he also writes, "what the intellect lays hold of is the natures or essences which are in existent things or subjects."[15]

As he turns to judgment, he emphasizes the point that the function of judgment is existential, and that judgment restores essence—the objects of thought—"to existence or to the world of subjects."[16] Maritain recalls that he had written in his *The Degrees of Knowledge* that when one forms a judgment, one accomplishes on one's *noemata* (objects of thought) "an operation that has meaning only because it relates to the fashion in which they exist (at least possibly) outside my thought."[17] As he continues in *Existence and the Existent* to quote from *Les Degrés du Savoir*:

> The function proper to judgment thus consists in transposing the mind from the plane of simple essence, of the simple *object* presented to thought, to the plane of the *thing*, of the subject possessing existence (actually or possibly) and of which the predicate-object of thought and the subject-object of thought are intelligible aspects.[18]

13. See *Existence and the Existent* [EE], English version, 11; French, 22.
14. English, 11–12; French, 22–23.
15. EE, English, 13, 15; French, 24, 25.
16. EE, English, 16; French, 26.
17. EE, English, 16–17; French, 26–27, citing *Les Degrés du Savoir*, 7th ed. (Paris: Desclée de Brouwer, 1963), 188.
18. EE, English, 17; French, 27, quoting *Les Degrés*, 188–89.

Shortly thereafter Maritain again quotes in *Existence and the Existent* from his *Degrees of Knowledge* to this effect: "Judgment is not content with the representation or apprehension of existence. It affirms existence, it projects into it, as effected or effectible outside the mind, the objects of [the] concept apprehended by the mind."[19] And here in *Existence and the Existent* he also indicates that existence as affirmed by and in the mind corresponds to the act of existing exercised by things outside the mind, and he refers to this act of existing as act or energy par excellence.[20]

But, as Maritain also rightly insists, existence itself is not an essence but belongs to an entirely different order. It is not an object of thought (or of the mind's first operation) in the way essences are. Maritain refers to it as a trans-objective act. And here he quotes from his earlier *De Bergson à Thomas Aquin*: "The intelligibility with which judgment deals is more mysterious than that which notions or ideas convey to us; it is not expressed in a concept but in the very act of affirming or denying. It is the super-intelligibility, if I may put it so, of the act of existing itself, either possible or actually given."[21]

From this description of judgment's relationship to the act of existing of extra-mental things, Maritain moves on to a Section entitled "*The Intuition of Being*"/*L'intuition de l'être*.[22] And so here *l'être* is translated as "being." This is interesting because Maritain has just been speaking of existence taken as the act of existing. As one follows his discussion of the intuition of *l'être*, one wonders whether he has in mind an intuition of *ens* or an intuition of *esse*. He begins by noting that Thomas places at the roots of metaphysical knowledge

> the intellectual intuition of that mysterious reality disguised under the most commonplace and commonly used word in the language, the word *to be* (*être* in the French text), a reality revealed to us as the uncircumscribable subject of a science which the gods begrudge us when we release in the values that appertain to it, the act of existing which is exercised by the humblest thing.[23]

Granted that Maritain is speaking almost poetically here, he also knows that for Thomas *esse* (the act of existing) is not the subject of metaphysics, but that *ens inquantum ens* is. And then in an oft-quoted remark he writes: "A

19. EE, English, 17; French, 27, citing *Les Degrés*, 191n1.
20. EE, English, 18; French, 27–28.
21. See EE, English, 18–19; French, 28, citing *De Bergson à Thomas d'Aquin*, in *Jacques et Raïssa Maritain. Oeuvres Complètes*, vol. 8 (Fribourg-Suisse: Editions Universitaires, 1989), 157.
22. EE, English, 19; French, 28.
23. EE, English, 19; French, 28–29.

philosopher is not a philosopher if he is not a metaphysician. And it is the intuition of being (*l'intuition de l'être*) ... that makes the metaphysician." But almost immediately after this he writes that by this he means the intuition of being *secundum quod est ens* (*l'intuition de l'être secundum quod est ens*). And the reader wonders again whether this is an intuition of *esse* or an intuition of *ens*. He continues with the important observation that being (*l'être*) as used here is not the vague being (*l'être*) of common sense and which, I would add, therefore seems to be very close to what I understand as Thomas's prephilosophical notion of being.[24] Rather, Maritain continues:

> It is being (*l'être*), attained or perceived at the summit of an abstractive intellection, of an eidetic or intensive visualisation which owes its purity and power of illumination only to the fact that the intellect, one day, was stirred to its depths and trans-illuminated by the impact of the act of existing (*par le choc de l'acte d'exister*) apprehended in things.[25]

Maritain goes on to list a number of different paths that may lead to this intuition, no one of which is more legitimate than any other, because here we are dealing with what he calls a primary fact. And he refers to what Aquinas calls the "judgment of sense" and notes that this "blind existential perception" plays a primordial and indispensable role, but one that is only preliminary. Among the avenues or paths leading to this intuition on the part of the intellect Maritain mentions that it might be owing to "the innate gift of an imperial intelligence" combined with a "pure and delicate flesh" and a "perfectly balanced sensibility," as seems to have been true of Aquinas himself; or it might spring up unexpectedly like a species of natural grace prompted by the sight of a blade of grass, or perhaps at one's perception of oneself, or perhaps from the implacability with which the being (*l'être*) of things independent from ourselves suddenly becomes evident to us; or one may move toward it by an inner experience of duration (here the implicit reference is to Bergson), or in still other ways. But whatever the path, what is important is that one takes the "leap, to release, in one authentic intellectual intuition, the sense of being (*l'être*), the sense of the value of the implications that lie in the act of existing (*l'acte d'exister*)."[26]

24. Ibid. In n. 8 he refers to Aquinas's Commentary on the *Metaphysics* IV, c. 1 (Cathala ed., nn. 530–535, mistakenly listed as pages in EE) where Thomas identifies *ens secundum quod est ens* as the subject of metaphysics.

25. EE, English, 20; French, 29–30.

26. EE, English, 21; French, 30.

And, as will be noted below, he thinks that very few, even among the greatest philosophers, have managed to do so in the formal sense.

But then a new section in his book begins with this title in English "The Concept of To-exist (*esse*) *and that of Being or of That-which is* (*Ens*)" or in French: "*Le concept de l'existence ou de l'exister* (esse) *et celui de l'être ou de 'ce qui est'* (*ens*)." Here, then, we have an important clarification: Maritain is using two terms in French to render the Latin *esse*, namely *l'existence* and *l'exister*, and two other words or expressions to translate the Latin *ens*, namely *l'être* or *ce qui est*.[27] He begins by noting a paradox: he has said that the intelligible apprehended in our ideas is essence, and that existence is not an essence. And so one may ask: How can existence be the object of the intellect, or be expressed by a concept?

In responding to this Maritain steps back for the moment from his discussion of the metaphysical intuition required to make the metaphysician to a consideration of how one arrives at what he will call the vague being known to common sense. As a premonition of his answer he recalls that he had said that essences are the objects of the intellect's first operation, and that it is the act of existing (*acte de exister*) that judgment confronts. He continues: because the intellect is present in each of its operations, in the initial upsurge of its activity arising from the world of sense experience, it apprehends and judges in one and the same instant. And so it "forms its first idea (that of being [*de l'être*]) while uttering its first judgment (of existence [*de l'existence*]), and utters its first judgment while forming its first idea.... [I]t thus lays hold of the treasure which properly belongs to judgment in order to envelop it in simple apprehension itself." And thus it expresses this in an original idea that does not result from simple apprehension alone but also from that which the intellect grasps through judgment—the act of existing—and makes this an object of thought.[28]

Here, then, Maritain speaks of a "concept of existence" (*l'existence ou l'exister*) and warns that it "cannot be *cut off* from the absolutely primary concept of being (*l'être=ens, ce-qui est, ce-qui existe, ce-qui a pour acte d'exister*)" because the judgment and affirmation of existence which provides content for this concept itself involves the composition of a subject with existence. It affirms that "something exists" (actually or possibly, simply or with some added predicate). Hence Maritain writes that this concept of being (that

27. EE, English, 22; French, 31.
28. EE, English, 23; French, 32.

which exists or can exist) in the order of "ideative perception" corresponds to this affirmation of existence in the order of judgment. Maritain also emphasizes that the concept of existence cannot be visualized completely apart from the concept of essence, for the two of them make up one and the same analogous concept, that of being.[29]

Maritain observes that being is the first of all concepts, although not explicitly formulated as such, because it "springs into the mind at the first awakening of thought, at the first intelligible coming to grips with the experience of sense" and transcends sense perception. Thus, when one points one's finger at an object and the eye sees and the sense power perceives in its blind fashion that "this exists," at this same instant the intellect judges that "this being is or exists" and expresses "being" in a concept.[30]

Maritain also brings out the reciprocal priority between this concept of being and the judgment "this being exists" in the sense that the idea of being ("this being") is prior to the judgment of existence in the order of material or subjective causality, whereas the judgment of existence is prior in the order of formal causality. This, he concludes, is the way one arrives at the idea of the "*vague* being known to common sense."[31] In an important footnote he explains that here he is not speaking of "verbally formulated operations, or even of operations explicitly thought. The essential thing is that they be there implicitly." He adds that some primitive languages lack the word "being" but comments that the idea of being is implicitly present in the minds of those using such languages, and also that the first idea formed by a child is not the idea of being but that the idea of being is implicit in the first idea the child has. Here one may recall my earlier remark above about Aquinas's references to being as that which is first in the order of resolution rather than in the chronological order.[32]

In another lengthy footnote, Maritain proposes in outline fashion the steps involved in arriving at this vague common sense notion of being. In the text which this note annotates, he is now ready to move on to what he calls "the higher intuition" which he will require for one to reach the subject of metaphysics. Hence this implies that formulation of the vague common sense notion of being also involves an intuition of being, although not the metaphysical and higher intuition which is restricted to only a few hu-

29. EE, English, 24–25; French, 32–33.

30. EE, English, 25; French, 33–34.

31. EE, English, 25–26; French, 34.

32. EE, English, 25n12; French, 34n12. See n. 9 above and my coresponding text.

man beings.[33] In the note itself he remarks that the extramental existence of a thing was given to the intellect from the very start in the intuition and concept of being, which I again take to refer to the common sense notion of being.[34] He distinguishes the following steps:

1. "Judgment" improperly so-named of the external senses and the aestimative power (French: *cogitative tel qu'il se trouve chez l'animal,* p. 35, n. 13), bearing upon a sensible existent that is perceived. This, he says, is "in the sphere of sense (with its treasury of intelligibility in potency, but in no wise in act) the 'blind equivalent' of what we express in saying, 'this exists.'"

2. Formation in a simultaneous awakening of the intellect and judgment of an idea ("this being" or simply "this thing" in which the idea of being is implicitly present) and a judgment that composes the object of thought with the *act* of existing itself (by asserting that "this thing exists" or "this being exists"). Maritain also explains that the intellect knows the subject as individual indirectly by "reflection on phantasms" but does not thereby affirm that it exercises the act of existing. It affirms this only "by and in this 'judgment' itself and in this intuition of sense which it grasps by immaterialising it. And thus the intellect reaches the *actus essendi* (in judging)—as it reaches essence (in conceiving)—*by the mediation of sensorial perception.*"

3. Formation of the idea of existence. From the moment when, conjointly with the first judgment of existence the idea of being emerges ("that which exists or can exist"), the intellect "grasps the *act* of existing affirmed in the first judgment of existence and makes of the act of existence an object of thought by formulating a concept or notion of existence (*existentia ut significata*).[35]

33. Already in his earlier *A Preface to Metaphysics* (New York: Sheed and Ward, 1948, but first published in 1939), Maritain had distinguished sharply between the notion of being first attained by the intellect (the being of common sense) and *ens secundum quod est ens* (the subject of metaphysics). See pp. 18–19; and especially pp. 27–33. See pp. 29–31 for his reference to the vague being of common sense as "pre-scientific knowledge" and as "infra-scientific knowledge" and, following Cajetan and John of St. Thomas, as being the object of *abstractio totalis* or of what one may call "extensive abstraction." Also, while in this book he does not spell out in detail the steps involved in the intellect's discovery of either the common sense notion of being or the metaphysical notion of being, he does refer to both as gained by intuition. There, in response to Gabriel Marcel's rejection of an intuition of being, Maritain refers to "the obscure intuition of being possessed by common sense, the perception of which I have termed vague being. It is only when the metaphysical intuition of being has occurred that this assurance refers to it also." P. 60, end of the long note 1 beginning on p. 59.

34. EE, 27n13; French, 35–36n13.

35. Ibid. Note that Maritain lists as step 4 the thinking subject's discovery of first princi-

Here I pause to compare this account with that of Aquinas as best as one can reconstruct his own position on the basis of his rather scattered references. I would first note that, at least on my reading of Thomas, both he and Maritain distinguish between a premetaphysical or prephilosophical notion of being and the metaphysical notion of being as being. As regards Maritain's three steps:

1. Both Thomas and Maritain argue that all of our knowledge begins in some way from sense experience. Maritain has referred in passing to the role played by the aestimative/cogitative power in our moving on to judgments of existence. Without rejecting some possible role for the cogitative power, here I would emphasize the role of the first internal sense power, the *sensus communis* in Thomas's theory of knowledge. For him this internal sense has two functions: (1) it distinguishes objects reported by different external senses appropriately such as this sound, as different from this color, this odor, etc.; (2) it enables a higher animal or a human being to be aware when such an agent is actually perceiving something with one or more external senses.[36]

2. Both Thomas and Maritain distinguish between the intellect's first operation which apprehends the essences or natures of things, and its second operation—judgment—which looks to a thing's *esse*; and I also think that Maritain's reference to this as a simultaneous awakening of both of these operations is a defensible presentation of Thomas's position.

3. While Maritain recognizes with Aquinas that the intellect knows the subject as individual by reflecting back on the phantasms preserved at the level of the imagination, I do not think that according to Aquinas, in the order of discovery one should hold that in its first judgment or judgments of existence the intellect explicitly grasps *esse* in the sense of the *actus essendi.* To recognize that there is such an act of existing requires some sophisticat-

---

ples and only as step 5 the subject's explicit awareness or consciousness of its own existence. I pass over additional consideration of these steps here in the interests of space, but would call the reader's attention to Therese Scarpelli Cory's recently published very thorough and helpful examination of Aquinas's own understanding of self-awareness: *Aquinas on Human Self-Knowledge* (Cambridge: Cambridge University Press, 2014).

36. See *Sententia libri De anima* II.24 (Leon. ed., vol. 45.1, c. 13, 120:99–105; note especially: "sensu enim communi percipimus nos videre et discernimus inter album et dulce"); c. 26, 178:8–14: "huiusmodi actiones sunt duae: una est secundum quod nos percipimus actiones sensuum propriorum, puta quod sentimus nos videre et audire; alia est secundum quod discernimus inter sensibilia diversorum sensuum, puta quod aliud sit dulce et aliud album."

ed metaphysical analysis, for instance, showing that one can reason from the fact that something exists to the presence of some ontological principle within that thing to account for that fact.[37]

But when an individual subject is explicitly recognized as existing in actuality, I see no textual warrant in Aquinas for saying that either its act of existing, or the notion of being itself is grasped by an intellectual intuition such as that described by Maritain. In accord with Aquinas's theory of knowledge, it is (1) by turning back (*per quamdam reflexionem*) to its own act, and then (2) to the species which is the principle of its act of understanding, and then (3) to the phantasms at the level of the imagination from which the species was abstracted, and by (4) reuniting the abstracted universal nature or essence with its individuating characteristics, that the intellect itself becomes aware of the object as individual. Here I would add, going beyond Maritain, it is by adverting to the common sense's awareness that one or more external sense is perceiving the object, that the intellect judges that such an object exists.[38] On the basis of one or more such existential judgments, the intellect then forms the general notion of being as "that which is."

For Aquinas our knowledge of an individual and hence of the subject of an individual judgment of existence is not direct, but indirect, and not unmediated but mediated through sense experience and so, too, it seems to me is an ensuing judgment (or judgments) of existence leading to a prephilosophical notion of being, disputed though this indeed is by certain interpreters of Aquinas.[39] Maritain himself, followed on this by a number

37. Interestingly, in his later *The Peasant of the Garonne*, translated by Michael Cuddihy and Elizabeth Hughes (Toronto: McMilllan, 1969; originally published in French in 1966), Maritain seems to recognize this: "It is in a judgment (or in a preconscious act equivalent to an unformulated judgment), and in a judgment of existence, that the intellectual intuition of being occurs. The philosophical concept of the *actus essendi*, of the act of existence, will only come later" (p. 163). There again he insists that this intellectual intuition of being has nothing to do with Bergsonian intuition which he thinks was spoiled by a quite accidental anti-intellectualism. Moreover, it did not focus directly on being, but on duration, which is only one of the aspects of being "which served him as a kind of substitute for being." But, adds Maritain, through the experience of duration it was actually being (*esse*) which Bergson attained without realizing it.

38. See, for instance, *De Veritate*, q. 10, a. 5 (Leon. ed., vol. 22.2, 309:73–81). Also see *In IV Sent.*, d. 50, q. 1, a. 3 (*S. Thomae Aquinatis Opera Omnia*, vol. 1, edited by Robertus Busa, 704).

39. For some who defend the presence of an intuition of being in Aquinas see James Hanink, "In Defence of the Intuition of Being," in *Distinctions of Being*, edited by Nikolaj Zunic (Washington, D.C.: The American Maritain Association, 2013; distributed by The Catholic University of America Press), 167–79; Joseph Owens, "Maritain's Three Concepts of Existence," *The New Scholasticism* 49 (1975): 295–309.

of those who would find his intuition in Aquinas, cites in support our understanding of first principles such as non-contradiction and identity.[40] For Aquinas, however, one's recognition of a principle such as noncontradiction as self-evident presupposes, at least in the order of nature, that one has already discovered the premetaphysical notion of being on which that principle is based. Such texts do not indicate that the discovery of being itself is based on an intuition. To put this another way, for me to recognize that being is not nonbeing presupposes that I have already reached a notion of being.

II. Our Discovery of the Subject of Metaphysics (*ens inquantum est ens*)

In *Existence and the Existent*, after having described the process whereby the intellect forms an idea of the "vague being known to common sense," Maritain distinguishes this from the higher intuition whereby

> the intellect disengages being (*l'être*) from the knowledge of the sensible in which it is immersed, in order to make it the object or rather the subject of metaphysics; when, in a word it conceptualises the metaphysical intuition of being ... what the intellect releases into that same light is, here again, first and foremost, the act of existing.[41]

Here again Maritain seems to put the cart before the horse because, on my reading of Aquinas, it is within the science of metaphysics itself that one becomes explicitly aware of *esse* understood as the *actus essendi*. Maritain notes that according to "classical Thomism," it has now reached the third degree of abstraction.[42]

Here in another long footnote in *Existence and the Existent*, Maritain quotes from a note in Louis-Bertrand Geiger's *La Participation dans la philosophie de saint Thomas d'Aquin* first published in 1942.[43] There Geiger cites excerpts from Thomas's extremely important Commentary on the *De Trinitate* of Boethius, q. 5, a. 3, taken from a transcription of the autograph, that is to say, from the manuscript in the extremely difficult handwriting of

40. See *Bergsonian Philosophy and Thomism*, in *The Collected Works of Jacques Maritain*, vol. 1 (Notre Dame, Indiana: University of Notre Dame Press, 2007), 152–54.

41. EE, English, 26; French, 34–35.

42. EE, English, 27–28; French, 35–36.

43. See Paris: J. Vrin, 1942; 2nd ed., 1953, which I am using here.

Thomas himself, which was made available to Geiger by Fr. A. Dondaine.[44] Here Thomas distinguishes between abstraction when it is taken broadly so as to signify any way in which the intellect can distinguish, and when it is applied strictly so as to signify distinguishing by the intellect in its first operation.[45] And so, Thomas writes, the intellect distinguishes one thing from another in different fashion in accord with its different operations. According to the operation whereby the intellect composes and divides (judges), it distinguishes one thing from another by understanding that one is not present in the other. But in the operation by which it understands what things are, it distinguishes one thing from another by understanding what that thing is without understanding anything about the other, neither that it is united with it or separated from it in reality. Because of this Thomas observes that this way of distinguishing on the part of the intellect should not be described as "separation" (*separatio*). That name should be reserved for the operation whereby the intellect distinguishes through judgment. It should rather be described as "abstraction," but only when one of those things that is distinguished by the intellect is in reality united with the other. Here, therefore, he is taking the name "abstraction" strictly rather than in the broad sense in which he had used it earlier in this article.[46]

Thomas then goes on to subdivide abstraction taken in the strict sense into abstraction of a whole from a part (abstraction of a universal from an individual) and abstraction of a form (abstraction of the accidental form of quantity from sensible matter). He associates the first of these especially with natural philosophy and the second with mathematics, meaning thereby that by means of the first one reaches the subject of natural philosophy (*ens mobile*) and by means of the second one reaches the subject of mathematics (*ens quantum*). Thomas contrasts these with another way in which the intellect distinguishes, this time only at the level of judgment by a negative judgment (*separatio*) and connects this with our discovery of the subject of metaphysics. In other texts within this same article Thomas

44. For these excerpted texts see Geiger, 318–19n.1.

45. See *Super Boetium De Trinitate* q. 5, a. 3 (Leon. ed., vol. 50, 146:86–147:95).

46. See 148:159–171: "Sic ergo intellectus distinguit unum ab altero aliter et aliter secundum diversas operationes: quia secundum operationem qua componit et dividit distinguit unum ab alio per hoc quod intelligit unum alii non inesse, in operatione vero qua intelligit quid est unumquodque, distinguit unum ab alio dum intelligit quid est hoc, nihil intelligendo de alio, neque quod sit cum eo, neque quod sit ab eo separatum; unde ista distinctio non proprie habet nomen separationis, sed prima tantum. Haec autem distinctio recte dicitur abstractio, sed tantum quando ea quorum unum sine altero intelligitur sunt simul secundum rem."

writes: "In those things which can be divided in the order of existence, separation obtains rather than abstraction," and also states: "Substance, however, which is the intelligible matter of quantity, can exist without quantity. Therefore to consider substance without quantity pertains to the genus of separation rather than that of abstraction."[47] As Maritain describes this: "It is in a judgment declaring that being is *not* necessarily linked to matter nor to any of its conditions that the intellect abstracts [here since he is commenting on q. 5, a. 3, he should have written "distinguishes"] being from all matter and makes for itself the metaphysical concept of being as being."[48]

One should recall here that in q. 5, a. 1 of this same treatise Thomas had distinguished the three theoretical sciences in accord with the differing degrees to which the objects they study (*speculabila*) depend on matter and motion. In the case of metaphysics he writes that metaphysics studies the kind of *speculabilia* that do not depend on matter *secundum esse* either in the sense that they are never present in matter (God and angels), or in the sense that they may or may not be present in matter. As examples of the latter he lists substance, quality, *ens*, potency, act, the one and the many, etc.[49]

In my fuller discussions of *separatio* elsewhere, I have referred to the first kind as positively immaterial, meaning thereby that they are never present in matter, and to the second kind as negatively or neutrally immaterial, meaning thereby that they may or may not be present in matter, but need not be.[50] Thomas includes being (*ens*) in this class, and in replying

47. See Leon. ed., 149:256–58: "In his autem quae secundum esse possunt esse divisa magis habet locum separatio quam abstractio"; and 149:270–74: "Substantia autem, quae est materia intelligibilis quantitatis, potest esse sine quantitate; unde considerare substantiam sine quantitate magis pertinet ad genus separationis quam abstractionis."

48. Also see near the end of the corpus: "Sic ergo in operatione intellectus triplex distinctio invenitur: una secundum operationem intellectus componentis et dividentis, quae separatio dicitur proprie, et haec competit scientiae divinae sive metaphysicae; alia secundum operationem qua formantur quidditates rerum, quae est abstractio formae a materia sensibili, et haec competit mathematicae; tertia secundum eandem operationem, universalis a particulari, et haec competit etiam physicae et est communis omnibus scientiis, quia in omni scientia praetermittitur quod per accidens est et accipitur quod per se est" (149:275–86). For Maritain's comment see EE, English, 29n14; French, 37n14.

49. See Leon. ed., vol. 50, 138:141–67. Note especially: "Quaedam vero speculabilia sunt quae non dependent a materia secundum esse, quia sine materia esse possunt, sive numquam sint in materia, sicut Deus et angelus, sive in quibusdam sint in materia et in quibusdam non, ut substantia, qualitas, ens, potentia, actus, unum et multa et huiusmodi" (lines 154–160).

50. See my *Metaphysical Themes in Thomas Aquinas* (Washington, D.C.: The Catholic University of America Press, 1984), 69–82; *The Metaphysical Thought of Thomas Aquinas* (Washington, D.C.: The Catholic University of America Press, 2000), 44–51. Dispute continues on the

to obj. 6 in this same q. 5, a. 1, he identifies being (*ens*) as the subject of metaphysics. Hence in noting that metaphysics is based on *separatio*, he is also speaking of one's discovery of its subject. As he again states explicitly in q. 5, a. 4, its subject is being insofar as it is being (*quae habet subiectum ens in quantum est ens*). Or as he also explains there, being and substance are separate from matter and motion in the sense that it is not necessary for them to exist in matter and motion although they may be present there.[51] It is this negative or neutral characteristic of being that is recognized and expressed by the negative judgment (*separatio*). Through this judgment one recognizes that that by reason of which something enjoys being need not be restricted to that by reason of which it enjoys any particular or restricted kind of being, such as material being or quantified being or living being or dead being. And thus, by negating any such limitation or restriction of being, by negating any such negation, one may say, one discovers the notion of being as being, the subject of metaphysics.

Credit should be given to Maritain for having recognized the role of *separatio* in the improved text of Aquinas's account. At the same time, he was so attached to the theory of three degrees of abstraction in the classical Thomism of Cajetan and John of St. Thomas that he mistakenly claimed that the difference between their approach and that of Aquinas himself in the text from q. 5, a. 3 of the Commentary on the *De Trinitate* was only verbal.[52] And so even in *Existence and the Existent* he unfortunately continues to refer to the third degree of abstraction rather than to *separatio* in presenting his understanding of Thomas's position. Thus he writes:

> If metaphysics is established at the highest degree of *abstraction,* the reason is precisely that, unlike all the other sciences, in concerning itself with being as being, as a proper object of analysis and scientific disquisition, it concerns itself with the

part of Thomistic scholars concerning whether in order to justify this negative judgment (*separatio*) and thereby discover the subject of metaphysics one must first have demonstrated the existence of some positively immaterial being such as a First Mover or God or a spiritual soul. For my own detailed discussion and rejection of any such claim both on historical and philosophical grounds see *Metaphysical Themes,* 82–104; *The Metaphysical Thought of Thomas Aquinas,* 51–62.

51. For his reply to obj. 6 in q. 5, a. 1, see Leon. ed., 141:322–33. For q. 5, a. 4, see 154:182–97.

52. EE, 30, continuation of the long n. 14; italics mine. There he notes that this *separatio,* since it ends in an idea, can be called an abstraction "in the general or rather proportional meaning of the word (but which is not produced in the line of simple apprehension of essences!)." The danger of referring to *separatio* as an abstraction without some such qualification consists in this, that readers may conclude that the resulting notion of being has been abstracted from the differences that obtain between beings and thereby treat it as univocal.

very act of existing.... In virtue of the type of *abstraction* which characterises it, metaphysics considers realities which exist, or are able to exist, without matter. It *abstracts* from the material conditions of empirical existence, but it does not abstract from existence![53]

Hence, after having referred to Aquinas's introduction of *separatio*, and its distinction from abstraction taken strictly, he seems to have set it aside for all practical purposes.

This becomes much more evident in Maritain's final treatment of all of this in his *Refléxions sur la nature blessée et sur l'intuition de l'être*, which was prepared for a seminar he held with the *Petits Frères de Jésus* at Kolbsheim on July 21, 1967, and was first published in the *Revue Thomiste* in 1968.[54]

There in a Section entitled "A Digression on the Intuition of Being (*L'être*): The Concept of Existence," Maritain speaks first of two concepts of existence, and then of three. He had anticipated this in the preceding Section by referring to an intellectual intuition of being which, he writes, is not the "peak of philosophical wisdom" but the "indispensable condition for attaining it."[55] He had singled out a number of philosophers who failed to reach this intuition of being such as Descartes, Hegel, and even Aristotle who, he says, did so only virtually and in implicit fashion.[56]

In this "Digression" Maritain insists that with the intuition of being one leaves the world of simple apprehension and enters that of judgment because this intuition is produced by a positive judgment of existence such as "I am" or "things exist." Again Maritain distinguishes this kind of judgment from those in which the verb "is" functions simply as a copula by which an attribute or predicate, grasped in the manner of an essence understood by abstraction, is connected to a subject. But in the case of the intellectual intuition of being (*l'être*), the idea or concept of existence is not prior to the judgment of existence but comes after it and arises from it.[57] In this case it

53. English, 31; French, 39.

54. See *Revue thomiste* 68 (1968): 5–40. For the English translation see "Reflections on Wounded Nature," in *Untrammeled Approaches*, vol. 20 of *The Collected Works of Jacques Maritain* (Notre Dame, Indiana: University of Notre Dame Press, 1977), 207–42.

55. Ibid., French, 14; English, 216. In terms of context, here Maritain wants to trace the failure of most philosophers to reach this intuition back to a wound of the intellect following from original sin.

56. Ibid., French, 16–17; English, 218–19.

57. Ibid., French, 17–18. There is an unfortunate mistake in the English translation, which I here present in corrected form: "but this judgment [read "*is not like*" rather than "*like*"] *those others* in which a subject endowed with a certain essence is linked, by the copulative *is*, to some

is the subject itself which is posited or affirmed in the mind just as it exists outside the mind and "to produce this judicative act, by really *thinking* it, is, for the intelligence, in the very heart of the spiritual intimacy of its own operation, to grasp intuitively, or to *see* the being (*l'être*), the existence (*l'exister*), the extra-mental *esse* of that subject." And this, writes Maritain, is the intuition of being (*l'être*).[58]

And, Maritain continues, after the intelligence has reached this intuition through judgment, it can by "a reflexive return" (*une reprise reflective*) of the intellect's first operation (simple apprehension) whereby it reflects on this intuition, produce an idea or concept of the *esse* that has originally been grasped through judgment and form what he will now call the "second concept of existence." This is what one means, he explains, when one says, for instance, "The soul communicates to the body its own *existence* or its own *esse*." Here, therefore, Maritain is holding that one grasps the act of existing itself through such a judgment of existence and intuition of being, and not merely the simple fact that something exists.[59]

Maritain stresses that this concept of existence is entirely different in origin from another concept, also called existence, that is produced from the intellect's first and abstractive operation in the way all other ideas are drawn from phantasms through abstraction. He now refers to that as his "first concept of existence" and laments having to use the same word "existence" to signify both. More important for our purposes, though, is the fact that he now seems to allow no place for judgment in the intellect's formation of this first concept of existence. He also says that it is formed before the intuition of being whereas the second concept is formed after that intuition. This first concept of existence seems to have replaced his earlier account of the formation of the vague and common-sense notion of existence which he had presented in *Existence and the Existent* and in which judgment would play an essential role. In this respect, therefore, this account now departs much more significantly from Aquinas's own position than that offered by Maritain in that earlier writing. To illustrate the difference between the first concept of existence and the second Maritain notes

attribute or predicate *by mode of essence,* that is, by means of an idea born of the abstractive operation" (220).

58. Ibid., French, 18; English, 220. Maritain immediately adds this comment which I quote in French: "Par elle je plonge dans le monde de l'exister, en m'évadant du monde des essence et de leurs relations."

59. Ibid.

the difference between one's saying that "the existence of a spy in our services *is* beyond doubt" [emphasis mine] and that "the soul communicates to the body its own *existence* or its own *esse*."[60]

Maritain also writes that Gilson seems to have been so fascinated by the intuition of being that, if Maritain recalls correctly, he wrote that there is no concept of existence,[61] a remark to which Gilson would respond rather sharply in 1974 as will be noted below. Against this claim Maritain comments that there are two concepts of existence, as he has just distinguished them and in a note he indicates that there is even a third as he will explain below and which like the first is of abstractive origin, but at the third degree of abstraction.[62] Neither the first concept nor the third plays any role in the intuition of being. He also points out that even those who have reached the intuition of being will use the first concept of existence in their ordinary speech, for instance when they say: "A visitor is *here*." For this, according to Maritain, is to use "is" as a copula that joins "here" to a subject and indicates that this subject is present to what Maritain refers to as "my world."[63]

Maritain points out that some true metaphysicians who have experienced the intuition of being will use the concept of existence arising from judgment and following upon the intuition as designating "an intelligible—*esse* or 'the act of existing'—*which was not drawn from phantasms by the abstractive operation, like all the other objects of concepts*."[64] But if this is true, Maritain asks rhetorically, how can the act of existing, which is material in the things our eye, for instance, sees, "become proportioned to the intelligence, and spiritualized, in such a way that the intelligence might

60. Ibid., French, 18; English, 220–21.

61. For Maritain see ibid., French, 18; English, 221. In the second edition of his *Being and Some Philosophers* (Toronto: Pontifical Institute of Mediaeval Studies, 1952), Gilson published as an Appendix a critique of certain aspects of own his position by L.-M. Régis that had originally appeared in *The Modern Schoolman* 28 (1951): 121–27. The first critique (217–18) responds to Gilson's denial that existence or "to be" can possibly be conceived and his rejection of a concept of existence (see 3, 202, 213–14). In light of certain texts taken from Aquinas himself and offered by Régis against this reading, in his response to Régis Gilson granted that in making this claim he was not using the language of Thomas himself and that for him every intellectual cognition is a "conception" (222) and might even be called a *conceptus* when that term is taken broadly. Also see Gilson's *L'Être et l'essence*, 2nd ed. (Paris: J. Vrin, 1962), 351, where he again addresses this issue, but warns that this should not be taken as meaning that one can have a "concept quidditatif de l'*esse*." Maritain himself was apparently referring to the position taken by Gilson in texts such as these, but without identifying what particular text or texts he had in mind.

62. Maritain, "Reflections on Wounded Nature," French, 18n1; English, 221n29.

63. Ibid., French, 19; English, 221.

64. Ibid., French, 19–20; English, 222.

come to *see* it, and *see it within itself*" by an act of judgment? Here Maritain indicates that he will proceed carefully in what he calls these "rather hasty notes."[65] He proposes three stages: In the first stage there is perception on the part of the external senses. For example, an act of the external sense of sight brings within my sense of sight the color of a rose by means of a sensible species received from without. Maritain explains that this "enters the mind by means of an intentional form which transfers into the sense the particular way in which the surface of the petals reflects the light acting on the organ (retina and cerebral center)." But at the same time it brings into the sense of sight the act of existence (*exister*) on the part of the rose without that sense "knowing what is going on." It does this not by means of a sensible species [presumably because there is no sensible species of the act of existing itself], but by an "intentional action exercised on the sense when it receives the *species* of the color of the rose."[66] Here I would again note Maritain's failure to distinguish between one's discovery of the fact that something exists, and the act of existing itself (*exister*), and also that unfortunately, perhaps in the interests of simplicity, here he now bypasses the role of the internal senses. As I have argued above, both the phantasms produced by the imagination and the role of the common sense are essential to Aquinas's account.

In presenting stage two Maritain writes that my intelligence does not need the imagination and its phantasms in order for it to be aware that *I am seeing* when my eye sees something. (But for Aquinas it does need awareness of the action of the common sense, as I have just noted.) For, Maritain continues, intelligence is present to the external sense and "penetrates with its own life" the life of the external sense. And it becomes conscious not only of the color of the rose that is perceived, but also of its own "seeing of that rose." The act of existing is made present in the sense of sight (though not perceived by that sense), owing to the intentional action the sense undergoes in receiving the sensible species, and is "made present to the intelligence in (a *totally implicit* way and without being grasped by it as of yet), as implied in *the rose*, … which it knows that *I see*." This occurs at the level of the first degree of abstraction where the intelligence says in its interior word: "That rose is there," which, says Maritain, is the *Dasein,* as he adopts a Heideggerian term, but only in the way a Thomist must understand this

65. Ibid., French, 20; English, 222.
66. Ibid., French, 20–21; English, 223.

expression—meaning that the rose is present to me.[67] Maritain denies that at this point the intelligence says: "The rose is" and so he continues to deny that a judgment of existence is involved in this stage. And so at this moment the rose's act of existing or *Sein* (another Heideggerian term, but again as understood by a Thomist) is not yet explicitly perceived but only potentially and implicitly. To repeat, it is only declared to be "present to me."[68]

As for the third stage, once the eye sees the rose and the intelligence says "The rose is there," the intelligence may pass, as if by a miracle which, Maritain writes, is really not a miracle but rather a "stroke of good fortune" and a gift of nature, to a higher level. This level is not merely at the third degree of abstraction, but at "a moment of natural contemplation in which thought is freed from abstraction." This is the intuition of being, which may happen supra-consciously in a child, or more or less supra-consciously in a poet, or consciously in a philosopher. Maritain describes this as follows:

> At this moment the intuition of being suddenly flashes in the mind like a bolt of lightning, and the rose's *act of existing* already intentionally present in the intelligence but only as spiritualized in proximate potency, or as implicitly and blindly contained in 'the rose is there' which the intelligence utters at the first degree of abstraction, is unveiled explicitly now as an object grasped, *spiritualized in act,* and made proportioned in act to the intelligence.[69]

And this privileged insight, this intuition, Maritain reminds us, is brought about by a true judgment of existence, asserting that "this rose, or this thing, exists" which Maritain also views as an affirmation of *Sein.*[70] The result from this intuition and the intellect's return of simple apprehension to reflect on it and on the judgment of existence that produces it is Maritain's "second concept of existence."[71] But missing from this account is any explicit mention of the role of *separatio,* which Maritain had at least recognized in *Existence and the Existent* as present in Aquinas's *In De Trinitate,* q. 5, a. 3 and which, as we have indicated above, according to Aquinas is required for us to discover being insofar as it is being—the subject of metaphysics.[72]

67. Ibid., French, 21; English, 223–24.

68. Ibid., French, 21–22; English, 224.

69. Ibid., French, 22; English, 224–25.

70. Ibid., French, 23; English, 225.

71. See ibid., French, 24; English, 226. On p. 227 there is another very misleading mistake in the English translation. One should read: "On the contrary, when we come to the second concept of existence, the one which [read: *proceeds from* instead of *precedes*] the intuition of being, we are in the register of [delete: "the"] *Sein.*" See p. 25 for the French version of the mistranslated text: "celui qui procède de l'intuition de l'être."

72. In the immediately following context, the need for some reference to *separatio* becomes

Maritain subsequently goes on to argue that many "great" philosophers have failed to reach this intuition, and that other truly great ones have reached it only in virtual fashion even though they were true or real metaphysicians, but seemed to be lacking something. He mentions Bergson here and writes that he did experience the intuition of being, but did not reach "the formal intuition of being in its full light" but only in a "disguised fashion, or by means of a substitute–*duration*," and that following from this his metaphysical thought suffered from a "doctrinal deviation."[73]

He then considers Aristotle who, he says, did have an admirable sense of the analogy of being but one still incomplete and deficient because even though he had a real experience of the intuition of being, this was only virtually and "*not formally and in full light.*" And in the course of developing the point that Aristotle never got "beyond the wall of essences," Maritain finds Aristotle reaching a third concept of existence, in addition to the two Maritain had already proposed. This third concept, he says, is of abstractive origin, like the first one and not based on a true judgment of existence, but now at a higher level, the third degree of abstraction, but which continues to treat *esse* in the manner of a "*quid* or of an essence *or in the manner of essence or of quality*," and so his metaphysics suffers from a grave deficiency.[74] But since Maritain does not attribute this third concept of existence to Aquinas, and since here I am interested in comparing Maritain and Aquinas, I will pass over any additional remarks about it.

III. Concluding Remarks

I have already remarked that Maritain's final presentation of how one discovers the subject of metaphysics—being as being—suffers greatly from the absence of any appeal to Thomas's negative judgment of separation. Moreover, in his consideration in this writing of what he calls the first concept of existence, Maritain is less Thomistic than was his presentation

very evident. Still referring to his second concept of existence which proceeds from the intuition of being and a real judgment of existence, Maritain writes: "Here being is grasped as such.... It is no longer taken in its relation to the sensible world; it is taken absolutely, in its limitless and intrinsically differentiated universality which embraces everything that *is* (and *is* in irreducibly varied ways)." Ibid., French, 25; English, 227–28. Perhaps Maritain had now concluded that his proposed intuition of being could accomplish all that Aquinas had attributed to *separatio*.

73. Ibid., French, 30; English, 232.

74. Ibid., French, 30–34; English, 234–36.

in *Existence and the Existent.* He omits and even explicitly rejects any role for judgments of existence in one's discovery of a prephilosophical and premetaphysical notion of being (or the "vague being of common sense," to use Maritain's earlier terminology).

But is there a doctrine of an intellectual intuition of being in the texts of Aquinas? Earlier on I have already expressed my reservations about finding such a doctrine in Aquinas himself. In connection with this I now turn to Gilson's response to the following remark by Maritain, mentioned above in passing: "Etienne Gilson seems to have been so fascinated by the intuition of being that he wrote, if I recall correctly, that there is no such thing as a *concept* of existence."[75] As will be recalled, to this Maritain had immediately replied that there are two such concepts and even three.

In his "Propos sur l'être et sa notion," Gilson quotes this text and responds that he also believes that he had written such a statement and affirms that he still holds such a view. He comments that he finds it somewhat scandalous that two followers of Thomas Aquinas, that is, Maritain and Gilson himself, after having spent so many years as members of his school, should disagree on such a fundamental point as the notion of being (*l'être*). But to say that there is no concept of existence and to hold that there are two or even three such concepts are incompatible propositions. Gilson points out that to ask whether there is a concept of existence may be taken in two ways—whether there is a concept of being (*conceptus entis*) or whether there is a concept of *esse*—and points out that he has not found Aquinas raising either of these questions in these words in his texts. And by speaking of a concept of existence, Gilson warns that one introduces a *conceptus existentiae* that is foreign to the language of Aquinas himself.[76]

As regards a concept of existence, Gilson responds along the lines of his earlier concession to Régis that in general there is a conception (*conceptio*) for every object of thought since to think is to conceive, and to conceive is to engender objects of thought. If therefore one wishes to name every object of this kind a "concept" then, if we grasp the meaning of the words "existence," "to be" (*être*), or "being" (*étant*), and understand the term concept in this broad sense, we may apply it to them.[77]

75. Ibid., French, 18; English, 221.

76. In *San Tommaso e il pensiero moderno,* edited by Antonio Piolanti (Citta Nuova: Pontificia Accademia Romana de S. Tommaso d'Aquino, 1974), 7–17; see 8.

77. Ibid., 9. See n. 61 above for Gilson's reply to Régis.

As regards intuitions of beings, Gilson acknowledges that we have sensible intuitions, but emphasizes very strongly that a sensible intuition of a being is not an intellectual intuition of its *esse* (*être*). He writes that for someone to see a being is to perceive something of which one knows that it has an *esse*, but that we do not have a distinct concept of that which makes it exist. While the most extensive quidditative concept is that of being (*ens*), or "that which has *esse*," Gilson comments that from the *esse* of a being one can only abstract the notion of *esse commune*. And the object of the notion of *esse commune* exists only in thought as a being of reason, not in reality as the act of a being. As he also expresses it, *esse* is that which makes of an essence a being. Here he is speaking of the *actus essendi*. And this, he points out, has no proper existence in itself apart from that of the substance which it makes a being. This is why, he continues, "one cannot have an intuitive understanding of the *esse* of a being (*de l'être d'un étant*) because it is only perceptible to us in the sensible perception of the substance which it actualizes."[78] And as regards *esse commune*, he repeats his point that it exists only in the intellect and cites *Summa contra gentiles* I, c. 26: "Much less, therefore is *esse commune* itself something outside of all existing things except in the intellect alone."[79]

To reinforce his rejection of any intellectual intuition of *esse*, Gilson recalls that if one wants to speak of degrees of abstraction, our apprehension of being will still be an abstraction based on sense experience. According to Aquinas the human intellect cannot think without images (phantasms). Since there is no image of being insofar as it is being, which is a pure intelligible, intellectual intuition of this is not possible in the present life even for the most experienced metaphysicians. Gilson also recalls that for Thomas it is the "that which," the quiddity of a being, that is the proper object of the human intellect in the present life.[80]

78. See "Propos," 10: "C'est même pourquoi on ne saurait avoir d'intellection intuitive de l'être d'un étant, parce qu'il ne nous est perceptible que dans la perception sensible de la substance qu'il actualise." He continues: "De l'acte de percevoir tel ou tel étant, nous pouvons abstraire la notion abstraite d'être, cet être commun et universel attribuable à tout ce qui est, mais l'être propre à chaque étant ne nous est connu que comme cause immanente à ce qu'il fait être."

79. See ibid. For Thomas see: "Multo igitur minus et ipsum esse commune est aliquid praeter omnes res existentes nisi in intellectu solum"; *Editio Leonina Manuelis* (Rome: Desclée, 1934), 27.

80. See "Propos," 11–12. On p. 12 Gilson cites ST I, q. 17, a. 3, ad 1 for support and then quotes from Thomas's Commentary on the *Liber de causis* in a French translation apparently based on a faulty Latin edition rather than on the critical edition by H. D. Saffrey, which I quote here:

Near the end of his article Gilson returns to Thomas's view that it is impossible for the human intellect, in the state of the present life whereby we are joined to a body, to understand something in actuality except by turning itself back to phantasms (ST I, q. 84, a. 7). Gilson concludes that because this rule is based on (human) nature, it admits of no exception.[81]

I myself regret the fact that, to the best of my knowledge, Gilson himself did not incorporate into his discussion of this issue and his account of how one discovers being as being the role of *separatio* in Aquinas's thought. And I have already criticized Maritain for omitting this from his final account of all of this. But concerning the presence of an intuition of being or of existence in the texts of Aquinas, I agree with Gilson in noting that I myself have not found it there, and conclude that it is not compatible with Thomas's theory of knowledge.

"Sed secundum rei veritatem causa prima est supra ens in quantum est ipsum esse infinitum, ens autem dicitur id quod finite participat esse, et hoc est proportionatum intellectui nostro cuius obiectum est quod quid est ut dicitur in *III° De anima,* unde illud solum est capabile ab intellectu nostro quod habet quidditatem participantem esse." See *Sancti Thomae de Aquino Super librum de causis expositio* (Fribourg: Société Philosophique, 1954), 47:11–17.

81. See "Propos," 16. For Thomas, see: "Impossibile est intellectum nostrum secundum praesentis vitae statum quo passibili corpori conjunimur, aliquid intelligere in actu, nisi convertendo se ad phantasmata" (Leon. ed., vol. 5, 325). On p. 17 Gilson notes that Maritain himself acknowledged that while the intuition of being had been lived *in actu exercito* by Thomas (and by the good Thomists), Maritain had not found any treatise or disquisition where Thomas had studied it *in actu signato*. Gilson comments rather wryly that another reason to account for the absence of any explicit discussion of this in Aquinas's texts may rather be that he held no such doctrine.

JASON WEST

Maritain and Dewan on the Intuition of Being and the Birth of Metaphysics

The intuition of being is not only the point of departure for metaphysics, but it is also the central point of reference in Jacques Maritain's thought. Implicit in every act of knowledge, in every statement, and in every experience is the act of being. Whatever is known by the intellect presents some mode of being to the mind, that is to say that everything is apprehended by the intellect as being embodied in some essence or nature. Being, however, is the first and formal object of the intellect, without which nothing can be thought, known, or even said.[1] This essay presents an explanation and defence of Maritain's articulation of the intuition of being as the appropriate point of departure for metaphysics as a science. I begin by presenting Maritain's account of intuition and its application in the metaphysical context. I then consider some objections to his position, notably the argument of Lawrence Dewan, O.P., that by assigning the mind's encounter with being to the act of judgment Maritain distinguishes too sharply between ordinary experience and metaphysical knowledge. Drawing upon Maritain's late writings on the topic, I argue that Maritain offers a much more dynamic and interactive presentation of the roles of abstraction and judgment than this objection seems to admit.

1. Jacques Maritain, *Introduction to Philosophy,* translated by E. I. Watkin (Lanham, Maryland: Rowan and Littlefield, 2005), 132; *Science and Wisdom,* translated by Bernard Wall (New York: Charles Scribner's Sons, 1940), 23; *A Preface to Metaphysics* (New York: Sheed and Ward, 1962), 12; and *The Degrees of Knowledge,* translated by Gerald B. Phelan (Notre Dame, Indiana: University of Notre Dame Press, 1995), 99–100.

Maritain distinguishes the general notion of being that is implied universally in judgments of common sense from the awareness of being that gives birth to metaphysics as a discipline. In common judgments about sense objects like "this is a beer," being is certainly apprehended, but here it is grasped in a manner that is clothed in a sensible nature. We do not encounter being as a common element of all things extracted in its purity, but being enveloped in a diversity of corporeal natures.[2] Accordingly, the apprehension of being present in common sense judgments is not the proper object of metaphysics. Being as an object of metaphysics requires reflection on being as such, being insofar as it is being. Here being is not enclosed in a sensible nature, but rather is abstracted from its particularized objects so far as possible. It is now considered in a way which is set apart in order to consider its pure intelligible values.[3] Clearly, this is also distinct from the particularized being studied by the scientist in considering the nature of physical things in motion. Being as such has no meaning for the scientist and cannot enter into her properly scientific work—that is ruled out by the empirio-logical method into which all her results are resolved. The being that interests the metaphysician cannot, therefore, be attained by moving to more and more general abstractions.

Throughout Maritain's work, he insists that metaphysics as a science (in the Aristotelian sense) has its origin in an intuition of being. The aspect of being of interest here is not the concrete being of common sense, the material and movable being of the sciences, nor the merely abstracted pseudo-being that prevails among logicians and essentialist or nominalist metaphysicians. Rather, the focus of attention ought to be in its most fundamental and irreducible act, being considered precisely as being. This is what is, and can only be, attained by way of intuition. Of course philosophers notoriously appeal to intuition in various and often confusing ways. Accordingly, it is extremely important to be attentive to the precise sense that Maritain gives to the phrase "intuition of being" in this context and the way it develops over the course of his various writings on the subject.

In this respect, it is well worth noting that intuition also played a central role in the thought of Maritain's mentor and nemesis Henri Bergson. Indeed, it is no mere coincidence that we encounter a lengthy and nuanced treatment of intuition in Maritain's first book *Bergsonian Philosophy and*

2. Maritain, *A Preface to Metaphysics*, 25.

3. Ibid., 26.

Thomism. Bergson had appealed to intuition in an attempt to highlight the shortcomings of the early positivism he fought against. Scientific knowledge, he pointed out, always views its object from the outside as something to be studied from various perspectives. This meant that it was a form of analysis that is by its nature restricted to a "symbolic" or "analytic" point of view. The scientist moves about the object, takes measurements, etc., and these symbolically represent the object to him.[4] He contrasted this approach with an "intuitive" perspective which would move beyond an external appraisal of the object in order to come into a direct affective union with it, to see the object not from without, but from within. Bergson notes that there is at least one case we all grasp intuitively, that of our own personalities. However, he argues that through intuition we can come to view other things from within as well, through a kind of affective sympathy with them. This is the task of metaphysics, the science that overcomes and dispenses with symbols.[5]

While Maritain will agree with Bergson on the need for intuition to go beyond the kind of analysis inherent in science, he is highly critical of the way in which Bergson characterizes this. Maritain makes his point by distinguishing a philosophical sense of intuition from a common sense everyday one. He explains intuition in the primary and philosophical sense as follows:

> The distinctive feature of intuition, taken in the very wide sense in which we understand it here, is that it is an *immediate* knowledge or perception, a *direct* knowledge or perception, in which the act of knowing terminates upon the thing known without any intermediary, without the interposition of a middle term—in which it is *seen* in a word.[6]

This understanding of intuition, which is Maritain's own, is radically different from that of Bergson as it is fundamentally a direct intellectual perception of the real that terminates in a word or concept. It is the perception of the real in a word. The second sense of intuition is how it is ordinarily understood by the non-philosopher as a hunch or gut feeling, in Maritain's words a "form of divination". This is the sense in which we speak of the

4. Henri Bergson, *An Introduction to Metaphysics*, translated by T. E. Hulme (Indianapolis, Indiana: Hackett, 1999), 21.

5. Ibid., 24.

6. Jacques Maritain, *Bergsonian Philosophy and Thomism*, translated by Mabelle L. Andison (Notre Dame, Indiana: University of Notre Dame Press, 2007), 149.

"intuitions of the heart". Here it is not the immediacy of knowledge that is at issue, but the spontaneity of the subject in arriving at it. The right idea is latched onto by sympathy and we are no longer dealing with the relation between the act of cognition and the subject that is known by it. This latter sense seems to be at work in many of Bergson's examples. Accordingly, Maritain credits Bergson with correctly identifying a key weakness in the positivism of the day, and rightly seeing that the need for intuition is the proper alternative. However, he rejects Bergson's own presentation of intuition as anti-intellectual, and thus an inadequate basis for a suitable metaphysical alternative.

Maritain is careful to qualify what he means by saying that intuition occurs directly without any intermediary. This does not mean that this knowledge occurs without any *subjective* intermediary. That would entail that the knowledge arises without any means of presenting the object within the knowing subject. Clearly, such a situation is impossible. If the object is not presented to the knowing agent, that agent can have no knowledge of it. Rather, the object is present within the knowing subject as a concept or mental word that serves as a likeness of the object. The key point is that the act of knowledge does not terminate in this concept, as if what we knew were the mental word. It is, rather, that this concept is a likeness through which and in which knowledge of the real can take place. It is a means of knowing the real thing in the world, it is not the thing that is known.[7]

Yet, this intuitive knowledge is complicated in the case of being, at least in the sense that interests the metaphysician, due to the fact that being cannot be attained through mere abstraction. The aspect of being that is relevant to metaphysics is the very act of existing that all things exercise in order to be. This is not something that can be attained only through a process of abstraction without falling into the Hegelian paradox in which being has been so abstracted from every particular quality that it is identical to nothing.

Yet, Maritain only gradually developed his position to emphasize that an intuition of being is not only possible, but utterly necessary to be a metaphysician at all."[8] In *The Degrees of Knowledge* (1934) he discusses "metaphysical experience" as an alternative to metaphysics as a science for some individu-

7. Ibid., 150–51.

8. Jacques Maritain, *Existence and the Existent,* translated by Lewis Glanatiere and Gerald B. Phelan (New York: Pantheon Books, 1948), 19.

als, but seems to deny that such intuitions are necessary for this science. In this text he writes, "Because for some men, the types of metaphysical experience of which we have just been speaking provide on some points, a substitute for metaphysical science properly so called that does not prove that, of itself metaphysics requires, in order to exist as a perfectly certain science and to reach being efficaciously, that it be completed by such intuitions."[9] But, it is important to note that this passage occurs in the context of a discussion of mysticism, and the primary concern seems to be to argue that mystical experience is not a necessary element of metaphysics as a science. However, the term "metaphysical experience" in this context seems somewhat ambiguous as what Maritain's later works advocate as necessary is a metaphysical, but certainly not mystical, experience.

However, in his later works such as *Existence and the Existent* (1947) and thereafter he advocates the necessity for an intuition of being in no uncertain terms: "A philosopher is not a philosopher if he is not a metaphysician. And it is the intuition of being—even when it is distorted by the error of a system, as in Plato or Spinoza—that makes a metaphysician."[10] Throughout his late works Maritain is uncompromising about the necessity of this intuition for the philosopher to rise to his primary task, the development of an adequate metaphysics.

But how are we to arrive at this intuition of being? Frequently he speaks of it as a "gift." Although, he is careful to distinguish it from a properly mystical grace, he is clear that it remains a gift nonetheless. What he means is that there is no step-by-step procedure we can go through to ensure that we will attain this intuition. It will always be one that some people acquire while others, some of them great philosophers, do not. The reason for this is that the key to attaining the intuition of being is not to construct an elaborate philosophical system, but simply to listen to the hymn to their being that all things whisper in virtue of the fact that they exist.[11] Nevertheless, there are several approaches that can lead one to this intuition. Maritain mentions a number of them: 1. Bergson's experience of duration in which motion becomes a unity; 2. Heidegger's experience of anguish in which we confront profoundly the fragility of our being as something saved from nothingness, and; 3. Marcel's metaphysical elaboration of ethical experi-

9. Maritain, *The Degrees of Knowledge*, 297.
10. Maritain, *Existence and the Existent*, 19.
11. See Maritain, *The Degrees of Knowledge*, 2, and *A Preface to Metaphysics*, 52–53.

ences in which existence loses its commonplace value so we can discover it existentially in an awareness of moral facts like fidelity.[12] All of these cases are examples of an experience that can reach fruition in the intuitive apprehension of being. Yet, Maritain insists we would make any intuition of being impossible if we rested content in the psychological or ethical aspects of these experiences. Something further is needed:

> What counts is to take the leap, to release, in one authentic intellectual intuition, the sense of being, the sense of the value of the implications that lie in the act of existing. What counts is to have seen that existence is not a simple empirical fact but a primitive datum for the mind itself, opening to the mind an infinite supra-observable field—in a word, the primary and super-intelligible source of intelligibility.[13]

Certainly, the empirical elements as well as the psychological or ethical factors may be more readily apparent, but the metaphysician needs to go further and see within those experiences a direct confrontation with being *qua* being disengaged for its own sake in its intelligible and transcendental values.[14]

These paths are all matters of experiences that can lead to an intuition of being if seen from a metaphysical perspective. However, Maritain suggests that it can also be prompted or confirmed through rational analysis. His examples are the classical arguments that show the inescapability of being: that events presuppose beings; Aquinas' argument in *De Veritate,* q. 1 a.1 that the first object of the intellect is being, to which it reduces all of its other concepts; and a metaphysical understanding of the principle of identity, that every being is what it is.[15] Such analyses are not optional extras, but necessary. Nevertheless, they would be empty unless they prompted us to go further to an experiential apprehension of being in an intuition.

> Were we content with the intuition without the rational analysis we should risk being landed with an intuition unconfirmed by reason, whose rational necessity therefore would not be manifest. Were we content with the analysis—as we are liable to be when we teach philosophy—though the analysis would indeed prove that we must arrive at the intuition of being as the goal of a necessary regress, it would not of itself furnish the intuition.[16]

12. Maritain, *A Preface to Metaphysics,* 52–53.
13. Maritain, *Existence and the Existent,* 21.
14. Maritain, *A Preface to Metaphysics,* 55–56.
15. See ibid., 58–61 and *The Degrees of Knowledge,* 228–29.
16. Maritain, *A Preface to Metaphysics,* 59.

Both the experiences and arguments given so far are philosophical. However, at times Maritain also speaks of non-philosophical experiences that can draw one into an intuition of being, "like a kind of natural grace at the sight of a blade of grass or a windmill, or at the sudden perception of the reality of self."[17] This seems to suggest that any experience, if viewed from the metaphysical perspective, might do the trick, becoming an occasion to sense the reality of being. A graphic example of this is supplied by Maritain's wife Raïssa, who speaks of feeling the presence of God while watching the forests go by while riding in a car. She goes on to note that such experiences placed her in contact with a direct awareness of being. "It also often happened, before I knew the things of faith, that I experienced through a sudden intuition the reality of my being, of the profound, first principle which placed me outside nothingness. The violence of this powerful intuition sometimes frightened me, and first gave me the knowledge of a metaphysical absolute."[18] However, whether it is a philosophical experience or not, the key thing is to take the leap beyond ordinary circumstances, the psychological or ethical factors implicit in them, and to see that reality from the perspective of the act of being that raises it outside of nothingness. Without that intuitive awareness of being, any attempt at metaphysics would be a mere arrangement of ideas without any object, an ideosophy rather than a philosophy.

What is it that we attain in the intuition of being? The aspect of being that is the object of this intuition and that gives rise to the birth of metaphysics is:

> ... being disengaged for its own sake, in the values and resources appertaining to its own intelligibility and reality; which is to say, in that richness, that analogical and transcendental amplitude which is *inviscerated* in the imperfect and multiple unity of its concept and which allows it to cover the infinitude of its analogates and causes it to overflow or superabound in transcendental values and in dynamic values of propensity through which the idea of being transgresses itself.[19]

The one who has apprehended being intuitively recognizes that being is not a mere fact, but an act. She has experienced the act of being in its transcendental and analogical nature as the bond that runs throughout all that is, that which holds all things outside of nothingness.

17. Maritain, *Existence and the Existent*, 21.

18. Raïssa Maritain, *We Have Been Friends Together* and *Adventures in Grace*, translated by Julie Kernan (New York: Image Books, 1961), 116. Also cited in Jacques Maritain, *The Degrees of Knowledge*, 297.

19. Maritain, *Existence and the Existent*, 20. Cf. *A Preface to Metaphysics*, 35–50.

Drawing on Aquinas' metaphysics Maritain sees two really distinct co-dependent aspects to any created real being or substance. First, there is the being of that thing, the act that makes it exist. Second, there is its essence that determines what kind of thing that entity is going to be. Both of these aspects are found in every real being. In coming to know a material being the mind in its first act abstracts the essence, so that this essence or form exists in the mind immaterially, but remains in the thing materially. However, this gives rise to a problem. As we have said, being is not an essence, in fact it is what is precisely contrasted with the essence. But, if the mind attains knowledge through abstracting an essence from matter, it would appear that being cannot be known.[20]

Obviously Maritain is far from willing to admit this conclusion. Rather, he suggests that in order to grasp how the mind attains its knowledge of existence we need to be attentive to the way in which judgment works in relation to the activity of abstraction. In typical cases judgment performs an existential function. Abstraction or eidetic visualization draws the essence from the thing to exist immaterially and intelligibly in the mind. Accordingly, this first operation comes to terms with what the thing is. Judgment on the other hand affirms or denies that what has been abstracted is the case. It asserts that it is so, and thereby reunites existence with the essence in the knowing agent.[21]

In judgment, a subject and a predicate that differ conceptually in the mind are asserted to be identical in the thing they signify existing outside of the mind. To use one of Maritain's examples, the notion "George Bernard Shaw" is different from the notion "dramatist." Yet, in the judgment "George Bernard Shaw is a dramatist," what is signified by these distinct objects of thought is identified in the order of real being. This consideration leads to the recognition of the existential function of judgment. As Maritain writes,

> Thus, the proper function of judgment consists in making the mind pass from the level of simple essence or simple object signified to the mind, to the level of thing or subject possessing existence (actually or possibly), a thing of which the object of thought (predicate) and the subject of thought (subject) are intelligible aspects....

20. See Maritain, *Existence and the Existent*, 22–23, and *A Preface to Metaphysics*, 67–68.
21. Maritain, *Existence and the Existent*, 16.

> ... The judgment restores to the transobjective subject the unity that the simple apprehension [i.e.abstraction] (by laying hold of different objects of thought in it) has shattered. That unity could not hold precedence in the mind since, quite to the contrary, the mind undoes it only to reconstitute it afterwards. It held precedence outside the mind, in existence (actual or possible) which, insofar as it is possessed, is outside the order of mere representation or simple apprehension.[22]

According to Maritain, judgment reunifies essence with the existence from which it had been abstracted in the first act of the intellect. Thus, it is in judgment that the mind comes into contact with being in the sense that the metaphysician is interested in, being disengaged for its own sake from the sensible nature in which it is clothed. The mind affirms and intentionally experiences existence in judgment in a way that makes existence the consummation of the mind's act of intelligibility.

There have certainly been objections to Maritain's use of an intuition of being as the sole entry point to metaphysical reflection. The classical objection is clearly formulated by Joseph Marechal in *Le Point de depart de la métaphysique*. The concern is that Maritain seems to require moving from an experience given in sensation to a judgment about the act of being (*esse*) disengaged from material bodies. Yet, the data does not show that being can actuate anything other than physical bodies.[23] It is true that Maritain refers to the beings (*ens*) apprehended in everyday common sense as "clothed" in a sensible nature, whereas the metaphysician begins by distinguishing the act of being in a judgment in its transcendental and analogical values. However, this need not entail that we have at this point shown that being really does actualize some immaterial entity in the way that Marechal's objection assumes. Rather, it simply involves recognizing that this entity is not merely present, but sustained in reality by an act that is transcendentally and analogically related to all other entities that exist, be they material or possibly immaterial. For Maritain's intuition to lead us to metaphysics, all that we need is an awareness of the fact that this being is like all others in some way, yet is utterly distinct from all others in another way. At that point being (*esse*) can be disengaged through reflection on the existential function of judgment for metaphysical analysis.

22. Maritain, *The Degrees of Knowledge,* 103 and 104. Maritain also quotes this text on p. 16 of *Existence and the Existent.*

23. See Joseph Marechal, *A Marechal Reader,* translated by Joseph Donceel (New York: Herder and Herder, 1970), 146.

A further objection has been raised by Lawrence Dewan, O.P., who argues that there is no hard and fast distinction between the way being is apprehended in common sense and the way it is attained in metaphysics as a science. In contrast to Maritain's emphasis on judgment as the path to being, Dewan argues that there is a quasi-quidditative knowledge of being in abstraction. Accordingly, he maintains that the ordinary awareness of being is already pregnant with the principles that lead us to metaphysical conclusions. For Dewan, the intuition of being that is the birth of metaphysics is not being as discovered through reflection upon judgment, but rather in "the drawing of the first metaphysical conclusion."[24]

However, this would not be an intuition in Maritain's sense at all, since the drawing of a conclusion must involve a process of deductive inference which is precisely what Maritain distinguishes from intuition. As we pointed out above, in *A Preface to Metaphysics* Maritain does suggest that we can confirm or even be led to the intuition of being through rational analysis and this is indeed necessary, even though it must be completed through the experience of intuition. Maritain seems to be suggesting that the rational analysis and the intuition are co-dependent.[25] This seems to rule out the possibility of locating the intuition of being in the drawing of the first metaphysical conclusion, without abandoning the sense of intuition that is at work in Maritain's thought altogether. For Maritain, the starting point of the discipline of metaphysics is not a conclusion at all, but an experience.

Yet, Dewan's main concern is to argue for the continuity between our ordinary experience of material beings and the conclusions we arrive at through developing metaphysical knowledge. In his view Maritain separates the beings considered in the everyday experience of common sense from being considered in the science of metaphysics too harshly.[26] In Maritain's defence, however, it is important to note that this is a distinction of two aspects within one and the same thing. A glass of milk is considered to exist in one way by the child who wants a drink and in another way by the metaphysician who wishes to know. Nevertheless what is known by both is the same existent thing, albeit objectified in two quite different ways. Moreover, Dewan suggests that the ordinary experience of being and the

24. Lawrence Dewan, "Jacques Maritain, St. Thomas, and the Birth of Metaphysics," *Maritain Studies/Etudes Maritainiennes* 13 (1997): 3–18, 16.

25. Maritain, *A Preface to Metaphysics*, 59.

26. Dewan, "Jacques Maritain, St. Thomas, and the Birth of Metaphysics," 15.

first operation of the intellect, abstraction, contains within it the principles that have the power to demonstrate metaphysical conclusions. These principles have just not been made explicit or applied yet.

Here I think it is important to emphasize that although Maritain distinguishes abstraction from judgment very clearly, he also insists that both are acts of the *entire intellect*. We are distinguishing in order to unite. This means that for Maritain being is apprehended in the different acts of understanding, but in different ways. In *Existence and the Existent* he explains,

> Essences are the object of the first operation of the intellect, or simple apprehension. It is judgment which the act of existing confronts. The intellect envelopes itself and is self contained, is wholly present in each of its operations.... [I]t apprehends and judges in the same instant. It forms its first idea (that of being) while uttering its first judgment (of existence), and utters its first judgment while forming its first idea. I say, therefore, that it lays hold of the treasure which properly belongs to judgment, in order to envelop it in simple apprehension itself.[27]

This is clearly more nuanced than a simple division that equates being confronted in simple apprehension or abstraction as common sense knowledge and being apprehended in judgment as metaphysical. The two acts of the intellect function together in producing the intuition of being that is the seed of all genuine metaphysical knowledge. The intellect, Maritain continues,

> visualizes that treasure in an initial and absolutely original idea, in a privileged idea which is not the result of the process of simple apprehension alone, but of the laying hold of that which the intellect affirms from the moment it judges, namely, the act of existing. It seizes upon the eminent intelligibility or the super-intelligibility which the act of judging deals with (that of existence), in order to make of it an object of thought.[28]

In the intuition of being both operations of the intellect are intimately involved. Judgment is placed in the role of rendering explicit what is contained in simple apprehension. This is made very explicit in Maritain's last discussion of the topic in a conference he gave in 1967 that was subsequently published as "Reflections on a Wounded Nature." In this essay he points to two distinct concepts of being that have different origins and meanings. Yet, they are nevertheless intimately related:

27. Maritain, *Existence and the Existent*, 23.
28. Ibid.

There is a concept of being (our second concept of existence), which arises in the mind after the intuition of being, by a turning back of simple apprehension, or of intelligence as formative of ideas, onto that intuition; all of this happens on a certain level, the level of metaphysical intellection (even in the case of someone who does not realize what is going on, in the case of a poet for instance). And there is another concept of existence (our first concept of existence), which is formed in the mind before the intuition of being has welled up within it: I mean on the level of the first degree of abstraction, which is the level on which man's thought moves ordinarily and in the first place. This concept of existence is of abstractive origin, not judicative, and, yes, it precedes the intuition of being, and is in no way an integral part of it. It remains completely foreign to it.[29]

This is certainly a stronger distinction between common sense apprehension and metaphysical knowledge than Dewan accepts. On his view, the principles of metaphysics are implicitly contained in the ordinary experience of beings known through the first operation of the mind by abstraction. There is some truth to this. However, I do not see how it suffices as a philosophical refutation of Maritain's view. In fact, he explicitly admits that as long as one remains at the level of abstraction, the awareness of being remains implicit.[30] Yet, the metaphysician is interested in making our knowledge explicit. One could just as easily say that these same principles are contained implicitly in human sense experience, for without sense experience there would be no way for us to know about them. Nevertheless, the question remains, How is that latent potentiality of metaphysical principles made known explicitly? Unfortunately, I do not find a clear answer to that question in Dewan's critique.[31]

As we have seen above, Maritain has a clear answer to the question of how the implicit awareness of being in ordinary common sense experience comes to be articulated explicitly by the metaphysician: through the mind's reflection on its acts of judgment. In most judgments, the idea or concept comes before the judgment. The judgment, "Truffle is a dog," for example, presupposes the concept "dog." The idea of being is unique, however, for in judgments like "I am" or "things are," it follows the judgment and is arrived

29. Jacques Maritain, *Untrammeled Approaches,* translated by Bernard Doering (Notre Dame, Indiana: University of Notre Dame Press, 1997), 221.

30. See ibid., 222.

31. I should note, however, that Dewan's focus is on the degree to which Maritain's presentation coincides with that of St. Thomas. The abundance of texts that he supplies from Aquinas is certainly helpful and deserve careful study. However, my only concern in this discussion is whether Maritain's argument is a defensible philosophical position in its own right.

at through it. It is important to keep in mind that linguistic analysis is not adequate to arrive at the intuition of being. These existential judgments do not merely apply a predicate to a subject.

> It is, rather, the subject itself that this judgment affirms or posits in the mind, as that subject itself is posited outside the mind, in extra-mental reality; and to produce this judicative act, by really *thinking* it, is, for the intelligence, in the very heart of the spiritual intimacy of its own operation, to grasp intuitively, or *to see*, the being, the existence, the extra-mental *esse* of that subject. This is what I call the intuition of being.[32]

In this text the existential character of judgment is made explicit. Judgment does not merely assert the predicate of the subject, but rather also asserts that it *is*. In this manner, it brings being into view of the intellect, and this encounter of the mind with the act of being is the authentic point of departure for metaphysics.

The aim of this essay has been to clearly articulate Maritain's position on the intuition of being. For Maritain this is the indispensable point of entry into the science of metaphysics. Of particular concern has been the emphasis that he places on the role of judgment within this intuition. Contrary to Dewan's position that metaphysics begins from a quasi-quidditative knowledge of being attained in the first metaphysical conclusion, I have argued that Maritain's account of being is defensible. While Maritain does distinguish ordinary experience from metaphysical knowledge, he is able to explain the transition from one mode to the other quite clearly. This does not lead him to separate the two, but rather to unify them in a dynamic interaction through which both abstraction and judgment share in the disclosure of being that serves as the vital originative experience that is the only foundation upon which the science of metaphysics can possibly build.

32. Maritain, *Untrammeled Approaches*, 220.

DOUG FLIPPEN

The Non-Abstractive and Non-Conceptual Character of Poetic Intuition in Maritain

I. Introduction

From the beginning to the end of his career, Maritain was concerned to understand how the human intellect could be involved in the appreciation and production of a beautiful material thing. In the end he decided that in order to make sense of our grasp of, or our production of, a beautiful thing we need to posit a twofold life or path of development of the intellect: one path leading to the formation of concepts by way of abstract intelligible species being imposed on the intellect, the second path leading to the obscure non-conceptual connatural knowing of a singular thing as such by way of a non-abstractive informing of the intellect by an emotion under the light of the illuminating intellect. The first life or path of development of the intellect is typically associated with speculative knowledge of universal aspects of material reality, while the second path of development of the intellect is uniquely associated with what Maritain calls creative or poetic intuition, by which the intellect focuses on singular things as such somehow through the senses. The question I am asking is whether poetic intuition can be defended as a mode of intellectual knowing that is both non-abstractive and non-conceptual and that has singular things taken as singulars as what it grasps. I will argue that the non-conceptual character of poetic intuition can be easily defended. On the other hand, I doubt whether the non-abstractive informing of the intellect with data taken from material singulars can be defended. In addition, I doubt whether the intellectual knowing of material singulars as such, in the manner Maritain takes to be unique to poetic intuition, can be defended.

II. Review of Selected Texts

The topic of poetic intuition in the writings of Jacques Maritain is adumbrated in Maritain's first work, *Bergsonian Philosophy and Thomism,*[1] and is then developed most of all in *Art and Scholasticism*[2] and *Creative Intuition in Art and Poetry.*[3] Maritain's treatment has been commented on a number of times. There have been at least three theses on the topic: *Maritain's Theory of Poetic Intuition,*[4] by Sean M. Sullivan; *Maritain's Theory of Poetic Knowledge,*[5] by Gerald Conrad Hay, and; *The Interrelation of Poetry, Beauty, and Contemplation in the Philosophy of Jacques Maritain,*[6] by John G. Trapani Jr. The subject was also covered by John W. Hanke in his *Maritain's Ontology of the Work of Art.*[7] John G. Trapani Jr. has dealt with poetic intuition in Maritain on at least four occasions, first in an address to an international Maritain conference in Ottawa in 1982,[8] second in his 1984 thesis, third in an article in *Beauty, Art and the Polis,*[9] and last in *Poetry, Beauty, and Contemplation: The Complete Aesthetics of Jacques Maritain.*[10]

1. Jacques Maritain, *Bergsonian Philosophy and Thomism,* translated by Mabelle Louise Andison (New York: Philosophical Library, 1955).

2. Jacques Maritain, *Art and Scholasticism and the Frontiers of Poetry,* translated by Joseph W. Evans (New York: Charles Scribner's Sons, 1962), 23–24.

3. Jacques Maritain, *Creative Intuition in Art and Poetry,* Bollingen Series XXXV, vol. 1 (New York: Pantheon Books, 1955).

4. Sean M. Sullivan, T.O.R., *Maritain's Theory of Poetic Intuition* (Fribourg: University of Fribourg, 1963).

5. Gerald C. Hay, *Maritain's Theory of Poetic Knowledge: A Critical Study* (Washington, D.C.: The Catholic University of America Press, 1964).

6. John G. Trapani Jr., *The Interrelation of Poetry, Beauty, and Contemplation in the Philosophy of Jacques Maritain* (New York: St. John's University, 1984).

7. John W. Hanke, *Maritain's Ontology of the Work of Art* (The Hague: Nijhoff, 1973).

8. John G. Trapani Jr., "Poetic Contemplation: An Undeveloped Aspect of Maritain's Epistemology," in *Jacques Maritain, A Philosopher in the World,* edited by Jean-Louis Allard (Ottawa: University of Ottawa Press, 1985), 197–206.

9. John G. Trapani Jr., "'Radiance': The Metaphysical Foundations of Maritain's Aesthetics," in *Beauty, Art and the Polis,* edited by Alice Ramos (Washington, D.C.: American Maritain Association, 2000), 11–19.

10. John G. Trapani, Jr., *Poetry, Beauty, and Contemplation: The Complete Aesthetics of Jacques Maritain* (Washington, DC: The Catholic University of America Press, 2011).

III. Connatural Knowing in the Realm of Fine Art

In his first published work, *Bergsonian Philosophy and Thomism*, Maritain had this to say about the role of the intellect in the connatural knowing of a beautiful thing in the realm of art:

> But most often the cogitative works with the other sensible powers in the service of the intellect. In this case we see why it can create in us, aside from our organic faculties, a certain sympathy or connaturality with beings that are themselves corporal or with material objects, in virtue of which the intellect will be spontaneously inclined toward this or that judgement.... In the same way, in his work the artist is directed by a kind of sensible sympathy which unites him to both the living reality he wishes to express and the means of expression he employs; thus he makes his model confess ... and the poet knows his heroes the better for the fact that it is always some aspect of himself that he expresses in them. One might say that art attempts precisely to make us divine sensibly in its very singularity that individual nature that our senses give us in its accidents and its material operations but not in itself, and which our intellect ... does not know directly as individual; that is why, even from the point of view of the perfection of our knowledge, we have so great a need of art and artists.[11]

Here Maritain notes that the senses grasp the singular thing, but only in its accidents and material operations, and the human intellect grasps the common nature of the thing, but does not grasp the nature of the individual as such. He then says that a value of art is that it attempts to make us grasp the individual nature sensibly and that this has to do with the perfection of our knowledge. If art is trying to make us grasp the nature of the singular thing, then it seems it is trying to conjoin the modes of knowing of both sense and intellect: sense so that we might grasp the singular, and intellect so that we might grasp the nature. In this early work Maritain stresses connatural knowledge as the way in which both sense and intellect are prepared to know things intuitively.

This notion of combining sense and intellect in the realm of art is elaborated on by Maritain in *Art and Scholasticism*, specifically in the chapter on art and beauty. In commenting on Saint Thomas' description of beauty as that which, being seen, pleases,[12] Maritain writes:

11. Maritain, *Bergsonian Philosophy and Thomism*, 165.
12. St. Thomas Aquinas, *Summa theologiae* I, q. 5, a. 4, ad 1.

> Beauty is essentially an object of intelligence.... But it also, in a way, falls under the grasp of the senses, in so far as in man they serve the intellect and can themselves take delight in knowing.... The part played by the senses in the perception of beauty is even rendered enormous in us, and well-nigh indispensable, by the very fact that our intelligence is not intuitive, as is the intelligence of the angel; it sees, to be sure, but on condition of abstracting and discoursing; only sense knowledge possesses perfectly in man the intuitiveness required for the perception of the beautiful. Thus man can doubtless enjoy purely intelligible beauty, but the beautiful that is connatural to man is the beautiful that delights the intellect through the senses and through their intuition. Such is also the beautiful that is proper to our art, which shapes a sensible matter in order to delight the spirit.[13]

The beautiful things that we as humans can most properly know are individual material things. We know these as the existing singulars they are only through the senses. Yet the senses do not know such things as beings, as good, or as beautiful. The intellect knows being, goodness, and beauty, but only by abstracting such aspects from things perceived by the senses. After abstraction, the intellect properly knows being, goodness, and beauty as universal and common aspects of sensible material things. As Maritain said above, "Beauty is essentially an object of intelligence." Yet Maritain seems to wonder whether a twofold and somewhat divided knowing of material things adequately explains our everyday experience of beautiful things. We do spontaneously delight in the goodness or the beauty of a material thing even as we see it or hear it; we do set out to make individual material things to be good and hence beautiful works. How do we explain this close connection between the senses and the intellect? This is what concerns Maritain.

He decides that there is a strong opposition between scientific knowledge and the intuition of artistic beauty. According to Maritain, "The intuition of artistic beauty thus stands at the opposite extreme from the abstraction of scientific truth. For with the former it is through the very apprehension of the sense that the light of being penetrates the intelligence."[14] This opposition is so extreme, according to Maritain, that no abstraction paves the way for the intuition of artistic beauty. He continues:

> The intelligence in this case, diverted from all effort of abstraction, rejoices without work and without discourse. It is dispensed from its usual labor; it does not

13. Maritain, *Art and Scholasticism*, 23–24.
14. Ibid., 25.

have to disengage an intelligible from the matter in which it is buried, in order to go over its different attributes step by step; like a stag at the gushing spring, intelligence has nothing to do but drink; it drinks the clarity of being. Caught up in the intuition of sense, it is irradiated by an intelligible light that is suddenly given to it, in the very sensible in which it glitters, and which it does not seize sub ratione veri, but rather sub ratione delectabilis.[15]

This is a somewhat puzzling text. Maritain tells us (1) that the intellect is "diverted from all effort of abstraction," in short, that it does not have to "disengage an intelligible from the matter in which it is bound," and yet (2) the intellect gets to "drink ... the clarity of being." If we wonder how the intellect can drink the clarity of being, i.e. perform an act of knowing, without being informed, and thus actuated, by abstraction, Maritain tells us (3) that something is indeed given to the intellect, since it is "irradiated by an intelligible light." If we wonder why this should not be considered abstraction, Maritain continues that (4) the intelligible light that is given to the intellect is given to it "in the very sensible in which it glitters." Supposedly the intelligible light is a light coming from the agent intellect acting on the sensible thing. Somehow the possible intellect is being informed but not by an intelligible form separated from a sensible thing but rather by an intelligible form as it is still contained in the sensible thing. How is this possible without the intellect and imagination somehow forming one power?

Maritain elaborates on this matter in a celebrated footnote. He immediately tells us that what we are dealing with is "a perception of the beautiful by the intellect using the senses as instruments."[16] If the perception of the beautiful is an act of "the intellect using the senses," then the distinction of intellect and sense is clearly not being denied. So we return to the question of how the intellect is able to act without being informed by abstraction. On the following page, Maritain shifts his focus slightly by arguing that the beautiful object is not grasped through concepts: "the splendor or radiance of the form glittering in the beautiful object is not presented to the mind by a concept or an idea, but rather by the sensible object intuitively grasped—in which there is transmitted, as through an instrumental cause, the radiance of a form."[17]

If we wonder why grasping the beautiful thing through a concept is a problem, Maritain gives us a reason. It is important here to keep in mind

15. Ibid., 26.

16. Ibid., 162n56.

17. Ibid., 163.

that Maritain still has Thomas' definition of beauty as "that which, being seen, pleases" in mind. It seems that beauty must please the intellect even as the beautiful thing is sensibly grasped. This, according to Maritain, excludes the formation of a concept. He writes:

> In the perception of the beautiful the intellect is, through the means of the sensible intuition itself, placed in the presence of a radiant intelligibility . . . which insofar as it produces the joy of the beautiful cannot be disengaged or separated from its sense matrix and consequently does not procure an intellectual knowledge expressible in a concept.[18]

The strong union between intellect and sense which these texts from *Art and Scholasticism* seem to demand is set forth very clearly by Maritain in the same place: "To understand this, let us recall that it is intellect and sense as forming but one, or, if one may so speak, intelligentiated sense, which gives rise in the heart to aesthetic joy."[19]

In these texts from *Art and Scholasticism* Maritain makes it clear that the grasping of a beautiful thing is essentially an intellectual act, but an intellectual act of a unique kind. The intellectual act is unique because it has a singular thing as its specific object. Because the human intellect cannot by itself grasp singular material things, Maritain must argue that the intellect is acting in and through the senses which are able to intuit a particular thing. To act at all, the intellect must be informed, but to grasp a singular thing the intellect must act in union with the senses grasping the singular themselves. How the intellect can act in a way both proper to its own nature as immaterial power and yet also act in and through the senses as if the two formed one power is not yet clear.

In a much later work, *Creative Intuition in Art and Poetry,* after stating that "poetic intuition, which in itself is an intellective flash,"[20] Maritain describes the thing grasped by such an artistic intuition:

> Poetic intuition is not directed toward essences, for essences are disengaged from concrete reality in a concept, a universal idea, and scrutinized by means of reasoning; they are an object for speculative knowledge, they are not the thing grasped by poetic intuition. Poetic intuition is directed toward concrete existence as connatural to the soul pierced by a given emotion: that is to say, each time toward some singular existent.[21]

18. Ibid., 163–64.
19. Ibid., 164.
20. Jacques Maritain, *Creative Intuition in Art and Poetry,* 123.
21. Ibid., 125–26.

In *Bergsonian Philosophy and Thomism* Maritain wrote that art makes us try to grasp the nature of the singular thing. Here he tells us that poetic intuition is not directed toward essences at all. If what Maritain means by not being directed toward essences is not being directed toward essences as abstract and common to many, then there is no disagreement between the texts. A little further in *Creative Intuition* he reiterates his point about the object of poetic intuition: "Such is, I think, the thing grasped by poetic intuition: the singular existent which resounds in the subjectivity of the poet, together with all the other realities which echo in this existent, and which it conveys in the manner of a sign."[22] When Maritain argues that essences are disengaged from concrete reality in a concept, he is presupposing that abstraction of an intelligible species and the informing of the intellect by that species has occurred, since that is what prepares the intellect to express something of that intelligible species in concepts. Hence it would seem that Maritain is claiming that in the case of poetic intuition neither abstraction nor the formation of concepts prepares the way and makes the act possible. Granting that the knowing of the beauty of a particular thing is essentially a work of the intellect, the questions we need to ask at this point are as follows: (1) Has the intellect been informed or actuated by the agent or illuminating intellect in order to prepare the way for poetic intuition? (2) If the intellect has been informed, then in what way has it been informed and by what has it been informed? (3) However the intellect has been prepared to perform an act of poetic intuition, why does Maritain think it reasonable to suppose that such an informing of the intellect is not properly called abstraction and does not lead to the formation of concepts?

1. Has the Possible Intellect Been Informed by the Agent Intellect in Poetic Intuition?

In response to the first question, as has already been indicated, Maritain makes it clear that the intellect is actuated and informed preparatory to an act of poetic intuition. Commenting on what he calls the twofold life of the human intellect, he writes:

> We must admit that in the spiritual unconscious of the intellect, at the single root of the soul's powers, there is, apart from the process which tends to knowledge by means of concepts and abstract ideas, something which is preconceptual or

22. Ibid., 126.

> nonconceptual and nevertheless in a state of definite intellectual actuation: not, therefore, a mere way to the concept, as was the "impressed pattern" I spoke of in the preceding chapter, but another kind of germ, which does not tend toward a concept to be formed, and which is already an intellective form or act fully determined though enveloped in the night of the spiritual unconscious. In other words, such a thing is knowledge in act, but nonconceptual knowledge.[23]

A little further on, in speaking of what makes poetic intuition possible and how both sense and intellect are involved, Maritain writes: "And through the vital though nonconceptual actuation of the intellect all the powers of the soul are also actuated in their roots."[24] That the intellect has been informed under the activity of the agent or illuminating intellect Maritain makes clear more than once. Speaking of the unity of powers that makes poetic intuition possible, he states: "The powers of the soul envelop one another, the universe of sense perception is in the universe of imagination, which is in the universe of intelligence. And they are all, within the intellect, stirred and activated by the light of the Illuminating Intellect."[25]

In the above three texts we see Maritain elaborating on the extremely close union between intellect and sense to which he referred in *Art and Scholasticism* as "intelligentiated sense." It is still not clear just how this union works and how it respects the immaterial nature of the intellect and the way in which it must be informed before it can act as the power it is. It is clear that, in preparation for the act of poetic intuition, the intellect has been informed under the influence of the agent or illuminating intellect. Such an informing of the possible intellect by the agent intellect has traditionally been understood as the result of an act of abstraction on the part of the agent intellect. Through its illumination of some image within the imagination, the agent intellect immaterializes or spiritualizes a form contained within an image in the imagination and imposes such an abstracted form on the possible intellect. Yet despite the fact that the agent intellect is informing or actuating the possible intellect by means of something that has been rendered immaterial and spiritual in preparation for poetic intuition,[26] Maritain argues that abstraction is not occurring. Let us consider what he has to say.

23. Ibid., 111–12.

24. Ibid., 124.

25. Ibid., 110.

26. Cf. ibid., 121, 123.

2. *In What Way and by What Has the Possible Intellect Been Informed?*

We are now dealing with the second question listed above, namely, if the intellect has been informed, then in what way has it been informed, and by what has it been informed? Recall that Maritain argues that there is a twofold life of the intellect, one which is exemplified in our abstract speculative knowledge of the essences of things, and the other which is exemplified in what Maritain is calling the connatural knowledge of poetic intuition and which has to do with the experiencing and production of a singular work of beauty.[27] This doctrine on a twofold manner of functioning of the human intellect, with one manner of functioning being peculiar to the production and experiencing of beautiful material things, goes back at least to Maritain's earlier work *Art and Scholasticism*. In that earlier work, as we have seen, Maritain wrote that the intuition of artistic beauty and the abstraction of scientific truth were opposed to one another as extremes.[28] In artistic intuition, according to Maritain, the intellect, with no effort of abstraction and without separating an intelligible content from the sensible in which it was contained, was yet able to grasp what was intelligible in the sensible in and through the intuition of the senses and by means of an intelligible light given to it, presumably by the light of the agent intellect.[29]

Let us now return to Maritain's account in *Creative Intuition*. In speaking of the first, or speculative, life of the intellect, Maritain argued as follows about the actuating of the intellect by way of the abstracting work of the illuminating intellect:

> [T]he knowing intellect, in order to know, must be actuated, and shaped, by what is drawn from the images, and the images are imbued with materiality. Thus, at a first step, the intelligible content present in the images ... is made intelligible in act in a spiritual form (species impressa, impressed pattern), let us say, in an intelligible germ, which is received from the images by the intellect, under the activation of the Illuminating Intellect.[30]

On the other hand, when he comes to speak of how the actuating of the intellect which leads to poetic intuition occurs, in the second life of the intellect, instead of having the agent intellect abstract or immaterialize the

27. Ibid., 110–11.
28. Maritain, *Art and Scholasticism*, 25.
29. Ibid., 26.
30. Maritain, *Creative Intuition*, 97.

intelligible content from an image in the imagination, Maritain looks to emotion as part of the explanation. He argues that it is an emotion, one which has been caused in us by our experience of things in the world about us, that is raised to the level of the intellect by the activity of the agent or illuminating intellect. Speaking of poetic intuition, he writes: "... poetic knowledge proceeds from the intellect in its most genuine and essential capacity as intellect, though through the indispensable instrumentality of feeling."[31] That this emotion comes from the level of the senses and, when immaterialized,[32] takes the place at least of the concept, if not of both concept and impressed intelligible species, is made clear by Maritain when he asks: "How can emotion be thus raised to the level of the intellect and, as it were, take the place of the concept in becoming for the intellect a determining means or instrumental vehicle through which reality is grasped?"[33] So, instead of the agent intellect acting simply on an image of some material thing and raising it to that level of immateriality whereby it may be received into the intellect as able to know, the agent intellect is acting on an emotion from the sensible realm and raising it to the level of the intellect as able to know. Because of the constant interaction between cognition and appetite, on both sense and intellectual levels, one assumes that the emotion that is being raised to the level of the intellect by the agent intellect is in the imagination as something sensibly known by it. That it is not a mere emotion as such that is immaterialized by the agent intellect, but rather an emotion that points to things in the world about us was indicated in the above quote, and is made abundantly clear in the following comment:

> It becomes for the intellect a determining means or instrumental vehicle through which the things which have impressed this emotion on the soul, and the deeper, invisible things that are contained in them or connected with them, and which have ineffable correspondence or coaptation with the soul thus affected, and which resound in it, are grasped and known obscurely. It is by means of such a spiritualized emotion that poetic intuition, which in itself is an intellective flash, is born in the unconscious of the spirit.[34]

Let us recall the second question we asked: if the intellect has been informed then in what way has it been informed and by what has it been informed? Maritain's response is that the intellect has been informed by an

31. Ibid., 119.
32. Cf. ibid., 123.
33. Ibid., 121.
34. Ibid., 123.

emotion raised from the level of sense to the level of the intellect by the illuminating intellect. The act of the agent intellect immaterialized or spiritualized the emotion and it was then received into the intellect. The emotion thus received into the intellect indirectly carried with it into the intellect those things in the material world that caused the emotion in the artist. Such material causes of the emotion were conveyed into the intellect not clearly but obscurely inasmuch as the emotion pointed to them as an effect and as a sign of them and by making the artist connaturally more aware of them. What is not clear at this point is why this emotion, immaterialized by the agent intellect and imposed on the intellect as able to know, should not be considered as one more example of abstraction. Abstraction, after all, is simply an activity of the agent intellect raising something from the level of the senses to its own properly immaterial level. And if the emotion has been spiritualized, as Maritain indicates, in being raised from the sensible level to the level of the intellect, then, because of how it exists in the intellect as something removed from the individuating conditions of matter, how can it still be a sign of or a pointer to a material singular as such? It can be readily admitted that what has been abstracted from the level of the senses always points in some way to a singular insofar as it is an abstract likeness of some singular thing. But that does not enable the human intellect as such to know directly material singulars as such. That remains the function of the senses, as Maritain ordinarily indicates. And yet in the matter of poetic intuition Maritain says that singulars are just what the human intellect somehow grasps. Recall what he said about the thing grasped by poetic intuition: "Poetic intuition is directed toward concrete existence as connatural to the soul pierced by a given emotion: that is to say, each time toward some singular existent."[35] An additional problem which suggests itself at this point is: either the things obscurely pointed to by the spiritualized emotion have also been immaterialized by the agent intellect or they have not. If the things obscurely pointed to by the immaterialized emotion are also raised up by the agent intellect and imposed somehow on the intellect as able to know, then they also will be abstract. If they are not raised up by the agent intellect, then how would the spiritualized emotion enable the intellect to grasp them at all?

35. Ibid., 126.

3. *Why Are Abstraction and Concept Formation Not Taking Place?*

We are now dealing with the third question asked above: However the intellect has been prepared to perform an act of poetic intuition, why does Maritain think it reasonable to suppose that such an informing of the intellect is not properly abstraction and does not lead properly to the forming of concepts? Why does Maritain refuse to call the informing of the intellect preparatory to poetic intuition a result of abstraction when he admits that the agent intellect is immaterializing or spiritualizing an emotion from the sense level before imposing it on the intellect? His response would seem to be twofold. First, because the very act of poetic intuition grasps a singular object and not a common essence or nature, Maritain is inclined to deny that the spiritualizing of a sensible emotion and the imposing of it on the possible intellect is properly abstraction. Second, Maritain seems to consider the process that begins with the illuminating intellect immaterializing an intelligible content from a sensible image in the imagination and imposing it on the intellect, a process he calls abstraction, to lead inevitably to the formation of concepts. If we ask what is wrong with that, the response is that the intellectual delighting in or production of a singular thing of beauty does not possess the clarity of conceptual activity. If the process of abstracting an essence from a sensible image and imposing it in the form of an intelligible species on the possible intellect leads inevitably to concept formation, then, since concepts are not directly and intrinsically involved in delighting in and producing works of art, we need to postulate another process. This is what Maritain is concerned to do.

What is distinctive, then, about the alternate process, the second life of the intellect which Maritain postulates? First we do not start with a sensible image of a material thing as that raw material on which the agent intellect will work. Instead, we begin with a sensible emotion which, because it has been caused in us by one or more material things which have affected us, points us to such things on the sensible level in a connatural way. Second, even though the emotion is being raised to the level of the intellect by being made immaterial, yet it is not being put into the intellect as an object to be understood, but rather as an emotion which, on the intellectual level now, according to Maritain, makes us connaturally like the material causes of the emotion, and thus somehow points the intellect in an obscure way to those singulars as such. Maritain is clear that it is not the intellect acting by itself that grasps material singulars; rather it is the intellect acting somehow through the senses that grasps material singulars. The intellect is able to grasp the singulars to which it has been connaturally inclined in and through the intuition of the senses themselves because of some especially strong union between the intellect and the senses, a union which Maritain has trouble clarifying.[36]

IV. Could Maritain Have Taken an Alternate Path?

Could Maritain have taken an alternate route, one that did not lead to the intellect somehow grasping singular material things in and through the intuition of the senses because of some strong union between sense and intellect that is difficult to understand? He could have written that a delight with a certain kind of beauty on both sensible and intellectual levels would suffice to connature a person to that type of beauty. This was the sole approach taken by Maritain in *Bergsonian Philosophy and Thomism*. The result would be that both sense and intellect would be more ready both to perceive beauty and to perceive how to bring about more beauty. The intellect would be informed, by way of abstraction, by aspects of sensible things in the normal way. The more connatured to beauty of a given type one is, the more the abstraction that occurred would be free from any hint of work or effort, even in the matter of the preparation of phantasms prior to abstraction. The intellect would also likely be informed, without abstraction, by the emotion of delight as existing in the will. It is clear that no abstraction occurs in the interaction between intellect and will since both are immaterial powers. Because of a strong desire for more beauty of a certain type, the intellect and cogitative power would both see, obscurely and a step at a time, how to bring about an instance of such beauty. No conceptualizing would occur because of the obscurity and piecemeal grasping of how to bring about a work. It would be as if the intellect and cogitative power, acting in conjunction with each other, would be groping their way toward a clearer vision of the work which would become as clear as it could only in the produced work itself. It would be somewhat as Maritain himself put it in

36. Cf. Maritain, "Art and Beauty," in *Art and Scholasticism*, and ibid., n. 56.

an essay entitled "The Freedom of Song": ". . . in itself the factive or creative idea is not a concept; it is an intellective gaze; it is an intellection having for concept, for intelligible fruit engendered—but exterior to the mind and born of matter –the work itself that is made, the object not of knowledge but of creation."[37] My contention is that such an obscure non-conceptual gaze is possible only following on abstraction. Abstraction informs the intellect by raising something from the level of the senses to the immaterial life proper to the intellect. Having been informed, the intellect is then able to know. Such knowing can in theory be no more than the simple activity of gazing Maritain refers to above. It need not involve the formation of concepts and the activity of reasoning. This is, after all, how knowing works in the external senses. Once informed, the act of sensing is able to follow with no expressing of what is sensed. Such an act of gazing that does not involve the formation of concepts and leads to the process of reasoning would be an intuiting that would involve the cooperation of sense and intellect, all without supposing the intellect itself intuits singulars somehow in and though sense intuition. It is the person who, using both sense and intellect, intuitively delights in the beauty of a singular thing.

V. What Seems to Have Gone Wrong in Maritain's Approach?

Two things seem to have gone wrong in Maritain's attempt to deal with the reality of our intellectual intuition of the beauty of a singular material thing and with the artist's ability to grope his way, using both sense and intellect, toward the creation of a singular thing of beauty: (1) Maritain seems to treat the various cognitive powers too much as if they were separate agents in their own right, and fails to emphasize sufficiently the unity of the person who acts using his various powers; (2) he treats abstraction and the consequent informing of the intellect as if it lead inevitably to the formation of concepts. What is wrong in each case?

In the first case, because our intuition of beauty in a singular material thing demands the close connection between intellect and sense, a connection so close that they seem to be united in one act, Maritain seems to try to find a way to unite the powers of intellect and sense so that they

37. Jacques Maritain, "The Freedom of Song," in *Art and Poetry*, translated by E. de P. Matthews (New York: Philosophical Library, 1943), 81–82.

might act as one power. Initially he speaks of "intelligentiated sense"; later he emphasizes the way the external senses have their root in the interior sense powers and the interior sense powers have their root in the intellect. Such an approach cannot work. Even though the sense powers are for the sake of the intellect, and intellect and sense work in close conjunction with one another, yet they remain separate powers. Each is informed in a different way. If we want to explain a seeming unity of powers, the only way to do so is to emphasize the unity of the person who acts using his various powers. The material world is constantly acting on our external senses, and the agent intellect is always in act, illuminating whatever is in the imagination and transferring the result to the intellect as able to know. Since the initial activity of both sense and intellect is an intuition, or a mere seeing of something, and because none of this involves labor or work and seems to happen automatically, nothing prevents a person from delighting in an intellectual intuition of something concerning which he also enjoys a sensible intuition. Since the intuitions of both sense and intellect seem to go together naturally and habitually, why would they not seem as if one to us?

In the second case, it is clear that a power must first be informed before it can act. The informing of the human intellect relative to the knowing of material things takes place via the action of the agent intellect transferring something from the level of the senses to that of the intellect. Ordinarily this is called abstraction. Yet Maritain does not want to speak of abstraction taking place prior and preparatory to an act of poetic intuition. His reason seems to be twofold: (1) abstraction is associated with what is abstract, i.e. what is lacking in singularity and is common to many; (2) abstraction seems to lead straight to the formation of concepts. What is wrong with abstraction giving us what is abstract and common to many is that poetic intuition is focused on the beauty of a singular thing. When it comes to poetic intuition, Maritain wants the intellect to grasp a material singular as such. This seems to be an unreasonable demand on Maritain's part. As already indicated, the unity of the person acting and the close conjunction between sense grasping the singular and intellect grasping something of being or beauty ought to suffice to explain our experience. In the second case, what is wrong with abstraction leading to the formation of concepts is that concepts are characterized by intellectual clarity, whereas poetic intuition is an obscure intellectual grasping of something of the object. This seems to be the case both when we experience and delight in a beautiful thing and are at a loss for words, and also when the artist is groping his way, via poetic intuition, to the making of a beautiful material thing. In order to explain how the intellect is informed by the agent intellect in such a way as to lead to an obscure intellectual intuition of a singular material thing as such, Maritain supposes that the agent intellect is spiritualizing an emotional response, on the level of the senses, to one or more singular material things. Because what is spiritualized and imposed on the possible intellect is both an emotion and only an indirect pointing to singular things, the result ought to be an intellectual act that is obscure, as well as an act that somehow grasps a singular as such. Maritain's theory here seems particularly weak. Emotion is involved, to be sure. But why not say that emotion is involved because sensible delight connatures the senses to intuit more quickly and readily what delights us sensibly, and intellectual delight connatures the intellect to intuit more quickly and readily what delights the intellect? Why not say that the person, having been connatured on both sense and intellectual levels to what is beautiful, abstracts an aspect of beauty from what his senses delight in and enjoys a poetic intuition that conjoins both a sense and an intellectual intuition? Abstraction need not lead to concept formation in every case.

IV

JACQUES MARITAIN, HENRI BERGSON, AND MYSTICISM

MARK MOES

Metaphysics, Epistemology, and Theology in Plato's *Theaetetus* 151d–187e and in Maritain's *Bergsonian Philosophy and Thomism*

Striking parallels exist between Socrates' arguments against Theaetetus and his teacher Theodorus in the first half of Plato's *Theaetetus* and Jacques Maritain's arguments against Bergson in chapters 6–9 of *Bergsonian Philosophy and Thomism*.[1] Maritain's critique of Bergson's metaphysics of pure duration is similar to Socrates' critique of the Heraclitean flux, and his critique of Bergson's theory of a-conceptual intuition—the theory that conceptual reasoning constitutes a distorting "arresting" of the vital flux—is similar to Socrates' critique of the thesis that knowledge is *aesthesis* unaided by any awareness of concepts or of unchanging universal forms. Furthermore, Maritain's exposition (especially in the Preface to the Second Edition of the book) of the way in which Bergson's errors in metaphysics and epistemology align him with certain potentially distorting theological tendencies of "Indian" mystical thought is similar to Socrates' attempt to show Theodorus that his philosophical errors are bound up with errors in *theology*.

1. Jacques Maritain, *Bergsonian Philosophy and Thomism*, 2nd edition, translated by Mabelle Andison in collaboration with J. Gordon Andison (New York: Philosophical Library, 1955). First edition originally published in French as *La philosophie bergsonienne: etudes critiques par J. Maritain* (Paris: Reviere et cie, 1914).

I. Metaphysics

Let us begin with Socrates' discussion of the metaphysics of flux in the *Theaetetus*. Responding to a query from Socrates, Theaetetus at 151e defines knowledge as "nothing other than" (*ouk allo ti he*) perceptual intuition (*aesthesis*).[2] *Aisthesis* in ancient Greek refers focally to direct perception by bodily senses, but by extension can refer to any kind of direct mental apprehension, sensory or intellectual. Socrates identifies this definition of knowledge with Protagoras' *homo mensura* doctrine, the doctrine that whatever anyone directly apprehends is unerringly the case for the person doing the apprehending. Furthermore, Socrates contends that this Protagorean doctrine presupposes a certain Heraclitean metaphysical doctrine of flux, a doctrine entailing that "there is nothing which in itself is just one thing, nothing which you could rightly call anything or any kind of thing" (152d). The flux doctrine entails that there are in reality no enduring substances and no fixed *kinds* or *forms* of substance or of anything else. There are particular events and particular bundles of events, but no event or bundle endures even for an instant as a substantial thing with any enduring attributes. According to this doctrine, a perceiver is an ever-changing bundle of unique event-movements. And if a perceiver has an experience of, say, a particular color, the experience results from a unique momentary interaction between a unique momentary perceiving-bundle and some other unique event or event-bundle. The color is "not itself a distinct entity, either outside your eyes or in your eyes" (153d). And the color experience is private to the individual percipient and therefore incorrigible, for there is no objective color essence that could provide a standard of sameness for diverse color experiences.

Theaetetus admits at 157d (and Theodorus admits at 161a) that the equation of knowledge with *aesthesis* presupposes a Protagorean theory of judgment and a Heraclitean metaphysics of flux. So Socrates proceeds to test the coherence and intelligibility of such theories. He begins at 152c–157d by discussing some problems faced by flux metaphysics concerning identity-over-time (a discussion resumed later at 179c–183c). If all is flux, he suggests, there is no way to make sense of the enduring identity of a perceiver who has a color experience, nor any way to make sense of any enduring color-event or bundle of events *other than* the perceiver. If neither

2. All translations of the Theatetus are from *The Theatetus of Plato*, translated by M. J. Levett, revised by Myles Burnyeat (Indianapolis, Indiana: Hackett, 1990).

perceiver nor perceived object can be identified as enduring even momentarily, then no putative *interaction* between the two can be identified. But on the flux theory it is precisely such an interaction that accounts for the coming into being of the putatively unique color experience. Socrates at 156a–157d expounds what he takes to be the most sophisticated version of the flux doctrine, and Theatetus judges it, initially, as "an extraordinarily reasonable view" (157d). According to this version, everything that exists is some motion (event). All events or bundles of events can come into active and/or passive relationships with other events or bundles of events and, sometimes, as in perceptual or intuitive events, these relationships generate new "offspring" events or bundles. These events have no *intrinsic properties* but only *relational properties* (157a: "There is nothing which in itself is just one thing; all things are coming into being relatively to something"). No particular *event* can have an enduring identity, for this would require it to endure as the substrate of certain *intrinsic* defining properties, but on the flux theory no event has any intrinsic property but is constituted only by its relations with other (inscrutably unique) events. Nor can any bundle or aggregate of events have an enduring identity *even as an aggregate*, for an aggregate that was identical over time would have to be an enduring aggregate of constituents that endured as long as the aggregate did. But since none of the aggregate-constitutive events can have enduring identities, since their relations with other events—the relational properties which supposedly define them—are ceaselessly changing, this is impossible.

We need now to attend to the similarity of Maritain's critique of Bergson's metaphysics to that of Socrates' critique of the Heraclitean flux.[3] Just as Socrates contends that Protagorean epistemology presupposes Heraclitean flux, so Maritain contends that for Bergson "what *being* is to *intelligence* [according to the perennial philosophy], *duration* is to *intuition* [in his system]."[4] Socrates points out that in the Heraclitean flux there are neither enduring things possessing substantial forms nor timeless properties or categories of property of any sort that might be recurrently exemplified

3. In order to understand Maritain's critique, we must realize that not only had he been a disciple of Bergson for a time but that even after coming to endorse Thomistic metaphysics he continued to hold great respect for Bergson's thought as a laudable struggle "against the so-called positive materialism and against the Kantian relativism," as something that had freed Bergson's disciples "from the heavy yoke of atheism," and as a significant attempt to undermine post-Cartesian rationalisms and cosmologies. Maritain, *Bergsonian Philosophy*, 119–23.

4. Ibid., 172.

in things or events as properties intrinsic to them, hence that there can be no enduring self-identical perceivers or events or objects perceived.

Maritain also draws out something implicit in Socrates' critique of the flux doctrine. He shows that the Heraclitean doctrine of flux shares with the Bergsonian doctrine of *duration* an inability to make sense of time. Both doctrines fail to conceive of time as constituted by the perseverance in being of finite temporal *things* which endure. Both conceive of change as continuous, like quantity, so that no matter how far we divide change we will never reach a temporal part that is not further divisible. Both fail to countenance Aristotle's insight that the parts of a continuum exist only potentially, because both fail to make use of any doctrine of potency and act.[5] In the end, then, both fail to account for the reality of any distinction between past, present, and future,[6] or any distinction between time and eternity, because they incoherently identify as the only reality a time/flux/duration that is not temporal but eternal. They replace the Parmenidean One with a Heraclitean One—a "pure change" that supposedly is the "substance of things." Maritain concedes that time involves flux, as pure quantity involves flux to the extent that it is not yet ordered mathematically. But he contends that real time presupposes both the *movement of the enduring thing which changes* and the *mind with a memory* that orders and numbers that movement. Time—the number of movement according to before and after—is not only a mode (quantity of duration) of an accident of an enduring *thing* (the movement of the thing), but also it is completely what it

5. Ibid., 174. "Modern philosophy," writes Maritain, "has an aversion for the doctrine of potency and act, which is the only possible foundation for the philosophical theory of movement and becoming.... Aristotle, founding metaphysics, has recognized that being, affirmed with evidence by the intellect, and change attested with evidence by the senses, are equally real and do not contradict one another in the least, because being in act comes neither from non-being, nor from another being in act, but from being *in potency*: that is to say that before change, the new being, the term of the change, was in no way given in act and nevertheless was not pure nothingness; but that before change, this new being, the term of the change, was in the mutable thing in the capacity of *real possibility*, which will be transformed into actual reality under the influence of a cause itself in act." Maritain perhaps was aware that this founding of metaphysics on the doctrine of potency and act was a development of ideas found in the discussion between the Eleatic Stranger and Theaetetus in Plato's *Sophist*. (Maritain quotes *Sophist* 248e on the activity, life, and intelligence of the divine nature.) Perhaps he was also aware that the "communion of the highest kinds" passage of *Sophist* 254b–257a contains a Platonic "proof" for the existence of a transcendent "One," suggesting that all distinct things that fall under the kinds of "being" and "identity" and "non-identity" and "change" and "rest" must ultimately derive from a higher Unity which transcends these categories.

6. Maritain, *Bergsonian Philosophy*, 176.

is only because the human mind measures it.[7] But neither the Heraclitean flux nor the Bergsonian duration allows metaphysical (or linguistic) room either for enduring self-identical temporal things or for embodied minds.

II. Epistemology

Maritain's critique of Bergson's theory of a-conceptual intuition is also quite similar to Socrates' critique of the thesis that knowledge is *aesthesis*. Socrates discusses in 157e–179b problems faced by the Protagorean theory of the incorrigibility of judgments of experience. This theory presupposes the flux metaphysics according to which no events or bundles of events have any intrinsic properties. On this metaphysics there can be no *truth* of the matter concerning either the quality of any subjective experience or concerning the real quality of any object perceived. Hence quality experience is incorrigible; no perceiver can make a wrong judgment about quality. But Socrates points out that this Protagorean-Heraclitean incorrigibility account of perceptual intuition flies in the face of judgments held true by almost everyone. For example, everybody agrees, first, that dreamers and madmen have perceptual intuitions that are mistaken; second, that people who are ill often make mistaken qualitative judgments about food and drink; third, that various wise men and wise connoisseurs are able to correct the mistaken perceptual-quality-judgments of unwise and untrained persons. Fourth, the content of certain kinds of perceptual intuitions are inextricably bound up with certain linguistically expressed *meaning contents* that are repeatable and stable over time. When people hear other persons speaking in a foreign language, they can be mistaken in a number of ways about what it is that they hear. They may, even if they understand the foreign language to some degree, mistake the meaning of what they hear, and they may, if they do not understand the foreign language at all, mistake for gibberish what they hear, what is in fact a meaningful utterance. Fifth, mistaken perceptual *memories* constitute counterexamples to the Protagorean incorrigibility thesis, if memories count as perceptual intuitions, and, if they do not, correct memories constitute counterexamples to the equation of knowledge with perceptual intuition. Sixth, common sense maintains that perceptual intuitions are events or states that can have many properties that events or states of knowing cannot have. For example, the

7. Ibid., 173.

former, but not the latter, can be dim or clear, from near at hand or from a distance, or intense or slight. Therefore, if identical things are indiscernible (have all the same properties), knowledge cannot be identical with perceptual intuition.

At *Theaetetus* 169d ff. Socrates recruits Theodorus to replace his student Theaetetus as his chief interlocutor, and then he expands upon his third criticism of the incorrigibility doctrine, the view that some men are wiser than others concerning certain subject matters and hence are able to correct the mistaken judgments of others. In this context Socrates focuses upon the frequent occurrence of mistaken *value judgments* made by unwise persons. He asserts that all men hold that, in matters of all kinds of craft expertise, master craftsmen exhibit a knowledge or wisdom that non-master-craftsmen lack, and that these masters most often have true intuitions whereas non-masters have false intuitions about the goods that are internal to their crafts—goods such as bodily health in medicine, the justice or piety of action or the goodness of virtue in ethics, the good of the community in statesmanship, etc. The fact that all men accord epistemic authority to craft masters undercuts in a very powerful way, suggests Socrates, Protagoras' incorrigibility thesis that every person's judgment about matters of value is true-for-that-person.[8] Socrates' craft-based argument against Protagoras gives him occasion to turn his attention to the craft of statesmanship, a craft he characterizes as having to do with questions "of what may or may not fittingly be done, of justice and injustice, and of what is sanctioned by religion and what is not" (172a). Socrates maintains that many persons who deny that such a craft of ethics/politics exists, and affirm instead that such matters are true or false only relative to particular communities under the sway of particular rulers, inconsistently hold at the same time that some laws are better than others *in the long run*. He reminds Theodorus that just as good trainers and doctors make true judgments about the future results of different kinds of lifestyles or treatments on individual clients, so good legislators and judges make true judgments about the future results of certain legal enactments and legal judgments on particular communities. Theodorus admits that the superi-

8. As an aside, Socrates maintains that in putting forward the incorrigibility thesis, Protagoras equivocates on the notion of "truth." He in effect redefines truth as a person-relative property (true-for-me) while at the same time asserting that the thesis itself is true in an objective non-person-relative sense of "true." If he were to claim that he uses "truth" in a univocal sense, his view becomes self-refuting, since then it entails that the incorrigibility thesis itself is not true *simpliciter* but only true-for-Protagoras, while false-for-those-who-reject-it (170d–171d).

or predictive power of the judgments of trainers, doctors, and adepts at the statesman's craft constitutes a powerful objection to the Protagorean thesis that every man's judgment is as true as any other man's.

At this point in the *Theaetetus* (183c–186e) Socrates turns to his final refutation of the thesis that perceptual intuition is identical with knowledge, and of its corollary thesis about the incorrigibility of judgment. Socrates maintains that persons become aware of various sensory qualities by means of various different sensory powers, but are only able to *think* in a unified way about sets of qualities grasped by these different powers by means of an intellectual power that is not identical with any of the sensory powers. Persons are able *to think* and *to reason* about the *existence* of any of these various qualities, about their *self-identity*, about the *non-identity* of some of these differing qualities with one another, about *similarity* or *dissimilarity* relations that hold among them, about their *number* or *intensity*, about their *beauty* or *goodness*, and so forth. They can do so only by means of a distinct intellectual power capable of grasping abstract qualities and relations that are exemplified in common by sets of these sensory qualities in such a way that cannot be accounted for by the powers of direct sensory awareness. And any true judgments, and hence any knowledge, about the existence, identity or non-identity, similarity or dissimilarity, or like abstract qualities or relations had by sensory qualities require the exercise of this intellectual power over and above that of the sensory powers. Hence knowledge expressible in conceptual judgments cannot be identical with sensory perceptual intuition.

Maritain begins his critique of Bergson in chapters 6–7 of *Bergsonian Philosophy* with a critical examination of Bergson's anti-intellectualism, just as Socrates concludes his critique of the thesis that knowledge is identical to *aesthesis* or intuition by arguing for the necessity for knowledge of a unified intellectual power that must make use of concepts. For Bergson, "the *critique of intellect* is at the very threshold of the temple of [a-conceptual] intuition,"[9] whereas for Socrates the *affirmation of intellect* is the crowning argument against the anti-intellectual "intuitionism" of Protagoras. Maritain begins by taking issue with Bergson's understanding of the *concept*:

> For Bergson, the abstract and general idea is not of a higher order or nature than the sensible image, it is even inferior to it, it is a diminution of it; it is only *this or*

9. Maritain, *Bergsonian Philosophy*, 132.

> *that one of our concrete perceptions elaborated, whittled down, subtilized,* arbitrarily chosen to represent the real and associated with a word. Thus the concept, being abstract in the above sense, allows everything essential in reality—reality which is above all original and individual, with the wealth of a thousand nuances—to escape. Always identical with itself, it immobilizes, it brutally solidifies reality, which it deprives of its life and its movement. Distinct from other concepts, it artificially cuts out and breaks up reality, the continuity of which it simply disregards.[10]

Maritain argues against Bergson's claim that concepts falsify the real by pointing out that it is tantamount to the claim that the concept 'quadruped' deforms reality because the concept itself does not have four feet. Bergson overlooks the way in which (for Thomistic Aristotelianism) conceptual aspects of the changing sensible object of knowledge are in the knowing intellect immaterially, with *esse intentionale* rather than with *esse naturale.* Maritain argues also against the Bergsonian claim that concepts falsify reality by *breaking up* real things, showing that the intellect knows in a composite way and by a multiplicity of concepts objects with substantial forms that are in themselves simple (though they constitute objects that have changing accidents): "Scholastic philosophy ... establishes that we can know in a composite way and by means of a certain multiplicity of concepts a reality which is in itself simple."[11] And he shows that Bergson confuses sensible knowledge with intellectual knowledge, sensibility and imagination with thought, by failing to see that in humans (though not in angels) there is a real distinction between sensibility and intellect, the former perceiving the individual and the latter intellectually intuiting the general. Bergson wrongly criticizes intelligence, says Maritain, because he confuses intelligence with imagination, claiming to find a means of knowing superior to intelligence in an "intuition" (not an "intellectual intuition") which is really only a form of imagination.

Maritain shows that *Bergsonian intuition,* a supposedly direct, immediate, and absolute contact with the real, is characterized essentially by its opposition to the intellectual intuition of the *philosophia perennis* (and hence, from the point of view of this essay, is closely similar to the non-conceptualized *aesthesis* opposed to the intellect by Theodorus in the *Theaetetus*). Maritain writes:

10. Ibid., 124; emphasis in original.
11. Ibid., 139.

> For Bergsonian philosophy, Aristotle and Plato are the source of all the trouble. They based the knowledge of reality on intelligence and ideas and, as a result, could only neglect becoming and movement.... But beyond these philosophers, victims of concept and language, the source of the trouble is in the very nature of the human mind; for Aristotelian metaphysics is *the natural metaphysics of the human intellect,* as Bergson, not without a great deal of irony, says; and if such metaphysics is illusory, it is because we have within us from birth, as a natural heritage, a principle of radical illusion.[12]

To this characterization of Bergson's anti-intellectualism, Maritain adds the following characterization of Bergson's theory of intuition:

> For Bergson, intuition is an absolutely original act, *sui generis,* an experimental knowledge which projects us into the object and makes us coincide with reality in its very depth. This intuition, according to Bergson, is related to animal instinct much more than to reason, and it goes so far beyond intellect that it cannot be expressed in a concept.... [I]t demands of us an effort contrary to nature. But the philosopher ... will pass halfway between scientific or pseudo-scientific materialism and classical spiritualism, which are like two eternally opposed and equally erroneous halves of the cursed conceptual *analysis,* which is incapable of grasping duration.[13]

Maritain counters this by pointing out that Bergson is wrong to suppose that in the "classical spiritualism" of the *philosophia perennis* the concept prevents us from coinciding with reality. Intellectual intuition, unlike Bergsonian intuition, has an immaterial content that is not the ultimate *object* of knowledge but the *means,* the "mental word" produced as the fruit of the vital operation of the power of noetic insight, often with the aid of discursive thought, *by* which the immaterial intellect knows something of the objective world.[14] According to Maritain, the essential vice of Bergson's way of conceiving intuition as the highest knowledge is that it dispenses with this inner word or concept, and with the "formal identity" of this inner word with some aspect(s) of the (physical) thing known. In unconscious continuity with the post-Cartesian tradition of the "veil of ideas," and in opposition to the epistemological tradition rooted in Plato's *Theaetetus* and carried forward by Aristotle, it understands the concept as a distorting screen interposed between the object and the intellect. The first principle of Bergson's way of thinking is "the radical inaptitude of the intellect for

12. Ibid., 129; emphasis in original.
13. Ibid., 126.
14. Ibid., 151.

the truth."[15] And Bergson makes true intuition an "identification of the object and the subject according to the mode of being of the object,"[16] so that Bergsonian intuition becomes a non-intellectual experience of losing one's mind by merging with the cosmic flux of "duration" (conceived of by Bergson as "the very stuff of things" and as a "flux"),[17] a distorted version of some kind of natural mysticism.

III. Theology

Theaetetus 151d–172c, as we have seen, depicts Socrates examining and refuting Protagorean-Heraclitean theses in metaphysics and epistemology held by Theaetetus and Theodorus, views that are in important respects similar to the views of Bergson opposed by Maritain. It is striking that, in the digression that follows that examination and refutation at 172c–177c, Socrates turns to *theology*. For Maritain, too, after refuting Bergson's flawed views on the intellect, intuition, and duration in chapters 6–8 of *Bergsonian Philosophy and Thomism*, proceeds in chapter 9 to unmask Bergson's theological errors that he takes to be bound up inevitably with those flawed views.

In the *Theaetetus* digression at 172c–177c, Socrates invites Theodorus to examine certain flawed conceptions of God, politics, and philosophy. Socrates' own very different conceptions go unexpressed but are hinted at in the second part of the digression. Readers of the *Theaetetus* have to wait until the *Statesman* to be introduced to conceptions of God, politics, and philosophy which are truly Socratic. These conceptions are expressed in mythical form by the Eleatic Stranger. The Stranger's myth replaces the conceptions of deity tied to the polytheism of the Olympian gods, conceptions that are implicitly pantheistic, with the conception of an altogether non-Olympian and non-traditional Athenian deity, who "fitted the universe together in the beginning" (269d) and who is free of all evils and wrongs.[18] Let

15. Ibid., 144.

16. Ibid., 155.

17. Ibid., 127–28.

18. The monotheism of the myth is perhaps not surprising, since the Stranger is a disciple of Parmenides, who was in turn a disciple of Xenophanes, who had re-described the supreme divinity as an unmoved being capable of moving everything by the power of thought alone. Socrates himself, according to Xenophon's treatment of him at *Memorabilia* 1.4.17–18, attributes to the supreme deity both omniscience and omnipresence. See David Sedley, *Creationism and Its Critics in Antiquity* (Berkeley, California: University of California Press, 2007), 78–86.

us look at the *Theaetetus* digression at 172c–177c and the complementary theological myth in the *Statesman*.

Socrates' digression in the *Theaetetus,* addressed to Theodorus, has two parts. In the first, it gives a sketch of the philosopher; in the second, it counsels living life in imitation of God. Socrates in the second part of the digression (176a–177c) seizes upon Theodorus' view that philosophers are like unto gods by calling to mind the practical maxim of *homoiosis theou* (assimilation to God). It stands to reason that if Theodorus thinks philosophers are god-like, and has a conception of philosophy as an otherworldly escape from politics that is unsatisfactory to Socrates, and cries out for examination, then his conception of the gods and of the god-like will be unsatisfactory to Socrates, and will likewise cry out for examination. And this is what we find when we turn to Socrates' moral advice in the second part of the digression, a passage that occupies the exact center of the dialogue. Theodorus has just said that if Socrates' portrait of philosophy as altogether apolitical convinced everyone as it does Theodorus, there would be more peace and fewer evils (*kaka*) on earth. Socrates adopts Theodorus' standpoint by making some rather pessimistic remarks about the evils of mortal nature and this earth, and then offers a way of escape. He says:

> It is not possible, Theodorus, that evil should be destroyed—for there must always be something opposed to the good; nor is it possible that it should have its seat in heaven. But it must inevitably haunt human life, and prowl upon this earth. That is why a man should make all haste to escape from earth to heaven; and escape means becoming as like God as possible, and a man becomes like God when he becomes just and pure, with understanding [*dikaion kai hosion meta phroneseos*]. But it is not at all an easy matter, my good friend, to persuade men that it is not for the reasons commonly alleged that one should try to escape from wickedness and pursue virtue. It is not in order to avoid a bad reputation and obtain a good one that virtue should be practiced and not vice.... In God there is no sort of wrong whatsoever; he is supremely just.... [I]t is the realization of this that is genuine wisdom and goodness, while the failure to realize it is manifest folly and wickedness.... We must therefore tell them [the vicious] that their very ignorance of their true state fixes them the more firmly therein. They do not know that the penalty of injustice ... is a penalty from which there is no escape.[19]

19. *Theaetetus* 176a–176d. Among Socrates' claims here are (1) "it is *impossible* that evils be done away with"; (2) "by *necessity* there is always something opposed to the good"; (3) "evils are not established (or do not have their place) among the gods"; and (4) "out of necessity evils must wander about mortal nature and this earth." (1) and (2) constitute a fatalism that it would

When at this point Theodorus asks Socrates what the penalty is, Socrates replies:

> My friend, there are two patterns set up in the world. One is divine and supremely happy; the other has nothing of God in it, and is the pattern of the deepest unhappiness. This truth the evildoer does not see; blinded by folly and utter lack of understanding, he fails to perceive that the effect of his unjust practices is to make him grow more and more like the one and less and less like the other. For this he pays the penalty of living the life that corresponds to the pattern he is coming to resemble.... [W]hen he dies the place that is pure of all evil will not receive him and he will forever go on living in this world a life after his own likeness, a bad man tied to bad company.[20]

We must of course keep in mind a distinction between the historical Socrates and the Socrates who is Plato's literary character. In Xenophon's *Memorabilia* 1.4 and 4.3, Socrates is credited with a radically unconventional theology, according to which true piety lies in appreciating divine gifts to man and thereby coming to understanding the bond that ties man to the divine. Socrates attributes to the supreme deity not only benevolence but also omniscience and omnipresence (1.4.17–18), developing the radical theology of Xenophanes (and no doubt Anaxagoras), and perhaps countering the views of his contemporary Democritus. Xenophon's Socrates, when his interlocutor Aristodemus chooses the poets and artists as the wisest of human beings, emphasizes the vast superiority to human craftsmanship of the *divine craftsmanship that must lie behind the origin of living beings.*

The Eleatic Stranger's Myth shows that the defective conceptions of the good held by wicked men, because of their forgetfulness of the transcendent God, account for the political plight of human beings in the later

---

be hard to attribute to Socrates. (3) is a thesis that Socrates rhetorically espouses when talking with an Adeimantus who would bowdlerize Homer and Hesiod and who distrusts the mystery religions. And (4) is an idea that he plays with when extracting and examining the doctrines of his dualistic Pythagorean interlocutors in the *Phaedo*. In this paper I want to avoid getting involved in the issue of Socrates' or Plato's conceptions of evil and of the source of evil. It is my view that Socrates is here just rehearsing some popular doctrines about evil familiar to Theodorus, as part of his rhetoric in dealing with and guiding his interlocutor. The view that the inevitability of evil on earth is a reason for "escaping from earth to heaven" echoes the counsel that he argues against in his discussion of suicide in the *Phaedo* in the presence of Pythagoreans and the severely abused and former-prisoner-of-war Phaedo. But here it is not the escape of suicide that he has in mind, for he introduces the new conception that "escape" from evil lies in knowledge of God and of the significance of God-likeness.

20. *Theaetetus* 176e–177a.

stages of the Age of Zeus. The myth suggests a conception of philosophy not radically different from Socrates' own. It suggests that a main task of philosophy is to elicit both the recognition of ignorance about the good and the recollection of the divine, and thereby to motivate the founding of an ethical and political project of dialectical inquiry into God and the good, and to serve that project.

We are now in position to recognize the striking *theological* similarity between the message Socrates attempts to convey to Theodorus in the *Theaetetus* digression, on the one hand, and Maritain's critique of the theology implicit in Bergson's thought in chapter 9 of *Bergsonian Philosophy*, on the other. For if in the *Theaetetus* digression Socrates corrects Theodorus' philosophical errors by employing a theology which, understood in light of the *Statesman* Myth, replaces the implicit pantheism and fatalism of Olympian theology with the conception of a single transcendent deity who provides the standard for human creative goodness, Maritain shows the way in which Bergson's errors in metaphysics and epistemology align him with certain potentially distorting theological tendencies of "Indian" mystical thought.

Maritain begins chapter 9 by discussing the cogency of the Thomistic conception of God. He summarizes Thomas' view as follows:

> This first mover, this first cause without cause and without any mixture of potentiality, this *pure act* absolutely immobile, not with the immobility of inertia—far from it—but with the immobility of pure and supreme activity, which has nothing to acquire and which can become nothing because it has in itself all that can be had and because it is by itself all that one can be, it is this that we call God.[21]

Maritain emphasizes that the Thomistic Five Ways rest upon a certain intellectual intuition of being which includes an intuition of "the principle of identity and the principles which are linked to this supreme principle."[22] Then he takes Bergson to task for thinking that none of the Thomistic proofs for the existence of God are sound, and for supposing that contingency is self-sufficient and self-asserting:

21. Maritain, *Bergsonian Philosophy*, 183; emphasis in original. On page 193 Maritain maintains: "This attribute of *aseity*, of existence by oneself, of absolute Independence in being itself, is the profoundest thing human reason can say on the subject. It is 'the fundamental truth of Christian philosophy'."

22. Ibid., 182, 185.

Bergson's argument, whatever his intentions may have been, can only end in one conclusion, namely that *contingent being* as well as being by itself has no need of cause, or in other words that the contingent exists by itself.[23]

Bergson thinks that, though our intelligence cannot infer the existence of God, the "intuition of pure duration" enables us to know the existence of God in a way that the intellect cannot know it. For Bergson our only resource for knowing this God is to to say that by the intuition of a created duration we manage to enter into contact with the divine essence, we manage to *perceive God intuitively*. Maritain summarizes Bergson's view as follows:

That by dint of dilating or transcending ourselves, and of intensifying the intuition of our duration, we should succeed, if only in a flash of evanescent intuition, in perceiving God intuitively: an obviously untenable thesis! As though there were not an infinite distance between the divine nature and our own, as though the intuitive knowledge of God were accessible to metaphysical effort and not the most supernatural gift of His mercy.

What, asks Maritain, is the nature of Bergson's God, so accessible to natural intuition? It is not that of the God of Christian philosophy, who is subsisting being itself, transcendent, without any admixture of potentiality or mutability, without limit, incomprehensibly rich in all perfection, simple and one without any composition, and the cause of all that is distinct from God.

In Bergsonian philosophy, which tries to do without being, it is not possible to establish, according to Maritain, *the real and essential distinction between God and things*.[24] Bergson's God is Pure Duration, a pantheistic, growing, creative Heraclitean One, a God like Hegel's God, a "pure change" that supposedly is the substance of things.[25] Bergson's theology is

23. Ibid., 187.

24. "Bergsonian philosophy, by the very fact that it tries to do without being, is logically incapable of establishing an *absolute and total, real and essential* distinction between God and things." Ibid., 196.

25. Bergson apparently makes a mistake that is common to many modern thinkers since Scotus, namely the adherence to the doctrine of the univocity of the concept of being, and the consequent forgetfulness of divine transcendence. Maritain discusses the *analogous* value of concepts applied to the transcendent God on pp. 194–202 in chapter 9 of *Bergsonian Philosophy*. He says that in knowing God by analogy we are able to conceive "at the same time the ineffable transcendence of the divine nature and the sovereign immanence of divine operation"; ibid., 195. Again, a little later on, Maritain writes: "there is nothing, absolutely nothing in common, except by analogy, between the being of God and the being of the world. And because in Bergsonian philosophy there cannot be between God and the world an absolute distinction of nature and

one according to which all things are one, not in a Spinozist substance, but in a pure becoming. Maritain quotes with endorsement an insightful passage from Garrigou-Lagrange's *Le Sens Commun, la Philosophie de l'etre et les Formules dogmatiques*:

> Bergson goes so far as to say that modern philosophy's last word, insofar as it is in opposition to ancient philosophy, consists in stating that the *fundamental reality is becoming*. Now that amounts to saying, as Hegel recognized, that *the intimate nature of things is a realized contradiction*. To deny the principle of identity as the fundamental law of the real is evidently to affirm that contradiction is at the very heart of the real, since the principle of non-contradiction is only the negative formula of the principle of identity. *To suppress pure Act which is to being as A is to A, to suppress divine transcendence, is to root everything in absurdity*. Bergson's anti-intellectualism is nothing more than Hegelianism turned upside down. These two extreme systems were bound to join one another in a common evolutionistic monism; if they did not exist they would have had to be invented for they constitute the most remarkable proofs by *reductio ad absurdum* of the existence of the transcendent God, absolutely One and immutable.... Only three positions are possible in general metaphysics and theodicy: (1) *Admit the primacy of being over becoming and deny potentiality*; then willy-nilly we must get back to Parmenides ..., absorb the world in God ... and *deny the world* in denying all multiplicity and all becoming. (2) *Admit the primacy of being and also admit potentiality*; then, with Aristotle, we *must affirm divine transcendence*, implied in the concept of pure Act; (3) *Deny the primacy of being and affirm that of becoming*, with Heraclitus, which is ... to deny the objective value of the principle of identity and place absurdity at the very heart of the real.... [A]bsorb God in the world ... and finally *deny God*.[26]

Bergson's God cannot be conceived without the world, and is a non-intelligent God who creates without an eternal plan.

Not valuing the intelligent use of concepts, much less the intelligent use of analogy, Bergson's theology can allow us to know God only with the same knowledge which allows us to know creatures, to perceive God only by an intuition whereby we coincide with him. Maritain, in the Preface to the second edition of *Bergsonian Philosophy and Thomism*—a text which Raïssa Maritain called "one of his most important writings"[27]—emphasizes the similarity between Bergson's doctrine of non-intellectual intuition

---

essence ... it must be said that Bergsonian metaphysics in spite of itself falls a prey to pantheism"; ibid. 199–201.

26. Ibid., 200n1; emphasis in original.

27. Raïssa Maritain, *We Have Been Friends Together and Adventures in Grace: The Memoirs of Raïssa Maritain*, translated Julie Kernan (Garden City, New York: Image Books, 1961), 348.

and certain aspects of "that characteristic heresy of Indian thought, Buddhist meditation."[28] He reminds us that "Socrates did not invent the concept but discovered it,"[29] and contends that theology suffers from a serious deficiency wherever Socrates' insight into the importance of the intellectual use of concepts is lacking. He takes Indian thought to be an important example of such deficient theology.[30] All movement of thought, he says, is determined by its goal. Aristotle, a second-generation student of Socrates, distinguished speculative intellect from practical intellect, and noted that the goal of the former is theoretical contemplation whereas the goal of the latter is the practical expression of the fruits of contemplation. Aristotle subordinated practice to theory, while emphasizing both the importance of theory's guidance of practice and the importance of practice in supporting theory and making it possible.[31] Indian thought from the fifth century B.C., on the other hand, completely subordinated theory to religious practice by considering the intellect as primarily aimed not at conceptualization of natures but at articulating a "practical science," an ascetic discipline aimed at a kind of concept-free meditation enabling a psychic deliverance from the world. Its very conception of mind was part of this practical science and not a theory of the nature of mind like the Aristotelian. But a meditation which does not aim at knowing the nature of things, but at freeing itself from human nature, dispenses with all ideas and essences. Maritain writes:

> Bearing heroic testimony to the postulations of the spirit in us she [India] has chosen at all costs to transcend human nature and reason.... [She, India, does this] with such courage that it is impossible to believe that sometimes grace's ways of compensating (for we know that God disguises Himself), or sometimes other influences less pure, do not nourish the soul in secret. But of itself, the goal toward which one aspires, loss of self in the absolute of the Vedanta, or in the Buddhist nirvana, if indeed it is other than a pure annihilation, is also something quite different from union with a divine Thou where all love is consummated.[32]

28. Preface to the Second Edition of Maritain, *Bergsonian Philosophy*, 42.

29. Ibid., 38.

30. Maritain, *Bergsonian Philosophy*, 38. It is impossible to convey in the present context the richness of Maritain's discussion of the kinship between Bergson's philosophy and "Indian thought" on pp. 38–43 of the Preface. It must be read in its entirety.

31. Maritain is careful here to point out that he is referring to the way in which Aristotle specified the goal of the *specific human power*, the speculative intellect, as he understood it, and not the goal of the human being as a whole. See *Bergsonian Philosophy*, 39n1.

32. Ibid., 41.

Maritain's discussion of this limitation of Indian thought confirms and further elaborates the insight expressed by Socrates when he suggested to Theodorus that the doctrine of knowledge as non-conceptualized *aesthesis* carries with it a deficient theology connected with an ethics or orthopraxy of escape from the world.

IV. "Natural Mysticism" and the Concept in Maritain's Later Writings

Before concluding this essay on Maritain's very first book, we should note, for the sake of readers unfamiliar with the whole corpus of his work, that Maritain eventually came to explore the possibility that the "natural mysticism" of Indian thought and of Zen Buddhism could be appreciated and embraced from a Thomistic standpoint, given certain cautions and qualifications. He came to maintain that natural mysticism was a valid, albeit potentially misleading, avenue of approach to an intellectual intuition of the existence of the transcendent God, a way to God complementary both to the way of the intellectual intuition of the divine *esse* by the metaphysician, and to the way of the experience of God through infused contemplation.[33]

We have seen that Maritain in *Bergsonian Philosophy and Thomism* attempted to reformulate in the light of St. Thomas the notions of intuition, intellect, and concept that he had received from Bergson. Admitting to himself that Bergson's understanding of concepts was wrong, and beginning his philosophical work anew, he insisted that the human mind needs both intellectual intuition and concepts, the latter being the means by which and through which we intellectually intuit real things, however gradually, by joining concepts, or intelligible aspects of things, together in judgments. But after 1913 the Maritain who had championed the concept in his disagreements with Bergson came eventually to defend more and more

33. When he wrote *Bergsonian Philosophy* in 1913, and even thirty-four years later when he wrote the Preface to the second edition, after having written *The Degrees of Knowledge* and *A Preface to Metaphysics*, Maritain was only beginning his reflections upon the "characteristic heresy of Indian thought, Buddhist meditation," and the related phenomenon of Zen meditation. James Arraj has written extensively about Maritain's relation to Eastern "natural mysticism" in general and to Zen in particular. Of particular interest are his *God, Zen and the Intuition of Being* (Midland, Oregon: Inner Growth Books, 1989), and *Mysticism, Metaphysics and Maritain: On the Road to the Spiritual Unconscious* (Midland, Oregon: Inner Growth Books, 2011).

certain forms of knowledge in which concepts play little or no role. He reflected often in his writings, beginning with *Bergsonian Philosophy* itself, on the Thomistic notion of "knowledge through connaturality"—intellectual intuition achieved without discursive preparation, a kind of knowledge produced in the intellect but not by virtue of conceptual connections or of discursive demonstrations. In these types of knowledge (Maritain insisted that they counted as knowledge in an analogous sense of the term) the intellect's non-conceptualized contact with the object is aided by a craftsman's or an artist's "estimative" powers of sense or by an agent's conative powers of will and heart.[34] James Arraj writes:

> In Maritain's hands, knowledge by connaturality becomes a fluid notion that embraces art [fine art and useful craft], poetry, morality and mystical experience. It extends to the hunches and image-laden primordial insights of the empirical scientist groping towards a new theory. It aids the artist whose dim perceptions do not reach the daylight of consciousness except in the work of art itself. Connatural knowledge is found in the conduct of the good man who consults his instinct rather than a text on moral theology in order to decide how to behave. Its intuition is divinatory, feeding not only on the input of the senses but on the imagination, emotions and heart.[35]

This conception of knowledge by connaturality came to play a role in Maritain's understanding of the mysticism of the East.

"Natural Mysticism and the Void"—originally published in 1939 when Maritain was fifty-eight—is perhaps the text that best represents his line of thought concerning natural mysticism. In this paper Maritain suggests that we have a natural awareness of the *esse* of our own natures as conscious knowers, but that this a-conceptual experiential knowledge of ourselves is unable to support any direct intellectual intuition of our own essence. "Existential" knowledge of ourselves from the inside is achieved without the

34. See, for example, Jacques Maritain, *The Degrees of Knowledge* (New York: Charles Scribner's Sons, 1938), Part II. (Originally published in French in 1932.) See also especially Jacques Maritain, "Natural Mysticism and the Void," in *Challenges and Renewals: Selected Readings*, edited by Joseph W. Evans and Leo R. Ward (Notre Dame, Indiana: University of Notre Dame Press, 1966), 76–106. (Article originally published in French in 1939.) See also a paper delivered by Maritain at the second annual meeting of the Metaphysical Society of America, Barnard College, New York City, February 24, 1951, reprinted in *Natural Law: Reflections on Theory and Practice*, edited by William Sweet (South Bend, Indiana: Saint Augustine's Press, 2001), 13–24. See also the early chapters of Jacques Maritain, *The Range of Reason* (New York: Charles Scribner's Sons, 1952).

35. Arraj, *God, Zen and the Intuition of Being*. Available online at http://www.innerexplorations.com/catew/gz4.htim. My quotation is from p. 8 of chap. 4 of the online text.

mediation of concepts and can actually be intensified by the practice of intentionally stopping all conceptual thought and all imagination. So intensified, "empty" consciousness becomes the means by which is achieved a reflective intellectual experience by connaturality of the substantial *esse* of the soul.[36] And since this experience of the soul requires the elimination of any finite essence which would limit and contract the existence of the reality intuited, it is at the same time an intellectual experience of the metaphysical amplitude an infinite openness of human conscious existence and, indirectly, of God as the source of this kind of existence. The specific limitation of this form of experience stems from the way in which the soul experiences its own *esse* without being able to distinguish it from the divine *esse*, for the human ability to understand the distinction between the divine *esse* and all finite *esse* requires the use of concepts. An experience of God is attained "in the mirror of the substantial *esse* of the soul," but what is mirrored cannot be distinguished from the mirror. The consequence is that a risk exists on the speculative level that, without the conceptual articulation of various sorts of identity and difference, the absolute that is the existence of the soul will be confused with, and identified with, the absolute which is God.

The chief difference between this natural mystical intuition of God and the intuition of God by the metaphysician (not to mention the experience of God by infused contemplation[37]) is the different relationship between

36. In the Barnard College paper Maritain writes cogently: "There is another kind of mystical experience [other than infused contemplation] ... which may be called natural mystical experience, and an example of which we can find in Plotinus and in the classical schools of Indian contemplation.... Here again, to my mind, we have to do with a particular type of knowledge both supra-conceptual and through connaturality. But the connaturality in question here is merely intellectual [by contrast to that of love in infused contemplation], and the essential part played by the will consists in forcing the intellect inwards, against the grain of nature, and in obliging it to empty itself of any particular representation. The Reality to be experienced is the very Existence, the very *Esse* of the Self in its pure metaphysical actuality—Atman—and as proceeding from the One Self: and it is by means of a supreme effort of intellectual and voluntary concentration, sweeping away any possible image, recollection or idea, any passing phenomenon and any distinct consciousness, in other words, it is through the void that the intellect is conatured to the unconceptualizable spiritual reality of the thing known." Sweet, *Natural Law*, 17.

37. Maritain finds something in Ramanuja that echoes his distinction between natural mysticism and infused contemplation. In a footnote he writes: "Let us note here the distinction made by Ramanuja between salvation by knowledge alone (the way of immanence, and of indifferentiation from the universal Brahman—its natural mystical experience as I have attempted to describe it), and salvation by grace (the way of friendship, and of access to the very Personality of Brahman). See Olivier Lacombe's fundamental work, *L'Absolu selon le Vedanta* (Paris: Geuthner, 1937), 372." Maritain, "Natural Mysticism and the Void," in *Challenges and Renewals*, 99n19.

the insight and its elaboration in concepts. Though both intuitions transcend the level of concepts, their transcendence is not of the same kind. The metaphysician's intuition of God is in continuity with the world of concepts even when it transcends them by pushing them to their limit analogically, intellectually intuiting the existence of God as the limit case of the pure perfections. The natural mystic who is innocent of the Thomistic tradition often mistakenly tends, after intuiting God's existence using as a means the elimination of all conceptual thought, to view conceptual thought as a tyranny that must be overthrown, *a la* Bergson. As a result, "Indian" thought, based on "natural mysticism" alone, often succumbs, as Bergson did (after Spinoza and Hegel had), to pantheism. But of course the pantheistic identification of the soul with God makes nonsense of various Christian doctrines. It had been in order to avoid this pantheism and to preserve the intelligibility of (and to understand the appropriateness of) God's revelation of articulate doctrines to the Church that Maritain originally rejected Bergson's philosophy after becoming a Catholic.

In later work, then, Maritain remains faithful to his original intention in writing *Bergsonian Philosophy and Thomism*, even while attempting to rehabilitate natural mysticism for Catholics. But he attempts to show that while Christianity can find a legitimate place for "natural mysticism" and even for Bergson's "intuition" suitably interpreted, religion based upon natural mysticism alone cannot find a place for truths about the Trinity, Incarnation, and Atonement.[38] Maritain continues to hold, both for reasons similar to those Socrates had adduced in the *Theaetetus* and for reasons connected with his faith in a *dogmatic* revelation to the Church, that mankind cannot do without concepts.

Let us re-emphasize what has been suggested earlier: the parallel between one aspect of Maritain's characterization of natural mysticism, on the one hand, and Socrates' suggestion in the *Theaetetus* digression that the Protagorean-Heraclitean metaphysics and epistemology are bound up with an orthopraxy of *escape from the world*, in the sense of escape from ordinary life and practical tasks, on the other. Socrates' characterization

Maritain also discusses a number of differences between natural mysticism and infused contemplation in the final section of "Natural Mysticism and the Void."

38. For some profound reflections upon ways in which the doctrines of Trinity, Incarnation, and Atonement complement and even complete the profound insights of Hinduism, Confucianism, Taoism, and Buddhism, see Yves Raguin, S.J., *The Depth of God*, translated from the French by Sr. Kathleen England, O.S.U. (St. Meinrad, Indiana: Abbey Press, 1975), esp. 99–129.

of theistic philosophy as an exercise in *craftsmanship* parallels nicely Maritain's exposition of the importance to human life of connatural knowledge (a primary example of which is for Maritain the embodied and to some extent tacit knowledge of the craftsman) and of the need to distinguish in order to unite theory and practice in philosophy and theology. Maritain captures the Socratic concern for embodied action in the world (yet, unlike Socrates, he does so for explicitly Christian reasons) in his comments upon natural mysticism. He emphasizes that despite the qualified validity and goodness of natural mysticism, the connaturality involved in it is, by contrast with the connaturality of love in infused contemplation, merely intellectual, and that the essential part played by the will in natural mysticism consists in forcing the intellect inwards to empty itself of any particular representation, "against the grain of nature." Toward the end of "Natural Mysticism and the Void" Maritain writes of natural mysticism:

> This experience goes directly—hence the host of techniques—against the grain of nature: it asks the soul to renounce all movement toward things, which amounts to quitting the world. Whereas in poetic recollection the world is drawn into the subjectivity and awakens it to itself, here, on the contrary, the subjectivity separates itself from the world, in order to seek within itself alone a sleep more intense than all awakenings. Then again it may be pointed out that the mystical experience of the Self requires the soul to quit the world in a manner altogether different from that required by Christian *ascesis* and contemplation. In both cases it is necessary to "cross the threshold," as Father Lallemant used to say; but in the natural effort against the grain of nature it is to satisfy the demands of an ascesis entirely ordered to gnosis—demands at once more negative and less profound than those of evangelic perfection. Demands more negative: for that which is required of the Christian is the utter *detachment from a world in which he exists more than ever, which he continues to know and to love, and for the salvation of which he suffers*; but that which is required of the soul in the other case is that it purely and simply *suppress the world*. . . . Demands less profound: for a detachment which attains only the roots of intelligence is less profound than a detachment which attains the roots of freedom itself and which causes one not only to quit the world but also to quit oneself (I do not mean merely egoism, the passions, etc. I mean the supreme governance of self).[39]

So in the end we are not only able justifiably to say that the metaphysical and epistemological criticisms that Socrates makes of the views of Theaetetus and of his teacher Theodorus exhibit striking parallels with the criti-

39. Maritain, "Natural Mysticism and the Void," in *Challenges and Renewals*, 95; emphasis added.

cisms Maritain makes of Bergson's metaphysics and epistemology. We are also able to claim with reason that Socrates' *theological* critique of (implicitly pantheistic) Greek polytheism , despite its pre-Christian character, exhibits striking parallels with Maritain's critique of Bergson's pantheism, and of the religion of mere natural mysticism that it resembles.[40]

40. Excellent reflections upon the relationships between Eastern and Western mysticisms can be found in Raymond Gawronski, S.J., *Word and Silence: Hans Urs von Balthasar and the Spiritual Encounter Between East and West* (Grand Rapids, Michigan: William B. Eerdmans, 1995); Paul Mommaers and Jan Van Bragt, *Mysticism, Buddhist and Christian: Encounters With Jan Van Ruusbroec* (New York: Crossroad Publishing, 1995); and Paul Mommaers, *The Riddle of Christian Mystical Experience: The Role of the Humanity of Jesus* (Louvain: Peeters Press, 2003).

HEATHER M. ERB

Springs of Abundant Life in the Philosophical and Theological Orders

Maritain, Bergson, and Aquinas

I. Introduction

In *The Three Ages of the Interior Life,*[1] Reginald Garrigou-Lagrange laments the seventeenth-century rupture of ascetical and mystical theology, noting that from that time, an individualist, experiential view of mysticism has consistently gained ground over the more theological and ecclesial approach favored by Aquinas and his followers. Union with God came to be seen as a hidden, mysterious, and intimate exercise accompanied by extraordinary graces and transitory supernatural phenomena, in contrast to the humdrum progress in the virtues, the practices of mortification, and exercises of piety. The tendency to identify stages of mystical ascent with subjective feeling-states was caused in part by ignoring the role of metaphysics and reason in worship and religion in general, and by distancing faith from philosophical wisdom. In recent times, this has given rise to critiques ranging from Bernard McGinn's historical approach to more apophatically inclined interlocutors such as Denys Turner.[2] The rupture of theologies is also mirrored

1. See Reginald Garrigou-Lagrange, *The Three Ages of the Interior Life: Prelude of Eternal Life* (New York: Herder, 1947) 2:628–43; cf. *Christian Perfection and Contemplation According to St. Thomas Aquinas and St. John of the Cross,* translated by Sr. Mary Timothea Doyle (St. Louis, Missouri: Herder, 1947), 25–26.

2. See Denys Turner, *The Darkness of God: Negativity in Christian Mysticism* (Cambridge: Cambridge University Press, 1995), 264–65; Bernard McGinn, *Foundations of Mysticism: Origins to the Fifth Century* (New York: Crossroad Publishing, 1991), General Introduction, xiv–xv, and Appendix.

in thinkers who retrieve the metaphysical spirit, such as Henri Bergson's theory of "dynamic" vs. "static" religion.[3] While Maritain critiqued Bergson's view of ethics and religion as a false interpretation of reason in relation to will and mystical experience,[4] Garrigou-Lagrange, Maritain's Dominican mentor, mapped the contents of mystical theology while giving several reasons behind the rupture between natural, revealed, and mystical theologies.[5] Both Maritain and Garrigou-Lagrange critique systems that divide experience from reason and mysticism from natural theology, errors introduced through pitting the practical against the speculative, reason against will, and by extolling the charismata at the expense of mapping the metaphysical principles of spiritual ascent. The list of errors includes, for Garrigou-Lagrange: blindness to the perfection found in the mystical life as a universal (even if remote) call; a carelessness in mapping how the spiritual Gifts inform and accompany the life of virtue; and a focus on states of consciousness and charismata as indicators of spiritual progress, instead of the threefold way of purgation, illumination and union, which involve the soul's natural faculties guided by the works of grace.

Maritain's review of the problems in Bergson's philosophy of religion is instructive in the project of regrafting mystical theology onto its metaphysical roots. This project also involves outlining and revealing links between the concepts of *vita, ordo,* and *visio spiritualis,* which signals an earlier unity and balance of theologies in Aquinas. Although often described as intellectual in tone, Aquinas's mystical theology balances the abstract (as in the metaphysical concepts of differentiated union, analogy, and order) and the affective (as in the analysis of beatitude as enjoyment, divine love as the cause of that beatitude through the Incarnation, and the Gifts of the Spir-

3. See Henri Bergson, *Two Sources of Morality and Religion,* translated by A. Ashley Audra and Cloudesley Brereton (Garden City, New York: Doubleday, 1977), originally published as *Les Deux Sources de la Morale et de la Religion* (Paris,1932).

4. See Jacques Maritain, *Bergsonian Philosophy and Thomism,* translated by Mabelle L. Andison, J. Gordon Andison (New York: Philosophical Library, 1955), 325–45, originally published as *La Philosophie Bergsonienne* (Paris: Marcel Rivière, 1914).

5. The artificial division of mystical and ascetical theologies since the seventeenth and eighteenth centuries, he says, "followed on lively discussions that were occasioned by abuses springing from a premature and erroneous teaching of the mystical ways," discussions stoked by the Jesuit/Dominican debate on grace and free will, and by suspicions of John of the Cross's "illuminism." Ascetical theology was seen to be practiced by those in the "ordinary" Christian life according to the virtues and the "three ways" (purgative, illuminative, unitive), while mystical theology treated only the extraordinary graces, supernatural contemplation and mystical union. Garrigou-Lagrange, *Christian Perfection and Contemplation,* 27–28.

it). Aquinas's deft intertwining of the analogous concepts of life, order, and spiritual vision provides evidence of the links he envisions between natural and supernatural orders.

A comparison of Bergson and Aquinas on the various meanings of "life" in relation to its role in religion (Bergson) and in natural, mystical and revealed theologies (Aquinas) involves a variety of tasks: (1) noting the foundations of Bergson's philosophy of religion, and in particular, his metaphysical first principle, the impulse of "life" or the *élan vital,* in relation to reason and natural theology; (2) outlining Bergson's description of two sources and types of morality and religion, with reference to the origins of social pressure, habit, and conformism, on the one hand, and to the aspiration to transcendence and universal love (identified by Bergson as the summit of "life" or the *élan vital*), on the other; (3) analyzing the weaknesses of Bergson's views on religion: First, he suppresses the role of reason and contemplation, which evinces his failure to link the mystical impulse and its native soil of natural theology. Second, the chasm he creates between the "two sources" of morality and religion ignores the rational character of the will, resulting in the complete absence of natural (vs. supernatural) morality, according to Maritain. Third, Bergson's philosophy of religion involves a methodological error, in ignoring the data of revealed theology. A final task (4) is to show the way in which Aquinas's senses of "life" provide a corrective to Bergson by illumining the continuity Aquinas envisions between natural, moral (ascetic), and mystical theologies through a harmony among the natural and supernatural senses of "life." The mutual causality of the intellect and will in spiritual progress appears in the supernatural sense of "life," in contrast to Bergson's sense of the sources of religion and morality.

II. Maritain and Garrigou-Lagrange on the Metaphysical Basis of Bergson's Philosophy of Religion

Bergson's theory of "dynamic" religion is grounded in his metaphysics of "intuition" and the *élan vital,* or impulse of life, which theory in turn is a reaction to the errors of scientific materialism and positivism. The notion of being as a self-creative *élan vital* or continual process of change perpetually struggling to overcome the entropy of matter, Bergson argues, is an alternative to both materialist mechanism and Aristotelian finality. Neither mechanism nor teleology account for the ebullience of energy at the heart of reality, which our concepts attempt to display but instead distort in a manner similar to the way cinematography freezes a continuous event for a moment in time, capturing only a momentary fragment of a larger whole.[6] Both mechanism and finality, he says, imply that everything is given or ready-made—the enemy of creative life, action, and nonrepetitive freedom. Bergson agrees with Nietzsche against Darwin to an extent, that life is not merely an adaptation of organisms to external conditions, or a fixed degree of reality, but a will to mastery from within, an ascending movement towards higher expression and organization.[7]

Life is coextensive with consciousness, but possesses variations in intensity in ascending creative movements,[8] and intensifies or slackens (in tension and release) in relation to its triumph over blind matter, which has no memory and thus is incapable of novelty or choice. Yet for Bergson, the mind's intuition is no more than a refined empiricism, at least according to the interpretations of Garrigou-Lagrange[9] and Maritain.[10] Despairing of reason's ability to know the truth or see the "inside" of things, Bergson made intuition's object pure duration or becoming. Maritain judged Bergson's thesis to be incorrect—Bergson's "intuition" was more a refined instinct than a speculative reflection on the nature of being, and in this sense failed to launch a coherent metaphysics. For Bergson, intellect evolved as a practical survival mechanism that distorts our grasp of the cosmos by revolting against the unpredictable flux and by making the unpredictable manageable.[11] Through concepts we grasp reality as discontinuous and immobile, whereas through intuition, which relates to the individual temporal particular, we are said to touch the stream of life directly through "sympathy" and involvement. In this respect, Bergson's philosophy is indeed "the revindication of intuition in a world dominated by intelligence and by our naturally 'Platonic' dispositions."[12]

6. See Henri Bergson, *Creative Evolution*, translated by Arthur Mitchell (New York: Henry Holt, 1911), 247.

7. See ibid., 238.

8. See Henri Bergson, *Mind-Energy: Lectures and Essays* (New York: Henry Holt, 1920; originally *L'Énergie Spirituelle* [1919]), 15.

9. See Reginald Garrigou-Lagrange, *Le sens commun, la philosophie de l'être et les formules dogmatiques* (Paris: Beauchesne,1909), 58–59.

10. See Maritain, *Bergsonian Philosophy and Thomism*, 329.

11. See Bergson, *Creative Evolution*, 29.

12. Leszek Kolakowski, *Bergson* (New York: Oxford University Press, 1985), 61.

Maritain's and Garrigou-Lagrange's correctives to Bergson center on an assertion of the intellect's speculative reach, by which truth is grounded in an analogous concept of being and natural theology is established.[13] Although Bergson revived metaphysics, he identified being with temporal becoming, flux, or "duration." Life (identified as consciousness) is containment of the past (memory) and anticipation of the future, in duration or time, he argues. This alignment of life with a consciousness devoid of the present involves identifying something as either the not-yet or the already-has-been. In responding to Bergson's Heraclitean first principle, Garrigou-Lagrange distinguished between becoming as known by the senses and as a principle of the real as such. Being is the formal object of the intellect, and metaphysical notions (potency/act, substance/accident, and the causes) have real reference; they are not just distortions of an original flux perceived by sense. Bergson goes so far as to deny the principle of contradiction (by stating that a thing is both itself and not itself) and with it the whole train of philosophical principles which flow from it, which approach Garrigou-Lagrange sees as halting reason's advance towards God.

Garrigou-Lagrange argued that the starting point of thought is not an intuition of one's "inner becoming"[14] but rather the insight into self-identity or the principle of contradiction, garnered through knowledge of the forms of things. Maritain agreed, noting that Bergson's intuition is reduced to a heightened instinct which grasps concrete particulars, resulting in the knowledge of being as "duration" in tension with the principle of contradiction.[15]

III. Bergson's *Two Sources of Morality and Religion*

In *Two Sources of Morality and Religion* Bergson applies his theories of the *élan vital* and intuition to the distinction of mysticism and cult. This, his final work, contains the following key themes: First, diverse sources, one infra-rational, the other supra-rational, specify the types of morality as "closed" or "open," and the types of religion as "static" or "dynamic." Sec-

13. However, Maritain's own theory of the "intuition" of being differs from Garrigou-Lagrange's more Thomistic view of abstraction and the judgment, and the metaphysical principles which follow in their train.

14. Bergson states that the duration which is the object of the intellect is primarily internal. See *The Creative Mind*, translated by Mabelle L. Andison (New York: Greenwood Press, 1968), 35.

15. Maritain, *The Degrees of Knowledge*, translated by Gerald Phelan (New York: Charles Scribners and Sons, 1964), 45.

ond, Christian mysticism is the summit of "dynamic" religion, as its activist quality is a perfect expression of the *élan vital* or cosmic dynamic impulse, or simply, "life" and as an extension of divine action in the world through love.[16] Third, contemplation, as linked to reason and the yearning for immutability found in Greek philosophy is, for Bergson, subordinate to action, which expresses the effervescence of life.

The first theme concerns the diverse sources of both morality and religion. Drawing on an Empedoclean-style attraction/pressure motif, Bergson says that the lower "morality of obligation" results from social pressure, where nature conforms the individual to society and its demands. He points to primitive ("closed") societies' identification of the moral and social selves—an identity which preserves society's existence and cohesion. "Open" societies, on the other hand, are led by outstanding individuals' aspiration to transcend society's rules, through responding to the "call of the hero." This call of attraction in the open morality stems, he says, from a supra-rational origin, in the creative source of life experienced by moral geniuses and expressed in the ideal of universal love. The vital impetus in the will, called "emotion," results in action which penetrates closed societies, leading them from obligation to inspiration. The morality of obligation mirrors animal instinct, as determined by repetitive mechanical laws, while the "open" morality arises when human consciousness sets itself free and true spiritual life emerges.[17]

In a similar way, Bergson distinguishes the lower "static" religion from more advanced "dynamic" religion.[18] The former involves nature's capacity to fend off anxieties brought on by speculative reason's questions about death, and to solidify individuals within society through stories and ritual. Dynamic religion has its source in the mystic's transcendence of societal and material conditions, in a personal union with the infinite—a confor-

16. Gilson admits that the concept of "life" is vague in Bergson: "He simply means by it [viz., "life"] the entirety of natural forces at work in living beings, and not a distinct energy such as those invoked by various vitalisms in order to explain specific matters in the vegetable and animal kingdoms. However that may be, Bergson speaks of it as a *vis a tergo*, a sort of initial push (*poussée*), the *élan vital*, which, similar to a rocket (*fusée*), opens out into a shower of beings." Étienne Gilson, *From Aristotle to Darwin and Back Again: A Journey in Final Causality, Species, and Evolution*, translated by John Lyon (Notre Dame, Indiana: University of Notre Dame Press, 1984), 99–100.

17. Bergson contrasts animal instinct (which is closer to the laws of matter and mechanism) with intuition, as a "direct vision of the spirit by the spirit." He uses this phrase in *The Creative Mind*, 48.

18. Bergson, *Two Sources*, chaps. 2–3.

mity or coincidence with the perfect activity of God. When authentic, this union bears the fruit of action in the world. Through "grand feats" in a gradual transformation of humanity, dynamic religion is an extension of divine power in creation. Christian mysticism alone is said to be complete in that through the Christian mystic, the current of divine love finds its broadest expanse in the mission to lead the process of human spiritual evolution. The twofold movement in humans towards transcendence and outwards into action is found in its fullness in Christian mystics, who incarnate the identity of the principle of life with love: "Beings have been called into existence who were destined to love and be loved, since creative energy is to be defined as love."[19] In *Two Sources,* the *élan vital* is called "love," a view in tension with *Creative Evolution's* non-Western God of "supra-consciousness" which is neither omnipotent nor omniscient, but a current of consciousness penetrating matter and guiding the path of evolution.

IV. Critique of Bergson's Philosophy of Religion

Bergson's theory of the *élan vital* in relation to religion suffers from three exclusions: First, his rejection of the claims of natural theology; second, his underestimation of the role of reason in morality and thus of the unique role of moral obligation in relation to conscience; and third, his suppression of the role of revealed theology and its concrete influence on both the development of Christianity and Judaism, and on mystics in particular.

1. Reason, Contemplation, and Natural Theology

Maritain echoes a key insight of Garrigou-Lagrange with respect to Bergson. The latter's rejection of classical metaphysics, Maritain held, stems from a skewed sense of the roles of reason, teleology, and contemplation, an error which resulted in a flawed priority of action over concerns about truth, dogma, and faith.[20] A kind of Manichaean cleavage between the forms of morality and religion is thus introduced which cannot be repaired due to the constricted role given to the intellect. In Bergson's "irrationalist philosophy," intelligence emerges only to make tools, and man is caught between the infra-rational impetus of social pressure and the supra-rational mystical impulse.

19. Ibid., 257.
20. See Maritain, *Bergsonian Philosophy and Thomism,* 332, 335, 336.

We can apply Bergson's language of the infra-rational and supra-rational to the static/dynamic religion distinction, where reason is subordinated to the *élan vital* represented by the mystical impulse. Using the metaphor of an erupting volcano, Bergson describes the mystical impulse of dynamic religion as the invisible seismic forces beneath the surface, which heave up the earth's crust and to the "fierce glow" of molten matter that cools into the "mold of doctrine." What we call religion is the crystallization of what a few privileged souls called "mystics" had poured hot, into the soul of man. Here, reason is a solidifying, even stultifying, force which refracts reality in a distorting kaleidoscope of concepts. Opposed to this is the movement of love, or superabundance of life which "pours itself into vast enterprises."[21] Several consequences follow. Free will becomes pure spontaneity, teleology and metaphysical perfections dissolve as static constructions of the mind, and contemplation is constricted and critiqued as a set of ideas—a "weakening of [the impulse] of life".[22]

Bergson's Kantian relegation of the intellect to its practical functions constricts the metaphysical trajectory of his philosophy of religion, exiling the mystical impulse from its native soil of natural theology, and collapsing contemplation into religious voluntarism. By the same token, Bergson views medieval natural theology as either a fruitless *a priori* exercise (deriving conclusions from predetermined conclusions of faith), or as a redundant *a posteriori* exercise by which we attempt to prove that which we have already encountered by experience.

Bergson's restriction of the scope of reason in the philosophy of religion contradicts the Aristotelian demands present in much of scholastic natural theology. Aquinas provides *quia,* not quidditative, proofs for God's existence, and proceeds *a posteriori,* not from God's essence to His properties, but from sensed features of material objects, to their metaphysical principles and extrinsic causes, which latter are inferentially known (not directly perceived) to exist. Natural theology does not start with preconceived *a priori* ideas any more than it commences with the raw data of mystical experience. Far from being divorced from the experience of God,

21. Bergson, *Two Sources,* 232.

22. Ibid., 212. Bergson inverts the Plotinian intellectualism, or view that "action is a weakening of contemplation." Ibid., 221. Arguably, when the classical metaphysics which grounds both ethics and authentic mysticism is absent, both morality and religion are seen as competing with intelligence, albeit a post-Enlightenment intelligence, which spins *a priori* ideas into neat but untrue systems, or procures goods set by our lower nature.

natural theology's *via negativa* approach to the divine attributes plays a key propadeutic role in the spiritual life by providing the mind with exercises of detachment. The link between metaphysics and mysticism is further secured in that some mystical claims (concerning monism, for example) can surely be corrected by metaphysical argument.[23]

Although absent in Maritain's analysis, Bergson's argument against reason sets the terms for his understanding of religion and mysticism. Bergson divorces both speculative and practical reason from the principle of life in his discussion of the problems with Greek metaphysics and the "false problems of philosophy." Aristotle's Unmoved Movers or Thought-thinking-Thought, and Plato's Ideas, are seen as instances of the confusion of intellect and being, which introduce insoluble riddles of a self-referential mind. In its drive for conceptual clarity, the mind suppresses movement and the current of becoming and posits the immutable as prior to change.[24] Describing our plight in his own version of an unhappy consciousness, Bergson says: "the intelligent being [is] not living in the present alone; there can be no reflection without foreknowledge; no foreknowledge without inquietude, no inquietude without a momentary slackening of the attachment to life."[25] As a withdrawal from life, reason leads to egoism, fear of annihilation, and despair, and must be suppressed either by the myth-making compensation nature provides through static religion, or by the mystical impulse which "transcends" questions about the soul, the First Cause, and even the problem of evil.

It is no surprise that a system which restricts reason's scope also suppresses contemplation as the ultimate *telos*, or recasts it as the triumph of love over reason. And the suppression of contemplation is also a brushing aside of faith and dogma, since the latter uses metaphysical reason for its scaffolding. It is actually surprising that in the absence of the glue of reason and faith, Bergson is able to develop an argument against the paranormal as the heart of mysticism. Mystical raptures, visions, and psychological aberrations are dismissed as a transitional stage between static and dynamic religion, when the soul is acclimatizing itself to heights of intuition. But

23. On this, see Heather M. Erb, "Being and the Mystic: The Metaphysical Foundations of Thomas Aquinas' Mystical Thought," *Verbum* [Budapest] 6 (2004): 135–59.

24. On the argument, and Bergson's treatment of the Greek philosophers, see Bergson, *Two Sources*, 142–45.

25. Ibid., 210.

why these phenomena are less a current of the *élan vital* than is mystic selflessness remains unclear without the insights of reason and faith. If the impulse of life is marked by novelty, creativity, and the absence of formal and final causality, why wouldn't the psychically bizarre be indicative precisely of the presence of the *élan vital*, rather than of a passing transition to a stable state?

In a rational schema of spiritual progress based on stages of perfection and a hierarchy of virtues, by contrast, paranormal phenomena are often less a sign of a divine incursion than they are of mental disturbance or even demonic activity. How psychic trauma anticipates "readjustment with a view to equilibrium on a higher level" requires narratives of virtue and grace, not just descriptions of felt undifferentiated union of ecstatic states followed by praise of spiritual activism (as an expression of divine energy) in contrast to "mere contemplation."[26] Bergson's failure to connect questions of natural theology with the spirit's search for union with the principle of being opens a chasm between metaphysics and mystical theology which is often quickly filled with an idealist activism, on the one hand, or with experientialism, on the other.

2. *The Will and Natural Morality*

Maritain argues that Bergson's account of the origins of the levels of morality and religion (in social pressures, aspirations, and mystical impulses or the "emotion" of charity) fails to account for the role of reason in moral obligation and in the "call of love," thus exposing a gap normally filled by natural law.[27] Invoking Aquinas's distinction of the orders of specification and exercise with respect to the will, he points to Bergson's failure to account for authentic moral obligation and conscience—a failure that stems from the diminished role given to intelligence in the moral life.

Authentic moral obligation, says Maritain, involves the formal causality of the intellect, giving to will its object (as well as ascertaining the *bonum honestum*, or the "good as right"[28]). This unique kind of influence is

26. Bergson, *Two Sources*, 229–33. While it is true that Bergson's views on mysticism serve his own metaphysical system of the *élan vital*, his Heraclitean vision propels the soul out of contemplation into action as its final perfection. He even reduces mystical contemplation to the state of rapture. See ibid., 232, 233.

27. Maritain argues this in *Bergsonian Philosophy and Thomism*, but more vigorously in *Moral Philosophy* (London: Geoffrey Bles, 1964), 428–35.

28. As contrasted to the "good as useful" or the "good as pleasurable."

in the order of specification, not exercise, such that the will is "formed in the light of the intellect" and bound by its dictates "as long as the gaze of the intellect is set on the law of human conduct."[29] Moral obligation is not an irruption of the sacred into the natural realm as Bergson argues, but is rather an "incommensurable" and unique reality stemming from the rational character of the will itself, whose thirst for being transcends utility and pleasure, being satisfied only by the good-in-itself, the *bonum honestum*. It is connatural to the will, says Maritain, to be formed in light of the intellect, and it is futile "to make a morality come forth from the mixture and interpenetration of an infra-morality of the social order and a supra-morality of the mystical order."[30]

3. *Revealed Theology and the Philosophy of Religion*

Both Gilson and Maritain note the methodological error involved in Bergson's attempt to trace the origins of religion and mysticism while ignoring the claims of revealed theology. For Gilson, Bergson's study of Christianity uses a method without an object, since he attempts to give an exhaustively philosophical account of religious life ("a natural theology of the supernatural life").[31] "Philosophism" (the exclusive use of philosophical reasoning to investigate reality) is powerless to gain entrance to a supernatural world which only faith can penetrate, and "Christian natural mysticism" does not exist, since it ignores the gratuitousness of faith.[32] We have seen Maritain's argument to the effect that lower or natural morality is not reducible to a social code without destroying authentic moral obligation, freedom, and conscience. But supernatural morality is equally incomplete without consulting the Faith itself, and even the mystics regularly claim the objective data of faith as the source from which their experience proceeds.[33]

29. Maritain, *Moral Philosophy*, 434. Maritain goes on to explain the misuse of free choice by voluntarily ceasing to "consider the rule," by detaching one's gaze from "the moral perspective." Ibid., 435.

30. Ibid., 434–35. This approach, he says, is as futile as trying to establish "a metaphysics by combining physics and religion" or wishing to "fabricate wine by mixing brandy and nectar." Ibid.

31. Étienne Gilson, *The Philosopher and Theology*, translated by Cécile Gilson (New York: Random House, 1962), 165–66. Further, Bergson "wanted to reach Christian mysticism by following the *élan vital* upstream to its source, and even if necessary, somewhat beyond; but the very essence of the Christian mystical life was that it came entirely from above as a gratuitous gift." Ibid.,167.

32. Ibid., 168.

33. Maritain, *Moral Philosophy*, 436. Bergson would deny the "contextualist" thesis con-

Maritain goes further than Gilson, positing that the supernatural lies at the very core of the moral life (in the order of being, not of discovery), thus implying the consequences of Bergson's oversight more clearly. Bergson was correct that the moral life is established in rectitude only by charity, but in reserving "open" morality (and "dynamic" religion) to elites (moral heroes and mystics), he missed the impact of the supernatural in the vast human family.[34] Moments of "secret inspiration" in acts of self-sacrifice, compassion and supererogation point to breadth and depth of charity in the "inner movements and invisible recesses where prior to every exterior act man already commits himself to decisive responsibilities." In these moments, ordinary persons may experience the paradox and bewilderment accompanying participation in "the breath of Uncreated Love."[35] The picture becomes more complex, of course, in analyzing the mutual conditioning of the theological virtues and the relation of faith, hope and charity to the moral virtues.[36]

V. Aquinas on Life (*vita*) as Corrective to Bergson's Theory

In contrast to Bergson's naturalistic analysis of the sources of morality and religion, Aquinas develops a robust view of *vita* in relation to the soul, spiritual vision (faith), and spiritual growth that maintains the links between natural, moral, and revealed theology. Unlike Bergson's activist emphasis on life as a force in competition with reason and contemplation, for Aquinas, *vita* is an analogous term moving across the natural and supernatural orders, finding its paradigm in God's immanent activities of love and knowledge.

Far from Bergson's vague mysticism represented as the source of "dynamic religion," Aquinas's mystical theology is fully incarnational and ecclesial, and is contemplative at its summit. Will and intellect are not juxtaposed but

cerning mystical experience, which promotes an unbridgeable diversity of religious experiences across the world religions, based on their unique doctrinal and cultural settings.

34. Ibid., 444.

35. Ibid., 446–47.

36. See, e.g., St. Thomas Aquinas, *Summa theologiae* (ST) I-II, q. 65 on the connection between the moral and the theological virtues, and on the mutual conditioning of faith, hope, and charity. Obviously, Maritain's view that even unbelievers may experience these bewildering encounters with grace needs qualification.

harmonized, and the supernatural order is not in tension with the natural organism, but is rather the fulfilment of its growth towards perfection. Further, Aquinas's robust account of intellect and will directs natural, revealed, and mystical theologies towards their unified Source. The creaturely senses of life found in form, operations, and *esse* recur in God, culminating in divine Self-knowledge and the plenitude of diffusive goodness. The signs of life (viz., self-motion and cognition) resonate in the theological themes of spiritual vision and in eternal life as inchoately experienced in the sacraments.

1. Philosophical Senses of "Life" in Aquinas

In the course of explaining the three ways in which the soul is the cause of the body (as the source of movement, the goal, and the form), Aristotle famously stated that "in the case of living things, their being is to live."[37] For Aristotle, the being of a thing is its form, which gives rise to the set of operations or activities the entity performs, and "to live" is to exist in such a way as to be capable of a set of operations. Form causes the being of a thing for it is by form that a thing is in possession of its essential predicates.

In his *Commentary on Aristotle's De Anima*, Aquinas repeats Aristotle's teaching that the soul is the cause of the living body as its form. Elsewhere, he diverges from Aristotle by positing *esse* as the act of either a substance or of the principle of substance, the form. At times, he interprets *vivere* as *esse* (in the Aristotelian maxim)—not as the operations exercised by the soul's powers, but rather as another act exercised through the essence of the soul, just as operations are exercised through the faculties.[38]

Life relates then either to a thing's *esse* or to its operations, depending on whether one is following the order of knowledge and discovery (here, life means operations, which are more manifest), or the order of causality (here, life is properly being). The soul gives actuality and unity of function or powers to the body. Life, he says, is displayed above all by two functions: cognition and movement.[39] In his *Commentary on Aristotle's De Anima* 2.1

37. *De Anima* 2.4, 1015b14–15. The famous Latin phrase is "vivere viventibus est esse."

38. Cf. Aquinas's *Summa Contra Gentiles* (SCG) I, chap. 98 [2]: "... Now, 'to live is for the living their very being,' as appears from the Philosopher in *De anima* II. For, since an animal is said to be living because it has a soul, through which it has being as through its proper form, it follows that to *live* is nothing other than *such* a being arising from *such* a form." *St. Thomas Aquinas on The Truth of the Catholic Faith, Summa Contra Gentiles Book I: God,* translated by Anton C. Pegis (Garden City, New York: Image Books, 1955).

39. See ST I, q. 75, a. 1.

(lectio 1), Aquinas develops the various meanings of life in relation to organisms and substances. The soul is both the cause of the being and operations of a thing, by fulfilling the potency of matter and giving life. The soul is first act, in relation to other operations, as knowledge is to the act of thinking. It gives life as causing self-motion in a thing, whose life is a self-propelling interiority generating an ascending ladder of functions, from vegetative to intellectual and volitional. Quoting *Metaphysics* 11.7 (1072b1ff), he includes in the notion of movement the activity of intellect, such that immaterial substances also have life.

The second meaning of life in the *Commentary on the Gospel of John* is that of the specific act of a living substance characteristic of its mode of being. So, "chief among the activities of life are the intellectual acts."[40] In the analogous notion of life encompassing both biological and intellectual levels, Aquinas gives a wider sweep to the notion than does Bergson, who aligns life more closely with irrational forces or instinct. The press towards interiority also distinguishes Aquinas's approach from Bergson's focus on transitive action and productivity.

In the *Summa theologiae,* Thomas continues the theme of the levels of life, focusing on the culmination of life that is God—life as the perfect life of self-love and understanding. He argues in ST I, q. 18, a. 3 that life in the highest degree is properly in God: if a thing *lives* insofar as it operates of itself (and not as moved by another), then the more perfect life is found alongside the most perfect power. He then traces a threefold ascending order among movers: First among these are things that move not by any inherent form or end, but only by executing their movements (their form and end being determined by nature); this is how plants grow and decay. Next are animals, which have more self-motion than plants. They receive through sense the principle of their motion but their cognition has a degree of immanence. Still higher are humans, whose knowledge is interiorized and ordered—not only can they propose an end to themselves, but can also discern the means to reach it. The fact that we experience the mind moving the senses specifies the kind of self-motion here. It is incomplete, however, in that the will is determined by the last end and the mind, by first principles. God has the highest form of life, in that His knowledge is not determined by another, but is identical with His essence. His perfect

40. In 14 Joann. lectio 2, no. 1869.

and eternally actual intellect signals that life is perfect when self-motion occurs without stain of potentiality in mover or moved. In God, perfect self-motion is purely immanent.[41]

Further, perfect life virtually contains all life as a cause contains the reality of its effects—"all things in Him are the divine life itself," Aquinas states. This occurs by being created and preserved by God, or having their forms or ideas in Him.[42] Things have life in God in two ways: first, as held together and preserved by the divine power, albeit existing in their own natures; in this way, things "live, and move, and have their being" in Him. Second, things are in God as known by Him, through their proper ideas and indistinct from God's essence.[43]

The theme of the plenitude of causal power of the divine life continues in the *Commentary on The Divine Names*, setting the stage for a theological concept of life involving regeneration through the Christ's Headship over His mystical body. God distributes life according to things' modes. Humans fall below angels in intellectual life, since their knowledge is weak, easily led into falsehood, and non-continuous.[44] The magician Simon of Acts 8 is said to err by ignoring the universality of the cause of being, resulting in a naturalistic concept of life based on sense appearances only.[45] The universal power of the First Cause grounds divine life as superabundant, containing all forms of life as fecund and ineffable.

Not only is there no contradiction between primary and secondary causal orders for Aquinas; in fact, the divine universal Cause conditions both the existence and operations of creatures, and is immanently present by causing them to operate according to their own natures. God gives

41. See ST I, q. 18, a. 3, ad 1.

42. See ST I, q. 18, a. 4 and ST I, q. 18, a. 4, ad 4.

43. ST I, q. 18, a. 4, ad 1. Aquinas says that considering them as forms only, they have truer perfection in the divine mind than in the natural order, as perfect, uncreated models; yet their existence as material particulars is more true to their nature, even if less noble. See ad 3. Taken from translation by Anton C. Pegis in *Basic Works of Saint Thomas Aquinas*, vol. 1 (New York: Random House, 1945).

44. See In De Div. Nom., chap. 6, lectio 1.

45. In de Div. Nom., chap. 6, lectio 2. Further, magic is a misuse of the intellect, diverting it away from the "goods of reason" towards lesser things. Aquinas also reasons that magic is unnatural inasmuch as it is a diversion of intellect and will from their proper objects of truth and goodness. He states that "false judgments in the area of intellectual operations are like monstrosities in natural things; they are not according to, but outside, nature; since the good and natural end of the intellect is the knowledge of truth." SCG III, chap. 107, no. 9. From translation by Anton C. Pegis in *Basic Writings of Saint Thomas Aquinas*, vol. 2.

things being, preserves them in being, and leads them to their end by relating their modes of operation to proper objects. Just as a good governor allows citizens to perform their own duties, so does God institute the natural order whereby things can reach their ends through their proper forms and operations. Providence does not cancel the existence of evil, contingency, free will, fortune, and chance, but invests creatures with forms and powers necessary for their fulfilment, such that humans are neither puppets nor "changers" of God, as determinism and process philosophy would have it.[46] God's inner life is communicated in part through the exercise of Providence, which as the wisdom or rule of reason in all things, works through the features of the temporal order.

2. *Theological Senses of "Life" and "Vision" in Aquinas*

Bergson's idealist, activist mysticism contrasts sharply with Aquinas's ecclesial, incarnational mysticism. While the former thinker pictures the expansive spiritual energy of the mystic in non-incarnational terms, Aquinas envisions mystical theology as a graced anthropology by which we are conformed by doctrine, conversion, and community, to Christ. This action occurs through sanctifying grace residing in and vivifying the essence of the soul, propelling us into natural and supernatural virtue, by help of the nourishing presence of Christ in the sacraments.

The ecclesial and Dominican context of religious experience, as well as the primacy of the theological virtues in the thought of Aquinas, also militates against quietism, contemplative elitism, and an interpretation of charity as an emotion or supra-rational impulse. Why is charity not an emotion but a virtue? Because theological virtues direct us to supernatural happiness in a way similar to the way natural inclinations direct us to our natural end, viz. through reason and rational appetite or will.[47] In his description of the theological virtues, Aquinas deftly combines the Aristotelian language of the stability of habit in relation to object, with the more fluid terminology of dynamic participation in the divine Nature.[48]

46. The magical view of prayer which forces God's hand is rejected by Aquinas: "For we do not pray that the eternal disposition of His providence may be changed, since this is impossible." SCG III, chap. 95, no. 1. From translation by Anton C. Pegis in *Basic Works of Saint Thomas Aquinas*, vol. 2.

47. It is important to note that these powers require divine help to conform to their higher end. See ST I-II, q. 62, a. 3.

48. In ST I-II, q. 62, a. 1, ad 1, he says that a nature may be ascribed to a thing either essentially,

Aquinas develops the theological concept of life in several texts, such as his *Commentary on the Gospel of John,* where he details both the effects of the sacraments (especially the Eucharist), and his theology of Christ's headship over the mystical body. In both cases, *visio spiritualis* is the means of entering into God's life, which is our *telos*. The fruitful exchange and complementarity between the various types of theology in Aquinas (in contrast to Bergson) is evident from four features of his theological thought: the mutual conditioning of intellect and will; the ecclesial context of spiritual growth; the frequent parallels of natural and supernatural orders; and the regular appeal to Scriptural authority. The Gospel of John provides Aquinas with an opportunity to link the ideas of eternal life, union with Christ, and spiritual vision as graced cognition involving intellect, emotions, and will. Here, three questions arise: What is eternal life? How do we know God by acquaintance? How does our spiritual rebirth figure in the process?

Eternal life refers primarily to God Himself as immutable truth and love. In the High Priestly Prayer of John 17, Jesus says that eternal life for man is to know the Father and the Son.[49] Since knowing is our chief operation, knowing is life in the best sense. Since the intellect actively knows by being united with its object, perfect understanding involves eternal life. His syllogism is as follows: "Since then intellectual understanding is living activity, and to understand is to live, it follows that to understand an eternal reality is to live with an eternal life. But God is an eternal reality, and so to understand and see God is eternal life."[50]

As directed to that object which is life, our knowing God is eternal life. In giving eternal life, God gives us Himself—so, eternal life is also enjoyment of God. The way to the bliss of eternal life is through the goodness of Christ bestowed through His Incarnation, Passion, and Resurrection, and made present in the sacraments. Although the divine intellect is in itself infinite and so incomprehensible to us, in the life of grace we are gradually conformed to God as He is in Himself.[51]

---

or by participation, "as kindled wood partakes of the nature of fire; and thus, after a fashion, man becomes a partaker of the divine nature." From translation by Anton C. Pegis in *Basic Works of Saint Thomas Aquinas,* vol. 2.

49. John 17.3: "Now this is eternal life: That they may know thee, the only true God, and Jesus Christ, whom thou hast sent." Translation from *Douay-Rheims Catholic Bible* (New York: The Douay Bible House, 1941).

50. In 17 Joann. lectio 1, no. 2186.

51. In 1 Joann. lectio 11, no. 213; lectio 10, no. 206.

In developing the theme of ascending degrees of participation in divine life, Thomas stresses the will's interaction with the intellect—a faith united with love has as its proper reward eternal life.[52] Love (*amor*) moves us to this spiritual vision, and the delight (*delectatio*) of beatitude is experienced in the enjoyment (*fruitio*) of God, as caused by charity (*caritas*).[53] Right formation of the mind and will introduces the notion of *ordo,* as well. Spiritual love, he says, begins with the intellectual vision of the lovable object—the spiritual vision of God in this life is through faith, which is propelled by the divine law, and leads us to enjoyment of God. Just as the divine plan and Trinitarian missions unfold the orders of nature and grace, which are vitalizing orientations from a life principle and towards a goal, so our spiritual life is established by the gift of grace inhering in the soul, giving it spiritual existence, and is developed by spiritual vision or the virtue of faith. This spiritual vision is subjectively possible by a right ordering of will and intellect through the divine law. Rationality is involved in the return to God, in that reception of divine law which forms the intellect and will to effect spiritual vision and faith. This view is far from Bergson's dynamic religion in which the mystic, in splendid isolation, possesses supra-rational insight (through an "emotion" of charity) and then draws others through example.

The doctrinal and ecclesial nature of Aquinas's doctrine on the spiritual life is further confirmed by his understanding of communion. To be conformed to God in love entails enjoyment of the divine Persons through sanctifying grace, which occurs on earth through an affective or experimental knowing (*affective seu experimentalis*) by which we taste the divine sweetness.[54] Our entry into the divine life involves connatural knowledge (through the Gift of Wisdom) of the highest degree of life, found in the immanent spiritual operations of the Trinitarian processions, as knowledge that is prepared in us by charity.[55]

52. In 3 Joann. lectio 5, no. 548.

53. In 17 Joann. lectio 1, no. 2186.

54. ST II-II, q. 97, a. 2. Dionysius "learned divine things through experiencing them." On this topic, see Heather M. Erb, "*Pati Divina*: Mystical Union in Aquinas," in *Faith, Scholarship, and Culture in the 21st Century*, edited by Alice Ramos (Washington, D.C.: The Catholic University of America Press, 2002), 73–96.

55. Garrigou-Lagrange discusses why this knowledge is only "quasi"-experimental in this life, noting that the *viator* does not experience God directly, but only through the filial love God works within us, and because of the lack of certainty of this knowledge in this life. See his *The Love of God and the Cross of Jesus*, vol. 1, translated by J. Marie (St. Louis: Herder, 1947), 155–57. Garrigou-Lagrange modified Aquinas's language by his qualification of this knowledge as "quasi"-experimental.

God is "in" Himself as the beloved is "in" the lover, since He loves Himself by His very essence, not by something beyond His essence.[56] God the Beloved is not in God the Lover *per accidens* (in the way that the objects of our love are in us who love them). The Holy Spirit pertains to the love whereby God is in Himself as the beloved is in the lover. As the supreme good that is God is loved, the love that is the Spirit is holy, as both pure and firm (or eternal), since the Object is perfect goodness. The relations are immanent to God in that to know and to love are identical with His essence,[57] although they are internally distinct as real relations. The dynamic, active, and intimate quality of life prized by Bergson is not sacrificed to transient action or production, but operates within a fruitful Trinitarian context and participated in by the *viator* through the aid of the Gifts.

The third question concerns spiritual rebirth as a path to eternal life. Aquinas says that Jesus responds to Nicodemus' question about rebirth and eternal life with gentleness instead of argument. Yet what follows is the argument that only spiritual rebirth gives access to the divine mysteries. Aquinas contrasts the sentient life which we share with all living things and the spiritual life by which we are conformed to God through spiritual vision. By the cleansing of spiritual regeneration we enter into spiritual life, increase in spiritual vision, and become conformed to God, knowing the mysteries of eternal salvation through the eyes of faith. The spiritual vision of the Old Covenant was distant and from afar, for spiritual regeneration in the patriarchs was imperfect and symbolic; the spiritual vision of the New Covenant is inward but still imperfect, since physical corruptibility remains; and the spiritual vision of heaven is perfect, since rebirth is both inner and outer. The gate to eternal life is decidedly sacramental in that we are reborn through the Church, the womb which renews flesh and soul through water and the Spirit. Even in eternal life we will rejoice in the humanity of Christ, as the instrument of His divinity; our eyes will see the king in his beauty and we will go in and out and find pasture (Isaiah 33.17; John 10.9).[58] Spiritual rebirth occurs and culminates in rational creatures, since everything that has an intellect desires to live forever.[59]

In contrast to Bergson's theory of the sources and nature of religion,

56. St. Thomas Aquinas, *Compendium of Theology*, chap. 48.

57. Ibid., chaps. 47 and 50.

58. See 17 Joann. lectio 1, no. 2188, where Aquinas argues against the Arian heresy.

59. Aquinas so reasons in his proof for immorality from natural desire: ST I, q. 75, a. 6.

Aquinas's doctrine of the spiritual life is clearly indebted to its Aristotelian metaphysical scaffolding. The path of spiritual rebirth and conformation to Christ depends on the prior gift of sanctifying grace inhering in the essence of the soul.[60] In this paradigmatic sense of life, grace is a form of life or a stable quality giving spiritual existence to the soul, and facilitates our participation in God's life through the infused virtues, Gifts, and beatitudes. As our very spiritual life, sanctifying grace works within an Aristotelian schema of forms, powers, and ends, paralleling life on the natural level:

> It is not suitable that God would provide more for creatures being led to a natural good by divine love than for those creatures to whom that love offers a supernatural good. For natural creatures God provides generously ... forms and powers which are principles of acts so that they are inclined to activity through their own beings.... Even more for those moved to reach an eternal supernatural good he infuses certain forms or qualities of the supernatural order according to which easily and enthusiastically they are moved by God to attain that good that is eternal. And so the gift of grace is a kind of quality.[61]

As the "beginning of glory in us," the gift of grace is higher than nature and even than charity (as more encompassing), making the soul capable and worthy of eternal life, embarking and sustaining it on its journey. The spiritual existence of sanctifying grace is God's presence to the rational creature not just in the "common mode" of His essence, presence, and power (by which God is present to all creation), but in the "special mode" of indwelling through love in the soul of the believer.[62]

It is true that sanctifying grace is an interior principle of motion and a participation in the deep levels of God's life. But as a supernatural moving principle, this grace is far from Bergson's *élan vital,* for it is not a transitory phenomenon. Transient spiritual phenomena belong to the category of transitory graces of the later Baroque, like those charismatic phenomena not necessarily allied with the life of grace.[63] In opposition to this more extrinsic understanding of spirituality, Aquinas's sanctifying grace is a sta-

60. See ST I-II, q. 110, a. 4.

61. ST I-II, q. 110, a. 2. The parallel between natural and supernatural life follows easily from Aquinas's view that "grace perfects nature and does not destroy it." ST I, q. 1, a. 8, ad 2; see also I, q. 60, a. 5.

62. ST I, q. 43, a. 3.

63. Grace is a supernatural principle moving one interiorly (ST II-II, q. 6, a. 1). Garrigou-Lagrange distinguishes sanctifying grace and infused contemplation from "extraordinary graces" such as visions, raptures, etc. (graces *gratis datae* which often belong to the charisms), which need not accompany mystical union.

ble, vivifying inner principle (albeit given from an external source), which enables us to act as true causes in a higher order through providing the ground of similitude between the divine source or goal and the soul. As a kind of life-giving nature directing the soul to its ultimate *telos*, grace not only facilitates and steers the supernatural virtues, but vivifies the natural moral order as well.

Knowing the sense in which the Gifts are habits helps situate Aquinas's mystical theology in relation to Bergson's theory of the sources of morality and religion. The Gifts, like all good habits, make the person more free in his actions, imparting both dominion and pleasure to them, whereas the ordinary, modern sense of "habit" connotes dull, repetitive routine. The Gifts condition the soul to respond to the promptings (*instinctus*) of the Holy Spirit and are habitual dispositions placed in our soul, lending docility to His inspirations. Although they lack the radical novelty and self-creation of Bergson's *élan vital*, they are, arguably, a Thomistic response to the desire for moral alertness to the unpredictable power of the transcendent, as examples of the way in which the moral life is not limited by human willpower or even by rationality, for their object is "intuitive familiarity with the divine."[64]

The Aristotelian natural desire to know puts the stamp of goodness on all knowledge of truth, for the soul is as wide as reality itself—and spiritual vision is an elevation of this natural desire.[65] But the false seeing of curiosity differs from the spiritual wonder involved in faith. It is not the knowledge of truth, but the striving or appetite for it that can be immoderate, says Thomas.[66] Curiosity is not only a secular drive, but is equally adaptable to a religious habitat in addition to its usual role of turning the soul out to the world.

Spiritual vision denotes not a superadded faculty or power, for Aquinas, in the way some argued for special "spiritual senses," but rather the act of judgment about spiritual matters when wisdom and charity are at work. The topic of Christ's Headship is one of the classic loci of the language of the spiritual vision. It is the Eucharist that allows us to see with the "mind

64. This phrase is used by Thomas F. O'Meara in "Interpreting Thomas Aquinas: Aspects of the Dominican School of Moral Theology in the Twentieth Century," in *The Ethics of Aquinas*, edited by Stephen J. Pope (Washington, D.C.: Georgetown University Press, 2002), 357.

65. Cf. De Malo q. 8, a. 2.

66. ST II-II, q. 166, a. 2. Curiosity differs from wonder in the way that the vivisection differs from a portrait-painting—the one type of seeing encloses, dominates, and measures things *to us*, to consume and control; spiritual sight is a contemplative gaze on things as they are—thus, wonder links religion to the poetic.

of Christ," the Head of His body the Church. Spiritual vision or knowledge is imparted by baptism, by which we are incorporated into Christ, as one of His members.[67]

Spiritual rebirth, the coming to participate in eternal life, is known only by revelation, for Aquinas. Yet the analogy with natural life maintains the connection with human reason, in contrast to Bergson's sense of dichotomy between nature, reason, and mystical experience. The benefits of spiritual rebirth are spiritual life, nourishment, and instruction. Regarding spiritual food, Aquinas argues for the power of the Eucharist to secure eternal life: "(Now) the reason why that bread which comes down from heaven gives a life which never ends is that all food nourishes according to the properties of its nature; but heavenly things are incorruptible: consequently, since this food is heavenly, it is not corrupted, and as long as it lasts, it gives life. So, he who eats it will not die."[68] The reversals of nature present in the spiritual life, patterned by the author of the Gospel of John, surface here. The spiritual logic whereby the internal and spiritual are prior to the external and physical now assimilates the one partaking spiritual food to the bread of life, not vice-versa.[69] We have eternal life "in its cause and in hope," and by gradual transformation in this life. The taste or experience of God's goodness builds up faith or certainty of the mind, he says, in commenting on another reversal implied in the Psalmist's words, "taste and see the goodness of the Lord." As he puts it in his *Commentary on the Psalms*: "Now, although in the physical world something is first seen and then tasted, in the spiritual world it is just the opposite. For one who does not taste does not know."[70] Again, the dialectic of knowledge, love, and affective response frame the discussion of our experience of God, which is far from Bergson's sidelining of the intellect in spiritual ascent.

Regarding instruction, Christ's doctrine gives eternal life as repelling the darkness of ignorance, guilt, and damnation. The perfection of our life is the perfection of our capacity to know by grace.[71] The link between *vita*,

67. ST III, q. 69, a. 5.

68. In 6 Joann. lectio 6, no. 955.

69. Spiritual nourishment reverses the causality of physical nourishment, for while bodily food is transformed into the flesh of the eater, spiritual food transforms the eater into itself: In 6 Joann. lectio 7, no. 972; cf. nos. 974–78.

70. In Psalmos 33, no. 9. Translated by Gregory Froelich, in DeSales University Aquinas Translation Project: http://www4.desales.edu/~philtheo/loughlin/ATP/Psalm_33.html.

71. See In 8 Joann. lectio 2, no. 1145.

ordo, and *visio spiritualis* is one of deepening conversion and conformity to Christ, and the integration of acts of intellect and will this process requires avoids the false dichotomies triggered by post-Kantian interpretations of religious experience.

VI. Conclusion

Bergson's philosophy of religion represents an example of the chasm between natural, revealed, and mystical theologies lamented by Garrigou-Lagrange, a divide which limits the vision of both reason and faith and obscures the link between religious experience and classical metaphysics. Aquinas, on the contrary, presents *vita* as moving seamlessly through philosophical and theological orders, guarding the mystical from irrationalism and securing natural theology as the scaffolding for mystical theology, faith, and dogma.

A sounding of salient texts of Aquinas on the spiritual life and philosophical anthropology reveals the breadth of the concept of life as it is used to establish harmony between natural and supernatural orders, while having its primary referent in the divine realm. Outlining the relation of life to both *esse* and to the notions of order, reason, and spiritual vision, highlighted Aquinas's creative adaptation of Aristotelian metaphysics as well as the depth, stability, and reach of *vita* in his thought.

Aquinas's rich concept of life allies it to intellect and interiority, universal causal power, eternal being, spiritual vision or faith, and to spiritual regeneration through the Church. As living water is united to its source and flows from it, grace stems from and joins us to eternal life itself.[72] For Maritain and his Dominican mentors, the enjoyment of God, which is proper to the perfect and the *telos* of all, is accessed through an integrated unity of reason, virtue, and an interior supernatural spring of abundant life, rather than through an evolutionary struggle with its problematic dualisms.

72. In 4 Joann. lectio 2, no. 577: "Now water is of two kinds: living and non-living. Non-living water is water which is not connected or united with the source from which it springs, but is collected from the rain or in other ways into ponds and cisterns, and there it stands, separated from its source. But living water is connected with its source and flows from it. So according to this understanding, the grace of the Holy Spirit is correctly called living water, because the grace of the Holy Spirit is given to man in such a way that the source itself of the grace is also given, that is, the Holy Spirit." Translation from *St. Thomas Aquinas: Commentary on the Gospel of John*, translated by Fabian Larcher and James A. Weisheipl, with an introduction and notes by Daniel Keating and Matthew Levering (Washington, D.C.: The Catholic University of America Press, 2010).

BERNADETTE E. O'CONNOR

Maritain's *Aufhebung* of Bergsonian Intuition

I. Introduction

In a footnote to the "Preface to the Second Edition" of his *Philosophie Bergsonienne*, Jacques Maritain suggests that what *"his first teacher,"* Henri Bergson (1859–1941), meant by "intuition" is, in reality, "an effort of the whole being which normally has its place ... in *the creative invention of the artist*."[1] In this paper I shall consider the similarity Maritain suggests between Bergsonian "intuition" and *"the creative invention of the artist."* I propose to show that Maritain effects a kind of Hegelian *Aufhebung* of Bergson's intuition. I will explicate and expand the part of Maritain's footnote which sets up a similarity between Bergsonian intuition and *"the creative invention of the artist"* by elucidating both how Maritain "cancels" Bergsonian intuition and how he "picks up" or "sublates" this intuition. In effecting this *Aufhebung*, Maritain preserves Bergsonian intuition but Bergsonian intuition only as corrected and "brought back to its true proportions" by eliminating Bergson's "exaggerated systematization" of it, his perversion of it in an "attempt to make a metaphysical instrument of it," and the excessive importance he attributes to "sense perception and instinct" in it.[2] I think of Maritain as having performed a Hegelian *Aufhebung* of Bergsonian intuition because he wants to "cancel" Bergsonian intuition as the instrument

1. Jacques Maritain, *Bergsonian Philosophy and Thomism*, translated by Mabelle L. Andison in collaboration with J. Gordon Andison (New York: Philosophical Library, 1955), 60 and 29n3. All the emphases in all the quotations throughout this chapter are in the originals cited.

2. Ibid., 29n3.

of philosophy while preserving what is valid in it by "picking it up" as poetic inspiration.

The Hegelian dialectic, then, gives us the structure for our considerations: in an *alpha* moment I describe intuition as Bergson understood it; in a *bēta* moment I explain why Maritain insists upon canceling Bergsonian intuition as the instrument of philosophy; and in a *gamma* moment I show how Maritain picks up Bergsonian intuition and preserves what is true in it by identifying it with poetic inspiration and artistic activity. Maritain's *Aufhebung* of Bergsonian intuition, his canceling it as the instrument of metaphysics and his picking it up as poetic intuition, can then be seen as another instance of his distinguishing what belongs properly to the intellect and what to the senses; what to the intellect and what to the will; and what to the speculative sphere and what to the productive sphere, in order to unify the properly distinguished powers and spheres in the experience of the concretely existing human person and in his holistic philosophy.

II. *Alpha* Moment: Bergsonian Intuition

First, then, what did Bergson mean by intuition? Bergsonian intuition is a special function of the human mind, distinct from that of intelligence and, as we shall see, moving in the opposite direction of intelligence. Intuition is the means by which we attain what Bergson calls "moving reality ... the absolute,"[3] or "real duration,"[4] or "reciprocal interpenetration."[5] Following the Aristotelian-Thomistic principle that faculties are specified by their objects, we take our first step toward understanding the Bergsonian faculty of intuition by considering its object. For Bergson the object of intuition is the absolute. This absolute, this ultimate reality, is *la durée*, and "*real duration* is," he writes, "what we have always called *time*, but time perceived as indivisible."[6] The Bergsonian ultimate is changing without a what-is-changed; he writes, famously, "*There are changes, but there are underneath the changes no things which change: change has no need of support. There are movements, but there is no inert or invariable object which moves:*

3. Henri Bergson, "Introduction to Metaphysics" in *The Creative Mind*, translated by Mabelle L. Andison (New York: Philosophical Library, 1946), 227.

4. Bergson, "The Perception of Change," in *The Creative Mind*, 176.

5. Henri Bergson, *Creative Evolution*, translated by Arthur Mitchell, with a Foreword by Irwin Edman (New York: Random House, 1944), 195.

6. Bergson, "The Perception of Change," in *The Creative Mind*, 176.

movement does not imply a mobile."[7] The fact that change or, more properly, changing has no need of support allows Bergson to write of "the *substantiality* of change" and both that "movement and change are substantial" and that "substance is movement and change."[8]

And this changing that is the object of Bergsonian intuition is creative: "as soon as we are confronted with true duration, we see that it means creation.... Thus will appear the necessity of a continual growth of the universe, I should say of a *life* of the real."[9] The famous Bergsonian *élan vital* is this creative tendency of real duration. Bergson identifies "the 'vital' order" with "creation." Out of this living, creative changing there issues matter: bodies, both non-living and living. Bergson writes of the creativity of duration using the imagery of "a center from which worlds shoot out like rockets in a fire-works display—provided, however, that I do not present this center as a *thing*, but as a continuity of shooting out."[10] And he immediately identifies that duration, that continuity of shooting out, with God: "God thus defined, has nothing of the already made; He is unceasing life, action, freedom."[11] And then Bergson identifies God, duration, unceasing life, action, and freedom with the "consciousness or rather supra-consciousness" "that is at the origin of life."[12] "Consciousness, or supra-consciousness, is the name for the rocket whose extinguished fragments fall back as matter; consciousness, again, is the name for that which subsists of the rocket itself, passing through the fragments and lighting them up into organisms."[13] For Bergson bodies are in some way the residue, the temporary concretizations of the creative duration.[14]

Bergson holds that we have two mental abilities by means of which to experience reality. Intelligence is our faculty for knowing real duration as it

7. Ibid., 173.

8. Ibid., 175 and 184.

9. Bergson, *Creative Evolution*, 373.

10. Ibid., 271. The active energy this "shooting out" suggests makes this an opportune point at which to note, if only parenthetically, that Maritain believes that what Bergson intuits in his theory of duration is "the irreducible metaphysical value of the act of being." *Bergsonian Philosophy*, 307.

11. Bergson, *Creative Evolution*, 271.

12. Ibid., 284.

13. Ibid., 284–85.

14. Ibid., 261. It is difficult to consider Bergson's doctrine of real duration without thinking that it is pantheistic. The changing out of which everything issues is God. While Maritain acknowledges that Bergson explicitly rejects pantheism, he also holds that the logic of Bergson's principles necessarily involves him in it. See Maritain, *Bergsonian Philosophy*, 13, 58n*, 198–99, and 342.

is congealed in matter, for knowing those sparks that fall from the rocket of real duration. And intelligence always makes the mistake of understanding matter spatially and mathematically rather than as the pure time, the real duration of which matter is a distillate. Intelligence makes its object, matter, discontinuous or discrete and immobile,[15] thus failing to attain the real at its deepest level. This intelligence is the instrument of practical action necessary for survival. Bergson indicates that both matter and intelligence, so defined, result from the same inversion of, the same falling back from, creative duration.[16]

For Bergson it is intuition that grasps, if only momentarily, creative duration itself. We should consider how intuition knows this real, indivisible duration. For Bergson intuition seems to bring about a very intimate unity between the human knower and the knower's ultimate principle, this surging life, pure duration. And this union appears to be an ontological union, not an intentional one. Bergson writes of "*intuitive knowledge which establishes itself in the moving reality and adopts the life itself of things*."[17] He writes that by means of intuition, "it is into pure duration that we then plunge back."[18] And again he asserts: "In order that our consciousness shall coincide with something of its principle, it must detach itself from the *already-made* and attach itself to the *being-made*."[19] And again Bergson states that our mind "can be installed in the mobile reality, adopt its ceaselessly changing direction, in short, grasp it intuitively."[20] Even "philosophy," whose instrument, Bergson believes, must be intuition, "can only be an effort to dissolve again into the Whole."[21]

We have indicated above that to exercise Bergsonian intuition is to reverse the normal direction of intelligence, preoccupied as it is with bodies (those extinguished fragments falling from the rocket that is duration), and to coincide with duration itself. Bergson writes that the intellect "cannot, without reversing its natural direction and twisting about on itself, think

15. See ibid., 170–71 and 182, and Bergson, "Philosophical Intuition" in *The Creative Mind*, 149–50.

16. Bergson, *Creative Evolution*, 225–26.

17. Bergson, "Introduction to Metaphysics," in *The Creative Mind*, 227.

18. Bergson, *Creative Evolution*, 219.

19. Ibid., 259.

20. Bergson, "Introduction to Metaphysics," in *The Creative Mind*, 224.

21. Bergson, *Creative Evolution*, 210. On intuition as the instrument of philosophy see also ibid., 260–61 and Bergson, ""Introduction II: Stating of Problems," in *The Creative Mind*, 33, 42, and "Introduction to Metaphysics," in *The Creative Mind*, 236–37.

true continuity, real mobility, and reciprocal penetration—in a word, that creative evolution which is life."[22] As a reversal of our normal, action-oriented mental activity by means of intelligence, intuition requires a kind of violence and thus is painful for us: our mind "must do itself violence."[23] Again, use of the faculty of intuition requires "an effort, often painful."[24]

Bergson writes that the intuitive turning from "the *already-made*" to "the *being-made*" requires that "turning back on itself and twisting on itself, the faculty of *seeing* should be made one with the act of *willing*."[25] Perhaps it is the difficulty of our reversing our consciousness' ordinary preoccupation with the material and spatialized condensations of real duration that causes Bergson to identify the exercise of intuition with willing. I think, however, that there may be more to this identity of intuition and willing. Bergson calls the creative impulse that operates in real duration the "*élan vital*." Real duration is identified with life and creativity; perhaps it is not reaching too far to suggest that duration itself is a kind of creative willing. In that case the human willing that Bergson identifies with intuition would be a re-immersion of it in the creative willing that is its principle. He writes: "When we put back our being into our will, and our will into the impulsion it prolongs, we understand, we feel, that reality is a perpetual growth, a creation without end."[26] It is difficult to read the impulsion that our will prolongs as anything other, ultimately, than duration itself. In any event, the connection between intuition and willing in Bergson appears to be something more than what a Thomist would mean by the will's commanding our intellects in our ordinary commanded acts of knowing.

And for Bergson intuition is above intelligence or intellect as we have described it; he writes of "an intuition of the psychical, and more generally of the vital, ... which would ... transcend the intellect.... [I]n other words, a supra-intellectual intuition."[27] And yet, notwithstanding his description of intuition as supra-intellectual, Bergson tends to identify our faculty of intuition with our senses, with instinct in particular, and to make intuition a feeling. We have seen that Bergsonian intuition is oriented in the opposite direction of intelligence; so is Bergsonian instinct. In fact, Bergson identifies intuition with instinct: "by intuition I mean instinct that

22. Bergson, *Creative Evolution*, 178. See also ibid., 179 and 291, and Bergson, "Introduction to Metaphysics," in *The Creative Mind*, 224.

23. Ibid., 224.

24. Ibid., 235.

25. Bergson, *Creative Evolution*, 259.

26. Ibid., 261.

27. Ibid., 391.

has become disinterested, self-conscious, capable of reflecting on its object and of enlarging it indefinitely."[28] And, to be clear, Bergson does mean that what he calls instinct, which functions very much like the estimative power in animals and the cogitative power in humans, is knowledge of individual material things; he writes: "*instinct implies the knowledge of a* matter."[29]

So, for Bergson, the intuition by which our minds plunge into the ultimate reality, into pure duration, and which transcends intelligence, is also identified with sense knowledge. This intuition is further characterized as a feeling and as sympathy. He asserts: "that each instant is a fresh endowment, that the new is ever up-springing, that the form just come into existence ... could never have been foreseen ... all this we can feel within ourselves and also divine, by sympathy, outside of ourselves, but we cannot think it, in the strict sense of the word, nor express it in terms of pure understanding."[30] This faculty by which we can (however briefly) attain the absolute, pure duration, and coincide with it, is tied to the internal senses and to feeling.

Before considering Maritain's critique of Bergsonian intuition, I want to make two remarks about the correlative terms in what Bergson called "the very centre [of his] doctrine: the intuition of duration."[31] My first observation is that there is a sense in which the intuition of duration is more like love than knowledge. St. Thomas writes that "the action of the intellect consists in this—that the idea of the thing understood is in the one who understands; while the act of the will consists in this—that the will is inclined to the thing itself as existing in itself."[32] This means that when we know we do, of course, know the real thing; but we do so by raising the intelligibility potential in it to the spiritual level of the intellect, such that the real thing known is known according to the mode of the intellectual knower. On the other hand, when we love we stand out in the direction of the thing loved; the thing loved, as it is or could be in reality, in its own mode, is the term of the motion that is love. Bergsonian intuition, especially when it as identified with willing and as transporting us into duration, resembles love, both in the faculty by which it is achieved and in its *terminus ad quem*.

28. Ibid. See also ibid., 182.

29. Bergson, *Creative Evolution*, 164.

30. Bergson, "The Perception of Change," in *The Creative Mind*, 180.

31. Bergson, "Letter to Harald Höffding," translated by Melissa McMahon, in *Henri Bergson: Key Writings*, edited by Keith Ansell Pearson and John Mullarkey (London: Continuum, 2002), 366.

32. ST I, q. 82, a. 3, in *Summa Theologica*, translated by the Fathers of the English Dominican Province (New York: Benzinger Brothers, 1947), 1:415.

The second observation is that Bergson seems to be struggling mightily with the mystery of the one and the many. This struggle makes Bergson blood-brother of many of the Pre-Socrates who sought a one, either physical or metaphysical, beneath the many of experience; of Plotinus who made the One the ultimate and everything else emanations of it; of Proclus who attempted to preserve both sameness and difference in the way he elucidated the non-temporal moments of Plotinian emanation, uniting the sameness of the first moment, *monē*, and the difference of the second moment, *proodos*, in a third moment, identity-and-difference, *epistrophē*[33]; of Hegel who also struggled, in his dialectic of the appearances of Absolute Spirit, to preserve both sameness and difference; and of Heidegger, whose lecture on "The Principle of Identity," which was published in a book titled *Identity and Difference*, brought Gilson to tears, as had the lectures of Bergson.[34] This is how Bergson expresses his engagement with the one and the many: "intuition may bring the intellect to recognize that life does not go into the category of the many nor yet into that of the one."[35] The living changing that is duration is a *one* from the forward propulsion of which fall the *many* of experience; among the human congealments of duration its creative thrust is prolonged and, through intuition, re-entered. For a philosophy that starts from Bergsonian intuition "reality no longer appears … in the static state, in its manner of being; it [duration, the one] affirms itself dynamically, in the continuity and variability [the many] of its tendency."[36]

I must applaud Bergson's effort, especially because he strives to maintain both terms of the mystery, the one and the many, and because he makes place in his philosophy for the findings of what was for him contemporary science. And yet, for reasons that will become clear in our *bēta* moment, for a philosophical explanation of the mystery of the one and the many, I subscribe to the doctrine of St. Thomas in which the analogical amplitude of *ipsum esse* is the one underlying and causing different *essentiae*, from which it is really distinct.

33. Proclus, *Elements of Theology*, translated by Thomas Taylor (Frome, Somerset: The Prometheus Trust, 1994), pp. 20–23, propositions 30–35, and *The Theology of Plato*, translated by Thomas Taylor (Frome, Somerset: The Prometheus Trust, 1995), p. 235, bk 4, chap. 1.

34. Laurence K. Shook, *Étienne Gilson* (Toronto: Pontifical Institute of Mediaeval Studies, 1984) 334: "[Gilson] always knew he was listening to a great philosopher when tears of emotion ran down his cheeks—he had cried before at Heidegger … and at Bergson." See also ibid., 227–28 of this text for Gilson's view of Heidegger as a failed Thomas.

35. Bergson, *Creative Evolution*, 195.

36. Bergson, "The Perception of Change," in *The Creative Mind*, 186.

III. *Bēta* Moment: Maritain's Critique of Bergsonian Intuition

Maritain believes that Bergson made a fundamental and fateful error in not elaborating an explicit metaphysics of knowledge. "If," Maritain writes, Bergson "had treated the problem of knowledge for itself as should be done, he might have been forced to ... entirely recast his critique of intellect."[37] There is, no doubt, a metaphysics of knowledge, "entirely implied and inviscerated," in the method Bergson used, and in this method Maritain finds "a criticism, less explicit and correspondingly more corrosive, of intellect as a faculty."[38] Maritain does not claim that Bergson "has in view the annihilation of intellect" but rather that "the conception he forms of it deprives it of its nature and of the function for which it exists in us."[39] This Bergsonian intellect cannot know the essences of real things by means of abstraction; its concepts are only diminished images; for it the essence or "the universal is nothing in things."[40] Thus Bergson falls into nominalism. But for him this intuition, that putative faculty which has duration, creative life, the ultimate reality, as its—I will not say "object," which would suggest an intentional means-by-which it is known, but rather as its—*terminus ad quem* is to be the very instrument of philosophy.

How does Maritain evaluate this intuition, proposed by Bergson as the instrument of metaphysics? First, says Maritain, intuition consigns itself and the one who would know by means of it to the sensible order. Intuition "is incommensurable with the idea" and "identifies us ... with what is unique, inexpressible, incommunicable in the thing, ... with matter itself—which, united to form, makes the singularity of the thing."[41] Thus, writes Maritain, "the philosopher who relies upon it as upon a true faculty of knowledge surrenders in reality to the divinations of his sensibility" and "he will henceforth attempt to think with images."[42]

And to think in images, to fail to achieve knowledge of extra-mental things by way of concepts, is to put an end to philosophy, because philosophy:

> passes through ... [concepts] and uses them indispensably. Thanks to them and to their apprehension of being, it attains in direct line (but by the properties which

37. Maritain, *Bergsonian Philosophy*, 49.
38. Ibid., 44 and 45.
39. Ibid., 44.
40. Ibid., 69.
41. Maritain, *Bergsonian Philosophy*, 108–109.
42. Ibid., 110.

manifest it), the suprasensible immanent in the sensible; and, by analogical refraction, the suprasensible separated from the sensible—the pure spiritual. It obtains, about the spiritual world and about God, certitudes in themselves firmer and more perfect than mathematical certitudes. By dint of logic it holds being in its grasp.[43]

Bergson would make intuition the instrument of philosophy; Maritain asserts that "one shatters in reality the philosophical instrument when one claims to exorcise from philosophy abstraction which is the proper mode of human intellection."[44]

There is, Maritain suggests, even a sense in which intuition falls below the level of the senses and is incapable of even the knowledge our senses achieve. Maritain calls Bergsonian intuition of pure duration "a lived identification of the mind and the thing in its *real* being."[45] Bergsonian intuition is not the identification of the mind with the real thing in its intentional existence.[46] In intuition, explains Maritain, "we do not possess things, we are possessed by them; we do not intellectualize matter, we materialize the mind."[47] Here again we have the transitive character of intuition that I likened to love earlier. In Bergsonian intuition "the union of the known and the knowing" is not the Thomistic union *secundum modum cognoscentis* but rather "*secundum modum cogniti*."[48] The reason why intuition, "supra-intellectual in the intention of Bergson," fails in reality to achieve the dignity even of sense knowledge is that it lacks "what the senses possess, an intra-psychic likeness of the object."[49] Bergsonian intuition does not allow the mind "to give light to things;" it gives us instead a contact with things "which changes us into them."[50]

The non-conceptual nature of Bergsonian intuition, Maritain further explains, deprives it of the ability to attain truth, no small privation in the supposed instrument of philosophy. But the privation is unavoidable on Bergsonian principles, for in order for us to possess truth as truth, it "must be in us as *thing known*," which is impossible without our possessing an intelligible likeness of the thing known and a judgment.[51] For all these rea-

43. Ibid., 42.
44. Ibid. 44.
45. Ibid. 109.
46. Ibid.
47. Ibid.
48. Ibid., 108.
49. Ibid., 109.
50. Ibid.
51. Ibid. Perhaps this would be an opportune point at which to note that duration, that correlate of intuition at the very heart of Bergsonian doctrine, comes in for severe criticism by Maritain as well. Maritain believes that the theory of duration reveals a misunderstanding of the natures of potentiality, change, and time and makes logically impossible a real difference between God and God's creation. See ibid., 13, 56–57, 58n*,127–30, 172–79, 199, and 342.

sons Maritain rejects or cancels Bergsonian intuition as the instrument of metaphysics. In doing so, however, especially in the preface he wrote for the second edition of *Bergsonian Philosophy*, he is careful to distinguish the Bergsonism of intention from the Bergsonism of fact. "This distinction between the *two Bergsonisms* is always necessary,"[52] he writes. "If it permits one to do justice to the great Bergsonian labour and to the intentions animating it, it also permits one to avoid the troublesome 'confusionism' and, strictly speaking, the *departures from truth* to which so human and natural a desire for sympathy and superficial effusion sometimes lead."[53]

Before taking up the similarities between Bergsonian intuition and Maritainian poetic inspiration, let us see what really discrete powers and acts Maritain believes are conflated in Bergsonian intuition. "In reality," he writes, "it seems clear that the intuition Bergson describes is composed of quite diverse elements artificially gathered together."[54] These diverse elements are, first, "intellectual perception properly so-called"; second, "the activity of that sensible faculty the scholastics call *estimative* in animals, *cogitative* in ... [humans], which is none other than instinct inferring from particular to particular"; third, "a sort of experimental knowledge, which proceeds by conformity to the inner inclinations of the subject and which is [according to Saint Thomas] 'a manner of judging that is affective or instinctive, or by inclination'"; fourth, "the kind of *sensible sympathy* which, for the artist, takes the place of the impossible intellection of the singular and which he [or she] needs in order to express in matter his [or her] model or ... idea, and which is wholly turned toward artistic *operation*, not toward speculation"; and, fifth, "a share of natural mysticism which would make this intuition akin to the ecstasy of Plotinus."[55] It is to the third and

52. Ibid., 19.

53. Ibid., 19–20.

54. Ibid., 109.

55. Ibid., 109–10. The quotation is from ST I, q. 1, a. 6, ad 3. The reference in the English translation is inaccurate; the one in the second French edition is correct. In translating from Latin Maritain adds the words "affective or instinctive or" to St. Thomas's "per modum inclinationis." *Summa Theologica*, vol. 1 (Rome: Forzani and Sodalisi, 1920), 21. In both *Distinguish in Order to Unite or The Degrees of Knowledge*, translated under the supervision of Gerald B. Phelan (New York: Charles Scribner's Sons, 1959), and in *Creative Intuition in Art and Poetry* (New York: Pantheon Books, 1953), Maritain associates Plotinus with "the old Brahmins" (*Degrees*, 5) or "the Indian wise men," and suggests—as he does of the Hindu sages in "The Natural Mystical Experience and the Void," in *Ransoming the Time*—that theirs was a "natural mystical experience ... in which supreme intellectual concentration is attained by means of the void, and through the abolition of any exercise of conceptual and discursive reason" (*Creative Intuition*, 93). In *Ransoming the Time* (272), what is known, however, is not God or some angelic being (see *Degrees*, 6) but

fourth of these elements (conflated in Bergsonian intuition) and to Maritainian poetic knowledge that we now turn our attention.

IV. *Gamma* Moment: Bergsonian Intuition Picked-Up in and Sublated as Poetic Experience

We have considered the object of Bergsonian intuition, pure duration, and the manner in which this intuition joins us to it, that is, by a kind of non- ("supra-") intellectual instinctual sympathy that carries us, volitionally and, apparently, substantially into the creative life that is duration. And we have seen that, inasmuch as Bergsonian intuition fails to achieve conceptual and analogical knowledge of the real, it cannot serve as the instrument of philosophy. Now we must consider the nature of that poetic knowledge which serves the creative invention of the artist and with which Maritain identifies Bergsonian intuition.

For Maritain, the poetic soul is blood kin to the metaphysician, over whose birth also "a sort of grace of the natural order presides."[56] Perhaps Bergson's error was that he felt their kinship too deeply to distinguish clearly the formalities of poetry and metaphysics. Maritain, on the other hand, while acknowledging their deep kinship, distinguishes them precisely. Now for Maritain there is no great art without what he means by poetry or poetic knowledge or poetic experience. This is how he defines and relates art and poetry:

> Art and poetry cannot do without one another. Yet the two words are far from being synonymous. By Art I mean the creative or producing, work-making activity of the human mind. By Poetry I mean, not the particular art which consists in writing verses, but a process both more general and more primary: that intercommunication between the inner being of things and the inner being of the human Self which is a kind of divination.... Poetry in this sense is the secret life of each and all of the arts....[57]

---

rather the substantial *esse* of the human soul itself. Given the "Wideness in God's Mercy" and the ubiquity with which grace is given I, however, would not want to preclude categorically—nor I do believe Maritain does—the possibility of graced mystical experience of God for these seekers, especially for the charitable Plotinus and the forgiving Bergson. The title is from a hymn by Frederick W. Faber; see *Bergsonian Philosophy*, 60, for a text suggestive of Bergson's forgiving Maritain for the harshness of his earliest criticism of his thought.

56. Maritain, *The Degrees of Knowledge*, 2.

57. Ibid.

So let us consider the nature of poetic experience, the indispensable soul of art.

What is it that a poet knows in poetic experience and by what kind of divination? The poet knows, in the depths of his or her own subjectivity, the things of the world and, in so doing, knows his or her subjectivity itself. This knowing is obscure, inasmuch as it is by *affective* connaturality, under the color of emotion, rather than by a cognitive grasp of them.

Both Maritains attempt to articulate the object and means of poetic knowledge, Jacques in many places. In a particularly clear and concise passage he writes that in poetic experience or poetic knowledge: "what is *most immediate* ... is the experience of things of the world ... but what is *most principal* is the experiencing of the subject."[58] This last is, of course, an objective genitive: the object experienced is the subject himself or herself. And the poet knows, is made kin to, the things of the world in all their particularities. The poet knows obscurely or suffers the "essences, quiddities, qualities, talities, haececities, ipseities with which the real and the singular abound."[59] And in these, perhaps, the poet intuitively grasps their "communication in the act of existing and in the spiritual flux from which existence proceeds, a communication which ... is in things as if the secret of [their] creative sources."[60] The poet brings all this, with himself or herself, known in and with them, "back to the mysterious nest of the soul," where they are "buried in the subjectivity itself."[61]

Poetic knowing is by connaturality; the poet is connaturalized "with the mystery that is scattered in things, ... the invisible powers at play in the universe."[62] Poetic knowledge, Jacques writes, "proceeds not per *modum cognitionis* but by way of affective connaturality or of resonance in the subject," and in it "the emotion or inclination becomes a grasping of the real, *amor transit in conditionem objecti*."[63] In poetic knowledge "the emotion or inclination bears the real which moves the soul," that is, "the world which affects it and which it suffers in the heart of its ... subjectivity."[64]

And the emotion from which poetic experience proceeds may be "any

58. Jacques Maritain, "The Experience of the Poet," in Jacques and Raïssa Maritain, *The Situation of Poetry* (New York: Philosophical Library, 1955), 83.

59. Ibid. 76.

60. Ibid., 79.

61. Ibid., 76 and 74.

62. Maritain, *The Degrees of Knowledge*, 281.

63. Jacques Maritain, "The Experience of the Poet," in *The Situation of Poetry*, 80.

64. Ibid., 81.

passion and emotion—even evil ones—and especially ... grief."[65] It is not a certain type of emotion that enables a kind of knowing but rather the fact that the emotion finds the poetic soul watching. The soul of the poet "remains available to itself, keeps as it were a reserve of spirituality not absorbed by the outside world and by the *work* of the faculties; and this deep unused reserve of the spirit, being *unused,* is like a sleep of the soul."[66] Raïssa, the poet, offers her own characterization of this sleep: "The brooding repose which is provided by such an experience acts as a refreshing bath, a rejuvenation and purification of the spirit.... We cannot esteem too highly the profundity of the quiet which all our faculties then enjoy. It is a concentration of all the energies of the soul, but a peaceful, tranquil concentration."[67]

The emotion, bearing the things of the world, "pierces" the subjectivity of the poet in "the depths of such a secretly vigilant sleep."[68] In so piercing, in falling into "the living waters" of the soul, "the emotion becomes intentional and intuitive" and "passes ... [into being] the condition of a grasp of the real."[69]

But the knowing of the things and of the self in them, as they communicate in the act of existence, is a knowing in the mode of unknowing. This communication is "what the poet receives and suffers.... [T]his is what he [or she] grasps without knowing it or knows as unknown."[70] Conditioned by emotion and the things emotion bears to the soul, poetic knowledge "cannot (because it attains the real only as buried in the subjectivity itself, and therefore non-conceptualisable) expand in a concept produced *ad intra,* in a mental word."[71] The truth revealed in poetic experience is "unproportioned to our intellectual grasp—since it is essential to it not to be conceptualisable, fleeting and impossible to seize by the means proper to reason."[72]

The gift of poetic knowledge is for the sake of, has as its *telos* or *finis,* the work or the artistic object. Everything we have seen about the receptive character of the gift of poetic knowledge remains true, but now we must see that this obscure knowledge gained by affective connaturality is ordained to

65. Ibid., 83.
66. Ibid., 81.
67. Raïssa Maritain, "Sense and Non-Sense in Poetry," in *The Situation of Poetry,* 21.
68. Jacques Maritain, "The Experience of the Poet," in *The Situation of Poetry,* 81.
69. Ibid., 82.
70. Ibid., 79–80.
71. Ibid., 74.
72. Ibid., 85.

the work to be made. Raïssa testifies that "for the poet ... the expression is a vital part of his [or her] experience, and as it were the fruit of that experience."[73] Again she asserts: "the obscure experience, if it attains a high degree of intensity, tends to fructify in an object."[74] And yet again the poet Raïssa insists that "poetic experience properly so called" is "oriented from the beginning toward expression" and that the poet returns from the obscure knowing "with words, sounds, forms and colors."[75]

The philosopher speaks explicitly of finality: "the end of art as such is not to know but to *create* ... in the way of spirit and of liberty; here it is a matter of the productivity of the intellect *ad extra*."[76] What the activity of art "aims at is to make an object according to the internal exigencies and proper good of that object."[77]

What is to be revealed in the object or work to be made? The philosopher answers: the obscure grasp of the realities which the poet suffers, and through which he or she grasps his or her own subjectivity. Jacques writes: "For if at the source of the poetic act there is the experience ... in which the obscure grasping of the real, resounding in the creative subjectivity, is at the same time an obscure grasping of the soul of the poet, it will be necessary that the work made be a manifestation of both at once."[78] Thus the art work makes manifest the double content of poetic experience.

V. Conclusion

We have seen the nature of Bergsonian intuition and of its object, pure duration. We have seen Bergson's intuition described by him as an activity which we can sustain only for moments and as both supra-intellectual and as moving in the manner of instinct, that is, as reversing the orientation of intelligence. We have seen that Bergsonian intuition depends on willing and causes us to coincide with our principle (*pure duration*) and thus that intuition has a transitive effect, making it more like love than knowledge. We have seen that Bergsonian intuition is the means by which we are somehow identified with ultimate reality and, implicitly at least, that intu-

73. Raïssa Maritain, "Magic, Poetry, and Mysticism" in *The Situation of Poetry*, 34.
74. Raïssa Maritain, "Sense and Non-Sense in Poetry, in *The Situation of Poetry*, 18.
75. Raïssa Maritain, "Magic, Poetry, and Mysticism," in *The Situation of Poetry*, 30–31.
76. Jacques Maritain, "Concerning Poetic Knowledge," in *The Situation of Poetry*, 47.
77. Ibid., 49.
78. Jacques Maritain, "The Experience of the Poet," in *The Situation of Poetry*, 84.

ition serves this finality; it is, therefore, not ordained to the goal of making. Because of its ability to unite us with the ultimate, we have seen, further, that intuition is, for Bergson, the proper instrument of metaphysics.

We have also seen Maritain criticize Bergsonian intuition as being sub-intellectual and more closely related to the senses and to our will than to our intellect. Our intellect, Maritain holds, knows, in its concepts, formed in the acts of abstraction and apprehension, the real essences in material things (and not merely the material distillates of duration organized in the form of spatiality). Bergsonian intellectual knowledge and the science it produces are only for the sake of our managing our environment, not for a speculative understanding of the nature of things. But Bergsonian intuitive knowledge, this putative instrument of metaphysics, being non-conceptual, causing us to coincide with duration in a substantial (or, at least, non-intentional) manner, cannot achieve human knowledge of the ultimate in the only natural ways we can, in concepts and through the analogical use of reason.

We are now in a position to summarize why Maritain identifies Bergsonian intuition with poetic knowledge and to consider what powers and spheres Maritain distinguishes in effecting his *Aufhebung* of this intuition. If we set aside, cancel, Bergson's aspiration to grasp the ultimate in intuition, to use it as the means of doing philosophy, we see that there are certain similarities between intuition as Bergson describes it and poetic experience or knowledge as the Maritains describe it. Both are experienced as gifts and are difficult to prolong in time. Both Bergsonian intuition and Maritainian poetic experience are supposedly means of knowing; both involve, at least, sense knowledge of, and emotive or sympathetic union with, their objects.

And inasmuch as Bergsonian intuition is on the level of sense and instinct (though Bergson would deny this), it can know only particulars; Maritainian poetic experience is of the particular things and of the individual subject in them, known under the color of emotion. Both are non-conceptual means of knowing. For Bergson intuition is a special faculty, distinct from intellect; for Maritain poetic knowledge is by means of affective connaturality in which the emotion, which bears the things of the world into the poetic soul, serves as the intentional presence of the particular object known. Emotion thus replaces the concept as the *medium a quo* of knowledge. Both Bergsonian intuition and Maritainian poetic experience in some way go over into their object. Bergsonian intuition issues in our substantial or non-intentional union with duration. Maritain's intuition issues in the emotive-intentional union of the poet with himself or herself and with the things known. Both intuition and poetic experience encounter, in some non-knowing mode, the existential energy of a philosophical ultimate: the teeming activity of duration, on the one hand, and the communication of particular things in the act of being and in their creative Source, on the other hand.

If Bergson conflates these powers and spheres in his doctrine of the intuition of duration, how does Maritain distinguish them? Maritain grasps the real more clearly in distinguishing our sense knowing powers and our intellectual knowing powers and their proper objects than Bergson does. The latter's intuition is clearly related to sense knowledge and yet aspires to be the instrument of metaphysics, the knowledge of being inasmuch as it is being, clearly not something graspable by the senses. Maritain understands and expresses more accurately than Bergson the distinction between the two properly human powers of intellect and will. The object of our intellect is being under the formality of the true; the object of our will is being under the aspect of the good. And again the intellect raises the potential intelligibility of material realities to its own spiritual mode of being; the will, when it loves, goes out to the beloved in the mode proper to the beloved. But Bergsonian intuition seems to conflate the natures and activities of our intellect and will: it knows the ultimate but seems to be *entitatively* rather than *intentionally* joined to it. Finally, if we grant (with Maritain) that what Bergson calls "intuition" is really poetic experience, then Bergson's thought conflated the speculative sphere with the productive sphere; that is, Bergson would have intuition serve speculative metaphysics while it is better suited to serve the artistic making which Maritain's poetic knowledge serves.

The questions of whether Maritain read Bergson accurately and whether his criticisms of Bergson were fair and conclusive are legitimate ones. And these questions arise on the level of rational judgment, where truth is either attained or is not attained. These questions, then, transcend what Maritain himself calls "the *tone* of ... [his] book," with its "uncompromising bombast" of style and "language at times so imperious, so lacking in deference."[79] The reader is entitled to know how I would answer these substantive questions. I have already expressed my sympathy for, and appre-

79. Maritain, *Bergsonian Philosophy*, 12.

ciation of, Bergson's effort to grapple with what I take to be his intuition of the mystery of the one and the many and cited Maritain's recognition of "the great Bergsonian labour and ... the intentions animating it."[80] But, although I am far from being an expert on Bergson's philosophy, I must concur with Maritain in holding that Bergson lacks an appropriate philosophical insight into the nature and function of intelligence and that his attempt to thematize his basic insight suffers from a "troublesome 'confusionism.'"[81] The greatness of Bergson is in his basic insight or intuition of a dynamic one underlying the many; however, when he goes to express this insight in philosophical concepts, he falters, identifying what he calls intuition as "supra-intellectual" while, by the very nature Bergson gives it, as Maritain asserts, "in reality, it can only be *infra-intellectual*."[82] If Bergson had chosen to express his poetic—in the Maritainian sense—intuition in the production of art objects, no one could possibly contradict it. However, he chose to express it as a philosophy, which must aim to express the real the way it is, but which in his case failed to do so.

I am struck by the similarity of errors with which Maritain grappled at the beginning of his philosophical life and at its end. In the beginning it is the error of Bergson, who mis-articulated a poetic intuition, making it the instrument of philosophy, with which Maritain contends. Near the end of his life it is the error of Père Teilhard de Chardin, who conflated "a poetic intuition—extremely powerful—of the sacred worth of created nature," "a religious awareness ... of the presence of God in the world," in which "natural mystique ... played the greater part," but which could also include "touches of supernatural mystique" with the scientific idea of evolution, with which he contends.[83] What Maritain writes of Chardin, I believe, could also be applied to Bergson. In both mis-articulations of initial inspirations, "the science of the scientists has been entirely outpaced, nay more, swept along and absorbed into a great torrent of ardent meditation, in which science, faith, mystique, theology and philosophy in a diffused state, are inextricably mingled and confounded."[84] But when one takes his or her stand in the realm of *lògos*, of rational discourse, be it scientific or

80. Ibid., 19–20.

81. Ibid., 20.

82. Ibid., 28.

83. Jacques Maritain, *The Peasant of the Garonne: An Old Layman Questions Himself about the Present Time*, translated by Michael Cuddihy and Elizabeth Hughes (Toronto: Macmillan, 1969), 139–40.

84. Ibid., 140.

philosophical or theological, one must be held to what Maritain calls "the intrinsic meaning and internal logic of the principles which specify ... [his or her] doctrine."[85] Had Bergson and Chardin stayed within the realm of *mythos*, they could not be faulted for the creative *poiēsis* in which they expressed their intuitions of the ineffable; but in the realm of *lògos* they "do not think as they wish, but as they can."[86] This is so because, as Gilson reminds us, "the interrelation of philosophical ideas is just as independent of us as are the laws of the physical world. A ... [person] is always free to choose his [or her] principles, but when he [or she] does he [or she] must face their consequences to the bitter end."[87]

I conclude, then, by concurring with Maritain's critique of Bergson. It is also worth remarking that in the case of Bergson's intuition (as in so many other cases over the course of his life), Maritain effectively served the human intellectual aspiration for truth by distinguishing in his thought and writings what are really different formalities while at the same time uniting and making place for what he had distinguished in the lived experience of the human subject.

85. Maritain, *Bergsonian Philosophy*, 22.

86. Étienne Gilson, *The Unity of Philosophical Experience* (New York: Charles Scribner's Sons, 1937), 120.

87. Ibid.

≈ V ≈

MIND, RELATIONS, AND CHRISTIAN PHILOSOPHY

JOHN N. DEELY

Gilson, Poinsot, Maritain, and the Future of Thomism

I. Introduction

Among those who are quite attentive to the work of Jacques Maritain, close to none even, I would dare say, have so far listened to Maritain on the one point most crucial for the "next stage" in the history of Thomism.[1] The point I have in mind is the claim by Maritain that the sign plays for hu-

1. Thomas Aquinas lived from c. 1224/25 to 1274, the first of his writings dating to 1244, the last to 1273 (among which was one of his most important and most neglected, his commentary *In libros de coelo et mundo*). A full century passed before a Latin commentary tradition on his writings (the "First Thomism," in effect) began with Joannes Capreolus (c. 1380–1444) and culminated with Joannes a Sancto Thoma (1589–1644), aka John Poinsot. But from the time of Descartes (†1650) until Pope Leo XIII launched the "modern revival" of Thomism in 1879 (the "Second Thomism"), as far as the mainstream modern development had been concerned, the summary of Latin Thomism as *mis*represented in the 1597 *Disputationes Metaphysicae* of Suárez (†1617) was assumed accurate and sufficient. Within the "Second Thomism," then, i.e., "Neothomism" (or "neoThomism"), the Thomistic revival in the modern national languages, no figures achieved a greater prominence and close association than did Maritain (†1973) and Gilson (†1978), which is the reason in part for my title of this essay. (On the history of Thomism after Thomas, see my *Four Ages of Understanding* [Toronto: University of Toronto Press, 2001], 358–62; and on the appropriateness of the label "Neothomism" for the late modern revival, see ibid., 342n200, and the Index entry for the term on p. 940.) The whole point of this present essay is to demonstrate, so far as possible, that the endless scholarship at play within Neothomism as the "Second Thomism" cannot conceal the fact that Neothomism as an important development within the modern period of philosophy's long history has reached its glass ceiling, as did the "First Thomism" after Galileo and Descartes. For there to emerge a *post*modern Thomism, a "Third Thomism," in the manner in which Maritain, in contrast to Gilson, conceived the proper mission of Thomistic interpretation over time, a new terminology and central focus is required, exactly of the sort that Poinsot presciently outlined in his *Tractatus de Signis* of 1632. See Section 4, "The Pill Hard to Swallow," in the "Foreword to the Corrected 2nd Ed." of Poinsot's *Tractatus* (South Bend, Indiana: St. Augustine's Press, 2013), xxvii–xxxviii.

man beings a role every bit as fundamental as the role that motion plays in the physical world.[2] From the earliest phase of his intellectual life, Maritain sought to establish that there is a foundation and framework in human understanding that not only antecedes but indeed makes possible in the first place that distinctively modern development that we call "science" in the modern sense. This is a subject that preoccupies Maritain from his earliest to his last years.[3]

In treating this foundational question of the framework enabling all knowledge, there is a source alongside St. Thomas himself upon whom Maritain constantly drew, namely, John Poinsot (1589–1644), known in Maritain's time more commonly (if at all) as "John of St. Thomas." Maritain considered Poinsot to be the greatest thinker in the Latin Thomistic line, to the extent that Poinsot became Maritain's principal teacher alongside St. Thomas himself. My purpose here is to make Maritain's voice regarding Poinsot heard so loudly and clearly that not even the heritage of Gilson will remain able any longer to cancel out Poinsot's work.

In this essay I wish to address the twin issues of signs as foundational to the totality of human knowledge, and Maritain's reliance on Poinsot for what Maritain himself had to say on the subject. I want to call attention not simply to Maritain's reverence for the work of Poinsot, but more crucially to what in Poinsot's work even Maritain never quite grasped (though he came "that close"!).

II. How Did Maritain Come to Listen to Poinsot?

How did Maritain come to the study of Thomas Aquinas? His first teacher, he tells us, was Bergson; but his main teacher alongside St. Thomas, he also tells us, came to be John Poinsot. As far as we can tell, it was Raïssa who first got her husband to read Thomas, beginning on 15 September 1910. Maritain got his first chair as a professor in the history of modern philosophy in 1914, a position that he held until 1928, when he became instead professor of logic and cosmology. Late in 1922 he published a book with a perhaps somewhat unfortunate title, *Antimoderne*. Now just what did he mean by "antimodern"? The theme of the book was that Maritain felt kind of trapped in the situation of modern philosophy, because, he said (much as Charles

2. Jacques Maritain, "Signe et Symbole," *Revue Thomiste* 44 (1938): 299–330.

3. As he reminded us as late as *Le Paysan de la Garonne* (Paris: Desclée de Brouwer, 1966), and as early as *Antimoderne* (Paris: Éditions de la Revue des jeunes, desclée et cie, 1922).

Peirce had said somewhat earlier), that the essence of nominalism consists in the denial that relation has a reality independent of awareness. "When I make a comparison between any two or more things," says the Nominalist, "then and only then does an actual relation arise between them." Outside of such awareness there are only the individual things.

Maritain tells us that Poinsot "was a dearly loved master and inspiration for me and my friends. But we were quite lonely in our admiration for him. French intellectual circles were sublimely ignorant of him. And nay more. A strong majority simply loathed all the commentators, and particularly John of St. Thomas."[4] Gilson was among those loathers. Thus Gilson and Maritain, over the years, had completely antithetical views when it came to the work of Poinsot. Gilson says—I find this hard to believe, but since he says it in a letter to me I know that he did indeed say it—that "one cannot present to readers a doctrine that would be common to both Aquinas and Poinsot. I never agreed with Jacques Maritain on that point."[5] Unbelievable!

Maritain says that "if we compare the work of Poinsot—latest of the great commentators—with that of St. Thomas himself, all important changes can be interpreted in terms of pure development."[6] Maritain calls Poinsot "the profound doctor"[7] and "the commentator with whom I fell in love."[8]

Speaking for myself, then, I would say that Gilson—without at all minimizing his enormous contribution to the recovery of Thomas's work from the oblivion into which it had fallen between the late seventeenth and late nineteenth (modern) centuries—has created followers primarily associated with a mired-in-modernity form of the Thomistic revival ("neoThomism",[9] or as I have come to call it overall, "rear-view mirror Thomism"), whereas Maritain must be associated rather with some forward-looking version of Thomistic revival that could move beyond modernity in philosophy.

III. Signs and Historical Background

Throughout his work one sees Maritain returning time and again to the subject of sign, with constant retouchings, and all turning on the central

4. Jacques Maritain, *Reflections on America* (New York: Scribner's, 1958).

5. Letter 30, the last in the 1968–1974 Gilson-Deely Correspondence, dated 10 July 1974.

6. "Preface" to *The Material Logic of John of St. Thomas*, trans. Yves R. Simon, John J. Glanville, and G. Donald Hollenhorst (Chicago: The University of Chicago Press, 1955), vii.

7. Martiain, *Antimoderne*, 124.

8. Maritain, *Le Paysan de la Garonne*, 149.

9. See Deely, *Four Ages of Understanding*, 342n200.

point that he made in the opening line of the 1938 essay: "No problems are more complex or more fundamental to the concerns of man and civilization than those regarding signs. The sign is relevant to the whole extent of knowledge and of human life; it is a universal instrument in the world of human beings, like motion in the world of physical nature."[10] When I had undertaken to provide the first complete independent or "stand-alone" edition of Poinsot's treatment of sign, the realization was forced on me that Maritain had come only "that close" really to getting Poinsot's guiding insight. Even Maritain did not manage fully to realize the trajectory or arc that made of Poinsot's thought on signs a revolution for our understanding of being as involving communication at every level (not only through the interactions of finite beings giving rise to relations, but more originally in the interior life of God consisting in the communication among Three Persons whose very being as Divine Persons consists in a triad of relations purely suprasubjective within the undivided unity of the Divine Being).

It is not obvious on the surface, but the moment you take communication seriously as a phenomenon of reality, you have cancelled out the basic modern notion of "epistemology." For if the only relations are those we make by comparing objects within our own awareness, we are indeed trapped inside a bubble with "no way out," with no way of knowing anything directly save for the workings of our own mind. Let me go back to Pope Leo XIII's *Aeterni Patris* encyclical of 1879, where he uses his authority as Pope to require Catholic institutions of higher learning to restore the study of the writings of St. Thomas Aquinas. Why did Pope Leo do this? He did it because, by that time, idealism in the modern sense, introduced most noticeably through the influence of Descartes—the doctrine that everything we directly know is (not "depends upon") a mental state subjective to our own mind—had, by the late nineteenth century, triumphed in the intellectual culture, making God, the world of things, and the soul "unknowable," as Kant put it. In medieval thought and in Catholic tradition there was a long-standing notion of truths of reason proving the existence of God and the likelihood of the immortality of intellectual souls, thereby providing "preambles to faith." But these "preambles" presupposed the knowability in awareness of awareness-independent reality, exactly what modern idealism had called into question and, in fact, by Leo's time, effectively placed "under erasure."

10. Maritain, "Signe et Symbole," *Revue Thomiste* 44 (1938): 299.

We might even say, looking back, that Leibniz and Berkeley are the two really great thinkers in the Rationalist and Empiricist lines, respectively; for these two independently recognized the consequent implied in the modern idealist doctrine that our own ideas provide the only direct objects of our apprehensions. Berkeley went so far as to deny not merely the knowability but indeed the very existence of an "external world," asserting that what we refer to as "the external world" amounts only to the dreams of God which have so much more reality than our own dreams that we are led naively to assume that ideas are not the whole of reality. Leibniz, on the Rationalist side, did not go quite that far, but summarized the situation rather with his formula that "Monads have no windows": nothing enters nor exits from the theater of our individual minds.

Yet what Leibniz saw as no problem most thinkers have seen rather as a conclusion unacceptable, and the history of modern philosophy can indeed be written, on the theoretical side, as a failed attempt to avoid the Kantian outcome, and, on the practical side, as a simple ignoring of the consequences which lead inescapably to the solipsist consequent. Maritain, among the late moderns, comes the closest to realizing Benedict XVI's point[11] that relation must be recognized alongside substance and in contrast to inherent accidents as an equiprimordial reality, and that indeed with this point we expose the essence of the nominalism which, as Peirce no less than Maritain has pointed out, both pervades the whole of modernity in philosophy and necessitates its consequent idealist (or solipsist!) character on the speculative side. Thus Leo XIII re-establishes Thomism in order to re-establish realism in the mainstream medieval sense in philosophy (the knowability of *ens reale*, being in its awareness-independent dimension) as a viable component of the late modern intellectual culture.

IV. Hearing Poinsot from Listening to Maritain

Consider the following text in Latin from Poinsot's *Artis Logicae, Secunda Pars*, Question XXI, "De Signo Secundum Se," Article 1, "Whether sign belongs to the order of relation", 117/20–24:

> Quaerimus ergo, an formalis ista ratio signi consistat in relatione secundum esse primo et per se, an in relatione secundum dici seu in aliquo absoluto, quod fundet talem relationem.

11. Joseph Ratzinger, *Introduction to Christianity* (New York: Herder and Herder, 1970), 132.

Now consider the English misinterpretation supplied by Yves Simon and his fellow translators:

> We propose to determine whether the formal notion of the sign consists, primarily and essentially, (a) in a relation according to existence or (b) in a relation according to expression, or (c) in a thing absolute which would ground the relation that the sign implies.[12]

There is a huge problem with this translation. For where Poinsot has posed the question of what a sign consists in according to an exclusive and exhaustive alternative between *two irreducibly distinct and exhaustive* forms or modalities of finite being, Simon and his associate translators propose *three* alternatives expressed in terminology so muddy that the reader cannot even see that he or she is being misled—and completely misled—from the outset, so far as concerns the standpoint of Poinsot's semiotic. In fact, anybody who approaches the thought of Poinsot on the subject of signs via the translation alone of Yves Simon and his colleagues is absolutely guaranteed never to understand Poinsot's treatment of sign: where Poinsot has provided but *two* alternatives which divide the order of finite being exclusively and exhaustively, the Simon translation sketches *three* alternatives, and in language which leaves quite unclear what the first two in particular (the sole key to Poinsot's understanding of sign) are.

The translation version that Simon and his colleagues have provided has to be completely abandoned in order to reach Poinsot's foundational point that the understanding of how signs work requires the adoption of a standpoint that transcends the terms of the late modern realism / idealism debate, inasmuch as to understand how signs work requires the analyst to begin from a standpoint that transcends the distinction between *ens reale* and *ens rationis* (being as having a dimension knowable but independent of awareness, and being as having a dimension dependent upon awareness).

You can see why I say that, for all his own devotion to Poinsot, Simon never came to see the alternative perspective Poinsot opened up in establishing the exact sense in which the positive being of relation makes possible in the first place the phenomenon of semiosis in nature and in culture alike. In Poinsot's Latin, "relativum secundum dici" refers wholly and exclusively to the realm of finite subjectivity as subjectivity. It refers, that is, wholly and exclusively to the *subjectum essendi* (the subject of finite existence or "sub-

12. *The Material Logic of John of St. Thomas*, 359.

stance") taken together with the characteristics which individuate that substance (its inherent "accidents" or subjective features) upon or on the basis of which relations can and do arise among individuals as a result of their similarities and differences, but especially and initially as a result of their interactions leaving behind in the subjects of existence the marks or traces of everywhere they go and everything they do. Thus a corpse, for example, has a story to tell, even if it takes a forensic scientist to read that story. For the traces of a finite being's interaction with and dependency upon its environment over time become veritable parts of its subjectivity as it goes along in time from its first moment of existence ("generatio") to its last moment ("corruptio"). In between, every mark left in the body of a "subject of existence" remains as a potential sign-vehicle that can under the right future circumstances tell part of the story of that subject's existential duration. "Relatio secundum dici" thus is *subjectivity as the bearer of a story which may or may not come to be told* in whole or in this or that particular part, but which could come to be told if examined by the right observer, the observer sufficiently trained in this or that aspect of material being. Thus the carpenter sees more in the grain of wood than does the financier, and the financier sees more in the development of a housing bubble than does the carpenter, and so on.

To get the story relations have to be formed. But those relations are not *secundum dici*. Those relations whether intersubjective here and now or purely objecctive are always suprasubjective (*relativum secundum esse*), *adesse* in contrast to *inesse*, even though dependent upon the latter. And whether those relations are awareness-dependent here and now or awareness- independent depends wholly and only on the prevailing circumstances, not upon the relations themselves.

A murderer to become a murderer has to be alive, and to find someone else alive. At the moment of discovery there is between the two a relation at once intersubjective and suprasubjective. Once the murder has been committed only the suprasubjective dimension of the relation survives, and that dimension will be revivable in awareness even after the murderer too is no longer alive. For someone else to find out who a particular murderer was does not necessarily depend upon that murderer being alive at the time that his or her identity comes to light. For a murderer to be identified requires the formation of a relation over and above the identity of both the detective, the one murdered, and the murderer. That relation will be founded upon evidence in the material order of subjective being, but it will not reduce to that order. Nor will it depend upon the murderer being alive at the time of the discovery, at the time that the relation of murderer to murdered enters into police awareness. The relation of murderer to murdered existed intersubjectively only while the murderer was alive and committing the murder. But when both the one murdered and the murderer are alike dead that relation as "intersubjective" has ceased, yet its potential positive being as suprasubjective, its possibility of being determined through investigation, remains part of the constitution of the universe of finite being and essential to the "synechism" or "continuity" as *ens reale.*

So the contrast between *secundum dici* and *secundum esse* is a contrast between the subjectivity or subjective dimension of finite being, and the relations that can arise among finite beings whether independently of or dependently upon finite awareness, depending upon the ever changing circumstances of existence here and now. All relations as *secundum esse* are suprasubjective, but only *some* of those relations are sometimes intersubjective as well. Relativity *secundum dici,* by contrast, refers not to suprasubjectivity directly, but directly to subjectivity as able to give rise to relations both independently of and also within awareness, according to the circumstances prevailing in the universe of finite beings at any given time.

So what Poinsot is asking in the text in question is, quite simply, whether a sign as sign exists primarily as does relation in an irreducibly suprasubjective mode of being dependent upon subjectivity indirectly, or is a sign rather some subjective thing ("that stop sign ahead") or characteristic of subjectivity ("that idea of camel that you have in your head")? His answer is that a sign always requires entanglement with suprasubjectivity in order to be a sign, while the subjectivity thus entangled—what we call a sign in ordinary usage—is not the sign formally but rather the sign materially (the sign-vehicle), the subjectivity upon which the suprasubjectivity may indirectly depend, but does not reduce to, for its existence.

Hence relation, "being toward another," viewed not simply (or simplistically!) as either "realis" or "rationis" but comprehensively as "secundum esse" (i.e., *esse ad* in the suprasubjectivity of its positive being, regardless of whether the circumstances of its occurrence make it awareness-independent or awareness-dependent), alone provides a standpoint from which the being proper to signs as indifferent to the *ens reale/ens rationis* status of their signifieds can be subjected to a complete analysis.

Relation "*secundum esse*" means relation as a suprasubjective mode of being in contrast to the subjectivity of substance with its inherent accidents. By contrast, relation "*secundum dici*" is indeed relative being but not "relation" at all,[13] but rather the "relativity" whereby finite beings depend upon interaction with their surrounding environment in order to survive, in order to maintain themselves in existence. The interactions are not relations; relations are what arise from interactions, as children arise from sexual intercourse. The relations resulting from physical interactions are intersubjective as long as the interactants both continue to exist; but in order to be intersubjective they (the resultant relations) have to be over and above subjectivity, and hence suprasubjective from the start. This dimension of suprasubjectivity in which the "positive being of relation as relation consists" is what makes it possible for a relation to continue in awareness even when its intersubjective status has ceased, or to be revived in awareness on the basis of "forensic evidence" uncovered by a later investigator.

You meet somebody new and take a liking to that person. You want to get to know the person. You ask: "Well, where were you born, who were your parents, what did your father do, where did you go to school, what do you want to do?", and so on. The person is not any of these things, but to get to know that person you have to establish in your awareness all these relations between that person and his or her surroundings, past and future as well as present. That is the *secundum dici* aspect or dimension of being and experience. But the *secundum esse* aspect is an actual relation itself, a relation as such.

Now here is a key point that Poinsot makes that I have never seen picked up on in the neoThomistic literature. The late modern Thomists distinguish between *ens reale* and *ens rationis*. But they have practically no interest in *ens rationis* except insofar as it enables logic as an instrument for the study of *ens reale*, and no appreciation at all of the fact that *ens rationis* is *relativum secundum esse* throughout, contrasting with subjective being as being *inter*subjective (*relativum secundum esse*) only in part. Yet as a matter of fact, says Poinsot, every relation is either an awareness-independent reality or an awareness-dependent reality, and which of the two any given re-

13. John Poinsot (Joannes a Sancto Thoma), *Tractatus de Signis: the Semiotic of John Poinsot*, 2nd edition, trans. John Deely with the assistance of Ralph Austin Powell, O.P. (South Bend, Indiana: St. Augustine's Press, 2013), Latin 89/47–90/5, English 89/47–90/6; cf. the Simon trans. in *The Material Logic of John of St. Thomas*, p. 314, lines 10–16 of last full paragraph.

lation is depends not on the relation but on the circumstances under which the relation happens to exist here and now. So one and the same relation under one set of circumstances will be *ens reale*, and that very same relation unchanged in its positive being as relation will become *ens rationis* under another set of circumstances sufficiently different.

Of course, there are some relations (e.g., grammatical relations, or purely logical relations) which are formed under circumstances which always require that they be *ens rationis*, awareness-dependent: such as grammatical relations, logical relations, or local relations such as "to the right or left." There are yet other relations the circumstances of which are such that they are perforce *ens reale* (and Thomas's prime example of relations perforce *ens reale* are the relations forming the three Persons of the Trinity in the One God). But all the other relations between these extremes are sometimes awareness-independent and sometimes awareness-dependent, while remaining in either case the exact same suprasubjectivity, the exact same relation.

V. What Makes Possible both Lying and Truth as Human Accomplishments

In one of his essays, Heidegger starts out defining "truth" in the medieval fashion as the conformity of thought with thing.[14] Then he asks, "Yes. But what is the basis for the prior possibility of such correspondence? How is this 'truth' in the medieval sense possible in the first place? How is correspondence possible between thoughts and things?" Heidegger provides no answer, just a posing of the question only the answer to which, he argues, would provide us with an understanding of the essence of truth. It is a profound point (yet one which I have yet to see faced in the neoThomistic literature).

When I read Poinsot on the singularity of relation as the only mode of being that is indifferent to being or not being in awareness, and the only mode of finite being that is suprasubjective even when dependent on some cognitive or cathectic subjective quality in order to provenate a relation establishing its terminus as an object whether that object does or does not (indifferently) have also a subjective physical dimension to its being, I real-

14. Martin Heidegger, "On the Essence of Truth," translated by R. F. C. Hull and Alan Crick, in *Existence and Being*, edited by Werner Brock (Chicago: Gateway, 1949), 292–324.

ized that Poinsot's *Tractatus de Signis* had in advance provided the answer to Heidegger's profound question. It is a pity that Heidegger never read Poinsot on signs, and an even greater pity that the neoThomists chose to follow Gilson in ignoring Poinsot rather than to follow Maritain in reading him. If Thomism has a future (and I am sure it does), this situation can only reverse, for only by this reversal do we pass from "late modern Thomism" to a "Thomism in the post-modern era". Listening to Maritain on the subject of sign as treated by Poinsot is as important to the future of Thomism as listening to Gilson on the subject of *esse* was important for recovering the past of Thomism from the oblivion into which it had fallen with the modern "turn to the subject."

Consider someone digging a garden who strikes a rock and casts it out of the way.[15] A friend comes over to visit who happens to be trained in paleontology. On seeing the stone he immediately grasps it and asks "Where did you find this? Do you realize what this is?"

"Yeah," says the gardener. "It's a stone."

"You mind if I take it?"

"No, go ahead."

The paleontologist has come into possession of a fossil bone, to the gardener a mere stone in the way of planting. The bone did not used to be stone. It used to be part of a Brontosaurus, really related thereto. It cannot be "really" (i.e., intersubjectively as a *relatio praedicamentalis seu realis*) related to a Brontosaurus any more, for there is no Brontosaurus to be related to any more. Under the current set of circumstances, the mind of the paleontologist has revived in an awareness-dependent mode ("ens rationis") *exactly the relation* that under past circumstances was an awareness-independent relation ("ens reale"). So we have from Poinsot (thanks in no small part to Maritain, who put both Sebeok and myself on to Poinsot's work on signs) the answer to Heidegger's question on the essence of truth.

Only human animals, and only at the intellectual level of concept-formation over and above the perceptual level of concept-formation, can come to recognize the difference within the objective world between purely objective dimensions of awareness and objective dimensions of awareness which have at the same time a corresponding subjective dimension. There is a reason for this recognition: only intellectual awareness is capa-

15. John Deely, *Basics of Semiotics* (Bloomington, Indiana: Indiana University Press, 1990), 48–49 and *passim*.

ble of distinguishing relations as such, which have no direct dimension of signate matter (and hence cannot be instantiated directly to sense perception), from related objects. For the same reason that alloanimals cannot distinguish their objects of awareness as such from things existing as such independently of awareness, the alloanimals cannot deal with relations directly but only indirectly via the medium of related objects. Thus, as Maritain says,[16] all animals make use of signs but only human animals come to perceive the relation of signification, i.e., the *relativum secundum esse* which makes of any subjectivity a sign in the ordinary sense.

Now St. Thomas is quite clear on the point that it is through the sensory partial apprehension of the surroundings (and which part depends entirely on the type of the animal body) that the process of objectification or "knowledge" (awareness) begins. Sensation prescissively considered, thus, is the nascence of objectivity. With the formation of concepts to interpret the sensed—that is, to structure objectivity to meet the needs and requirements of animal development and life—*entia rationis* enter into the realm of objects, not only for human animals but also for alloanimals,[17] and not only via mistaken interpretations but also in terms of imagined alternative structurings of the "physically given," such as the beaver makes in deciding when and where to build its dam, or the bird makes in constructing a nest, and so on. The animal sees real possibilities (sometimes mistakenly!), and these "possibilities" prior to their realization are purely objective (*entia rationis*) in contrast to their realization as physical realities—such as the beaver's dam upon completion.

Deception is widespread in nature, but outright lies are restricted to the cultural world of human animals, for the reason that only human animals can deal with relations directly as such, i.e., in their proper dimension as a mode of being irreducible to anything directly sensed. Only the human animal can compare the purely objective with the subjective as such. For precisely this reason intellectual awareness, in contrast to sense perception, is required explicitly to form objects as prescissively awareness-dependent.

St. Thomas is quite clear on the point that, given the priority of *sentire*

16. Jacques Maritain, "Language and the Theory of Sign," in *Frontiers in Semiotics*, edited by J. Deely, F. Kruse, and B. Williams Deely (Bloomington, Indiana: Indiana University Press, 1986), 53. Cf. Charles Peirce c. 1905, in his *Collected Papers*, vol. 5, ed. C. Hartshorne and P. Weiss (Cambridge, Massachusetts: Harvard University Press, 1934), par. 534.

17. Poinsot, *Tractatus de Signis*, 1st Preamble, Art. 3, esp. 66/46–51, 68/36–39, and 76/19–28.

over *phantasiari* and *intelligere* alike in the process of concept-formation as occurring only at the latter two "levels" or (rather) "dimensions" of animal awareness, awareness of *ens reale* is presupposed to the possibility of forming *entia rationis*; and intellectual awareness is presupposed only to the explicit or deliberate, i.e., the consciously controlled and reflexive formation, of *ens rationis*. But in this matter of an intellectual (as opposed to a perceptual) formation of *ens rationis*, a prior pattern of *ens reale* is provided for the intellect in only two forms: there are subjective patterns of *ens reale* provided by substances with their inherent accidents, and when the intellect forms an *ens rationis* on this pattern (such as Hamlet, Sherlock Holmes, or Colombo) the resultant object is not what its pattern is, to wit, an *esse in se*; and there are the intersubjective patterns provided by the intellectual awareness of the difference between relations as such and things related, and when the intellect forms an *ens rationis* on this pattern (such as Hamlet's mother, Sherlock Holmes' father, or Colombo's family tree) both that which is formed and that on the pattern of which it is formed are relations.

Yet fully to appreciate the importance of Thomas' and Poinsot's *secundum esse/secundum dici* distinction we must, slow learners that we are, go yet one step further. The whole of finite being is exclusively and exhaustively divided between the relativity of subjective being and the suprasubjectivity of the positive being of relation. That means that the whole of *ens rationis*, every being of reason objectively formed, every one without exception, is a relation in its positive structure as suprasubjectively establishing a terminus of awareness lacking subjectivity in its own right. This consequent is already implicit in Thomas's distinction of "negation" from "relation," in that both the negations and relations "of reason" consist wholly in a being suprasubjectively patterned after *entia realia* (whether 1. the *esse in* case of subjectivity comprising material individuals, or 2. the *esse ad* case of intersubjectivity comprising *relationes* suprasubjectively as *praedicamentales seu reales*). Thus "being patterned after" is the shared or common positive and defining characteristic of "negations" and "relations" alike respecting the subjective order, the order of physical being as including the suprasubjectivity presupposed within intersubjectivity.

Thus the approach since Aristotle of beginning the treatment of being in terms of "being in itself" and "being in another" (history of philosophy more than proves the point I am about to make) tends to blind thinkers to seeing suprasubjectivity as what is proper to relation and crucial for the possibility of communication among finite beings wherever it might occur. Neither the traditional division of *ens reale* into substance and accident nor the traditional division of *ens rationis* into negation and relation helps one to see either the singularity of relation (as the only form of *ens reale* capable of positive realization with essence unchanged also in the order of *ens rationis*), or the positively relational character of *every ens rationis whatever*. Such proves to be the case whether we objectify *ens rationis* in its positive being by emphasizing the dependency of terminus as terminus upon the relation as such (which is why objects as terminating relations can do so even when they cease to be or never were or even never could be things subjectively existing), or whether we emphasize the positive being of the relation itself as necessarily suprasubjective while being only contingently intersubjective (which is why objects as terminating cognitive and cathectic relations are public in principle even though the cognitive and cathectic psychological states as provenating those relations are subjective qualities of an individual animal substance).

Thus, in those few texts—about sixteen in all[18]—where Thomas approached being from the point of view of *secundum esse* (suprasubjectivity) / *secundum dici* (subjectivity), instead of—or perhaps rather: as superordinate to—the point of view of Aristotle's being-*in-se* (substance) / being-*in-alio* (accident) distinction, we remove both the Nominalist risk of failing to see that "*inesse*" is not the whole of *ens reale*, and the epistemological failure to realize that "*adesse*" (as a suprasubjective mode open to *ens reale* and *ens rationis* alike and equally) is what makes for the possibility in the first place (the "prior possibility") of truth as correspondence.

From Aristotle to the present, the opening gambit in the treatment of being has been to make the distinction between substance and (inherent) accident as constituting the order of *ens reale*, and then also, since Boethius (c. 480–524/5) and Avicenna (c. 980–1037), to *contrast simply* (over-simply!) this *ens reale* order with the order of *ens rationis*. The Thomists in general, but

18. Seven locations, eight passages in the 1252/56a *Scriptum super libros Sententiarum*, all in Book I: (1) liber 1 d. 3, q. 5, a. 1 expositio; (2) d. 7, q. 1, a. 2, corpus; (3) d. 30, q. 1, a. 2, c.; (4) d. 30, q. 1, a. 3, arg. 4; (5) d. 30, q. 1, a. 3, ad 4; (6 and 7) d. 33, q. 1, a. 1, arg. 1: two passages; (8) d. 33, q. 1, a. 1, ad 1. Two locations and passages in the 1256–59 *Quaestiones disputatae de veritate*: (9) q. 4, art. 5, arg. 2; (10) q. 4, art. 5, ad 2. One location and passage in the 1257 *Quodlibeta* 9: (11) Quodlibet IX, q. 2, a. 3, arg. 3. Two locations, four passages in the 1265/66 *Quaestiones disputatae De potentia dei:* (12) q. 7, art. 10, arg. 11; (13, 14, 15) q. 7, art. 10, ad 11. And one location and passage in the 1266–1268 *Summa theologiae* Prima Pars: (16) I, q. 13, a. 7, ad 1.

the neoThomists in particular continue to employ this opening gambit, in effect closing the way to understanding semiosis.

The time has come, not so much as to leave Aristotle's approach behind as to assimilate that approach to the approach which begins from the realization that "absolute being" properly speaking refers to God alone as creator, while "relative being" includes the entire finite order in its subjectivity (*relativum secundum dici*) and suprasubjectivity (*relativum secundum esse*) alike.

We, students of Aquinas especially, need to stop disguising the fact that relation is neither *esse in se* nor *esse in alio*, nor reducible to either thereof despite being directly dependent on *esse in alio* while only indirectly dependent upon *esse in se*. We have here the reason why both truths and lies can be "free floating." As Benedict XVI put it some years ago, the time for "the undivided sway of thinking in terms of substance [as "*ens absolutum*"] is ended"; the time has arrived finally when "relation is discovered as an equally primordial mode of reality."[19] In order to display that discovery in its foreground importance, it is time and necessary to pivot from the substance/accident distinction to the suprasubjectivity/subjectivity distinction. This distinction not only gives us the traction needed from the start to understand the action of signs, but also the traction needed to deal philosophically with evolution as it pertains to the entire universe of finite beings interacting.

Maritain considered the problem of thing and object to be "the nub of the critical problem."[20] He was right about this, but what he did not see clearly is that an object as object in contrast to thing is always necessarily a terminus of a cognitive or cathectic relation "solummodo in ratione puri termini," while even when those same objects have also the subjectivity of being things as well as objects they do not "in ratione puri termini ipsum respiciunt" as things. For the terminus of a relation as terminus depends upon the relation, while as thing it is independent of that psychologically founded relation. Hence insofar as a thing becomes cognized it exists "in ratione puri termini," while insofar it exists also as a thing it does not exist only "in ratione puri termini." And that is exactly why "the problem of thing and object" cannot be solved without bringing relation to the front and center of the analysis, for the very reasons Poinsot gives (as we saw

19. Ratzinger, *Introduction to Christianity*, 132.

20. Jacques Maritain, *Distinguish to Unite, or The Degrees of Knowledge*, translated under the supervision of Gerald B. Phelan (New York: Charles Scribner's Sons, 1959), 107.

above) in posing the choice between the relativity of subjective being (*relativum secundum dici*) and the suprasubjectivity of relation itself (*relativum secundum esse*) as the key to understanding semiosis.

A thing can be what it is whether it be known or not. But in order to become known it must become involved in a relation to a finite mind in the position of the terminus of that relation. When that occurs, the thing in the very respect in which it is known becomes simultaneously an object of awareness or apprehension.

Still, it is not its status as terminating the relation with a finite mind that determines its status as thing; as thing, its status is determined by the existence it exercises independently of that finite mind. At the same time, its status as object is determined by its being in that relation as terminus, and therein lies the reason why it can continue to exist objectively even when its subjective existence is lost.

For a relation to have as its terminus a thing, that relation must exist both as suprasubjective and as intersubjective. But if the relation in question is a relation of awareness, the subjectivity upon which it is founded has to be a psychological state, cognitive or cathectic. Since such relations provenate from their foundation of necessity (and that is the essence of "intentionality" or "relations as intentional"), the status of their objective terminus participates in that necessity, whether or not the terminus at the same time exists subjectively as a thing in the order of awareness-independent being. In other words, a thing as object exists in the awareness-independent realm while it also exists partially in the awareness of some animal; but that very object as once existing in some animal's awareness can continue to exist as object even after it has ceased to exist as a thing.

The reason for this partial indifference to having awareness-independent status on the side of objects lies in the indifference of relation as a mode of being to the circumstances which determine its status as obtaining awareness-independently (intersubjectively)—whether or not in awareness as well, or only in awareness. In the latter case, where the cognitive relation exists *only* in awareness, the terminus of the relation continues to exist objectively even though no longer subjectively as thing.

The nascence of objectivity in sensation (what I have called "animal realism"[21]) guarantees the involvement of animal awareness with *ens reale*.

21. "The Quo/Quod Fallacy in the Discussion of Realism," *Człowiek W Kulturze. Pismo poświęcone filozofii i kulturze*, Part 1 in vol. 19 (2007), 389–425; Part 2 in vol. 20 (2008), 289–316.

The full development of that objectivity into a world of objects structured requires not only concepts but (as a result of conceptualizations) the additional inclusion into objectivity of the component of *ens rationis*, a component which can be recognized as such only by an intellectual power, because only intellection is able, unlike the powers of sense perception, to objectify something which is uninstantiable[22] to sense. Even though only materially and not formally, as we noted above, this *ens rationis* component is both formed and utilized by animal imagination, memory, and estimation no less than by the human animal's intellection so far as concerns negotiating the animal's environmental surroundings.

Relations in sensation are relations in awareness, to be sure, but, prescissively taken, they can continue to exist in sensation only as long as the animal and the thing sensed continue to be involved in a physical interaction (*agere et pati*). But this relation of sensation as incorporated into perception loses that immediate dependency on physical interaction, whence as a perceptual relation it sustains in memory, imagination, and estimation the existence of the object regardless of whether the object continues to have its subjective existence (*esse in se* or *esse in alio*) or not.

VI. Evening's Twilight and Morning's Dawn

Neothomism is in the same position today that Latin scholasticism was in at the time of Descartes. Neothomism is in the twilight zone; it is finished. Something new has to come about in order for there to be a future for Thomism—a philosophical future, that is, not merely a scholarly future (which is easily assured). That future, if it is to be more than "scholarly," cannot be simply a repeat or endless reproduction of the late modern realism-idealism struggle.

Listen to Maritain, and on this point listen closely: "The Thomist philosopher is dubbed scholastic, a name derived from his most painful affliction. Scholastic pedantry is his peculiar foe. He must constantly triumph over his domestic adversary, the Professor."[23] A way has to be found from within Thomistic thought to explain the public character of socially constructed reality. That way is the way of signs.

22. See John Deely, "Uninstantiability," *Semiotica* 208 (2016): 1–20.

23. Jacques Maritain, *Quatre essais sur l'ésprit dans sa condition charnelle*, 1st edition (Paris: Desclée de Brouwer, 1939), 24.

In the physical universe everything begins from touch, physical interaction between bodies, causal interactions. These interactions are not relations. Relations are what arise and result from the interactions, and survive when the interactions are over and finished. Relations are the offspring of interactions, and so crucial to the understanding of nature throughout. So all those divisions—substance, accident, *ens reale, ens rationis,* negation, relation—collapse down into the *secundum dici/secundum esse* distinction. That distinction not only gives you, on the "secundum esse" side, the foundation for understanding the action and theory of signs, but something also on the "secundum dici" side that transforms the whole picture of the universe of interacting substances in a manner consistent with the evolutionary universe—as definitely was not the "terrestrial/celestial matter" picture with which Thomas worked.

Let me recall a classroom incident from my River Forest days. Fr. Raymond Nogar once began his class on evolution by asking the students, "What does the average person see when he or she looks out on reality? I'll tell you what they see. They see exactly what you see when you look out this window this morning," he said, pointing to the window. It was completely covered with ice. We couldn't see a thing!

That is where we are today in philosophy when we bury the irreducibly distinctive and crucial nature of relation by approaching the analysis of being first of all from the side of *ens reale* as distinguished into substance and accident. By listening to Maritain in what he says about John Poinsot, then by understanding in turn what Poinsot himself says, we come to recognize that Poinsot's work stands not only as an evening star for the Latin Age. His work stands now also as a morning star for postmodernity, in his demonstration of the importance of realizing that truly "absolute" being applies only to God as Creator (source of existence here and now), while finite being in its entire extent is a relative interplay of substances in which, through the suprasubjectivity of pure relations, the future is able to change through the indirect consequences of present interactions the relevance thereto of past events. This "influence of the future" ("*vis a prospecto*"[24]) thereby makes of the universe of finite beings an evolutionary whole into which the human animal alone among material substances introduces a dimension of moral responsibility. This new understanding of the whole of

24. Jesper Hoffmeyer, "Biology is immature biosemiotics," in *Semiotics 2008,* edited by J. Deely and L. Sbrocchi (Ottawa: Legas, 2009), 939.

finite being is tied up with the necessity of understanding the singularity of relation as transcending the nature/culture divide, by the fact that, as Poinsot put it, "solum in his, quae sunt ad aliquid, invenitur aliqua relatio realis et aliqua rationis, ... quia pure relatio est et non aliquid absolutum importat"[25]—the very reason Aquinas gives in his attempt to explain why the Trinity of Persons in the One God does not involve a compromise of the divine unity, still less any contradiction (for the Persons are subsisting relations, as such presupposing but introducing nothing of the divine unity as "*ens absolutum*").

25. *Tractatus de Signis,* Book I, Question 1, 118/12–18: only in the order of being as suprasubjective do we find objects to be both awareness-independent and awareness dependent ("solum in his, quae sunt ad aliquid, invenitur aliqua relatio realis et aliqua rationis").

JAMES M. JACOBS

Christian Philosophy

Reconciling the Temporal and the Eternal

I. Introduction: The Difficult Duty of Christian Philosophers

The conversion of Jacques and Raïssa Maritain may be told in broad strokes.[1] Having been educated in the materialism and determinism of modern science, they had also accepted the inescapable corollary that human existence is meaningless, leading the young couple to propose a suicide pact. They were saved from this tragic fate only by their discovery of the philosophy of Henri Bergson, which revealed a spiritual dimension that endowed reality with meaning. This philosophical discovery was in turn magnified by their embrace of the transcendent and eternal truths of the Christian faith, particularly in the lucid formulations of St. Thomas. These two discoveries conspired to reveal to Jacques his life's project: to be a Christian philosopher. It is as a Christian philosopher that Maritain spoke to the world. The pursuit of this project continued even into the last years of his life, when he was still passionately arguing for the integral unity of faith and reason: "Charity has to do with persons; truth, with ideas and with reality attained through them. Perfect charity toward our neighbor and complete fidelity to the truth are not only compatible; they call for one another."[2] Indeed, I would venture that it is precisely Maritain's ability to

1. A brief review of the significance of this conversion for Maritain's biography is presented in John G. Trapani Jr., *Poetry, Beauty, and Contemplation: The Complete Aesthetics of Jacques Maritain* (Washington, D.C.: The Catholic University of America Press, 2011), 11–26.

2. Jacques Maritain, *The Peasant of the Garonne:An Old Layman Questions Himself about the*

unite wisdom and charity as a Christian philosopher that has drawn many to become students of his work.

Yet, from the beginning of this life project, Maritain realized that being a Christian philosopher is a uniquely difficult vocation. In *Bergsonian Philosophy and Thomism,* Maritain offers this stern admonition to those who would be Christian philosophers:

> Christianity, as I have often said, does not make things easier; it does not facilitate art and, in a certain sense, it does not facilitate philosophy.... It is easier to be a stone than a shrub, a shrub than a bird, a bird than a man, a businessman than a poet or a philosopher, a poet or a philosopher than a Christian, a poet and a Christian or a philosopher and a Christian than a Christian poet or a Christian philosopher.[3]

The profound difficulty in being a Christian philosopher lies in the fact that the purely speculative spirit of the philosopher must at the same time accept the discipline of revealed truth. Accordingly, speculation for the Christian philosopher cannot be ordered merely to the immanent satisfaction of temporal curiosity, for when it is so debased, as it is in much modern thought, that speculation becomes an end in itself, leading man not to truth but to a narcissistic apotheosis of his own ideas.

In the more prophetic voice of *The Peasant of the Garonne,* Maritain makes the argument this way: "By being concerned for truth, and by grasping it, the spirit transcends time. To make the things of the spirit pass under the law of the ephemeral—which is the law of matter and the purely biological—to act as if the spirit were subject to the lord of the flies, is the first sign, the first symptom of the sickness denounced by St. Paul."[4] The Christian philosopher, on the other hand, humbly acknowledges that there can be no novelty to the truth he proclaims. Relatedly, Étienne Gilson argues that it is this sort of humility in the face of truth that set Thomas Aquinas apart:

> While so many men were trying to base philosophy on theological foundations, a very simple and modest man was putting everything in its place. His name was

Present Time, translated by Michael Cuddihy and Elizabeth Hughes (New York: Holt, Rinehart and Winston, 1968), 90. Throughout the book, Maritain personifies the task of the Christian philosopher in lamenting the state of modern secular philosophy which "cheats" the soul in its erotic quest for eternal realities (105ff) and makes it blind to spiritual truth.

3. Jacques Maritain, *Bergsonian Philosophy and Thomism,* translated by Mabelle L. Andison and J. Gordon Andison (New York: The Philosophical Library, 1955), 13–14.

4. Maritain, *The Peasant of the Garonne,* 14.

Thomas Aquinas, and he was saying things so obviously true that, from his time down to our own day, very few people have been sufficiently self-forgetful to accept them. There is an ethical problem at the root of our philosophical difficulties; for men are most anxious to find truth, but very reluctant to accept it. We do not like to be cornered by rational evidence, and even when truth is there, in its impersonal and commanding objectivity, our greatest difficulty still remains; it is for me to bow to it in spite of the fact that it is not exclusively mine, for you to accept it though it cannot be exclusively yours. In short, finding out truth is not so hard; what is hard is not to run away from truth once we have found it.[5]

Yet, despite the conservative nature of this truth, Maritain was certainly not one to seek refuge from contemporary debate in a nostalgia for the past. To the contrary, he is well-known for his attempts to bring the principles of Thomism into conversation with the modern world, be it with respect to abstract art, democratic politics, or contemporary science. But in all these areas, Maritain realized that the critical point for the Christian philosopher is to receive these new insights according to the unchanging principles of being, rather than trying to fit the eternal truths into the ephemeral methods of the day. Just as Augustine could make use of Plato[6] and Aquinas could adapt the truths of Aristotle, Maritain demonstrated how what is of value in modernity could be appropriated by Christians. Yet should the Christian philosopher surrender too readily to the currents of his time, he will be led not to truth but to error; thus, for every Augustine, there is an Origen; for every Thomas, there is a Siger. It is just this defect that vitiates Bergson's thought for Maritain: in accepting the anti-metaphysical prejudices of modernity, he diminishes of the true power of the intellect: "The most serious objection one must raise here against Bergsonism is that it was not daring enough, that in the very exercise of philosophy it failed to recognize the power of intellect and of philosophy and that it recoiled from any recognition of the autonomy of metaphysical knowledge."[7]

5. Étienne Gilson, *The Unity of Philosophical Experience* (San Francisco: Ignatius Press, 1999), 49.

6. Cf. St. Augustine, *On Christian Doctrine,* translated by D. W. Robertson Jr. (Upper Saddle River, New Jersey: Prentice Hall, 1997), II.40.60: "If those who are called philosophers, especially the Platonists, have said things which are indeed true and are well accommodated to our faith, they should not be feared; rather, what they have said should be taken from them as from unjust possessors and converted to our use. Just as the Egyptians had not only idols and grave burdens which the people of Israel detested and avoided, so also they had vases and ornaments of gold and silver and clothing which the Israelites took with them secretly when they fled, as if to put them to a better use."

7. Maritain, *Bergsonian Philosophy and Thomism,* 49.

This clearly illustrates the hazards which are to be faced by the Christian philosopher. To be relevant, he must engage the issues of contemporary philosophy; at the same time, he must exercise discretion in employing contemporary ideas, lest he be led away from truth. This dilemma is especially acute when he turns his philosophical attention to God. A true Christian philosopher will see God as the source of Being, Truth, and Goodness; a faulty philosophical method will inevitably distort this understanding of God. This problem is particularly acute when that argument is intended as an apologetic in defense of faith, for an inadequate understanding of God invites anti-theists to attack this illusory God as if it were the God of the Christian faith.[8]

Using Maritain's work as a guide, in what follows I will survey three examples of Christian philosophers who were moved to defend theism from the challenges arising from the philosophical suppositions of their time; in exploring their responses, we will also ascertain to what extent each stayed true to, or departed from, the eternal verities they aimed to defend. Descartes, seeking to repudiate skepticism, aims to defend theism with the certitude of a mathematical method; but he is left with an impersonal God and a valueless, mechanistic universe. On the other hand, Newman is faced with the atheism of scientific positivism, but he is able to adapt the canons of British empiricism in defense of theism and discover an innovative account of certainty in religious belief. Finally, in our own day, Alvin Plantinga sees the need to respond to the scientistic reductionism of the "New Atheism." His response is to show that scientific explanations leave room for divine activity; but in giving precedence to the principles of contemporary science, especially its univocal metaphysics, his God can only exercise a restricted causality which never transcends the operations of the material universe. The varying fates of these attempts at Christian philosophy can be seen to provide both edifying examples and cautionary tales for students of Maritain who aim faithfully to imitate his life-project of being a Christian philosopher.

8. Even St. Thomas exhorts Christian philosophers to be wary of making such an error, as in *Summa theologiae* I, q. 46, a. 2: "It is useful to consider this, lest anyone, presuming to demonstrate what is of faith, should bring forward reasons that are not cogent, so as to give occasion to unbelievers to laugh." All quotations from the *Summa theologiae* are taken from *Summa Theologica*, translated by the Fathers of the English Dominican Province (1948; reprint, Allen, Texas: Christian Classics, 1981).

II. The Example of Maritain

Before considering the other philosophers, let us briefly consider how Maritain himself fulfilled this call to formulate a fully adequate natural theology. An inadequate natural theology subordinates God to a certain philosophical method, thereby constricting the nature of God in a way contrary to the orthodox faith. An adequate method, on the other hand, does not allow God to be so constricted. As noted above, Maritain's insistence on the true power of the intellect and the autonomy of metaphysical knowledge is crucial to his method's adequacy. Indeed, the defense of a method adequate to the analogical hierarchy of *being* lay at the heart of Maritain's vocation as a Christian philosopher: "My real purpose [is] ... to turn men's minds toward the powerfully coherent but indefinitely progressive doctrine of Saint Thomas Aquinas, as toward the sole philosophy exclusively commanded by *what is*."[9] This is precisely where he critiques Bergson, for the notion of intuition of *duration* is oblivious of the objective *fact* of existence; in its place, Maritain advocates the Thomistic idea of intuition of *being* as the sole foundation for an adequate metaphysics.[10] This idea takes full form in his presentation of ananoetic intuition associated with the "third degree" of abstraction as the foundation for metaphysical knowledge, yet in continuity with the modes of abstraction constituting scientific knowledge.[11] While fully accepting scientific knowledge of particular causal relations, Maritain shows the intellect is also capable of a higher knowledge, grasping the universal intrinsic cause *being*; yet in grasping being, we analogically grasp everything that participates in being in any way. This enables man to know God as the necessary cause of all contingent being. But Maritain is careful here to recognize that the intuition of being in no way limits God, for while we clearly grasp *that God exists* by means of this ananoetic intellection, we cannot grasp His essence, for He transcends the finite powers of human cognition: "Even in the knowledge by which our mind knows *that God is* it submits to the absolute transcendence of a reality which ananoetic intellection attains only in recognizing itself surpassed

9. Maritain, *Bergsonian Philosophy and Thomism*, 15; emphasis in original.

10. See ibid., 22–35.

11. Maritain, *The Degrees of Knowledge, or Distinguish to Unite*, revised edition, translated under the supervision of Gerald B. Phelan (Notre Dame, Indiana: University of Notre Dame Press, 1995), 215–59.

on every side by it."[12] This metaphysical approach to the analogy of being allows for knowledge of God without any anthropomorphic constriction of God's infinite reality. In that sense, it is a model which all Christian philosophers, whatever their chosen method, should strive to imitate. With this in mind, let us now consider how the developments of science in other eras were dealt with by three noted philosophers.

III. Cartesian Certainty?

The early modern period had undergone tremendous intellectual dislocation as a result of the rejection of scholasticism and the uncertain rise of scientific discovery in its place. This anxiety is well illustrated by John Donne in his poem "An Anatomy of the World":

> And now the springs and summers which we see,
> Like sons of women after fifty be.
> And new philosophy calls all in doubt,
> The element of fire is quite put out,
> The sun is lost, and th'earth, and no man's wit
> Can well direct him where to look for it.
> And freely men confess that this world's spent,
> When in the planets and the firmament
> They seek so many new; they see that this
> Is crumbled out again to his atomies.
> 'Tis all in pieces, all coherence gone,
> All just supply, and all relation;
> Prince, subject, father, son, are things forgot,
> For every man alone thinks he hath got
> To be a phoenix, and that then can be
> None of that kind, of which he is, but he.[13]

Science had banished the old elements and the stability of their formal causes; in their place the telescope and microscope revealed a disconcertingly infinite vastness and multiplicity. All sense of intelligible order and contextual horizon was thereby undermined. This obliteration of common

12. Ibid., 236; emphasis in original.

13. John Donne, *An Anatomy of the World*, lines 203–219, cited in Stephen Toulmin, *Cosmopolis: The Hidden Agenda of Modernity* (Chicago: The University of Chicago Press, 1990), 65. Toulmin points out the striking similarity of this passage with Yeats's post-war elegy of despair, *The Second Coming*: "Things fall apart; the centre cannot hold; / Mere anarchy is loosed upon the world."

principles led to a revival of skepticism, which seeks peace in nescience, exemplified particularly in Montaigne. Included in this general skepticism was, of course, a direct assault on the possibility of religious knowledge.

These circumstances provided the occasion for Descartes's attempt to secure the truth of theism. Michael Buckley narrates this fateful event:

> Perhaps the best scene to capture Descartes' entry into Western philosophy would be the conference in Paris of November, 1628. The gentle Oratorian Pierre Cardinal de Bérulle, the Minim friar Marin Mersenne, René Descartes, and a "grande et sçavant compagnie" were summoned by the Papal Nuncio, Monsigneur de Baigné, to hear the Sieur de Chandoux savage scholastic philosophy and propose "sa nouvelle philosophie." La Rochelle had fallen in October to the troops of Richelieu, and Chandoux envisaged a similar fate for the methods of the schools. It would be an easy victory, one often won in the drawing rooms and among the clerics and literati of newly centralized France. When Chandoux had finished, the assembly applauded with a general enthusiasm. Only Descartes sat quietly. The Cardinal noted his silence and pressed him for a response. Descartes, after some halfhearted attempts to escape the charge, finally "praised the address, but did not praise the assembly because they had allowed themselves to be satisfied with what was only probable." ... And how [would Descartes] build [knowledge with certainty]? "He replied that he knew of no [method] more infallible than the one he himself was wont to employ, adding that he had drawn it *from the treasury of the mathematical sciences*, and that there was, he believed, no truth which he could not, by its means, clearly demonstrate, in conformity with his own principles." ... The Cardinal and the assembly were conquered. Bérulle asked for an interview, in which they discussed "those thoughts on philosophy that had first occurred to him after he had come to recognize the usefulness of the methods commonly employed in treating it." He indicated further effects which this method of philosophizing might obtain in medicine and mechanics. This colloquy, however, subtly reversed their roles. Descartes told the Cardinal about the method to be followed if one wished to obtain certainty in knowledge; Bérulle, one of the greatest spiritual directors of his century, told Descartes about the obligations he had in conscience to pursue these studies if he wished to obtain salvation from the "Sovereign Judge." Bérulle gave Descartes a mission that reinforced his own natural inclinations, a mission that was to last all his life, "to publish his doctrine against the skeptics and atheists." Never were two adversaries more fatefully merged in one mission.[14]

Despite this ecclesiastical commissioning, the failed results of this project are the stuff of every introductory course in philosophy. By subordinating

14. See Michael J. Buckley, S.J., *At the Origins of Modern Atheism* (New Haven, Connecticut: Yale University Press, 1987), 71–72; emphasis in original.

God to the mathematical method in order to obtain certainty, Descartes reduces God to a step in a deductive argument. As Buckley points out, this is revolutionary in Western philosophy, for Descartes' predecessors had seen in the universe proof for the existence of a transcendent Creator; Descartes, on the other hand, sees in his idea of God a means to prove the existence of the universe. But that universe itself is now Godless, a purely mathematical and mechanical universe for which God simply provides epistemic justification. Descartes's method, in effect, discovers a Deistic God, a God who is readily pushed aside in the face of scientific discoveries concerning the physical causes of the universe.[15] The end result is as bad as the original problem, for as Pascal observes, deism and atheism are the two things Christians hate equally.[16] Thus the ironic conclusion: Descartes' scientifically certain method undermines man's knowledge of God.

IV. Newman's Illative Sense

Move forward two centuries. A different kind of atheism is once again challenging the Christian worldview[17]; but this time the rebellion against faith is fueled not by a general skepticism, but by the scientism that restricts evidence to the empirical. Unlike Descartes, however, John Henry Newman will offer a response that accords with orthodoxy.[18] Newman himself, upon being created Cardinal, confessed that his life's work had been to preserve orthodoxy against the challenge of what he called *liberalism* in religion. "Liberalism in religion consists in looking at all conclusions (in religion) in proportion to the strength of their premises ... or resolving all beliefs into opinions."[19] Liberalism, thus, has two manifestations: On the one hand, the notion that all beliefs should be proportioned to producible evidence led some to the conclusion that an educated man ought to embrace a chaste agnosticism. On the other hand, some believers reacted to

15. On this, see Étienne Gilson, *God and Philosophy*, 2nd edition (New Haven, Connecticut: Yale University Press, 2002), 74–108.

16. See *Pensées* 556 (Brunschvicg number = Sellier 690/Lafuma 449).

17. On the differences in the nature of atheism in these two eras, see Charles Taylor, *A Secular Age* (Cambridge, Massachusetts: Harvard University Press, 2007), 221–98 and 322–51.

18. For a catalogue of other attempts to adhere to secular canons of evidence during the Enlightenment, see Charles Taliaferro, *Evidence and Faith: Philosophy and Religion since the Seventeenth Century* (Cambridge: Cambridge University Press, 2005).

19. Quoted in Paul F. Sands, *The Justification of Religious Faith in Soren Kierkegaard, John Henry Newman, and William James* (Piscataway, New Jersey: Gorgias Press, 2003), 103.

this by adopting a "romantic" view of religion, which asserted that Christianity is based on feeling and imagination. Newman understood that this cure was worse than the illness, for it reduces religion to subjective opinion and destroys religion's claim to truth.[20] Newman's great achievement was to accept the demand for evidence, but then to widen the scope of rationality so as to discover a new kind of empirical evidence for religious faith.

In response to his positivist contemporaries who were opposing religious faith and scientific reason, Newman worked to reconcile them. But this was a new kind of reconciliation, for as a convert to the Catholic faith, Newman was rather self-conscious about not being typical of traditional Catholic scholasticism. Moreover, he believed that that scholastic method had become insulated from the concerns of the modern world, and so was not the most appropriate vehicle for his argument.[21] The new conditions of his era compelled him to compose an argument appropriate to the assumptions of his time. As he wrote to another convert, William Brownlow: "I have not insisted on the argument from *design*, because I am writing for the 19th century, by which, as represented by its philosophers, design is not admitted as proved.... I believe in design because I believe in God; not in a God because I see design."[22]

Newman's attempt to justify religious belief will face one further constriction due to the particularity of his circumstances. Newman was thoroughly British, and he absorbed the empiricism so characteristic of that people; this fact would shape his presentation of an argument thoroughly unlike scholastic metaphysical arguments. The originality of Newman's argument is readily seen in the two most significant innovations of the *Grammar of Assent*: the distinction between real knowledge and notional knowledge; and the role of the illative sense in justifying religious knowledge from the accumulation of particular facts.[23] These insights allow Newman

20. This objection to a religion based on feeling is clearly articulated in Newman's critique of the fideism associated with the Protestant worldview; see *The Idea of a University* II.4, edited by Daniel M. O'Connell (Chicago: Loyola University Press, 1927), 45–46.

21. See Ian Ker, *John Henry Newman: A Biography* (Oxford: Oxford University Press, 1988), 631–38.

22. Cited by Nicholas Lash in his introduction to John Henry Newman, *An Essay in Aid of A Grammar of Assent* (Notre Dame, Indiana: University of Notre Dame Press, 1979), 13; emphasis in original. This should not be taken to mean that the scholastic argument was an argument from design.

23. On the importance of Newman grounding his philosophical and theological investigations on his real-world experiences, see Frederick D. Aquino, *An Integrative Habit of Mind: John*

to point to empirical evidence as proof for the existence of a truly Christian God. Let us briefly consider these.

Newman's justification of belief begins with the recognition that the concreteness of the individual believer requires a sort of phenomenology of belief instead of an abstract metaphysics. This analysis reveals to him two critical points that contradict the Enlightenment ideology that truth is the product of a disinterested and universal reason. First, Newman sees that all thinking, for believer and unbeliever alike, must begin with some assumed first principle.[24] These principles, though, are shaped by individual experience and so give divergent "antecedent probabilities" in the formation of convictions, for what is seen as relevant evidence varies among individuals according to the diversity of their first principles. Accordingly, Newman claims that unbelief "criticizes the evidence of Religion only because it does not like it, and really goes upon presumptions and prejudices as much as Faith does, only presumptions of the opposite nature."[25] Second, although the events of salvation history are particular and not universal, we can nevertheless attain certitude about them through the "assemblage of concurring and converging probabilities,"[26] compounding individual bits of evidence, just as a steel cable intertwines strands of iron to create greater strength than can be found in any one rod. In this way, the concrete personal experience extolled by Enlightenment science is used to justify the religious faith of Catholic Christianity.

Newman deploys the first insight in his analysis of conscience, which he sees as a first principle concerning the nature of moral obligation. As a prelude to this, he introduces his distinction between real knowledge, which concerns singulars and individuals, and notional knowledge, which is about generalities and common nouns.[27] Because real knowledge is more

Henry Newman and the Path to Wisdom (DeKalb, Illinois: Northern Illinois University Press, 2012), esp. at 18.

24. See Ian Ker, *The Achievement of John Henry Newman* (Notre Dame, Indiana: University of Notre Dame Press, 1990), 36: "The realization that differences between people rest on positions and states of mind not open to obvious view came early to Newman as one of his deepest insights into the workings of the human mind. He also saw clearly that without 'first principles' it would be impossible to think at all. 'Resolve to believe nothing . . . and you must prove your proofs and analyze your elements, sinking further and further . . . till you come to the broad bosom of skepticism.'"

25. Cited in Ker, *The Achievement of John Henry Newman*, 41.

26. The phrase is taken from John Henry Newman, *Apologia Pro Vita Sua* (Garden City, New York: Image Books, 1956), 140.

27. It is important to note that even here his idea of general notions is much closer to Locke's

immediate, it exercises greater motivating force; in turn, it is the source of all notional assents reached by inference. Thus, direct personal experience lies at the foundation for all reliable knowledge.[28] This includes religious beliefs, which must be based on an immediate experience associated with real knowledge, while theological reflections are the *notional* assents derived from it. Newman will then point to the personal experience of moral obligation as the basis for a real knowledge of God. In conscience, man recognizes a moral authority independent of himself; if there were no moral authority other than the self, there would be no sanctioning obligation to conscience. Appropriating the personal significance of this fact allows one to move quickly from experiencing God as the Sovereign Judge to forming full personal relations with Him as Creator and Redeemer. Thus, personal experience, especially as real and not notional, gives evidence for the reality of God.

Yet if the believer is to be justified in this, he needs to show he can be certain about these experiences. Most philosophers assert that only abstract, deductive arguments can yield certainty. Newman replies to this by arguing that, in addition to formal inference, certainty may also be attained by the accumulation of evidence from particular experiences. This informal reasoning about concrete particulars operates implicitly over the majority of human life, and so ought to be as valid as abstract formal reasoning. It is for the sake of this sort of reasoning that Newman emphasizes the need for a broad education, for a well-educated person can adequately interpret and order information from as many sciences as possible[29]; lacking this catholic background, personal prejudice obscures the relevance of certain facts. The well-prepared mind, then, can attain certainty about many things that are outside the province of formal logic, for man's most natural mode of inference is not from proposition to proposition, but from the experience of concrete things to other concrete things. Newman calls this faculty of informal inference the illative sense, which, like Aristotle's *phronesis* (prudence), reasons about particulars. It is this power that surveys the concrete experiences that compose religious life and concludes that, taken together, they meaningfully answer the most substantial questions of human exis-

nominalist version of abstraction as confused generalities than the Aristotelian idea of abstraction of formal essences, which is why real knowledge has greater authority for him.

28. See *A Grammar of Assent*, 80–85, for Newman's analysis of this.

29. See *The Idea of a University*, VI.5 (153–54) for Newman's description of how this works.

tence, such that the believer can be justified in accepting these answers.

Thus, like Descartes, Newman felt the pressures of irreligion rising in his time; and like Descartes, he made direct reference to the canons of truth current in his time. Yet, very much unlike Descartes, his method does not distort religious truth by reducing it to fit the presumptions of those canons. Rather, the challenge of atheism led him to an innovative approach to human reason in which the very notion of evidence is expanded to include a wider range of human experience. For Newman, the human mind is capable of truth when we respect its natural immanent movement without the arbitrary constraints emerging from scientism, and so the truth even of religion can be defended according to the rational principles that are operative in all human experience.

V. Plantinga's Design

It is in light of these historical observations that I wish to discuss a philosopher of our own day who is in a position similar to these esteemed predecessors. Alvin Plantinga addresses the arguments of the current crop of atheists—Dawkins, Dennett, Pinker, and others—in his recent book, *Where the Conflict Really Lies.*[30] In general, their argument against theism is that the scientific evidence of cosmology and evolution points to a causally closed universe which precludes any recourse to a theistic explanation. Plantinga refutes this argument by pointing out that this position *assumes* a metaphysical naturalism, for the notion of a causally closed universe goes beyond what scientific evidence can justify. Moreover, he attacks metaphysical naturalism as being unable to sustain the scientific enterprise, for it can explain neither why the intelligible regularity of the material world exists at all, nor how it can be objectively known by man; theism, on the other hand, offers a perfectly plausible explanation for both of these. Thus, his thesis is that that "there is a superficial conflict but deep concord between science and theistic religion, but superficial concord and deep conflict between science and naturalism."[31] I will argue, however, that in making his argument, Plantinga cedes too much to the methods of the scientists he is engaging. By adapting his argument for theism to the assumptions of sci-

30. Alvin Plantinga, *Where the Conflict Really Lies: Science, Religion, and Naturalism* (Oxford: Oxford University Press, 2011).

31. Ibid., ix.

ence, he establishes only that scientific theory *leaves room* for divine action; but I will argue that this is far too weak a basis on which to argue for the existence of God, for it at best shows divine action is *possible*, not *necessary*. Indeed, by trying to find evidence for divine activity in the discrete facts of empirical science, Plantinga illicitly restricts God's activity to be particular causes of events in the universe, which obscures the more important—and probative—point that He is the universal cause of the most universal effect; that He is, in other words, the transcendent source of being itself. The inadequacies of this approach to God's causality will be evident in considering Plantinga's attempt to make divine activity accord with the principles of evolution and physics.

Plantinga first shows that the theory of evolution is not incompatible with divine action. While Dawkins and Dennett both insist that unguided evolution by way of random genetic mutation adequately explains the existence of all life on earth, Plantinga points out that the facts of evolution, taken on their own, can never establish that it was unguided: "Take biological possibility . . . and suppose that all terrestrial life has indeed come to be by way of natural selection. It doesn't follow that life has come to be by way of *unguided* natural selection, and it doesn't even follow that it is *biologically possible* that life has come to be that way."[32] While science reveals the facts, the metabiological cause of the process of evolution is necessarily unknowable; the dogma that it must be unguided is a metaphysical assumption illicitly imported from naturalism, and need not be accepted in order to accept the facts of evolution itself. In fact, one can just as easily postulate that evolution is a perfect illustration of the doctrine of Providence, with God directing the activity of natural selection, for there is nothing in the facts of the evolutionary record to prevent God from having acted in the events of history.

This mode of argument is extended to divine miraculous intervention. That God cannot miraculously interfere in the world, and that all things are deterministically controlled by the laws of physics, assumes once again a causally closed physical universe; and this assumption is again a metaphysical assumption. Since whatever is freely asserted is freely denied, Plantinga offers in rejoinder that "any occasion on which God performs a miracle is an occasion when the universe is not causally closed; and the laws say

32. Ibid., 39; emphasis in original.

nothing about what happens when the universe is not causally closed."[33] Indeed, Plantinga offers an explanation of how God can act in the universe without "interfering" in it: the indeterminacy arising from quantum mechanics opens the door for God's activity. "God can cause quantum events, and, because the laws are merely statistical, do so without 'suspending' those laws. This action on his part can perhaps be amplified . . . to the macroscopic level; in this way, perhaps, God can cause dramatic effects at the level of everyday life, and do so without falling into intervention."[34] Thus, even within the parameters dictated by modern science, Plantinga shows that God can act in the universe and accomplish miraculous outcomes.

While one can sympathize with Plantinga's well-intentioned attempt to show that God may be acting in the physical universe, it is impossible to ignore how this mode of argumentation necessarily reduces God's activity to being just another cause *in* the universe, as opposed to the transcendent cause *of* the universe as a whole. Plantinga defends God's acting in evolution and miracles because the laws of science are open to His acting immanently in the world in very specific ways; thus, the world has natural laws, yet God can act without violating them.[35] But the fundamental error here is that in trying to discover God within the scientific order of causality, Plantinga assumes that divine activity is on the same ontological level as the natural and finite causes of change which science investigates. Thus, in any natural event, God's activities can only compete with the activity of nature, and so it is either one or the other acting. Plantinga defends divine causality by locating a gap in scientific causality in which God could possibly be present. Yet this fails to recognize the more significant fact that the entirety of the scientific causal order is ontologically dependent on God; it is much better to see God as acting not in, but above the immanent empirical order. In fact, God is active in *every* scientifically explicable event, yet his action is of a different ontological sort since it constitutes the being of the event, and not only the change in question. Plantinga's error is the result of a denial of the analogy of being, which forces him to see every causal act as exclusively either natural or supernatural. That is, since action

33. Ibid., 82–83. Indeed, as he will argue, "Given contemporary quantum mechanics, there isn't any sensible way to say what [divine] intervention *is*, let alone find something in science with which it is incompatible." Ibid., 96–97.

34. Ibid., 114.

35. See ibid., 116–17.

follows from being, if all being is univocal, all causal activity happens in the same way, so effects must be accomplished either by nature or by God.[36] This reduces the evidence for God to discrete facts in the universe since God is just another causal source *in* the universe.[37] But any finite characteristic can never point to an infinite cause, and so while divine causality might possibly explain the event, this is very far from demonstrative proof.

This tendency to view God's causality in a univocal fashion is reflected in Plantinga's anthropomorphic assertion that God is a *person* (not *personal* or *three persons*),[38] which obliterates the ontological distance between God and creation. This completely ignores the fact that personhood is itself analogical: while persons are, as St. Thomas says, the highest of substances because they exercise dominion over their activities,[39] the nature of that self-sufficiency varies between divine, angelic, and human persons, with the human person being radically constricted in the order of creation by its predetermined *telos* and the material mode of acting.[40] This reduction to a univocal idea of person leads to the consequent assumption that man can come to know God by reflecting on human personhood.[41] For example, when Plantinga addresses those who object to divine intervention because God would be acting arbitrarily and inconsistently in violating the laws

36. On the problems emerging from the nominalist tendency to view God as a univocal cause, as in Scotus and Ockham, see Brad S. Gregory, *The Unintended Reformation: How a Religious Revolution Secularized Society* (Cambridge, Massachusetts: Harvard University Press, 2012), 25–73.

37. This difference is spelled out clearly by David Bentley Hart, *The Experience of God: Being Consciousness, Bliss* (New Haven: Yale University Press, 2013), 302–303: "In either case, [in design arguments] 'God' has become the name of some special physical force or causal principle located somewhere out there among all the other forces and principles found in the universe; not the Logos filling and forming all things, not the infinity of being and consciousness in which all things necessarily subsist, but a thing among other things, an item among all the other items encompassed within nature."

38. For example, see *Where the Conflict Really Lies*, 66: "According to Christian and theistic views of God, he is a *person.*" He clarifies this by explaining that God has knowledge, affections, ends, and acts on the basis of knowledge to achieve ends.

39. See ST I, q. 29, aa. 1–3.

40. *Summa Contra Gentiles*, IV, chap. 11, no. 5.

41. Plantinga, *Where the Conflict Really Lies*, 298–99: "Insofar as we have been created in God's image, it is reasonable to think our intellectual preferences resemble his. We value simplicity, elegance, beauty; it is therefore reasonable to think that the same goes for God." Brian Davies has critiqued this position, which he calls theistic personalism, as a rejection of classical theism because in denying simplicity it severely limits God's knowledge and power, and so also undermines immutability. See also Brian Davies, *An Introduction to the Philosophy of Religion*, 3rd edition (Oxford: Oxford University Press, 2004), 9–15.

He has established, he replies that it is only arbitrary if God does not have "special reason for acting contrary to the usual regularities; but of course he might very well have such reasons."[42] All this speculation about God having reasons to act as a determinate cause in nature assumes a creaturely finitude inappropriate for the Creator; as Charles Journet points out, what remains is really a pagan divinity, since the "aberration of paganism … lay not in denying God but in submerging him in the universe."[43] God is pictured here not as the self-sufficient and transcendent Creator, but as one who manipulates the world to get what He wants.

More troubling, this approach diminishes even the nature of God's miraculous activity. By putting God in univocal competition with natural causes, a miracle can no longer be defined according to *how an event is brought about* (since this assumes the distinction between primary and secondary causes), but solely as an event inconsistent with the laws of nature, for which divine causality is the only apparent alternative. This reduces divine activity to a "God of the gaps," a ploy both futile in light of science, and impious in light of the orthodox notion of God as primary cause of being.[44] As a God of the gaps, He can only be a finite explanation of a finite event. Ironically, this mode of argument is the same that David Hume critiqued as being unable ever to demonstrate the existence of God.[45] Herein lies the problem: Plantinga, in order to accommodate the assumptions of modern science, uncritically embraces the Humean assumptions of those scientists about causality and knowledge, thereby adopting a method which inherently undercuts his attempts to defend theism. Of course, neither Plantinga nor modern scientists are skeptical about causality as Hume was; yet both, lacking a sense of ontological dependence based on causal necessity, tend to view causality in terms of regular conjunctions. For example, he writes: "We expect the future to resemble the past in relevant respects; but specifying the relevant respects is far from easy.… We learn these things only by virtue of exercising [a] habit [of making generalizations from experi-

42. Plantinga, *Where the Conflict Really Lies*, 106.

43. Charles Journet, *The Meaning of Grace*, translated by A. V. Littledale (New York: Scepter, 1996), 125.

44. For an explanation of miracles from the perspective of God as the primary cause of being acting without the mediation of secondary causes, see *Summa Contra Gentiles* III, chaps. 99–102.

45. David Hume, *Enquiry Concerning Human Understanding*, edited by L .A. Selby-Bigge, 3rd edition (Oxford: Clarendon Press, 1975), section XI, 132–148.

ence]."[46] The tenuousness of these inductive generalizations is grounded in his estimation of human epistemic powers, in which there is no real notion of intelligence as a power able to ascertain necessary causal relations.[47]

To defend properly God as the primary cause requires recognizing that natural and supernatural causes always cooperate in bringing about effects by acting on different levels of being. Thomas concisely adumbrates this distinction in *Summa Contra Gentiles:*

> And so, when we ask the reason why, in regard to a natural effect, we can give a reason based on a proximate cause; provided, of course, that we trace back all things to the divine will as a first cause. Thus, if the question is asked: "Why is wood heated in the presence of fire?" it is answered: "Because heating is the natural activity of fire"; and this is so "because heat is its proper accident." But this is the result of its proper form, and so on, until we come to the divine will.[48]

VI. Conclusion: Philosophy and Discipleship

The cautionary tales of Descartes and Plantinga well illustrate what Jacques Maritain knew as he began his life's work: to be a Christian philosopher is hard, for one must attend first to the eternal truths of the faith, not the ephemeral intellectual standards of the day. In being too eager to employ contemporary methods, philosophers end up misrepresenting God; but misrepresenting Him only leads those same scientific minds to scoff at God, for a God who is domesticated by the scientific method, a God who is not transcendent, does not merit worship. Kierkegaard warns against this in his provocative essay, "On the Difference Between a Genius and an Apostle."[49] Where the genius is a man who speaks to his time, the apostle—the Christian philosopher—has the duty of speaking for eternity:

> A genius and an Apostle are qualitatively different, they are definitions which each belong to their own spheres: *the sphere of immanence, and the sphere of tran-*

46. Plantinga, *Where the Conflict Really Lies,* 292.

47. See ibid., 292–94. On this note, see his list of cognitive faculties on pp. 311–312, which names all sorts of interior and exterior sensitive powers (memory, perception, intuition, sympathy, introspection, testimony, etc.), but fails to include anything like the traditional power of intellect ordered to universal principles.

48. SCG III, chap. 97, no. 17; translation by Vernon J. Bourke (Notre Dame, Indiana: University of Notre Dame Press, 1975).

49. Soren Kierkegaard, "On the Difference Between a Genius and an Apostle" in *The Present Age: On the Death of Rebellion,* translated by Alexander Dru (New York: Harper Perennial, 1962), 63–87.

> *scendence.* Genius may, therefore, have something new to bring forth, but what it brings forth disappears again as it becomes assimilated by the human race . . . ; the Apostle has, paradoxically, something new to bring, the newness of which, precisely because it is essentially paradoxical . . . always remains.[50]

Kierkegaard then notes that the greatest violence that can be done to the Apostle is to call him a mere genius, for that saps his truth of its transcendent authority. This eviscerated teaching, even if it aims to defend theism, can only constitute a departure (however unintentional and well-meaning) from the orthodox faith. Descartes and Plantinga are geniuses.[51] But we who call ourselves Christian philosophers are happier if, like Maritain, we aim to be Apostles, no matter how difficult that vocation might be.

50. Ibid., 67; emphasis in original.

51. Gilson makes this pertinent comment about Descartes' genius: "No man can fall a victim to his own genius unless he has genius; but those who have none are fully justified in refusing to be victimized by the genius of others. Not having made the mathematical discoveries of Descartes and Leibniz, we cannot be tempted to submit all questions to the rules of mathematics; but our very mediocrity should at least help us to avoid such a mistake. There is more than one excuse for being a Descartes, but there is no excuse whatsoever for being a Cartesian." *The Unity of Philosophical Experience*, 6.

JAMES V. SCHALL, S.J.

Why are there Minds in the Universe?

Before all things else wisdom was created; and prudent understanding, from eternity. To whom has wisdom's root been revealed? Who knows her subtleties? There is but one, wise and truly awe-inspiring, seated upon his throne: It is the Lord; he created her, has seen her and taken note of her. He has poured her forth on all his works, upon every living thing according to his bounty; he has lavished her upon his friends.[1]

Reality is immensely complex, and the truth about it must also be immensely complex. Only by long and painstaking work can mankind assimilate some, not much, but at least some of it.[2]

Is there an infinite body, as the majority of the ancient philosophers thought, or is it an impossibility? The decision of this question, either way, is not unimportant, but rather all-important, to our search for the truth. It is this problem which has practically always been the source of the differences of those who have written about nature as a whole. So it has been; and so it must be; since the least initial deviation from the truth is multiplied later a thousand-fold.[3]

—Aristotle, *De Caelo,* 1:5, 271b6–10.

I

A human race has appeared on the planet Earth, the third from the Sun, itself a bright, but still size-wise one of the lesser of billions of stars in the cosmos. While all such dates are controversial and subject to radical revi-

1. Sirach 1:4–8. New American Bible.
2. J. M. Bochenski, *Philosophy: An Introduction* (New York: Harper Torchbooks, 1972), 41.
3. Aristotle, *De Caelo*, 1.5, 271b6–10. Translation taken from W. D. Ross, *Basic Works of Aristotle.*

sion, the age of the universe is now given as around 13.7 billion years old. What we know as time and space began then, immediately. Our Sun is calculated at 4.5 billion years. That is, it took about seven billion years for it to show up. Our race, whose appearance on this planet is relatively recent, has itself manifested a human form that has gradually increased in numbers, within the last centuries or so, to billions of individual persons.

Each of these existing persons lives a certain amount of time, usually at most up to eighty or ninety years, if they are strong, as Psalm 90 has it. Most human beings, of course, die younger. Not a few never make it out of the womb of their mothers. With today's bio-genetic, in *vitro* techniques, others do not even make it into the womb of women, let alone that their own mother's. Many fertilized ova are frozen or discarded. Since 1980 alone, through deliberate human agency, over one billion three hundred million abortions have been carried out world-wide. What we call "natural" deaths, go on at their usual rate, but wide-spread state assisted or imposed euthanasia is on the horizon or already in place.

Estimates have it that perhaps ninety to one hundred billion human beings, give or take considerable room for error, have lived on this planet since mankind first appeared some widely disputed number of years ago. Some seven billion human beings are currently alive, with some being born and some dying daily. A general population decline is developing in the so-called advanced countries. This decline appears to be the result of a loss of human purpose.

The billions who have preceded us over the ages have left a record of their presence among us. We have accounts of their deeds and thoughts in writings, in the ruins of their cities and buildings, and by memories of their faces and voices in statues, photos, and, more recently, recordings. Because of this human presence, scientists have taken to referring to the post-Ice Age in which we now live as the Anthropocene Age. This phrase means that the men who have been present in this era have reconfigured much of the earth in their image. Some even experiment with reconfiguring the human corpus itself.

The human race, however, does not exist all at once or in one place. At least for now, it only exists, as an intelligible whole, in the mind. But in its actuality, the whole human race includes the living and the dead plus whoever might live in the future if they actually come into existence. Each existing person seems both to belong to nature and yet to possess something that transcends the concrete cycles of nature. Ever since Genesis, it has been assumed that the primary purpose of the earth is not simply to continue it untouched down the ages, but to provide for the existence and flourishing of man if he sets himself to using it. The purpose of the human race in time cannot simply to be to leave the earth and its riches untouched, as if man has no real purpose for being where and what he is. In some basic sense, he obviously comes from the same ultimate source that everything else does.

The question that I want to address here is perhaps unusual, if not downright rash. But it is, I think, a legitimate one. Why, in this universe, do we find, in addition to things inanimate and things living by instinct, also a strain of living beings with minds? Can it be merely an accident? To be sure, we do not have disembodied "minds" in this world. We are not "ghosts in a machine"—to use Gilbert Ryle's description of Descartes' understanding of man. Our minds and bodies are not absolutely independent of each other, as we sometimes think in reading Plato or certain spiritual writers. We are "living beings with *logos*," as Aristotle put it. We are a race of beings who think. That fact sets us apart, but does not deny that we also have bodies that are involved in the very process of our thinking.

We have a power both of understanding things and of being able to act on them through our understanding. Our very bodies, as Leon Kass graphically points out in his great book *The Hungry Soul*, seem, in comparison to animals, to be "modified" in such a way that they facilitate our thinking.[4] This intricate inter-twining of mind and body is why our eyes are where they are, why we stand erect, and why we hear. Josef Pieper made the same point in this way: "The whole living human body acts as an infinitely differentiated and sensitive receptacle of this direct contact with reality and thus forms one whole organ of possible experience."[5] We take it for granted that the purpose of a person with mind, if we wonder what it is, is first to know what is not himself. And what is it that a mind knows when it is actively knowing?

The first thing that a mind knows, or, better, the first thing that a human person knows through his mind, is not the mind itself or the knowing person. Unlike God or the angels, the minds that we have, evidently, become

4. Leon Kass, *The Hungry Soul* (New York: The Free Press, 1994).

5. Josef Pieper, *In Defense of Philosophy* (San Francisco: Ignatius Press, 1992), 104.

active, as it were, become luminous to themselves, only when they know something besides themselves. We ourselves are not the first objects of our knowing powers. Even to know what we look like, we need mirrors, that is, some artifact besides ourselves.

We do not in fact know ourselves except reflexively when we know something else besides ourselves. Then, we realize that it is "I" who knows that tree or that person out there beyond myself. When we say "I know," we always have to name something else that we know besides ourselves. Knowing does not happen unless a something is being known. Our "I" is not the object of our immediate knowledge. Yet, we are certain that it is "I" who knows what is not myself when we know anything at all.

The great Delphic admonition—"Know thyself!"—was not a formula to bypass things other than ourselves. Rather it advised us to know ourselves by how we knew and dealt with others.[6] We might say that the first time that we know anything at all besides ourselves becomes an indirect gift to us of ourselves from outside of ourselves. We do not know that we know until we know something not ourselves. To "know ourselves," we must spend much time, even our lifetime, being made alert and intellectually active by what is not ourselves. The wondrous existence of myriads of things that are not ourselves make it possible that the one unique being that is ourselves knows that *he is*.

Yves Simon once wisely put it this way: the only way that we can be ourselves is that we are not anything else but our selves.[7] To be myself, it is imperative that I am not someone or something else. But if there were not something else, I could not know that I exist. Knowledge of someone or something else as such has the marvelous ability to leave the person or thing known as it is. What is not ourselves lives in us by an intentional, not real, existence. Otherwise, every time we knew something, we would consume or destroy it by our knowing.

We must add one more thing. In the case of other human beings, if we simply know their exteriors, their height, weight, and other particulars about their statures, we do not really know them. To know someone else as he really is, he has to want us to know him. He has to invite us to know him.

6. See E. F. Schumacher, *A Guide for the Perplexed* (New York: Harper Colophon, 1977), 62–80.

7. See Yves R. Simon, *A General Theory of Authority* (Notre Dame, Indiana: University of Notre Dame Press, 1980), 91–94, 152–53.

He has to tell us about himself. We can, to be sure, guess or intuit some inner characteristics or qualities of others, both good and bad. But we are beings who have to reveal ourselves if we want to be known by someone else and vice versa. This fact brings up at many levels the whole realm of friendship among human beings, indeed within the divine being also. The fact is, as Aristotle said, that we can only know a few people, probably very few, in one life time, if we mean "know" them well. And this restriction is a good thing, not an evil, though it is a loss.

Walker Percy wondered early in *Lost in the Cosmos*: "Why it is that we cannot look in the eyes of someone else for more than ten seconds without turning away?" This question is relevant to the counter biblical refrain that we want to see God "face-to-face." We want to see each other "face-to-face." We have to suspect from these striking experiences that the ultimate object of our knowing is not exclusively another human being, even though we are told to love our neighbor as ourselves. We usually have no trouble accepting this admonition as the worthiest human happiness. But we are also aware, by the same logic, of the millions or billions of other, likewise human beings, whom we will never meet or know in this life. We have to conclude that this "meeting and loving absolutely everyone else" is not necessary for our purposes here in this life. Chesterton, I believe, put it well when he remarked that we are to love the neighbor next door because he exists there, not the abstraction "mankind," which involves loving no actual human being.

II

"What is the point of these reflections?" It is this: something in the universe exists besides just a multiplicity of other things that do not know themselves. In addition to non-rational beings, the existence of a knowing being in the universe changes everything. In addition to things, we have thoughts about things. Why? Lucy and Charlie Brown are in a strategic huddle before Charlie Brown sends Lucy in to bat in a crucial game. "Lucy, you're the next batter," he tells her. "Here's what I want you to do." Lucy listens with growing perplexity. Charlie Brown explains: "The situation calls for a bunt. Now the other team knows that we know the situation.... But we know that they know that we know."

As Lucy becomes ever more dazed, Charlie Brown goes on calmly: "But it just may be that they know that they know we know ... so ..." In the final scene, Lucy turns on a confused Charlie Brown. She tells him: "Start over."[8] The mind not only seeks to cover all possibilities, as Charlie Brown was trying to do, but it seeks to know what other minds are thinking in the light of what we are thinking. Thus, we not only have the existence of things that are knowable, we also have a world of thought about these things, even a world of thought about thought which can itself be thought about.

And learning anything really well usually involves a series of "start overs." On the basis of experience, the intellect "intuits" what the thing it observes is. It seeks to know ever more clearly what it is by examining what it does—*agere sequitur esse*, as the Scholastics put it, the action of a thing follows the *what is* of a thing. We do not expect ducks to bark. If they in fact do bark or say "good morning," we look for a cause beyond the duck.

As Bochenski remarks, even if reality is immensely complicated, we seek to know what we can of it. Presumably, reality remains mostly what it is even when we know it. And if something does, perchance, become something else, we want to know the process, the reasons, whereby it changed. We do not find rocks or even toads out there trying to figure out what they are. They are what they are. But human beings are not content with the fact that they just are. And "Upon every living thing according to His bounty" something has been "lavished." It is called wisdom. It suggests that everything, if it exists, possesses an act of being that cannot be explained by anything that is not existence itself.

Aristotle was most perceptive when he told us that we cannot really escape the question of the infinite body, at least if we want to know the truth. Aristotle presumed that we did want to know the truth. The "least deviation from the truth leads" to "a thousand-fold" number of errors. I suspect this multiplication is true. It shows that there is much at stake when we think about things, both when we think correctly of them and erroneously.

The Book of Sirach tells us that the Lord has poured forth his wisdom on all His works and "upon every living thing according to his bounty." These are curious words. In everything, we find not only the thing itself but also a "wisdom," as if to say that it is not *what it is* simply by itself. No finite thing caused itself to be *what it is* or to be at all. This relation to wisdom would imply what poets have long seen, namely, that we see even in a flower or a bird something that connects us with all things. It is not surprising

8. Charles Schulz, *You're the Greatest, Charlie Brown* (Greenwich, Connecticut: Fawcett, 1964).

then that the intellect is best defined as that power or capacity that we have whereby we know all things. Our minds are *capax omnium*.

We might surmise, then, that some fundamental relationship exists between things and knowing things. We can legitimately wonder why? Is there something incomplete about a thing if it is not also known? One of the further curiosities about knowing is that, in principle, to know a thing does not change the thing known. It is true that on the basis of knowledge, a knower can become a maker. He can change something about a thing. He can take wood and make a chair. He can even make a plastic chair, that is, a chair from a substance which itself depends on his mind and the making capacities of the person who possesses it. But in itself, my knowing of a thing or a person does not change a thing without some transference or application of knowledge by will and hand.

Aristotle was perceptive when he defined man as that being in the universe with both a mind and a hand. Man's soul, his formal cause, makes his very body an apt instrument for him to know what is not himself. His memory and hands make it possible for what is inside of him, his acquired knowledge, to have an effect outside of himself. It enables him to become present, to make himself manifest in the world. Indeed, he can make something "that works." It may take many centuries to perfect an idea—say a self-moving vehicle to get rapidly from place to place. But the record of the improvement is written in every automobile that we now drive.

Am I implying that the reason we have minds is so that we can drive cars? Hundreds of thousands are killed every year in automobiles throughout the world. Our deeds seem always to be capable of either good or bad usage. While we do not trust madmen or apes with our Toyotas, we evidently soon will trust our robots with them. But robots are just a sophisticated form of human intelligence and human hand working together, as are machines that land us on the planets of our solar system or those that enable us almost instantaneously to communicate with one another across the world.

Man exists as an individual personal being that has a transcendent end for himself, but who exists in a world in which some sort of primordial fall seems to cloud his personal and corporate history. The fact that he is not primarily a spirit, even though he has a soul, means that he changes gradually, often slowly. He is responsible for himself, both for what he does that is good and what he does that is evil. All utopian schemes that try to eliminate evil by some sort of impersonal means—economic, political, or psychological—usually end up making him worse. They do not want to understand that present in the world is also a revelation that can redeem each man but only by its own terms.

The primary purpose of this revelation is not "world improvement" either now or down the ages. Rather it is the salvation of each soul in whatever civil or economic condition a man finds himself. This is not an individualism but a personalism that sees the relation to others and the given status of mankind to be the context of his salvation. The greatest enemy to this view, as Benedict XVI pointed out in *Spe Salvi*, is an inner worldly utopianism, usually called modernism, that promises every transcendent Christian principle as attainable in this world by human means.

III

Here, however, I am not asking primarily about man's transcendent destiny, though its proper understanding, I think, is what makes possible our sense of why we find minds in the universe. Rather, I am asking a question about the existence of a finite mind itself. In a way, I am asking: "Could God create a world in which no rational being existed?" I know that for God "all things are possible." So logically I have to say that a world without man in it would be an incomplete world. Even God could not create an incomplete world. If He did, it would indicate that God, even while knowing in what it consisted, did not complete what He began. That would, in my opinion, be a defect, a contradiction, in the Godhead. I do not mean that God had to make everything He could conceive. Rather I mean that if He actually began a thing He did not complete, it would show a defect in His intelligence as He already knew the end He rejected. No purpose would exist in half completed things.

Such issues may sound silly to scientists or anyone else who might worry about such esoterica. But I think that the scientists are key in the answer to this question, provided that they do not, in principle, exclude the primary issue. The cosmos itself is the place in which each rational being, to participate in his personal and corporate destiny, decides freely, by the way he lives, his relation to his transcendent origin. The physical universe exists as the arena in which our purposes are revealed—high, evil, or banal. It makes possible the conditions for real action.[9]

9. See James V. Schall, *Rational Pleasures* (San Francisco: Ignatius Press, 2013), 167–89.

That being said, however, we can still inquire: "Is anything lacking within the world itself, even if we do know what man's final end may be from a source outside of the world?" I emphasize again that nothing in a thing known when it is known is changed. The change takes place in the knower. That change in the knower, as such, is invisible to all but the knower and those to whom he reveals it. Logically, then, the last and most important "change" in the universe is when the human knower finally understands why the world exists and his place in it. Contrary to much modern ideology of sundry origins, the world does not exist in order that, somehow down through the ages, a perfect inner-worldly city will exist in this world. We have to conduct our lives on the premise of the abidingness of sin and evil among us, including in our leaders.

Following St. Augustine, I would argue that this perfect inner-worldly city simply will not happen. To pretend or predict that it will can only make it difficult or impossible to concentrate on what can be done. One reason to deny that this perfect city is our purpose is that if it were, that fact would make all earlier generations, who did not live in the later best regime, unable to reach the purpose of their existence. I take this to be the historic lesson of political philosophy. The inner-worldly purpose of the cosmos has to be achievable even by the imperfect, sinful men in it, each of whom lives at most fourscore years and ten in imperfect polities.

So what is left? What happens over time with human intelligence? It learns more about what is not itself. Some of this knowledge it also forgets or loses. In doing so, it is also more aware of itself as a being who seeks to know and who does know all of *what is*. He learns that this thing is not that thing. He distinguishes. In so doing, he finds similarities and dissimilarities. Nothing he encounters caused itself to be or to be the kind of thing it is. He says: "This is not that." "That is this kind of a thing." That does not "exist." He says such things because what he sees and knows are the same or not the same. He is hardly prepared for the wide variety of things that he knows. But he rejoices in their abundance.

At a certain point, man realizes that the cosmos out there is not watching him. It has no capacity to do what he can do. Nothing in the cosmos, except himself, knows *all there is* as "the cosmos." He not only knows the separate things in the cosmos, but also, in some sense, that their unity is an order, not a chaos. But if the cosmos is not watching man, he is watching it. Why? To know *what it is*. If the different things in the universe can be known, they are made to be known. They are a communication of knowledge of what does not know itself to a knower who knows it. Thus, the universe is not complete unless we find something within it, not just outside of it, that can know it, can know the *what is* that is in it.

Aquinas says in his Treatise on Law that the Eternal Law is the order of all things as they exist in the mind of God. But the natural law is that same order now resident in the things themselves. It is these latter things we know when we know. And Aquinas does tell us in the *Summa Contra Gentiles* (II, 46), that "the perfection of the universe does require that there be some intellectual creatures" in it. It is only when the universe is known that it can be freely praised and returned to its Beginning. This is why Plato says in his *Laws*, that we should, in response, spend our lives "singing, sacrificing, and dancing."[10]

Aquinas further tells us that we cannot love a thing unless we first know it. Without the knowledge of a thing, including a human thing in the only way he can be known, we cannot really love it. Love follows upon knowledge as well as leading to it. Socrates tells us in the *Phaedrus* that "to be unaware of the difference between a dream-image and the reality of what is just and unjust, good and bad, must truly be grounds for reproach, even if the crowd praises it with one voice" (277e). That we be not unaware of this difference between just and unjust, good and bad, is why minds are found in the universe.

And in the *Symposium*, Diotima says to Socrates: "What is the real purpose of love, can you say?" He tells her that, if he could answer, he would not be her student but her teacher. So she answers him: "Well, I'll tell you. It's giving birth in beauty whether of body or of soul" (206b).[11] That we be not unaware that we are known and loved, both by God and by one another, is the reason why minds exist in the universe. The universe could not be complete without such knowledge within it.

But, not to forget that we are but men passing through a vale of tears to our transcendent end, let me recall, in conclusion, a passage in Boswell's *Life of Johnson*. It is April 26, 1776. Boswell complains that he has "dined at a splendid table without hearing one sentence of conversation worthy

10. See James V. Schall, *On the Unseriousness of Human Affairs* (Wilmington, Delaware: ISI Books, 2001).

11. From Plato, *Complete Works*, edited by John M. Cooper (Indianapolis, Indiana: Hackett, 1997).

of being remembered." Johnson responded: "Sir, there is seldom any such conversation; for when there is, people differ in opinion, and get into bad humour, or some of the company who are not capable of such conversation, are left out, and feel themselves uneasy."[12]

We will, I think, find no more sober and concrete reminder of the way most of us are and live than in this classic Johnsonian exchange. Philosophy exists in conversation. *Caritas* (charity) is directed to *logos* (reason) and *logos* in turn to *esse* (being). Mind also exists in the universe. Ordinary things do go on. Revelation exists that even those who differ radically in opinion or are not much capable of high conversation may not be ultimately left out of that final conversation and love that was given to us if we choose to accept it. Thus, revelation is itself directed to philosophy, to the distinction of good and bad, of *what is* and what is not. That such things might be known, might be pondered, accepted or rejected, is the final reason that we find minds in this universe.

12. *Boswell's Life of Johnson* (London: Oxford, 1931), II, 38.

VI

THOMISTIC ETHICS AND POLITICAL THEORY

JOSHUA SCHULZ

Scale, Anonymity, and Political *Akrasia* in Aristotle's *Politics* 7.4

I. Introduction

Many philosophers and social scientists have held that the intensity of interpersonal interaction within a society varies inversely with the scale of a society, that is, that living in large communities increases the superficiality of our relationships. So obvious is this connection between scale and community that some thinkers have distinguished between kinds of communities in ways that are ultimately reducible to scale: Tonnies's distinction between *Gemeinschaft* and *Gesellschaft*, Durkheim's distinction between organic and mechanical solidarity, Maine's distinction between societies defined by status and contract, and Redfield's distinction between folk and urban cultures all fit this paradigm.[1]

However, as Gerald Berreman has noted, "scale" is an ambiguous term, as is "social interaction."[2] Does the relation between scale and social interaction simply inhere in the sheer population of a community, or is it also dependent on the density of settlement, on the heterogeneity of the population, on the extensiveness of communication networks, or on the complexity of a community's political, economic, and social organization? How reliable are the generalizations of social scientists about the relationship

1. See Ferdinand Tönnies, *Community and Civil Society,* edited by Jose Harris (Cambridge: Cambridge University Press, 2001); Emile Durkheim, *The Division of Labor in Society,* translated by W. D. Halls (New York: Free Press, 1997); Henry Maine, *The Ancient Law, Its Connection with the Early History of Society, and Its Relation to Modern Ideas* (1861), chapter 5; Robert Redfield, "The Folk Society," *American Journal of Sociology* 52 (1947): 293–308.

2. Gerald Berreman, *Current Anthropology* 19 (1978): 225–45.

between scale and the variable social characteristics of societies? Clearly, no mere quantity of people directly correlates with intensity of social interaction. A community of Carthusian monks is small and dense, but short on interpersonal interaction, for instance. The interesting questions lie in the other direction: at what point does scale (however we analyze that term) inhibit social interactivity (whatever that is), and how?

This essay suggests that Aristotle provides a coherent and insightful theoretical and normative framework for thinking about the relation between scale and properly *political* activity. First, Aristotle provides a defensible justification for the concept of "proper size." Second, he develops useful criteria for evaluating the relationship between scale and social interactivity by analyzing the relation between interpersonal familiarity and successful political deliberation. The key thesis in Aristotle's thinking about this relation is that interpersonal anonymity is destructive of the virtue of prudence, which is a requisite for political justice and the well-functioning of the *polis* as such. After developing and defending Aristotle's principal argument for this thesis, we will outline several important implications of the argument should it prove to be sound.

II. The "Proper Size" Argument of *Politics* 7.4

The proper size of the state (or city, or *polis*) is a qualitative rather than a quantitative question for Aristotle.[3] If "the city, like the individual, has a work to do, and the city which is best adapted to the fulfillment of its work is to be deemed greatest," he argues, we should judge a city not by the number of its inhabitants, but by its ability (*dunamis*) to do that work.[4] "A great city is not the same as a populous one."[5]

In these brief lines, Aristotle articulates several theses. The first is that the city has a *telos*, an end or purpose following from its nature as a city. That purpose is to facilitate human *eudaimonia*, as he has previously ar-

3. I will be using the terms "city," "state," and "polis" interchangeably, though following Aristotle in *Politics* (hereafter *Pol.*) 5.3 and 7.4, as distinct from "nation." Aristotle indicates these are normative terms. Cities possess a principle of unity, whereas nations lack such a principle due to their excessive size. All citations taken from Aristotle's text refer to translations in *The Complete Works of Aristotle*, edited by Jonathan Barnes (Princeton, New Jersey: Princeton University Press, 1984).

4. *Pol.* 7.4, 1362a10–14.

5. *Pol.* 7.4, 1326a24–25.

gued.[6] Second, he asserts that a human population is the material in which the statesman works his craft, and third, that size is an accidental rather than essential feature of the *polis* as such.[7] One cannot create a state simply by drawing random lines on a map or by "surrounding all Peloponnesus with a wall."[8]

It is nevertheless obvious that every city has some size, and arguably the case that size plays a determinative role in a city's ability to accomplish its *telos* and thus to be a city at all.[9] As Aristotle puts it, "a very populous city can rarely, if ever, be well governed."[10] This is the fourth thesis in this section, the one to be proved. While Aristotle suggests that it is substantiated by experience, he is aware that the one-time reputation of a few (now defunct) city-states is a thin basis on which to build a philosophical argument. We should keep in mind, then, that while Aristotle thinks experience will confirm the relevance of size to the well-functioning of the state, the thesis itself is established by an argument premised on the nature of the *polis* rather than by an inductive generalization.

Suitably reconstructed, the first half of Aristotle's *Limit Argument* runs thus:

1. Organized bodies are directed towards an end (*telos*).
2. Size affects the ability of organized bodies to achieve their ends, since:
   a. Size can cause an organized body to lose its ability to achieve its end, and
   b. Size can cause an organized body to lose its original end by becoming a different kind of being altogether.[11]

6. *Pol.*, 7.1, 1324a22–23: "That form of government is best in which every man, whoever he is, can act best and live happily."

7. *Pol.*, 7.4, 1325b37–1326a4: "As the weaver or shipbuilder or any other artisan must have the material proper for his work ... so the statesman or legislator must also have materials suited to him," including "a certain number of citizens, a country in which to place them, and the like."

8. *Pol.*, 3.3, 1276a26–29.

9. Bodies bear the same relation to the flourishing of the state as external goods bear to the flourishing of the individual: they are limited "like any other instrument, [for] all things useful are useful for a purpose, and where there is too much they must either do harm, or at any rate be of no use, to their possessors"—unlike goods of the soul. *Pol.*, 7.1, 1323b7–10.

10. *Pol.*, 7.4, 1326a25–26: "Experience shows that a very populous city can rarely, if ever, be well governed; since all cities which have a reputation for good government have a limit for population."

11. The passage on which premise (2) is based reads: "To the size of states there is a limit, as there is to other things, plants, animals, implements; for none of these retain their natural power when they are too large or too small, but they either wholly lose their nature, or are spoiled." *Pol.*, 7.4, 1326a35–38.

3. Therefore, there is a rational limit to the size of organized bodies, a "proper size" for them to be.

Let us consider each premise individually.

Premise (1). Putting aside homogenous materials, we immediately see that the first premise articulates a foundational principle of Aristotelian natural philosophy.[12] Aristotle's hylomorphic metaphysics holds that every substance is a composite of matter and form. Matter is a *substratum* that persists through change and is organized by form, whereas form is the *rational principle* which explains the structure and powers of a substance and thus accounts for the intelligibility of something as a member of a kind.[13]

Aristotle further argues that this formal organizing principle can be *internal* or *external* to the being it organizes. Being "the material of a tree" is what makes wood woody, for instance, whereas being "the material of a bed" does not conceptually specify any specific material of which beds are made (beds can be made of metal, plastic, wood, or marshmallows).[14] Internally organized substances behave "always or for the most part" through change, that is, *regularly*: water freezes at 0° C, living things grow and reproduce, men act for reasons. Since chance is not a sufficient explanation for causal regularity, some other explanatory principle is required, which Aristotle calls the *final cause* or *telos* of a substance.[15] The *telos* of internally organized or "natural" substances is identical with the *form* of a thing: that something has the chemical structure of water explains both why it is water and why it freezes at 0° C.[16] In every case, the final cause explains the regularity of something's behavior or powers, allowing us to classify substances (e.g., in the Periodic table) and thus to engage in practical and productive reasoning.

12. While Aristotle argues that every substance is organized in *some* way by form, Aristotle uses the term "organized body" more specifically in his biological and political writings to indicate a substance possessing parts whose operations are coordinated towards a corporate end; see *De anima* 2.1 and *Pol.* 7.3, 1326a25. Premise (1) clearly refers to non-homogenous ("corporate") organisms as opposed to homogenous substances, such as copper.

13. Aristotle, *Physics* (hereafter *Phys.*) 2.3, 194b23–35.

14. Thus, Aristotle quips in *Phys.* 2, "man is born from man, but not bed from bed. That is why people say that the figure is not the nature of a bed, but the wood is—if the bed sprouted not a bed but wood would come up." See the discussion at 193a9–193b21.

15. See *Phys.* 2.8, 198b32–199a8

16. See *Phys.,* 2.1, 192b13–15 for the definition of natural substance, and 2.7, 198a25–26 for the assertion that the formal, efficient, and final causes are often identical in natural substances.

The fruits of productive reasoning are artifacts, things created by human beings for a purpose. Artifacts are externally organized: wood does not spontaneously become a bed, but can be made into a bed by a carpenter who understands how to make use of it for that purpose.[17] The formal and final causes of artifacts are not identical, for they originate in the mind and will of an artificer rather than in the material on which she works her art. Nevertheless, just as final causality was necessary to explain the causal regularity of natural substances, so too is final causality necessary to ground the intelligibility and value of artifacts.[18] If a pen is an instrument for writing with ink, for example, what cannot write with ink is not a pen, and what cannot write well with ink is not a good pen. One cannot coherently evaluate a pen *qua* pen by asking whether it is useful for hunting or war.

Premise (2). The second premise of Aristotle's argument asserts that size affects the ability of both naturally and artificially organized beings to achieve their ends. Consider writing instruments again. A pen can be too small or too large to be used for writing. An ungraspable, microscopic pen and an unliftable, three-ton pen would be pens in name only, as good for writing as a drawing of an eye would be good for seeing. On the other hand, a worn-down nub of a pencil is *hardly* a pencil, and a pen the size of a baseball bat is *hardly* a pen, because both are bad for writing.[19]

That is true at least for an average sized person, anyway. As Aristotle argues in *Nicomachean Ethics*, "virtue" or "excellence" is a term whose instantiation is relative to acts, subjects, and circumstances. What counts as a better-making property of *F* depends on what *F* is, the condition of *F* at the time, and the circumstances in which *F* finds itself. Whether the size of a pen is a better or worse-making property of that pen depends on whom the pen is used by, just as what constitutes a "healthy" amount of food de-

17. *Phys.* 192b30–31. Note that Aristotle's distinction between natural and artificial substances is not a distinction between real and nominal essences. Artificial substances possess real forms necessary for explaining their structure, function, powers, and purpose. No such explanations can be given for nominal substances.

18. See Aristotle's distinction between use and exchange value at *Pol.* 1.9, 1257a6–15, which is indebted to Plato's arguments (for instance) at *Republic* 352e–354a, *Euthydemus* 279a–281d, and *Meno* 87e–88d.

19. Aristotle himself illustrates premise (2) using the example of a ship, arguing that "a ship that is only a span long will not be a ship at all, nor a ship a quarter of a mile long; yet there may be a ship of a certain size, either too large or too small which will still be a ship, but bad for sailing." *Pol.* 7.4, 1326a39–1326b2.

pends on whether one is Milo the wrestler or Fifi the ballerina.[20] The pens useful for Tom Thumb and Jack's Giant are not the same size. Likewise, what counts as a well-sized pen depends on whether one is young or old, skilled or unskilled at writing, as well as where one finds oneself: underwater, among rich business associates, etc. As these reflections show, Aristotle is not asserting that there is *one* best size for every kind of artifact. Rather, he is asserting that an instrument that cannot be used for its purpose is not an *F*, while the degree to which an instrument accomplishes its purpose—the more useful and qualitatively better it is—the more it both satisfies its definition as an *F* and maximizes its value. "Being," "end," and "good" are in this sense coextensive, though not synonymous. That which accomplishes the *telos* of F best has the best claim to be *F*, since if *kinesis* is the reduction of potentiality to actuality, then "the form of a thing emerges in its activity of striving toward its actuality from its potentiality to do so."[21]

Nevertheless, it remains the case that in order to be a pen at all, the instrument must be sized in such a way that it is capable of being easily used for writing. The *telos* of a thing functions as a limit on the size of an organized being relative to both its nature and its use. The concept of "proper size" is therefore coherent insofar as there is some purpose *F* can succeed or fail at and the size of *F* contributes to its success or failure at that purpose.

Does the same follow for natural things? The point is obvious in the case of living things. There are many goods whose acquisition or achievement is made more difficult, or even impossible, by the size of Tom Thumb and Jack's Giant.[22] Using pencils and having sex come to mind, of course, but so do goods of the soul, like friendship and wisdom. As Aristotle argues throughout the *Politics*, human beings require social structures such as families, friends, teachers, and neighbors both to *acquire* moral and intellectual excellences and to *exercise* them: one cannot learn to speak or

20. See *Nicomachean Ethics* (hereafter *EN*) 2.6, 1106b3.

21. For an excellent technical discussion of this point, see Adriel Trott, *Aristotle on the Nature of Community* (Cambridge: Cambridge University Press, 2014), 25–28. Aristotle defines change as the "fulfillment of what is potentially, qua potential" at *Phys.* 201b5 ff. He asserts that "actuality" and "good" are coextensive in many places, including *Metaphysics* 5.16 and the opening arguments of the *Pol.* at 1252b32–1253a2.

22. We might also offer a vegetable example. Evolutionary theory would posit that insofar as size affects an organism's ability to survive and reproduce, non-optimally sized organisms will fail at both tasks. Thus the size of a plant's leaves and the depth of its root structure respond to climate, etc.

philosophize well alone.[23] If Tom's voice is too quiet for us to hear and the Giant's voice too loud for us to endure, neither will be capable of participating in the life of the *polis* or achieving *eudaimonia*. Insofar as natural things have a *telos* at which they aim, giantism and dwarfism will be defects of those things and their parts insofar as each constitutes a disability, a frustration of an organism's capacity to exercise the activities characteristic of its kind.

In sum, Aristotle makes a plausible case that the rational limit of organized bodies is a *relative limit* in the case of artifacts and an *intrinsic limit* in the case of natural beings.

III. The Organized State Claim

Having established (3), that there is a rational limit to the size of organized bodies, Aristotle makes a key assertion: "In like manner a state when composed of too few is not, as a state ought to be, self-sufficient; when of too many, though self-sufficient in all mere necessaries, as a nation may be, it is not a state, being almost incapable of constitutional government."[24] Formally stated, Aristotle is asserting that

1. The *polis* is a relevantly organized body.

From this he can infer,

5. Therefore, there is a rational limit to the size of the *polis*.

We should note here that Aristotle is not inferring (5) by way of an *analogy* between the *polis* and other organized beings (e.g., "plants, animals, implements"). Rather, he is asserting in (4) that the *polis* is an *instance* of something being so organized that its size affects both its nature and its ability to achieve its *telos*. This is clear in his explanation: a state that is too small will lack the necessary conditions of being a *polis*, such as the ability to satisfy the basic needs of its citizens, while a *polis* that is too large is incapable of rational order, that is, rule by law—and therefore will not be a *polis*, but something else.[25]

23. See V. Bradley Lewis's analysis in "Wealth, Happiness, and Politics: Aristotelian Questions," in *Wealth, Poverty, and Human Destiny*, edited by Doug Bandow and David Schindler (Wilmington, Delaware: ISI Books, 2003).

24. *Pol.* 7.4, 1326b2–5.

25. Aristotle suggests that it has become a nation, both here and at *Pol.* 3.3.

Several objections can be raised against this fourth premise. First, one might argue with Hobbes that a *polis* is only a nominal substance in the way a pile of stones is. That a pile of stones has a location in space makes it *one thing* for some practical and conceptual purposes, but it does not make it *one substance* in the same way that you and I are individual persons rather than collections of organs. We possess, and piles lack, a principle of organization coordinating the powers of our parts so as to act as a unified whole. However, as we noted in our analysis of premise (3) above, only things which have a *telos* can have a proper size. If the nominalists are correct, then, there is no proper size for the *polis* because the *polis* lacks a *telos*.

Second, one might argue that even if some polities are organized according to a rational principle, there is no one principle that organizes all polities. As evidence one might point out that polities can be organized by many political principles and for many ends, even the mere production and consumption of material goods. Thus, one might conclude that size is relevant to the success of some polities but not others: it might be the case that for polities aimed at market growth, bigger *is* always better.

In favor of (4), however, stands Aristotle's political naturalism.[26] Aristotle explicitly argues in a number of places that the *polis* is an organism whose form is its constitution. For instance, he argues that the constitution of a *polis* is its principle of identity. The *polis* remains one city despite the cyclic birth and death of its members, but does not remain the same city if it acquires a new form of government even if the members of the city remain identical.[27] For example, the American Revolutionary War caused the American colonies to cease to exist as colonies and to begin to exist as the United States, even though the members of each polity were roughly the same. Second, as Aristotle argues in *Motion of Animals*, the state is an organism like an animal insofar as the proper work of each of its parts is coordinated towards the work of the whole.[28] Finally, Aristotle famously

26. This section, and the discussion of the *akratic* state below, was greatly assisted by Carlos Cortissoz's unpublished paper, "The Soul-State Analogy in Aristotle's Politics," presented at the *Society for Ancient Greek Philosophy Annual Meeting*, October 2009, New York, New York.

27. *Pol.* 3.3, 1276b2–10

28. "The animal organism must be conceived after the similitude of a well-governed commonwealth. When order is once established in it there is no more need of a separate monarch to preside over each several task. The individuals each play their assigned part as it is ordered, and one thing follows another in its accustomed order. So in animals there is the same orderliness—nature taking the place of custom—and each part naturally doing his own work as nature has composed them" *De. Mot. An.* 10, 703a30–35.

argues in *Politics* 1.2 that as a political organism, the state is prior to its parts in the way that a body is prior to a hand: a stateless human being is a nominal person in the way a hand unattached to a body is a nominal rather than a real hand, since what it is to be a person or hand includes being a part of a *polis* or body, respectively. Thus, Aristotle concludes, the state is an organic, natural compound whose constitution stands to its members as form or soul to its matter.[29] For such reasons, Aristotle would find both nominalist objections mistaken in principle.

A further argument in defense of (4) can be developed from Aristotle's account of the origin of states. Aristotle posits two individually necessary and jointly sufficient causes of human association: sex and speech. As he famously puts it,

> In the first place there must be a union of those who cannot exist without each other, namely, of male and female, that the race may continue ... and of a natural ruler and subject, that both may be preserved. For that which can foresee by the exercise of mind is by nature lord and master, and that which can with its body give effect to such foresight is a subject, and by nature a slave.[30]

Lest we mistake Aristotle's "natural ruler" to designate some persons rather than other persons, Aristotle adds that "man is the only animal who has the gift of speech," the purpose of which is to determine what is expedient and what is just. Therefore only man "has any sense of good and evil ... and the association of living beings who have this sense makes a family and a state."[31] In other words, Aristotle's natural ruler—and the second necessary condition of both the family and the state—is *logos,* which is expressed in speech. It is for this reason that Aristotle says man is not simply a gregarious animal, but a political one: human beings spring from our loins but require the sharing of *logoi* to fully actualize their end as virtuous persons engaged in leisurely *philosophia,* and "what each thing is when fully developed, we call its nature."[32] *Logos,* in other words, is the internal cause of the *polis,* for it is natural to human beings and associations that our character-

29. *Pol.* 1.2, 1253a18–29.

30. *Pol.* 1.2, 1252a25–32.

31. *Pol.* 1253a10–18.

32. *Pol.* 1.2, 1252b34. Cf. Eric Voegelin, *Plato and Aristotle,* vol. 3 of *Order and History* (Columbia, Missouri: University of Missouri Press, 1999), 251: "The growth of the polis is not an inevitable biological process; men are not forced into the polis by an urge or instinct. Man is not a gregarious animal [*agelaion zoon*]; he is a *politikon zoon* and that means that the end, the *telos,* of the community lies in the realm of conscious, deliberate recognition of good and evil, of right and wrong."

istic excellences are exercised through deliberation, social intercourse, and choice. As Aristotle puts it, "justice is the bond of men in states; for the administration of justice, which is the determination of what is just, is the principle of order in political society."[33]

Two things follow from this analysis. The first is that the only suitable material for states is man, for it is only such a being that the state can bring to conscious, deliberate perception and the choice of good and evil. One cannot make cities of rocks, animals, children, or madmen. The second is that a good *polis* is one which makes good reasons available to individuals and promotes them as choiceworthy.[34] Since reasons are causes for rational animals, a community of rational persons must provide sufficient material as well as formal causes—reasons—for the reproduction and flourishing of human culture. As V. Bradley Lewis puts it,

> One's development into a person fitted to pursue happiness, a life of rational action in accord with the virtues, is made possible by a complex of relationships to other persons often structured as associations or communities for the pursuit of goods common to many persons.[35]

Because material goods are sought for the sake of the soul, Aristotle argues, the primary *telos* of the city is to habituate its citizens in virtue—to promote "living well" over and above "mere living"—by means of law[36]; the highest work of the *polis* is moral education.[37] This raises an important question: If "the happy state may be shown to be that which is best and acts rightly; and it cannot act rightly without doing right actions, and neither individual nor state can do right actions without excellence and wisdom," where precisely do these reasons come from?

Aristotle believes the answer is clear: from the public, political, and philosophical discourse of citizens with one another—that is, from the contemplative action proper to human society. The burden of proof for premise (4) thus lies in proving that the size of a state affects its ability to develop, utilize and display virtuous reasons for action.

33. *Pol.* 1.2, 1253a37–39.

34. See *EN* 1099b29–32; 1102a7–13; 1103b3–6; 1129b14–25; 1179b20–1180a24.

35. V. Bradley Lewis, "The Common Good in Classical Political Philosophy," *Current Issues in Catholic Higher Education* 25, no. 1 (2006): 25–41.

36. *Pol.* 1280a21–1281a4. Aristotle makes claims about the best *polis* on this basis at 1283a23–26, 1284a1–3, and 1323b29–1324a13.

37. *EN* 1129b24–25.

IV. Friendship, Anonymity, and the Akratic State

If the state is an organism, as Aristotle holds, then its parts have a proper work as much as the state as a whole does. Speaking roughly, Aristotle suggests that the basic governing function within the state is to adjudicate disputes among citizens through the creation of law and the judgment of lawsuits, while the basic function of the citizen is to decide who is most capable of exercising the duties of governance.[38] The marked inability of a community to agree either about how to judge cases or about how to distribute public offices is therefore a symptom of political *akrasia*, which Aristotle discusses in *Politics* 5.1 and *Nicomachean Ethics* 7.10. These political failures promote the development of factional associations within the state, leading to instability, political violence, revolt, or revolution.[39] The presence of factions in a *polis* is thus a symptom of a deep loss of a necessary condition of human society, namely, constructive political discourse. Although such a city may continue to reproduce itself without public philosophy, it will lack the necessary unity of a real *polis*, possessing only the nominal and unstable unity of a (growing) pile of stones.

However, Aristotle argues, "if the citizens of a state are to judge and to distribute offices according to merit, *then they must know each other's characters*; where they do not possess this knowledge, both the election to offices and the decision of lawsuits will go wrong."[40] In other words, on Aristotle's diagnosis, a *lack of familiarity* with one's fellow citizens brings about the failure of political discourse, factionalism, and the ultimate dissolution of the city. Let us call this the *Anonymity Thesis*:

7. Aristotle's Anonymity Thesis: It is difficult or impossible to judge and distribute goods according to justice without knowledge of someone's character.

Importantly, the *Anonymity Thesis* assumes that character is the basis of desert. This is unsurprising, since if virtue makes a person better as a human being, and Aristotelian justice requires distributing goods in proportion to worth or excellence, then the virtuous person is the one most deserving of

38. "For both governors and governed have duties to perform; the special functions of a governor are to command and to judge … [and] the citizens of a state are to judge and to distribute offices according to merit." *Pol.* 7.4, 1326b11–14.

39. *Pol.* 5.1, 1301a37–1301b10

40. *Pol.* 7.4, 1326b15–19; my emphasis.

real goods. It follows, then, that goods cannot be justly distributed in the face of ignorance of someone's character, since such ignorance deprives us of the necessary conditions for making true judgments about the distribution of goods. This principle will hold at both the interpersonal and the political level. If a constitution is "an ordering of offices in a *polis* in respect of the way they are distributed," for instance, then a constitution is a kind of distributive justice, as Richard Kraut has argued.[41] Anonymity will thus entail that the state either cannot deliberate, or will be unable to put its conclusions (i.e., laws) into effect, the political equivalence of moral *akrasia*.

One justification of Aristotle's Anonymity Thesis is found in his account of friendship in *Nicomachean Ethics* 8 and 9. Just as "pleasure coming through sight originates erotic passion," Aristotle argues, friendly affection is spurred by the recognition of some excellence in another person called ευνοια.[42] Reciprocal and recognized *eunoia* is friendship.[43] One important difference between erotic passion and *eunoia*, however, is that *eunoia* constitutes a judgment that can be false; it is difficult to be "falsely attracted" to someone, but not difficult to wrongly esteem someone. Thus, Aristotle adds, to truly call people friends, the friendship must have developed over a sufficient period of time and the friends must have become familiar, that is, have been found loveable and trustworthy to each other.[44] As he puts it,

> those who quickly show the marks of friendship to each other wish to be friends, but are not friends unless they are both loveable and know the fact; for a wish for friendship may arise quickly, but friendship does not.[45]

Friendship requires developed familiarity because personal knowledge, *justified eunoia*, requires an understanding of the causes of someone's character, and such knowledge—like character—develops of necessity over

41. *Pol.* 4.1,1289a15–18; cf. 3.1, 1274b38; 3.6, 1278b8–11. Richard Kraut, "Aristotle's Theory of Distributive Justice," in *A Companion to Aristotle's Politics*, edited by David Keyt and Fred Miller (Oxford: Blackwell Publishing, 1991), 238.

42. *EN* 9.5, 1167a4–5. See Peter Hadreas, "Ευνοια: Aristotle on the Beginning of Friendship," *Ancient Philosophy* 15 (1995): 393–401. Hadreas defines *eunoia* as an allogenic "recognition of another's worthiness," an intellectual response to some feature of a person we find valuable. Note that *eunoia* does not require that the excellence we recognize in another is virtue: Aristotle's own example is of a spectator recognizing the skill, *techne*, of an athlete. See *EN* 9.5, 1166b35 and 1167a19–20. In fact, Aristotle will distinguish the kinds of friendship precisely according to the various ways we perceive the goodness of others.

43. *EN* 8.2, 1155b33–1156a3.

44. *EN* 8.3, 1156b26–30.

45. *EN* 8.3, 1156b30–32.

time.[46] It is precisely knowledge that so-and-so is lovable because he is virtuous that justifies the extreme level of trust and loyalty accorded to friends.

It follows from this analysis that those who lack familiarity with one another—and *a forteriori* persons who are anonymous to each other—will lack the epistemic basis for making prudent judgments about one another's character, and therefore about what each deserves in truth. Since the political function of the governor is to exercise political prudence, then, citizens who are unfamiliar with the character of political candidates will lack the epistemic basis for making their own prudent judgments about the relative worth of those candidates. This conclusion will hold for all political associations. Just as no stranger will be able to judge whether a particular thirteen-year old teenager is capable of babysitting her five year old sister without knowledge of the teenager's character, so too no *polis* will be capable of judging which candidate is qualified for executive office when their only interaction with the candidate occurs through rumors, office memo, or the television set.

Since the size of a polis—the number of its inhabitants and their proximity to one another—is arguably the most basic circumstance of familiarity, it follows that giantism in a *polis* will create political anonymity which undermines the conditions for political discourse required for a well-functioning city. As Aristotle concludes: "Clearly then the best limit of the population of a state is the largest number which suffices for the purposes of life, and can be taken in at a single view."[47] Put otherwise, the exercise of political prudence is coextensive with familiarity between persons.

V. Conclusion

If this argument is sound, then several surprising and important consequences follow. The first is that, if Aristotle's argument truly applies to

46. Cf. *Metaphysics* 1.1, 981a27–29: "For men of experience know that the thing is so, but do not know why, while the others [wise persons of knowledge and understanding] know the 'why' and the cause." Though this passage discusses the nature of theoretical knowledge, it also provides a suitable description of the knowledge of others required for friendship. The practical knowledge of how to make such judgments (including what facts about people are relevant to the judgment that a person is lovable, and which are not) is a function of our intellectual maturity and moral character.

47. *Pol.* 7.4, 1326b24–25.

all human associations, it follows as a general principle that for each kind of social relation, some level of familiarity is necessary for the exercise of prudence and the achievement of justice. Likewise, for each kind of social relation, some degree of anonymity will frustrate the exercise of prudence and justice.

Second, it follows that those views of social relations which presuppose methodological anonymity will necessarily frustrate the exercise of prudence and justice. For instance, Aristotle's Anonymity Thesis presents an *a priori* challenge to the coherence of using many anonymous citizens methodologically hidden behind a Rawlsian "Veil of Ignorance" to determine the just distribution of political goods. Likewise, Aristotle's argument is relevant for current debates about the political value of "Big Data," namely, whether large-set analytics entails the "end of theory," as Chris Anderson, Jonathan Rauch, and others have argued, or whether political decisions will always require human prudence.[48] Likewise, Aristotle's argument will undermine the normative value of economic approaches to analyses of citizen behavior in democracies as found in "Public Choice Theory," since Aristotle would attribute the irrational outcomes of democratic processes not to discrepancies between the costs of informed political participation and the negligible impact of individual votes, but to failures of political prudence due to the anonymity of candidates (not *policies*) to voters.[49]

48. Philosophically, both "Big Data" methodologies and "Public Choice" theories of politics have their roots in Hayek's arguments against Socialism, namely, that the knowledge required for a successful state cannot be located in one person unless—as Aristotle himself suggests—that person is a god (the only being who can introduce order into the unlimited; see *Pol.* 7.4). Rather, they hold, knowledge is widely distributed among individual agents. Like Adam Smith, Hayek argued that the free, self-interested exchange of goods between rational agents naturally tends towards optimal consequences without intentional direction. The question then arises as to how that knowledge can be harnessed by processes whose consequences are identical to those which would be exercised by an Aristotelian god, were there such a being, and whether such processes can be intentionally or unintentionally directed. According to modern theories of political "Datafication," widely distributed knowledge can be "mined" for intentional use by algorithms. Critics argue that even if algorithms can make data patterns available to theorists, context and human judgment are still necessary for interpreting those patterns, and such judgments remain beyond the scope of human prudence. See the debate between, e.g., C. Anderson, "The End of Theory: The Data Deluge Makes the Scientific Method Obsolete," *Wired Magazine*, June 2008; Shvetank Shah, Andrew Horne, and Jaime Capellá, "Good Data Won't Guarantee Good Decisions," *Harvard Business Review*, April 2012; M. Graham, "Big data and the end of theory?" *The Guardian*, March 9, 2012; and Jonathan Rauch, "Seeing Around Corners," *The Atlantic*, April 2002.

49. See for instance James Buchanan and Gordon Tullock, *The Calculus of Consent: Logical Foundations of Constitutional Democracy* (Indianapolis, Indiana: Liberty Fund, 2003).

Third, Aristotle's argument may prove to be relevant for issues in moral psychology. For instance, his argument suggests that moral character itself is a kind of *reason* over and above abstract "rights" claims in deliberations about justice—something Aristotle emphasizes in his *Rhetoric*, but not in his *Politics*. There he argues that "[a speaker's] character may be the most effective means of persuasion he possesses."[50] The argument we have been examining suggests this might be grounded in the nature of prudence as a *moral necessity* rather than in the art of *rhetoric* as a condition of psychological persuasiveness.

Finally, Aristotle's argument has implications for thinking about democratic theory. Nothing in Aristotle's argument precludes us from *scaling* familiarity at the political level. That is, it might well be the case that good political judgment can be scaled if, at each level of election and judgment, those responsible for choosing leaders are familiar with the character of the leaders they elect. Thus, while Aristotle would give a negative prognosis to the American democratic system in which every citizen has an equal vote in the election of unfamiliar candidates to legislative and executive office,[51] he would probably argue that the hierarchical governance of an institution like the Catholic Church constitutes a more virtuous structure of political authority, since each leader is—in theory—selected by a small group of familiars.

50. Aristotle, *Rhetoric* 1356a2–13.
51. I here put aside the Electoral College as an unnecessary complication.

HEIDI M. GIEBEL AND BENJAMIN I. HUFF

Justice, Benevolence, and Friendship

A Confucian Revision to Thomistic Ethics?

I. Introduction

Thomas Aquinas presents a remarkably comprehensive theory of virtue ethics in the second part of his *Summa theologiae*.[1] There he analyzes and defends the classical Western cardinal virtues: prudence, temperance, fortitude, and justice. These four virtues, he systematically and plausibly argues, include and direct all of the other moral virtues. Aquinas's ethical theory represents a synthesis of Western philosophical and religious thought on the virtues, reaching back to Aristotle, Plato, and the Stoics as well as to the Christian scriptures and Church Fathers; it has been among the most influential accounts of virtue ethics in Western Christianity.[2]

As appealing as Aquinas's theory is in its own right, comparing it with other theories of the virtues may be valuable both to better assess its merits and to cast it in a fresh light. In this paper we present a provocation arising

1. Thomas Aquinas, *Summa Theologica*, 2nd revised edition, translated by Fathers of the English Dominican Province (New York: Benzinger Brothers, 1920). All quotations of the *Summa* are taken from this translation.

2. As MacIntyre notes, however, Aquinas's influence on the philosophical development of the Aristotelian virtue tradition has been "unexpectedly marginal" outside of explicitly Christian ethics. See Alasdair MacIntyre, *After Virtue*, 3rd edition (Notre Dame, Indiana: University of Notre Dame Press, 2007), 178. Even within Christianity, Aquinas's influence has been stronger in Catholic circles than, for example, Orthodox ones. See Marcus Plested, *Orthodox Readings of Aquinas* (Oxford: Oxford University Press, 2012). For a very helpful discussion of the non-Aristotelian elements in Aquinas's virtue theory, see Andrew Pinsent, *The Second-Person Perspective in Aquinas's Ethics* (New York: Routledge, 2012), especially 13–22; see also Eleonore Stump, "The Non-Aristotelian Character of Aquinas's Ethics: Aquinas on the Passions," *Faith and Philosophy* 28 (2011): 29–43.

from a comparison with the Confucian thinker Mencius and explore the resources Aquinas offers for responding. This provocation brings to light gaps and tensions within Aquinas's account that may be easily overlooked given the impressive manner in which he lays out his system; it also calls forth intriguing possibilities and promising resources. As a result, we discover important features of Aquinas's positive conception of the virtues that may be obscured by the structure of his presentation in the *Summa theologiae*.[3]

Like Aquinas, Mencius systematized and expanded key elements of a significant moral tradition in a manner highly influential for centuries afterward: the impact of Confucianism in East Asia is comparable to that of Christianity in the West. Mencius also presents a moral theory involving four cardinal virtues: benevolence or humaneness (*ren* 仁), rightness (*yi* 義), ritual propriety (*li* 禮), and wisdom (*zhi* 智). There are some striking similarities in the two lists of virtues: Mencius's notions of rightness and wisdom have significant parallels with Aquinas's notions of justice and prudence.

The differences in their lists are equally striking, however, and for an ethicist interested in an objective account of the virtues, these differences prompt serious reflection. In particular, the absence of counterparts to temperance and fortitude in Mencius's list, and the absence of a counterpart to benevolence in Aquinas's list, seem to call for explanation. In this paper we take up the latter point.

Given the prominence of the virtue of benevolence in Mencius's account of the virtues, two main questions arise: (1) where might a counterpart to it appear in Aquinas's account of the virtues, and (2) does his account give it the importance it deserves? We look first among the usual suspects, considering the possibility that benevolence is already among the Thomistic cardinal virtues (at least implicitly) as a potential part of justice. Then we look around the near Thomistic neighborhood to consider whether a good Thomist might identify benevolence with mercy, an effect of the theological virtue of charity, in addition to annexing it to justice. Next, we widen the search a bit more to consider revisions to Thomas's system, while remaining faithful to his fundamental approach. Drawing on insights from Aquinas's predecessors and successors in the tradition of the

3. Aquinas himself remarks that the manner in which a given book is organized (its "plan") tends to make some aspects of a subject more obvious while obscuring others: see ST I, Prologue.

virtues, we consider a super-cardinal virtue including both justice and benevolence, which we provisionally name "fellowship."

Finally, by combining our search tactics, we identify the missing virtue of benevolence as follows: drawing on Thomas's arguments for the four cardinal virtues and some underdeveloped aspects of his account of justice, we propose that the cardinal virtue of justice be defined widely enough to include all fitting actions toward our neighbor, renaming it "justice-fellowship." We then identify "justice-fairness" and benevolence (or mercy) as the two main species of justice-fellowship and as themselves cardinal: that is, some justice-fellowship-related virtues are categorized under fairness and others under benevolence. This suggestion has several advantages: (1) it offers a plausible interpretation of Aquinas's complex and often puzzling account of justice; (2) it provides a place for benevolence among Aquinas's cardinal virtues, as well as more natural homes for liberality and magnificence; (3) it clarifies the importance of mercy in Thomistic ethics; (4) it draws on Aristotelian and Ambrosian virtue ethics, both of which Thomas endorses; (5) it harmonizes with more recent work in the Thomistic tradition, such as that of Maritain and MacIntyre, on the relationship between justice and generosity, friendship, and love; and (6) it leaves Thomas's arguments for the cardinal virtues intact.

II. Cardinal Virtues, Confucian and Thomistic

One of the chief virtues in Confucian thought is *ren* 仁, which in the context of Mencius' thought is naturally translated as "benevolence" or "humaneness." As Mencius describes it, the most basic manifestation of benevolence is compassion for the suffering or potential suffering of another human being. He famously argues that this sense of compassion is innate:

> Suppose someone suddenly saw a child about to fall into a well: anyone in such a situation would have a feeling of alarm and compassion.... From this we can see that if one is without the feeling of compassion, one is not human.... The feeling of compassion is the sprout of benevolence.[4]

4. Mencius [Mengzi], *Mengzi*, translated by B. Van Norden (Indianapolis, Indiana: Hackett, 2008), 2A6; cf. 6A6.

Our innate sense of compassion is a rudimentary form of benevolence and provides a necessary basis for a more complete moral development. When this "sprout" is developed through education and good habits into the full virtue of benevolence, it is not just a feeling but a consistent *disposition* of heartfelt, dedicated, and thoughtful care for others.

Aquinas defends his four cardinal virtues in two main ways. First, since virtue is good as defined by reason, we need a virtue (prudence) for practical reason itself and virtues for what it orders: justice for operations, and temperance and fortitude for passions.[5] Second, we might consider the subjects of virtue, or the faculties of our minds in need of moral excellence: reason, the will, the irascible faculty, and the concupiscible faculty.[6] Again, we arrive at the same four cardinal virtues.

On Aquinas's account, every non-cardinal moral virtue is categorized as "part" of one of the four cardinal virtues. Thomas recognizes three kinds of virtue-parts: (1) integral parts: components necessary for exercise of the virtue; (2) subjective parts: species or subtypes of the virtue, and; (3) potential parts: related virtues that share a significant feature in common with the cardinal virtue but fall short of it in some way.[7]

While the idea that all moral virtues fit under the four cardinal virtues is attractive, the details can be surprising. For example, liberality is "part" of justice even though, unlike justice, it is *not* about giving anyone what he or she deserves or is owed. Meanwhile, magnificence seems similar to liberality insofar as both address dispossession of material wealth, but magnificence is "part" of a different cardinal virtue: fortitude. In the last main section of this essay we will suggest a solution to these and related puzzles in Thomistic virtue ethics.

For now, let us consider where within Aquinas's account of the virtues we might locate a reasonable counterpart to the Confucian virtue of benevolence. Let us assume that we will find it, though the form it takes may surprise us. We can approach this process in three different ways. First, we will look among the usual suspects: the Thomistic cardinal virtues. Perhaps, suitably interpreted, they already include benevolence. Second,

5. ST I-II, q. 61, a. 2. More specifically, we need temperance to curb our passions when they tempt us to pursue our desires contrary to reason, and we need fortitude to strengthen us to follow reason when our passions incline us to shrink unreasonably from the pursuit of a difficult good.

6. For more on the concupiscible and irascible faculties, see ST I-II, q. 23, a. 1.

7. ST II-II, q. 48, a. 1.

we will search the near Thomistic neighborhood: it may be that although Aquinas does not include benevolence among his cardinal virtues, we can locate it elsewhere in his ethical theory. Third, we will look just a bit farther and wider within the Thomistic tradition—among Aquinas's predecessors and followers—bringing further resources to clarify, interpret, and perhaps supplement Aquinas's theory in a way consistent with his approach to ethics. In the following sections, we will discuss promising possibilities using each of these search tactics; then we will develop and defend our solution combining all three.

III. Looking for Benevolence Among Aquinas's Natural Virtues

A first approach to finding a counterpart to Mencian benevolence—and probably the most attractive to a Thomist—is to argue that benevolence is perfectly at home under one of Aquinas's cardinal virtues as he defines them. The most obvious place to look for benevolence is under the umbrella of justice, since among the Thomistic cardinal virtues justice deals most directly with our relationships to other people and since Aquinas already places the somewhat similar virtue of liberality under justice as a "potential part."

According to St. Thomas, the virtue of justice is "a habit whereby a man renders to each one his due by a constant and perpetual will."[8] As he goes on to explain, "each man's own is that which is due to him according to equality of proportion. Therefore the proper act of justice is nothing else than to render to each one his own."[9] In light of this definition, we can already see that it is somewhat awkward to locate benevolence within the category of justice. As it happens, this is also true of liberality. Liberality is about giving others what rightfully belongs to oneself—not what is theirs, as Aquinas acknowledges.[10] Indeed, liberality might be a better candidate for a part of benevolence than of justice—if benevolence were among Aquinas's cardinal virtues.

As Aquinas correctly notes, liberality resembles justice in that it deals with actions toward others. If that really is all that is necessary, perhaps benevolence has implicitly been there all along as well: it too concerns actions toward others. At times Aquinas does seem to think this is sufficient:

8. ST II-II, q. 58, a. 1.

9. ST II-II, q. 58, a. 11.

10. ST II-II, q. 117, a. 5.

"since justice is of one man to another ..., all the virtues that are directed to another person may ... be annexed to justice."[11]

Yet as tempting as this simple interpretive approach may be, it seems problematic for at least three reasons. First, given Aquinas's more specific definition of justice as "a habit whereby a man renders to each one his due by a constant and perpetual will," it is odd to label as its "parts" virtues that are completely unrelated to the desert of the recipient.[12]

A second difficulty is that the Confucian virtue of benevolence is a central aspect of both Confucian ethical life and ethical theory—important enough, one might argue, that benevolence should not be just an implicit potential part in Aquinas's account of cardinal virtue. Mencius often pairs benevolence with rightness (*yi* 義) to refer to morality as a whole. In fact, for Confucius *ren* 仁, which we are translating as *benevolence*, is *the* chief moral virtue, and while there are significant differences in Mencius' account of it, that prominence lingers to a degree. Can it really be that the ethical life is so culturally variable that such a central Confucian virtue can be nearly ignored by a Thomist?

A third problem with attempting to categorize benevolence under justice is that, unlike the Thomistic virtue of liberality, Mencian benevolence fundamentally arises from compassion. That suggests it should involve the sensitive appetite (emotions) as well as the rational appetite (will). So even if liberality really does belong under justice, it looks like benevolence does not.[13]

A more promising interpretive strategy might be to argue that benevolence is part of the nature of justice itself in Thomistic ethics: it is an integral or quasi-integral part of justice.[14] In fact, several passages in Aquinas's

11. ST II-II, q. 80, a. 1.

12. ST II-II, q. 58, a. 1. We discuss this point further in section IV below.

13. That is, compassion-based benevolence cannot fit solely under "justice" as Aquinas defines it. However, Aquinas does suggest elsewhere that the emotions can be involved in a secondary way when there is an "intense" movement of the will: "among powers hierarchically connected the situation is such that an intense movement in one, and especially in the higher, overflows into the other. Accordingly, when by a choice the movement of the will is directed to something intensely, even the irascible and the concupiscible powers follow the movement of the will." See Thomas Aquinas, *De Veritate*, translated by R. W. Schmitt (Chicago: Henry Regnery Company, 1954), q. 25, a. 4. (We thank Scott Cleveland for this reference.) Later in the paper we will discuss additional possibilities for including both will and emotions in a Thomistic account of benevolence, along with possibilities for broadening the definition of "justice" and for one virtue's being related to two or more other virtues as potential parts.

14. Aquinas (ST II-II, q. 79) lists only two quasi-integral parts of justice: "do good" and "avoid evil." Perhaps benevolence can be partly identified with doing good?

text lend themselves to this interpretation. For example, he claims, following Aristotle, that justice can be described as "the good of the other."[15] In a later discussion, he includes "obligations of justice" that look more like obligations of benevolence, including feeding the hungry and clothing the naked.[16] Finally, in his article regarding virtues annexed to justice he comments on the relationship of liberality and friendliness to "another due that is necessary in the sense that it conduces to greater rectitude, although without it rectitude may be ensured."[17] So one might construe the moral "due" of justice to be broad enough to include benevolent actions.[18]

While designating benevolence as a quasi-integral part of justice may well be satisfying to many Thomists despite the departure from Aquinas's definition of "justice" as tied to what is owed, this strategy is less likely to satisfy Confucians for two reasons. First, it continues to focus solely on justice's requirement of *actions* similar to those of Mencian benevolence: it does not address the virtue's affective foundation. Second, while an integral part of a cardinal virtue enjoys some pride of place in Thomistic ethics (since the main virtue cannot be exercised without its integral parts), a Confucian might hesitate to accept an account that renders benevolence part of another virtue at all—especially if it is a part that one must look closely to see. However, this interpretive solution may become more palatable to Confucians with the addition of an insight from Aquinas's account of theological virtues. It is to this insight that we next turn.

IV. The "Near Neighborhood": Looking for Benevolence Elsewhere in Aquinas's Ethics

When seeking a suitable place for benevolence within Thomistic ethics, perhaps the next place to look is the account of theological virtues of faith, hope, and charity found just before the cardinal virtues in Aquinas's

15. ST II-II, q. 58, a. 12; cf. Aristotle, *Nicomachean Ethics*, translated by R. Crisp (Cambridge: Cambridge University Press, 2000), 5.1, 1130a4–5.

16. ST II-II, q. 66, a. 7. Indeed, these obligations are called "corporal works of mercy" in the Catholic tradition; in the next section we will argue that mercy is a promising counterpart for Mencian benevolence.

17. ST II-II, q. 80, a. 1.

18. Stump makes a related point, arguing that Thomistic justice implies an ethics of care in its inclusion of almsdeeds under distributive justice. See Eleonore Stump, "Aquinas on Justice," *Proceedings of the American Catholic Philosophical Association* 71 (1997): 61–78.

Summa. In some ways the theological virtues seem an unlikely place to look, because the theological virtues are presented as being available only through grace, and oriented toward God, while Confucian thought is not even theistic, let alone Christian. However, several qualities falling under the theological virtue of charity or love—which, like the cardinal virtue of justice, is primarily other-directed—display important similarities with Mencian benevolence in content and function.

Our first candidate there is *benevolentia*, an aspect of love, which is the principal act of charity. It at first seems an obvious fit: the Latin is even frequently transliterated "benevolence." However, it is more appropriately translated "goodwill" (from *bene voluntas*) because it is simply the act of wishing well to another. Goodwill is not a good counterpart to Confucian benevolence, since it does not involve (let alone stem from) a feeling of compassion. Perhaps an even more important problem with identifying *benevolentia* with benevolence is that Aquinas argues that *benevolentia* is not a virtue at all but merely one aspect of the exercise of charity.[19]

One might turn next to another aspect of the virtue of charity: *beneficentia*, an effect usually translated "beneficence." Like *benevolentia*, this effect also is verbally similar to benevolence, and in content sounds quite similar to benevolence: performance of kind acts toward others.[20] Appearances are deceiving once again, however: Thomistic beneficence is merely an external manifestation of the virtue of charity; it is not itself a virtue.[21] So neither *benevolentia* nor *beneficentia* is a good counterpart to the Mencian cardinal virtue of benevolence.

A much more promising parallel for Mencian benevolence in Thomistic ethical thought seems to be the virtue of mercy (*misericordia*—literally "compassionate heart"), which Aquinas defines as "heartfelt sympathy for another's distress, impelling us to succor him if we can."[22] This description corresponds strikingly with Mencian description of benevolence as arising from a "feeling of alarm and compassion" at another's distress.[23]

Perhaps the most obvious objection to identifying mercy with Mencian benevolence is the fact that it is categorized under charity. If mercy is an effect of a Christian theological virtue, is it not, then, necessarily unavailable to Confucians?

19. ST II-II, q. 27, a. 2.
20. ST II-II, q. 31, a. 1.
21. ST II-II, q. 31, a. 4.
22. ST II-II, q. 30, a. 1.
23. See Mencius, *Mengzi*, 2A2.

Fortunately, the answer for Aquinas is "no." If mercy were a *species* (subtype) of charity, one might plausibly argue that one could have it only by having charity itself. There is not, however, such a tight connection between virtues and their *effects*: the efficacy of one cause in bringing about a particular effect does not rule out the possibility that a similar effect could arise from another cause. In the case of virtues, of course, the obvious alternate cause is habituation, which is the standard way of acquiring the natural moral virtues.[24] Moreover, Aquinas allows for the same virtue to be related in different ways to multiple main virtues insofar as it is in several powers of the soul: "so that it is in one chiefly, while it extends to others by a kind of diffusion, or by way of a disposition."[25] In fact, he even suggests in passing that mercy may be categorized under the cardinal virtue of justice (presumably as a potential part): "to succor the needy, which belongs to mercy or pity, and to be liberally beneficent, which pertains to liberality, are by a kind of reduction ascribed to justice as to their principal virtue."[26]

A second objection will likely reassert itself at this point: won't a Confucian object to the "potential part" status of mercy, as we suggested earlier? As we noted, potential parts of cardinal virtues are related to the main virtue in some way but fall significantly short of it. It seems, then, that being a potential part would relegate mercy to a second-class status among the virtues.

Two considerations can at least partly address this concern. First and more generally, Aquinas's arguments about the preeminence of the cardinal virtues do not imply that they are superior to their part virtues in every respect. St. Thomas acknowledges multiple ways in which virtues might be ordered hierarchically: e.g., according to the faculty they perfect or the object toward which they are directed. So while Aquinas does speak of cardinal virtues as especially important in various respects,[27] he also argues that a potential part of a cardinal virtue can be in some ways superior to the cardinal virtue itself. For instance, he calls the virtue of religion, a potential

24. For a thorough discussion of the similarities and differences between acquired and infused versions of the moral virtues, see Pinsent, *The Second-Person Perspective in Aquinas's Ethics*, especially chapter 3; and Angela McKay Knobel, "Aquinas and the Pagan Virtues," *International Philosophical Quarterly* 51, no. 3 (2011): 339–54.

25. ST I-II, q. 56, a. 2; for further discussion see Oderberg, "On the Cardinality of the Cardinal Virtues," *International Journal of Philosophical Studies* 7, no. 3 (1999): 305–22.

26. ST II-II, q. 58, a. 11, ad 1. Aquinas promises to substantiate this claim in q. 80, a. 1 but does not.

27. See, for example, ST I-II, q. 61, a. 1 and I-II, q. 66, a. 4.

part of justice (falling short of its equality aspect), the most excellent of all the moral virtues because it involves giving what is due to God, and our obligations to God are our most important obligations.[28]

Second and more specifically, Aquinas explicitly raises the question of whether mercy is the greatest virtue. Considered as a virtue in itself, he argues that it *is* the greatest, pointing particularly to God's mercy, in which "His omnipotence is ... chiefly manifested."[29] For human beings, mercy is not the greatest virtue because it is directed toward our suffering neighbor rather than to God, who is a greater object. Still, Aquinas contends that "of all the virtues which relate to our neighbor, mercy is the greatest,"[30] even greater than the cardinal virtue of justice.

Mercy thus has many advantages as a counterpart virtue to Confucian benevolence. Its primary manifestations are caring for others and pursuing their good, with a strong affective component of compassion. In these central respects, then, it is closely analogous to benevolence. Further, it is the greatest virtue involving our relationships to our fellow human beings. However, a Confucian might still find this account unsatisfactory because, despite the high esteem Aquinas gives mercy, he does not give it sufficient pride of place in the *structure* of the account: as we noted earlier, it appears in just one question of the *Summa* as an effect of the Christian theological virtue of charity. A Confucian—or anyone who thinks benevolence is essential to an ethical life—presumably would prefer to see it placed prominently among the moral virtues. Hence we will now consider one possibility for doing so.

V. The "Wider Neighborhood": Insights from the Broader Thomistic Tradition

As mentioned earlier, there are reasons for leaving the structure of Aquinas's ethics intact: he gives plausible arguments for his cardinal virtues and a similarly impressive account of his theological virtues. If his arguments succeed, any genuine virtue must fit under one of these seven virtues. More pragmatically, leaving the system intact may result in less resistance from fellow Thomists: they will rightly be cautious about modifying an ethical theory that is systematic, well-defended, influential, and in keeping with

28. See ST II-II, q. 81, a. 6.

29. ST II-II, q. 30, a. 4.

30. Ibid.

millennia of tradition. So we are motivated to keep the structure of Thomistic ethics as intact as possible while looking for ways to highlight the importance of benevolence within Aquinas's account. In this section, we make a suggestion regarding the interpretation of his cardinal virtues in which justice—or a broader virtue encompassing it—more clearly has room for benevolence and related virtues.

Rather than identify Mencian benevolence with an existing Thomistic virtue, one might instead posit a broad, other-directed virtue which includes both justice and benevolence, either as species or as integral parts. Since it includes other cardinal virtues, this broader virtue would be a "super-cardinal virtue" ("SCV" for short), as we will explain. As Aquinas himself seems to recognize, moral virtues may be categorized on more than two levels of generality: following Daniel Russell, we will call virtue *y* "cardinal" with respect to virtue *x* if, in addition to being a virtue in its own right, *y* is a category of which *x* is a member. But *y* may itself be classified under a yet more general virtue *z*, which is cardinal with respect to it: for example, in Aquinas's account of the moral virtues justice is clearly cardinal with respect to observance, which in turn appears to be cardinal with respect to gratitude, truth, affability, and liberality.[31] So our posited SCV would be super-cardinal in that justice and benevolence, while each being cardinal with respect to some other virtues, would themselves be categorized under this more general virtue.

While it sounds rather bold, this proposal is not so dramatic as one might expect, and it has significant advantages. First, this SCV provides a suitable place for an important virtue—benevolence—that previously received little attention in Aquinas's account of moral virtue. Second, insofar as benevolence can be identified with Aquinas's virtue of mercy—the most important virtue we can exercise toward our neighbors—it would seem to deserve greater structural prominence even on Aquinas's own estimation. Third, this SCV provides a more natural home for liberality and magnif-

31. See ST II-II, qq. 58, 102, 106, 109, 114, and 117. For further discussion of levels of cardinality, see Daniel Russell, *Practical Intelligence and the Virtues* (New York: Oxford University Press, 2009), 198 ff. According to Russell, virtue *x* is cardinal with respect to virtue *y* if the reasons for being *y*, upon reflection, boil down to reasons for being *x*. But the reasons for being *x* may in some cases boil down to reasons for being *v*, where *v* is some other, more cardinal, virtue. As we see in his arguments for identification of the four cardinal virtues, Aquinas himself tends to individuate virtues with reference to their objects and to the powers of the soul they perfect. (We owe this point to Alina Beary.)

icence, which are placed awkwardly under justice and fortitude, respectively, but would now be regarded as parts of benevolence.[32] Fourth, this move fits well with important threads in the Thomistic tradition, as we will explain.

The idea that justice and benevolence are both species of some larger ethical category is not new to Christian virtue theory: in fact, Thomas quotes Ambrose's claim to that effect in support of placing liberality under justice. Ambrose states, "Justice has to do with the fellowship of mankind. For the notion of fellowship is divided into two parts, justice and beneficence, also called liberality or kind-heartedness."[33] Aquinas seems to misinterpret this passage as equating liberality with justice and kind-heartedness with beneficence, but it is clear in Ambrose's original text that both liberality and kind-heartedness are synonymous with beneficence. Thus Ambrose seems to be describing a virtue rather like our SCV, referring to it as "fellowship."[34] And since Aquinas himself appeals to him as an authority, it seems reasonable for a Thomist to draw on Ambrose's views.

Further, Maritain also might naturally be interpreted as endorsing a similar approach in his discussions of friendship, love, and justice. To take just one example among many, in "The Conquest of Freedom," Maritain states, "If the person has the opportunity of being treated as a person in social life … it is first of all due to the development of law and to institutions of law. But it is also and indispensably due to the development of civic friendship, with the confidence and mutual devotion it implies."[35] Thus while Maritain sees an important distinction between justice and friend-

32. We are of course far from alone in noticing the awkward placement of magnificence under fortitude on Aquinas's account. Russell notes it briefly in his discussion of magnificence in chapter 7 of *Practical Intelligence and the Virtues,* and Yearley makes a similar observation. See Lee H. Yearley, *Mencius and Aquinas: Theories of Virtue and Conceptions of Courage* (Albany, New York: SUNY Press, 1990), 33–34.

33. Ambrose, *De Officiis* I, q. 130, translated by H. de Romestin, edited by E. de Romestin and H. Duckworth. K. Knight, 1896, accessible online at http://www.newadvent.org/fathers/3401.htm, and quoted in ST II-II, q. 117, a. 5. Ambrose in turn is heavily influenced by Cicero's work of the same name, in which one finds a nearly identical passage: cf. Cicero, *De officiis,* translated by W. Miller (Cambridge, Massachusetts: Harvard University Press, 1913), I, q. 20.

34. We say it *seems* to be like SCV because it is possible that for Ambrose fellowship represents something other than a virtue though related to virtues. Note that Ambrose's "beneficence," being synonymous with kindheartedness, seems closer to Confucian benevolence than to Thomistic beneficence, which is not a virtue and includes no affective component.

35. Jacques Maritain, "The Conquest of Freedom," in *The Education of Man: The Educational Philosophy of Jacques Maritain,* edited by Donald and Idella Gallagher (Garden City, New Jersey: Doubleday, 1962), 172–73.

ship in civic life, he also envisions them as mutually supporting and jointly necessary for human flourishing. Maritain's conception of friendship thus displays a rather similar form to Ambrose's fellowship, and to our SCV.

A similar modification would be to call justice and benevolence both integral parts or necessary conditions of this SCV, so that one exercising it must simultaneously exercise justice and benevolence. Alasdair MacIntyre makes a proposal along these lines, describing the virtue of "just generosity" as a chief virtue of acknowledged dependence, and arguing that justice and generosity must be exercised in light of one another.[36] Since generosity may be either a species of benevolence or, as Ambrose suggests, identical with benevolence, MacIntyre may be proposing the same SCV. In fact, Ambrose may be interpreted as taking this integral-part approach when he supports his earlier points regarding fellowship: for example, he states, "the Gospel contains many instances in which a just liberality is inculcated."[37] We might also see a similar pattern in Aquinas's claim that all of God's actions display both justice and mercy.[38]

While the idea that there is an SCV including both justice and benevolence seems promising and fits well with several threads in the Thomistic tradition, enough questions may remain to give a good Thomist pause: for example, what effect does the SCV have on the structure of the cardinal virtues in Aquinas's theory? Must we now reject his arguments for justice, fortitude, temperance, and prudence as the four cardinal virtues? And how does this SCV relate to the broader notion of justice that Aquinas occasionally seems to endorse? In the final section of this essay, we propose combining the SCV approach with the considerations we raised earlier regarding justice and mercy, to arrive at an account of Thomistic benevolence that can answer these questions while providing an attractive and plausible interpretation of Aquinas's account of justice, as well as providing a satisfying response to Confucians.

36. Alasdair MacIntyre, *Dependent Rational Animals* (Chicago: Open Court, 2001), chapter 10. Interestingly, MacIntyre seems to include mercy as itself a necessary condition of just generosity: see especially p. 126. Equally interesting (to the present authors, anyway) is the fact that he does not comment regarding the effect his interpretation may have on the structure of Thomistic virtue theory.

37. Ambrose, *De Officiis* I, q. 143.

38. ST I, q. 21, a. 4.

VI. Super-Cardinal Justice: A Combined Strategy

To respond adequately to the questions just raised, we will have to return to our first suspect in our search for benevolence: the Thomistic cardinal virtue of justice. As we recall, justice has its place as one of the four cardinal virtues in Aquinas's system because it fills two roles: (1) it primarily orders our actions (as opposed to our reason or passions), and; (2) it functions via the will.[39] But the cardinal virtue filling these roles need not be directed exclusively or even primarily toward giving others that to which they have a right—such roles are broad enough to include extending material goods or aid to any fitting recipient, whether the fittingness is derived from desert or need. And in fact Aquinas himself occasionally speaks of justice in this broader way, as we noted earlier, speaking of liberality as directed toward "another due" that goes beyond what is strictly owed the recipient but "is necessary in the sense that it conduces to greater rectitude."[40] He could—but does not—emphasize this other due in his justification of categorizing liberality under justice: instead, he rather non-committally bases its annexation to justice by "some" upon its relation to external objects and persons.[41]

What might cardinal justice look like were it to address more explicitly the "other due" on which Aquinas occasionally relies but which he leaves underdeveloped and underemphasized? We propose interpreting the cardinal virtue of justice in a way that incorporates the form of the super-cardinal virtue we described in the previous section of this essay. Following Ambrose, we refer to this broad, super-cardinal form of justice as "fellowship," or "justice-fellowship," to clarify that it is a form of justice, as distinct from the narrower form of justice, which we will call "justice-fairness." Thus, justice-fellowship is composed of two main species: one is justice-fairness, the narrower form of justice as "rendering to each one his right"[42]; the oth-

39. ST I-II, q. 61, a. 2.

40. ST II-II, q. 80, a. 1.

41. ST II-II, q. 117, a. 5. Aquinas does refer to the other due in his response to objection 1 of the same article, but downplays it even there: "Although liberality does not consider the legal due that justice considers, it considers a certain moral due. This due is based on a certain fittingness and not on an obligation: so that it answers to the idea of due in the lowest degree." Here he seems to use "legal" in a narrower and more individualistic and desert-related sense than in the term "legal justice," which is synonymous with "general justice" in his account and deals with the common good as such.

42. ST II-II, q. 58, a. 1.

er is benevolence—or mercy. Both of these species of fellowship are in turn cardinal themselves, with desert-related virtues such as piety and gratitude falling under the narrower justice-fairness, while those related to moral fittingness but not strict desert, such as liberality and affability, fall under benevolence/mercy. Thus justice-fellowship, as a will-based, action-governing virtue, provides standards and direction for all actions toward others, whether we are interacting with them in a manner merited by their actions or special relations to us (as in justice-fairness), or in a manner fitting given their particular needs or simply their status as fellow human beings (as in mercy or benevolence).

In addition to interpreting our first suspect, justice, as being the super-cardinal virtue suggested by our reading of Aquinas's predecessors and followers, then, we have returned to the prime suspect from the near Thomistic neighborhood—mercy. Recall that mercy is an effect of the infused theological virtue of charity, but can also take a natural (acquired) form, which is closely comparable to Mencian benevolence. We now draw once again on insights from Aquinas's account of the theological virtues to further develop and defend our account of justice-fellowship as a (super-) cardinal virtue.

Charity is the greatest of the virtues for Aquinas. It functions via the will as does justice. Yet as a type of friendship—"friendship of man for God"—it allows for affective components such as "union of affections" with its object, so that one considers his friend's good to be his own. Thus charity is extended beyond love solely of God to love of those God loves—our neighbors—such that we "rejoice and grieve with them," as Aristotle would put it.[43] Hence it includes the compassion-based virtue of mercy, which looks very much like Mencian benevolence, among its primary effects. And as we noted earlier, Aquinas gives an exalted standing to the virtue of mercy, calling it the greatest of the virtues directed toward our neighbor.[44] Further, its neighbor-directedness makes it a lot less "theological" than the virtue of charity of which it is an effect.

It therefore seems reasonable to interpret justice so that it resembles Ambrosian fellowship, being based on fitting interactions with our neighbors, including those of desert-based justice as well as compassion-based benevolence. It thus forms a secular counterpart to charity among the cardinal virtues. In fact, Aquinas himself suggests in one of just two articles

43. ST II-II, q. 23, a. 1. See also *Nicomachean Ethics* 9.4, 1166a9.

44. ST II-II, q. 30, a. 4.

devoted to general justice that it is just such a counterpart, saying: "just as charity may be called a general virtue in so far as it directs the acts of all the virtues to the Divine good, so too is legal justice, in so far as it directs the acts of all the virtues to the common good."[45] Since mercy is a manifestation of the Christian friendship of charity, it seems reasonable that a secular virtue of benevolence or an acquired version of mercy could be a manifestation of human fellowship. Like charity, this friendship or fellowship would function via the will, order our actions, and cause union of affections with its object(s): the other people in our communities.

Moreover, the proposed parallel between charity and human fellowship reflects the moral teaching of the Gospels. Upon being asked which commandment is the greatest, Christ replies, "You shall love the Lord, your God, with all your heart, with all your soul, and with all your mind. This is the greatest and the first commandment. The second is like it: You shall love your neighbor as yourself."[46]

This role for friendship also seems especially fitting within Aquinas's thought because he repeatedly appeals to Aristotle's account of friendship to illuminate specific features of charity.[47] Hence Aquinas clearly recogniz-

45. ST II-II, q. 58, a. 6; we thank Daniel Shields for pointing out this connection. As some recent commentators have noted, Aquinas—mistakenly believing that he is following Aristotle—considers general (legal) justice to be a particular virtue: he handily interprets away Aristotle's claim that "justice is every virtue" both in this article of the *Summa* and in his commentary on the *Nicomachean Ethics*: see *Commentary on Aristotle's "Nicomachean Ethics,"* translated by C. I. Litzinger (Notre Dame, Indiana: Dumb Ox Books, 1993), book 5. For further discussion of this point, see Jeffrey Hause, "Aquinas on Aristotelian Justice: Defender, Destroyer, Subverter, or Surveyor?" in *Aquinas and the "Nicomachean Ethics,"* edited by T. Hoffmann et al. (Cambridge: Cambridge University Press, 2013), 146–64; and Mary M. Keys, *Aquinas, Aristotle, and the Promise of the Common Good* (Cambridge: Cambridge University Press, 2006), chapter 7. Thus it may be tempting to equate the broader justice-fellowship with Thomistic general justice and the narrower justice-fairness with particular justice. However, while Aquinas divides general from particular justice based on the virtues' aims (the common good as such versus that of other individuals), our suggested division of justice into justice-fellowship and justice-fairness is based on the nature of the moral due (fittingness versus strict desert).

46. Matthew 22:37–40, New American Bible. For an interesting analysis of how love of God and neighbor relates to Aquinas's ethics, and particularly to his theory of natural law, see Kevin Flannery, *Acts Amid Precepts* (Washington, D.C.: The Catholic University of America Press, 2001), 41–45.

47. See, e.g., ST II-II, qq. 23, 25, 27, and 31. We considered identifying SCV with Aristotelian *philia*; but despite the promising connections we have noted, there are enough differences between Aristotelian and Thomistic accounts of friendship to make such an identification misleading. For helpful discussions of such differences, see Gerald B. Phelan, "Justice and Friendship," *Thomist* 5 (1943): 153–70; and Marko Fuchs, "*Philia* and *Caritas*: Some Aspects of Aqui-

es the existence of a kind of friendship available to non-Christians, with a similar structure to that of charity, and directed primarily toward other human beings, rather than toward God. Indeed, at times he refers to them together as closely parallel concepts. For example, in discussing beneficence he attributes it equally to friendship and to charity: "beneficence in its general acceptation is an act of friendship or charity."[48] Elsewhere, he similarly associates friendship with goodwill[49] and describes charity as acting alongside but perfecting "natural friendship" which we have "for those who are connected with us,"[50] while extending friendship, in the form of charity, even to strangers. Thus human friendship is strongly present in Aquinas's thought, although it receives little formal treatment in the *Summa*. To discern where to situate human friendship or (justice-) fellowship within his scheme of virtues, then, we first had to draw on other sources in the Thomistic tradition.[51]

Natural friendship or fellowship starts with and is primarily directed toward those closest to us, but when fully developed is extended to all. Aquinas acknowledges this pattern to hold of love and beneficence,[52] as Mencius describes it with regard to benevolence.[53] The fact that friendship involves a union of affections also nicely handles the problem of locating benevolence in the will rather than in the sensitive appetite: although it is primarily in the

nas's Reception of Aristotle's Theory of Friendship," in *Aquinas and the "Nicomachean Ethics,"* edited by T. Hoffmann et al. (Cambridge: Cambridge University Press, 2013), 203–19. For an extensive treatment of Aquinas's account of friendship and its relation to justice, see Daniel Schwartz, *Aquinas on Friendship* (Oxford: Oxford University Press, 2007), especially chapter 6.

48. ST II-II, q. 31, a. 1.

49. ST II-II, q. 80, a. 11.

50. ST II-II, q. 26, aa. 7–8.

51. Aquinas expresses ambivalence regarding whether friendship is a virtue. In the *Summa*, he says "we might say that it is a moral virtue about works done in respect of another person, but under a different aspect from justice," but seems to retract that view in the same article, stating, "it may be admitted that it is not a virtue distinct of itself from the other virtues" and "not every friendship is praiseworthy and virtuous, as in the case of friendship based on pleasure or utility. Wherefore friendship for the virtuous is something consequent to virtue rather than a virtue." ST II-II, q. 23, a. 3. In his *Commentary on Aristotle's "Nicomachean Ethics"* (§1538) he states, "Friendship is a kind of virtue inasmuch as it is a habit of free choice." However, in his *Disputed Questions on Virtue* he says that human "friendship is not a virtue properly speaking, but something following on virtue. For because one is virtuous it follows that he will love those like himself. It is otherwise with charity, which is a friendship with God that lifts man up to that which exceeds the limits of his nature." Thomas Aquinas, *Disputed Questions on Virtue*, translated by Ralph McInerny (South Bend, Indiana: St. Augustine's Press, 1999), I, q. 5.

52. See ST II-II, q. 27, a .7; q. 31, aa. 2–3.

53. See *Mengzi* 1A7, 7B31.

will in that it involves willing and doing good for the other, it involves the passions of the sensitive appetite through shared joy and sorrow.[54]

This conception of fellowship also closely follows the prominent role that friendship plays in Aristotle's thought. Aristotle explicitly states that friendship encompasses and surpasses even (particular) justice: "when people are friends, they have no need of justice, while when they are just, they need friendship as well; and the highest form of justice seems to be a matter of friendship."[55] Our proposed interpretation of the super-cardinal virtue of justice-fellowship fits that description quite well. It also fits fairly well with Augustine's claim that "justice is the love of God and our neighbor which pervades the other virtues, that is to say, is the common principle of the entire order between one man and another"—a claim that Aquinas quotes with approval in his own discussion of justice.[56]

In short, our solution of reinterpreting the cardinal virtue of justice as the super-cardinal virtue of justice-fellowship has several advantages in addition to those outlined in the previous section: (1) it provides a plausible and attractive interpretation of the Thomistic virtue of justice; (2) it develops the parallels between the Thomistic cardinal virtues and the theological virtues, in which charity (friendship with God) is the highest virtue; (3) it elevates and gives a formal place to human friendship, which figures prominently in Aristotle's *Nicomachean Ethics* and is a strong influence in Aquinas's account of charity; (4) it builds on Ambrose's division of fellowship into justice and beneficence, which Aquinas endorses but seems to misinterpret; and (5) it leaves Aquinas's virtue classification scheme, and his arguments for it, surprisingly intact. Finally, by offering a robust Thomistic account of benevolence that reflects an emphasis on compassion, (6) this interpretation of cardinal justice as fellowship resonates deeply with the moral teaching of Christ.

Since Aquinas writes primarily for a Christian audience, it is fitting that

54. Here, friendship follows the pattern Aquinas describes for mercy: "Mercy signifies grief for another's distress," including "a movement of the sensitive appetite" or "passion" as well as "a movement of the intellective appetite." Since these both "may be ruled in accordance with reason ... it follows that mercy is a virtue." ST II-II, q. 30, a. 3.

55. Aristotle, *Nicomachean Ethics* 8.1, 1155a27–8.

56. ST II-II, q. 58, a. 8. While Augustine's description may appear to fit the virtue of charity better than even a super-cardinal interpretation of Aquinas's virtue of justice, we once again see in Thomas's work hints of support: in ST I-II, q. 109, a. 3 he argues that man is capable by nature (i.e., without grace) of loving God above all things, and his reasoning in that article is based upon God's being our common good—the sort of good at which general justice aims. (We thank Daniel Shields for this point.)

he emphasize how mercy, friendship, benevolence, and beneficence function in the context of charity. However, if we read the account of the natural virtues in the *Summa* without incorporating this material from the discussion of the theological virtues, we may acquire an incomplete and even misleading conception. It is clear that mercy and friendship are extremely important outside a Christian context as well, and Aquinas both acknowledges and relies on this fact in his exposition of charity.

Though the Confucian challenge comes from a distant time, place, and culture, in pursuing it we have explored many important and even surprising features of Aquinas's thought, features which might otherwise remain obscure. In fact, by drawing out the importance of mercy and justice-fellowship as natural virtues, we present a picture that in some respects may be more faithful to Aquinas's moral vision than is the organizational scheme of cardinal virtues in the *Summa*.

DANIEL SHIELDS

St. Bonaventure, St. Thomas, and Eudaimonism

Eudaimonism is the belief that happiness, understood as the full flourishing of human nature, is the ultimate end and thus first principle of human and moral action. Eudaimonism is highly attractive in that it avoids the bifurcation of the right and the good characteristic of Kantian positions, and the subjective understanding of happiness as preference satisfaction characteristic of utilitarian positions. Eudaimonism renders moral propositions immediately and obviously relevant: they matter to each individual's interests, and they claim to be more than somebody's purely private, personal preference. Eudaimonism, however, is open to the objection that it is a self-centered moral theory in that it claims that one ought always to do what will make oneself most happy. Even on an Aristotelian understanding, my happiness is a private good, namely my full actualization as a human being, my rational activity.[1] St. Augustine, on the other hand, held that the virtues of the pagans were bound up with the sin of pride, an inordinate desire for one's own excellence. Eudaimonism clearly avoids the charge of hedonism, but in making one's own *eudaimonia* or perfection the center of one's life, it is easy prey to, and in some forms may even constitute, the sin of pride.

There are many possible ways of defending eudaimonism against such a charge, of course, but rather than evaluating them, I want to show how Aquinas and Bonaventure, although often regarded as eudaimonists, each in fact provide an alternative to eudaimonism while incorporating all of its

1. On happiness as rational activity, see Aristotle, *Nicomachean Ethics* 1.7, 1097b21–1098a20.

strengths. Aquinas and Bonaventure provide theoretical articulation of an ethics of humility by holding that not the private good of personal happiness, but rather the common good is the ultimate end of the individual's moral life. For both, God, the most common good, is the ultimate end of the moral life strictly speaking, *not happiness,* even though happiness is a legitimate and essential subordinate end. I start with Bonaventure.

I. St. Bonaventure: Three Senses of End

In distinction 38 of the second book of his *Sentences,* Peter Lombard says that rightly ordered wills have one ultimate end: charity or God, which in his view are the same thing, since charity is nothing other than the Holy Spirit dwelling in the believer. All other actions must be done for the sake of charity, or they are not right. Since both Bonaventure and Aquinas commented on this distinction of Lombard's *Sentences,* and because it directly addresses the question of the human being's ultimate end, it is helpful to compare their commentaries. Both saints hold, unlike Lombard, that charity is a *created* habit infused into the soul by God,[2] and so neither can endorse Lombard's claim in distinction 38 without making some distinctions of their own.

Bonaventure explains in the second question of his commentary on this distinction that it is perfectly right for Lombard to say that charity is the ultimate end of rightly ordered wills, because there is a created charity, and an uncreated charity.

> "End" is said in three ways, namely, an end *in which* (*in quo*) one rests, and an end *by which* (*quo*) one rests; and "end *by which* one rests" is said in two ways, either *simply speaking* or *for now.* In any of these ways charity is the end of a good will. For the end *in which* one rests is uncreated charity, which is God, concerning which it is said in the first letter of John "God is charity." Created and consummate charity, however, namely the charity of heaven, is the end *by which* one rests *simply speaking* in God. Inchoate charity, however, namely the charity of the wayfarer, is the end *by which* one rests in God *for now.*[3]

Aquinas in other places similarly distinguishes between two main senses of end, and the basic idea, for both Aquinas and Bonaventure, is that

2. Bonaventure, *Commentaria in Quatuor Libros Sententiarum Magistri Petri Lombardi,* lib. I (hereafter *In I/II/III/IV Sent.*), d. 17, a. 1, q. 1; Aquinas, *Scriptum super Sententiis,* lib. I (hereafter *In I/II/III/IV Sent.*), d. 17, q. 1, a. 1.

3. Bonaventure, *In II Sent.*, d. 38, a. 1, q. 2, c. (Quaracchi ed., 2:884). Emphasis in original. All translations of St. Bonaventure are my own.

God is our goal, but one can also say that our *attainment* of God is our goal; we have to somehow reach Him, and the state in which we reach Him can rightly be called our ultimate end. "Happiness," when said of human beings, names this state. For Bonaventure, the state in which we reach God is charity, by which we love Him above all things, including even ourselves.[4] This state is a created good, and is distinct from uncreated happiness, namely God Himself.

The fifth objection in Bonaventure's text, however argues that love or created charity cannot be the end in any sense, because "'what weight is in bodies, that love is in spirits'; but weight in bodies is in no way said to be the end of locomotion; therefore love in spirits will in no way be said to be the end of the rational appetite."[5] The idea behind this objection is that while weight is the principle that moves a body to its proper place, the place that constitutes its end, nevertheless having weight is not the same thing as being in one's proper place. So too, love may move us towards God, but it is not the same thing as attaining God. As we will see, Aquinas will use just this argument to claim that loving God does not constitute a human being's happiness.

Bonaventure's response to the objection is as follows: "There is no similarity, because weight is found in bodies both when they are out of their proper place and when they are in it. Charity, however, is never in the soul unless God is present. Whence everyone who has charity, has God."[6] Thus, for Bonaventure, God is the ultimate end in which we rest, and love for God is the ultimate end by which we rest in God; in other words, having charity is the same thing as attaining God. We are united to God principally by means of affection, not knowledge; one can see this play out in Bonaventure's *Itinerarium Mentis ad Deum*. The first six days are concerned with knowing God better so as to inflame one's love for Him. On the seventh day the intellect ceases its activity and rests, and the soul passes over to God by love.[7] (Bonaventure does not, however, deny that in heaven,

4. Bonaventure says in *Itinerarium Mentis in Deum*, cap. 1 (Quar. 5:296), that "beatitudo nihil aliud sit, quam summi boni fruitio." In *In I Sent.*, d. 1, a. 2, q. 1 he explains that *fruitio* is essentially an act of the will (love), but dispositively an act of vision.

5. Bonaventure, *In II Sent.*, d. 38, a. 1, q. 2, s.c. 5 (Quar. 2:884).

6. Bonaventure, *In II Sent.*, d. 38, a. 1, q. 2, ad 5 (Quar. 2:885).

7. Bonaventure, *Itinerarium Mentis ad Deum*, ch. 7 (Quar. 5:312): "His igitur sex considerationibus excursis ... tanquam etiam *sex diebus primis*, in quibus mens exercitari habet, ut tandem perveniat ad sabbatum quietis ... In hoc autem transitu, si sit perfectus, oportet quod relin-

where we are perfectly united to God, we will see and know Him as He is. But love is the primary factor in union with or attainment of God.)

II. St. Bonaventure: Ultimate and Penultimate Ends

Now a straight-forward eudaimonist might think that since happiness is a condition of the moral agent, by which he is brought to full perfection and flourishes, one's attainment, or fruition, or enjoyment of God must be one's end in a more ultimate sense than God is. One is perfected not just by the fact that God exists, as would seem to be the case if God were one's end irrespective of one's fruition of Him; one is perfected, rather, by *attaining* God (otherwise we would all be happy automatically, from the first moment of our existence, because there is no potency in God to be actualized). A more subtle eudaimonist might claim that neither God nor one's attainment of God is one's end in a sense more ultimate than the other; they are just two sides of the same coin, or rather ultimate ends in two irreducible senses of end.

Bonaventure, however, does not see things this way. As he argues in the very next question of his commentary, a rightly ordered will has just one ultimate end, God. Any other end that a rightly ordered will has must be an "end under an end (*finis sub fine*)"[8] by being ordered to God. To have an end that is not actually ordered to God is a venial sin if one does not at the same time actually make it an *ultimate* end. It is a *mortal* sin if one actually sets something else besides God up as a second ultimate end.[9]

The second objection, however, argues that created happiness, in addition to God, can be our ultimate end:

---

quantur omnes intellectuales operationes, et apex affectus totus transferatur et transformetur in Deum." Emphasis in original.

8. This phrase also shows up in Aquinas' commentary on this distinction (q. 1, a. 2, c.) See n. 19 below.

9. Bonaventure, *In II Sent.*, d. 38, a. 1, q. 3, c. (Quar. 2:886): "Quod plures fines statuere hoc potest esse tripliciter. Uno modo ita, quod finis sit *sub* fine et *propter* finem; alio modo ita, quod unus sit finis *principalis*, alter *non principalis*, ita tamen, quod finis non principalis non referatur ad principalem actualiter; tertio modo ita, quod uterque sit finis *principalis*.... Primo modo statuere diversos fines est bonum et meritorium et pertinent ad bonam voluntatem. Secundo modo statuere diversos fines non est bonae voluntatis, loquendo formaliter; attamen non sic repugnat, quin possit cum ea stare; est enim ibi peccatum veniale, non mortale.... Tertio vero modo statuere diversos fines non est bonae voluntatis, immo contra bonam voluntatem; talis enim vult *duobus dominis servire;* et hoc est impossibile, sicut Matthaei sexto dicitur." Emphasis in original.

A mercenary sets for himself a created end, namely some reward, which is created beatitude. For if he set for himself only an uncreated end, he would be already not a mercenary, but a son; therefore, if it happens that there are good mercenaries, it can happen that a good will has several ends.[10]

Bonaventure responds by distinguishing between a good mercenary and a bad mercenary. "A bad mercenary sets for himself a created end as a principal [end]; a good mercenary, however, establishes for himself a created end as an end under an end (*finem sub fine*); for he does not love God for the sake of fruition, but fruition for the sake of God."[11] For Bonaventure, God Himself, not happiness, is the ultimate end of human beings. Happiness in attaining God is a penultimate end.

In the next question (q. 4), Bonaventure confirms this with a distinction between the common good (*bonum commune*) and private goods (*bona propria*). The question asked is whether bad wills have a single end, and Bonaventure answers that only good wills have a single end; each good person has only one ultimate end, namely God. Bad people have many ultimate ends because nothing they pursue can satisfy them. But there is also another sense in which good wills have a single ultimate end, and bad wills multiple ultimate ends. Numerically many good persons have numerically one ultimate end:

The contrary is the case in good wills and in bad ones. For the end of good wills is one, whether the good wills be diverse by *numerical* diversity, or by *formal* diversity. I call the diversity *numerical* when many human beings are affected in regards to something by the same kind of affection; I call the diversity *formal*, however, when one and the same human being is affected in regards to diverse things by diverse habits of virtue. For in either way, although one happens to assign many proximate and private (*proprios*) ends, nevertheless it is necessary that the ultimate and principal end be one, namely God Himself.

And the reason for this is both the perfection of the *motivating love* and the perfection of the *satisfying desirable object* (*appetibilis quietantis*). For *the love* of charity is liberal, and *does not seek what is its own*, but rather the common good; hence it is that many men, moved by charity, desire ultimately the same good. *Again*, because that *desirable object* [, namely God,] is most complete, in which not only does one happen to find perfect good, but even every good; hence it is that all wills, no matter how numerous, find [in Him] their end in which they rest.

10. Bonaventure, *In II Sent.*, d. 38, a. 1, q. 3, s.c. 2 (Quar. 2:886).

11. Bonaventure, *In II Sent.*, d. 38, a. 1, q. 3, ad 2 (Quar. 2:887). Emphasis in original. See also ad 4.

It is the opposite in bad wills because of the imperfection *of the love* and *of the desirable object*. For because of the imperfection of licentious *love* (*amoris libidinosi*) wills dfferent only in number have diverse ends, because licentious love always *seeks what is its own*; and because it always seeks *its own private* good (*bonum proprium*), therefore even if many human beings out of licentious love agree in one act, nevertheless each seeks his own private end (*finem suum proprium*), as is clear in the case of an adulterer and a prostitute, because the one seeks pleasure and the other money.[12]

Happiness, a human being's attainment of God, cannot be the ultimate end, because it is a private good. My happiness is my happiness, and no one else's. Upright wills order themselves to the common good, which is one and the same for all, namely God Himself as He is in Himself, not each individual's participation in Him. God is the single end of all human beings, uniting them together. Each person's own happiness is merely a penultimate end, a *finis sub fine*.

Bonaventure argues that we ought to love God more than ourselves, not only with a love of desire but with a love of friendship.[13] He and His honor should be more important to us than our own happiness. This does not mean, however, that we might ever have to choose to renounce beatitude for the sake of God: "It is true that God's honor ought to outweigh in our heart our own advantage (*nostrum commodum*); nevertheless charity never separates God's honor from our spiritual advantage; nor does it belong to the divine will that we desire for the sake of His honor anything which be to the detriment of our salvation."[14]

For Bonaventure, the point of the moral life is to fall totally in love with God, such that our concern is with Him above all, not with our own happiness or perfection, even though these things will also come to us. All contemplative knowledge, in fact, is ordered towards inflaming our love for God. Theology is neither a practical science, ordered towards action, nor a

12. Bonaventure, *In II Sent.*, d. 38, a. 1, q. 4, c. (Quar. 2:888–89). Emphasis in original.

13. Bonaventure, *In III Sent.*, d. 29, a. 1, q. 2, c. and ad 4; cf. also *In II Sent.*, d. 3, p. 2, a. 3, q. 1, where love of God above all things, even oneself, is said to be natural, although natural love for God above all differs somewhat from supernatural love for God above all, namely charity. A discussion of this latter text may be found in Thomas Osbourne, *Love of Self and Love of God in Thirteenth-Century Ethics* (Notre Dame, Indiana: University of Notre Dame Press, 2005), 57–61.

14. Bonaventure, *In III Sent.*, d. 29, a. 1, q. 3, ad 6 (Quar. 3:645). Bonaventure adds: "Sicut enim essentiale est *naturae* appetere *esse*, sic essentiale est *gratiae* appetere *Deo placere* et *Deo adhaerere;* ideo Deus nunquam illud a nobis exigit, ut magis salutem alienam quam propriam diligamus." Emphasis in original.

speculative science, pursuing knowledge for its own sake. Theology is wisdom, knowledge for the sake of nourishing our affection; by contemplating God and what He has done for us, we are set on fire with love for Him, and He becomes everything for us.[15] For us, to live is Christ.

III. St. Thomas: Two Senses of End[16]

In his commentary on distinction 38 of book II of the *Sentences*, Aquinas similarly appeals to the notion of the common good:

> In the procession of things from a principle there is found one *first* principle of things common to them all, under which are found other proper principles, which differ in different things. So, too, in referring things to an end there is found one end common to them all, which is the ultimate end; but different proper ends are found according to the diversity of beings.... And since things are referred to an ultimate common end by means of the end proper to each, therefore a diversity in the proper end brings about diverse relations of things to an ultimate end.
>
> Accordingly, therefore, it should be said that *as there is a single ultimate end of all things, namely God, so there is a single ultimate end of all wills, namely God*; nevertheless, there are other proximate ends, and if the due relation of the will to the ultimate end is preserved in regard to those ends, the will will be right; but if not, it will be perverse. Now the due relation of the will to the ultimate end is preserved in accordance with that end through which the will is naturally able to participate in the ultimate end, in which it is distinguished from other things that participate in the ultimate end in another way; and this is charity or beatitude. And therefore it is not only God, but also charity, that is the end of all right wills.[17]

15. Bonaventure, *In I Sent.*, proem., q. 3, c. (Quar. 1:13): "Perfectibile a scientia est intellectus noster. Hunc autem contingit considerare tripliciter, scilicet *in se*, vel prout extenditur *ad affectum*, vel prout extenditur *ad opus*.... Nam si consideremus intellectum *in se*, sic est proprie speculativus et perficitur ab habitu, qui est contemplationis gratia, qui dicitur *scientia speculativa*. Si autem consideremus ipsum ut natum extendi *ad opus*, sic perficitur ab habitu, qui est, ut boni fiamus; et hic est *scientia practica* sive moralis. Si autem medio modo consideretur ut natus extendi *ad affectum*, sic perficitur ab habitu medio inter pure speculativum et practicum, qui complectitur utrumque; et hic habitus dicitur *sapientia*, quae simul dicit cognitionem et affectum: *Sapientia enim doctrinae est secundum nomen eius*, Ecclesiastici sexto. Unde hic est contemplationis gratia, et ut boni fiamus, principaliter tamen, ut boni fiamus.... Nam haec cognitio, quod Christus pro nobis mortuus est, et consimiles, nisi sit homo peccator et durus, movet ad amorem; non sic ista: quod diameter est asymeter costae." Emphasis in original.

16. I have treated Aquinas' views on this topic in a more complete and systematic way in my article "On Ultimate Ends: Aquinas' Thesis that Loving God is Better than Knowing Him," *The Thomist* 78 (2014): 581–607. My treatment here draws on, but also adds in some ways to, what I have written there.

17. Aquinas, *In II Sent.*, d. 38, q. 1, a. 1, c. (Mandonnet ed., 2:968–69). See also ad 1 (Mandonnet

God is the common good of the universe, and also the "single ultimate end of all [rightly ordered] wills." But subordinate to this ultimate end, common to all things, is a proximate end, proper to each creature, by means of which it participates in God the ultimate end. For rational creatures this proximate, proper end is beatitude. Aquinas clarifies in the next article that beatitude is an activity having God as its object, and that charity is the habit that renders this activity perfect. The activity in question is the intellect's act of seeing God.[18]

Although he has here referred to it as a penultimate end,[19] Aquinas often speaks of happiness as the human being's *ultimate* end, and leaves it at that. But how can happiness *and* God both be the ultimate end? Aquinas distinguishes, in a fashion similar to Bonaventure, between two senses of end in the *Prima Secundae*:

> Our end is twofold. First, there is the thing itself which we desire to attain: thus for the miser the end is money. Secondly there is the attainment or possession, the use or enjoyment of the thing desired; thus we may say that the end of the miser is the possession of money.... In the first sense, then, man's ultimate end is the uncreated good, namely God, Who alone by His infinite goodness can perfectly satisfy man's will. But in the second way, man's ultimate end is something created, existing in him, and this is nothing else than the attainment or enjoyment of the ultimate end.[20]

---

ed., 2:969): "Ad primum ergo dicendum, quod charitas non est finis ultimus, cum non sit finis communis quem omnia desiderant: sed est finis proprius voluntatis per quem pertingit ad finem ultimum; et ideo non sequitur esse plures fines ultimos." For those passages from the *Commentary on the Sentences* which it includes, I have used the translation of Peter Kwasniewski, Thomas Bolin, O.S.B., and Joseph Bolin, *On Love and Charity: Readings from the "Commentary on the Sentences of Peter Lombard"* (Washington, D.C.: The Catholic University of America Press, 2008), although I have altered it at times. This text is found on pp. 88–89 of *On Love and Charity*; emphasis added.

18. Aquinas, *In II Sent.*, d. 38, q. 1, a. 2, c. (Mandonnet ed., 2:971): "Ipsa autem operatio perfecta beatitudo est, objectum autem altissimum Deus est, habitus autem perfectissimus charitas est, delectatio autem purissima est spiritualis delectatio." Aquinas does not specify in the body what the activity is, seemingly because he does not want to trumpet his disagreement with Lombard, or give the appearance of disagreeing with the authorities Lombard cites. He quietly identifies the activity as seeing God in the response to the third objection. That happiness is the intellect's activity of seeing God is stated straightforwardly in *In IV Sent.*, d. 49, q. 1, a. 1, sol. 2, c., as well as *Summa Theologiae* (hereafter ST) I-II, q. 3, aa. 4 and 8.

19. Aquinas, *In II Sent.*, d. 38, q. 1, a. 2, c. (Mandonnet ed., 2:971): "Therefore it is said in the text of Lombard that God is the end of right wills, and that charity, good delight, and beatitude are also the end of right wills—in such a way that God is nonetheless the ultimate end, and beatitude, embracing charity and pleasure, is like "an end under the end," conjoining one to the ultimate end, since activity tends to the object itself; nor is there a right relation of the will to God except by the mediation of these three things."

20. ST I-II, q. 3, a. 1, c. (Leon. 6:26). Aquinas adds: "Si ergo beatitudo hominis consideretur

God is the ultimate, uncreated good. He is the ultimate end in the sense of object. Man's highest created perfection consists in his most perfect activity, by which he attains God. Although this activity has God as its object, it is a created good, an accident inhering in the human substance. It is this created activity that the word "happiness" properly signifies,[21] and it is a human being's ultimate end in the sense of attainment.

Aquinas goes on to argue, in both the *Prima Secundae* and the *Sentences* commentary, that the activity by which we attain God cannot be an act of the will, but must be an act of the intellect:

> Happiness is the attainment of the ultimate end. (*Beatitudo est consecutio finis ultimi.*) But the attainment of the end does not consist in the act of the will itself. For the will is directed to the end, both absent, when it desires it, and present, when it is delighted by resting in it. Now it is evident that the desire itself of the end is not the attainment of the end, but is a movement towards the end, while delight comes to the will from the end being present; and a thing, conversely, is not made present by the fact that the will delights in it. Therefore, that the end be present to him who desires it must be due to something else than an act of the will. . . . Therefore, the essence of happiness consists in an act of the intellect.[22]

The will's act of love for God leads one to desire God when He is absent, and to delight in Him when He is present. Love is the will's weight, and this weight can be possessed in the absence of that towards which it tends.[23] The attainment of God consists not in love, but in knowledge, in particular the beatific vision, which renders the God one loves present and thus makes one happy.[24] Aquinas differs on this score from Bonaventure; the human being's end in the sense of attainment, by which his desire rests in God, is an act of knowledge, not of love. The wayfarer who has charity does not have God, although he does dearly want to have Him.

---

quantum ad causam vel obiectum, sic est aliquid increatum: si autem consideretur quantum ad ipsam essentiam beatitudinis, sic est aliquid creatum." See also ad 2 and ad 3. For ST I have used the translation of the Fathers of the English Dominican Province throughout (*Summa Theologica* [New York: Benziger Brothers, 1948]), although I have altered it at times.

21. If, of course, we are speaking of *a human being's* happiness. *God's* happiness, which is His substance, is happiness in the highest sense, and a human being's happiness is a participation in God's happiness: ST I-II, q. 3, a. 1, ad 1.

22. ST I-II, q. 3, a. 4, c. (Leon. 6:29). See also Aquinas, *In IV Sent.*, d. 49, q. 1, a. 1, sol. 2, c.

23. At ST I-II, q. 26, a. 2, c., Aquinas says that *love* leads to *desire* when the object loved is absent, and to *pleasure* when it is present, and compares these three to the weight of a heavy body, its movement downwards, and its rest in its proper place, respectively.

24. On the natural level also, God is the ultimate end of the moral life, but He is attained in a far less perfect way, by means of speculative knowledge and imitative action through the moral virtues.

IV. St. Thomas: God, and not Happiness, is Man's Ultimate End Strictly Speaking

In the case of Aquinas, just as in the case of Bonaventure, a eudaimonist might think that, since happiness is the ultimate end of the moral life, God must be desired as the source of one's created happiness, and thus, in a constitutive sense, as a means. A Thomistic eudaimonist is far more likely to think that Aquinas' two senses of end are simply incommensurable. It makes no sense, one might say, to claim that one's happiness is the end of God, or that God is the end of one's happiness. Aquinas, however, surprises us on this score, because he does say that God, and *not one's own happiness*, is the ultimate end simply speaking. For him, happiness is ordered to God as to its end.[25]

St. Thomas, like St. Bonaventure and others, distinguishes between the love of desire (*amor concupiscentiae*) and the love of friendship or love of benevolence (*amor amicitae vel amor benevolentiae*):

> As the Philosopher says (*Rhet.* ii. 4), *to love is to wish good to someone.* Hence the movement of love has a twofold tendency: towards the good which a man wishes to someone—to himself or to another—and towards that to which he wishes some good. Accordingly, man has love of desire towards the good that he wishes to another, and love of friendship towards him to whom he wishes good. Now the members of this division are related as primary and secondary: since that which is loved with the love of friendship is loved simply and for itself; whereas that which is loved with the love of desire is loved not simply and for itself, but for something else.[26]

When one wants something for himself or for someone else, he has the love of desire for the wanted object. He has the love of friendship for the person for whom he wants the object.[27] Nothing loved with the love of de-

25. We can already see this in Aquinas, *In II Sent.*, d. 38, q. 1, a. 1, c., quoted above. Further evidence is provided in this section of the article.

26. ST I-II, q. 26, a. 4, c. (Leon. 6:190). Aquinas adds: "Sicut enim ens simpliciter est quod habet esse, ens autem secundum quid quod est in alio; ita bonum, quod convertitur cum ente, simpliciter quidem est quod ipsum habet bonitatem; quod autem est bonum alterius, est bonum secundum quid. Et per consequens amor quo amatur aliquid ut ei sit bonum, est amor simpliciter: amor autem quo amatur aliquid ut sit bonum alterius, est amor secundum quid."

27. The love of friendship involves wishing well to someone. However, goodwill is not really the essence of the love of friendship. ST II-II, q. 27, a. 2, c. and ad 1 (Leon. 8:225–26): "The love which is in the intellective appetite also differs from goodwill, because it denotes a certain union of affection between the lover and the beloved, inasmuch as the lover deems the beloved as somewhat united to him, or belonging to him, and so tends towards him. On the other hand,

sire can be a strictly speaking ultimate end, because it is ordered to some person who is loved with the love of friendship.

Happiness is clearly the greatest good that can be desired for anyone (and is hence the ultimate end of the love of concupiscence), but whom should one love most with the love of friendship?[28] Not oneself:

> Since any part whatever is imperfect in itself but has perfection in its whole, it follows that even by natural love the part tends more to the preservation of the whole than to its own conservation. Accordingly, an animal naturally interposes its arm in defense of the head on which the health of the whole animal depends, and particular men, too, expose themselves to death for the preservation of the community of which they are a part. Since therefore our good is perfect in God, as in the first and perfect universal cause of good things, it follows that the good's being in him naturally pleases us more than the good's being in us. And thus, too, *with love of friendship, God is naturally loved by a man more than a man loves himself.* And since charity perfects nature, it follows according to charity as well that man loves God above himself and above all other particular goods.... The inclination of human nature, as such, never contradicts the inclination of virtue, but is in conformity with it.[29]

Aquinas uses this argument consistently throughout his career: God is the common good of the universe, and every part of the universe, the human being included, naturally loves the common good more than its own private good as a part.[30] The common good is not instrumental to one's own private good; the common good itself is one's ultimate end.[31] God is in fact the source of one's own happiness, but He Himself is a greater good than the happiness He causes, and so He is to be loved with both the love of desire and the love of friendship, but more with the love of friendship than

---

goodwill is a simple act of the will, whereby we wish a person well, even without presupposing the aforesaid union of the affections with him.... The Philosopher, by thus defining to love [as *to wish good to someone, Rhet.* ii. 4], does not describe it fully, but mentions only that part of its definition in which the act of love is chiefly manifested."

28. ST I-II, q. 2, a. 7, ad 2 (Leon. 6:23): "Happiness is loved above all as the good desired (*concupitum*), whereas a friend is loved as that for which good is desired, and in this way too a man loves himself. Consequently, it is not the same kind of love in both cases. As to whether man loves anything more than himself with the love of friendship, there will be occasion to inquire when we treat of charity."

29. Aquinas, *In III Sent.*, d. 29, q. 1, a. 3, c. (Moos ed., vol. 3, 929). Emphasis added.

30. In addition to Aquinas, *In III Sent.*, d. 29, q. 1, a. 3, quoted above, see ST I, q. 60, a. 5; II-II, q. 26, a. 3; I-II, q. 109, a. 3; *Quaestio Disputata de Spe*, a. 1, ad 9; *Quodlibet* I, q. 4, a. 3. Cf. Aquinas, *In II Sent.*, d. 3, q. 4, a. 1.

31. ST II-II, q. 26, a. 3, ad 2.

with the love of desire.[32] Hence God Himself is, most properly speaking, the ultimate end of human life, and our private happiness in attaining God is only a secondary, or penultimate end.

If there be any lingering doubt, one need only turn to distinction 49 of the fourth book of Aquinas' commentary on the *Sentences*, where Aquinas himself explicitly states that happiness is only the ultimate end of the love of desire, and that it is therefore to be ordered to God as its end, because He is the primary object of the love of friendship:

> An object of love is of two kinds. There is an object that is loved in the manner of benevolence, when we will the good of another on account of himself, as we love our friends, even if nothing should come to us from them. And there is an object that is loved by the love of desire; and this is either a good that is within us, or because from it something good comes to be in us, as we love pleasure, or wine inasmuch as it produces pleasure. *Now whatever is loved with a love of desire cannot be the ultimate object of love, since it is referred to the good of another* (*his, namely, who has a desire for it*); *but that which is loved by a love of benevolence can be the ultimate object of love*. Therefore the created beatitude that is within us is loved only by a love of desire; hence we refer the love of it to ourselves, *and consequently we refer it to God, since we ought to refer even ourselves to God*; and thus it cannot be the ultimate object of love. Nevertheless it is the ultimate object of desire by the very fact that it is the greatest good that comes *to us* from union with God, and so it is said to be sought or desired for its own sake (*propter se*); for each signifies something ultimate among the things that are loved with a love of desire. For although God [Himself] is desired, it is the same to *desire* God (*concupiscere Deum*) and to desire the greatest of goods that come to us from God, just as it is the same to desire wine and to desire the effect of wine in us, say, pleasure.[33]

Happiness is not God; it is a human activity that has God for its object. But this activity, human happiness, is simply less good than God is, and so is not the human being's ultimate end. Happiness is ordered to God as to its end. We are to desire happiness *because* we love God—who created us to be with Him—and not only to love God *because* we desire happiness. This is why Aquinas can hold, for example, that one who is perfect in charity would be willing to leave for a time the happiness of contemplation, which he desires most, to serve or preach to his neighbors for God's sake.[34]

32. ST II-II, q. 26, a. 3, ad 3.

33. Aquinas, *In IV Sent.* d. 49, q. 1, a. 2, sol. 1, ad 3 (*Sancti Thomae Aquinatis Opera Omnia* (Parma: Typis Petri Fiaccadori, 1858), tome 7, vol. 2, 1188). Emphasis added.

34. *Quaestio Disputata de Caritate*, a. 11, ad 6.

V. St. Thomas: Loving God is Better than Knowing Him

Even though Aquinas holds, contrary to Bonaventure, that happiness consists in the knowledge of God, and *not* in the love of God, he nevertheless claims, consistently throughout his career, that loving God is better than knowing Him, even better than the beatific vision:

> The perfection and dignity of the intellect consists in this, that the species of the thing which is understood is in the intellect itself, since in this way it actually understands, and from this its whole dignity is seen. The nobility of the will and of its act, however, consists in this, that the soul is directed to some noble thing in the very existence which that thing has in itself. Now it is more perfect, simply and absolutely speaking, to have within oneself the nobility of another thing than to be related to a noble thing outside oneself. Hence if the will and the intellect are considered absolutely, and not with reference to this or that particular thing, they have this order, that the intellect is simply more excellent than the will. But it may happen that to be related in some way to some noble thing is more excellent than to have its nobility within oneself. This is the case, for instance, when the nobility of that thing is possessed in a way much inferior to that in which the thing has it within itself.... *With reference to divine things, which are superior to the soul, in this way to will is more excellent than to understand, as to will God or to love Him is more excellent than to know Him.* This is because the divine goodness itself is more perfectly in God Himself as He is desired by the will than it is participated in us as known by the intellect.[35]

This may seem surprising, but once it is understood that God *and not happiness* is the human being's ultimate end strictly speaking, the seeming contradiction is resolved: happiness (knowing God) is not the best thing a human being can do because it is not his ultimate end. But neither is loving God the human being's ultimate end, not even in the sense of attainment—that is rather Bonaventure's position. God Himself as He is in Himself is the ultimate end, and loving Him is what subordinates our own happiness and perfection to Him. Love puts us in the proper relationship to God—making Him our ultimate end—and so loving God is the best thing a human being

35. *Quaestiones Disputatae de Veritate*, q. 22, a. 11, c. (Leon. 22.3.1:639). I have used the translation by Robert W. Schmidt, S.J. (*Truth*, vol. III [Indianapolis: Hackett, 1994]), although I have altered it. Emphasis added. See also ST I, q. 82, a. 3, c.; Aquinas, *In III Sent.*, d. 27, q. 1, a. 4, c.; cf. also ST II-II, q. 23, a. 6, ad 1. That the superiority of love for God over knowledge of Him holds even in regards to the beatific vision is evidenced by ST I, q. 108, a. 6, ob. 3 and ad 3. On this, see my paper "On Ultimate Ends."

can do. It is more important to be in proper subordination to the common good, the true ultimate end, than to attain one's own immanent perfection through knowledge.

Of course, someone who loves God for His own sake and above all things will want dearly to be in His presence, and will be unable to rest until he is. One who loves God yearns to be with God face-to-face, which happens in the beatific vision, an act of the intellect. Thus happiness, the final resting of a human being's desires, consists in an act of the intellect. This intellectual act is the full actualization of human potential, the highest act of a human being's highest power in regards to its highest object. It makes one as perfect an intellectual being as one can be. But such knowledge of God is itself perfected by the habit of charity or love for God above self,[36] which turns one's attention away from one's own finite perfection as an intellectual being and focuses it, instead, on God's infinite goodness.

I conclude, as is fitting, with Maritain. In his essay "The Immanent Dialectic of the First Act of Freedom," he says that each person makes, in the depths of his being, a choice either for or against God. A person who chooses against God, a "true atheist," may in fact pursue moral goodness, but for him "moral good, duty, virtue inevitably become demands of his own perfection viewed as an absolute center, or a desolate rite of his own grandeur, ... and thus moral good, duty, virtue lose their true nature."[37] They become, in Augustinian terms, "splendid vices."

What is at stake in the question of whether God or *eudaimonia* is the human being's ultimate end is a life of either pride or humility. Will we dedicate our whole lives to our own immanent perfection, striving to be the most perfect beings we can be? If so, we will have to acquire moral virtues and wisdom to flourish as rational beings. We will have to gain knowledge of the ultimate principle of reality, namely God. But we will do all of this for the sake of our own excellence, out of pride, an inordinate desire to excel.[38] Or will we fall totally in love with God's infinite goodness, seeing ourselves and everything else in relationship to Him? If so, we will strive to

36. Aquinas, *In II Sent.*, d. 38, q. 1, a. 2, c.

37. Jacques Maritain, "The Immanent Dialectic of the First Act of Freedom," in *The Range of Reason* (London: Geoffrey Bles, 1953), 85.

38. ST I-II, q. 84, a. 2. To seek happiness or *eudaimonia* as one's ultimate, currently active end is not necessarily an act of pride and may even be the tool God uses to set someone on the path to loving Him above all. What matters is whether someone is closed or open to subordinating his *eudaimonia* to a higher, more ultimate end. See Aquinas, ST II-II, q. 27, a. 3.

fulfill His will, and we will not cease until we have accomplished it and rest in His presence. But God gave us our nature and so wants us to flourish by obtaining the virtues, living as an image of Himself, and ultimately resting in His presence, all for which we will strive even more for His sake than for our own.[39] Eudaimonism threatens to nourish the sin of pride, but St. Thomas and St. Bonaventure present an ethics of humility.

39. The virtuous agent wills his happiness primarily for God's sake, but also wills it for his own sake. There is a natural love of friendship for oneself that remains even when the theological virtue of charity is infused into one's soul, although it is subordinated to, and less intense than, the love of friendship for God. See ST II-II, q. 19, a. 6.

About the Authors

PRUDENCE ALLEN, R.S.M., PH.D. taught philosophy at Concordia University, Montreal, Quebec, Canada and was named Professor Emeritus in 1996. She was then Professor at the Department of Philosophy, St. John Vianney Theological Seminary, Denver, Colorado and named to the Charles J. Chaput, O.F.M. cap. Chair of Philosophy in 2011. Sister Allen has published a two volume work on *The Concept of Woman* with the third and final volume forthcoming. Retired from academic teaching, she is presently working as the Bishops' Archivist for the Diocese of Lancaster, England and was recently appointed to the International Theological Commission for the term 2015–2019.

JOHN N. DEELY was a founding member of the AMA and the Secretary of the original Constitution Committee. In fact, it was at the second AMA meeting in Washington that Deely met the Maritain scholar (author of *Jacques Maritain: Antimodern or Ultramodern,* Elsevier 1976) Brooke Williams Smith, now Brooke Williams Deely. In 1965–66 the River Forest students were moved to St. Rose Priory in Dubuque, Iowa, where Deely as a Dominican in simple vows ("Brother Nathaniel") found in his assigned choir stall the 1956 edition of Maritain's *Quatre Essais sur L'Esprit dans sa condition charnelle.* This book first acquainted Deely with both Maritain's works on signs and the work of John Poinsot ("*Joannes a Sancto Thoma*"), identified by Maritain as his principal teacher alongside Thomas himself. In 1966–67, in his first year teaching at St. Joseph's College in Rennselaer, Indiana, it was the reading of Maritain's *Les Degrés du Savoir* which led Deely to realize that Heidegger's *Sein* had little to do with the *esse* of Aquinas but everything to do with *esse intentionale* in Aquinas. This enabled him to complete his doctoral dissertation, *The Tradition via Heidegger,* dedicated upon publication (Nijhoff, 1971) to the Maritains. John Howard

Griffin (1920–1980), Maritain's "official photographer" after Jacques joined the Little Brothers of Jesus after Raïssa's death, provided a "letter of introduction" which paved the way for a personal meeting of Deely with Maritain over several hours at Kolbsheim in August of 1972. It was agreed that Deely would attend the following year Maritain's seminar with the Little Brothers, but Jacques' death in April of 1973 made Deely's next visit simply a visit to what had been in 1972 Raïssa's grave, but was now in 1973 also the grave of Jacques himself. Deely is currently "Philosopher in Residence" for Saint Vincent Seminary and College in Latrobe, Pennsylvania.

E. JANE DOERING is Professor emerita of the University of Notre Dame. She has been reading French philosopher Simone Weil for over two decades, starting with a particular interest in her social and political ideas and how that thought evolved after her mystical experience. As a member and officer in both the American Weil Society and the international Association pour l'étude de la pensée de Simone Weil, Professor Doering strives to facilitate communication among Weil scholars around the globe. Her publications include a co-edited volume, *The Christian Platonism of Simone Weil* (Notre Dame Press, 2004), *Simone Weil and the Specter of Self-perpetuating Force* (Notre Dame Press 2010), and over three dozen articles in English, French, and Italian on the multi-dimensional thought of Simone Weil. A recipient of many research grants, she is also very proud to have received the Notre Dame Kaneb Teaching Award. Doering is presently extending her research to include Raïssa Maritain and Flannery O'Connor as contemporaries of Simone Weil.

HEATHER M. ERB is a moderator for the Great Books Academy of the Ignatius-Angelicum Liberal Arts Program. She has served as Assistant Professor of Philosophy at Lock Haven University of Pennsylvania, Fordham, and other universities, and as a senior lecturer in Religious Studies at Penn State. Her publications focus on the nexus between metaphysics and mystical theology in the thought of Aquinas, and her articles on Catholic culture and Aquinas have appeared in *New Oxford Review*, *Verbum* (Hungary), and in Catholic University of America, American Maritain Association, and Vatican collections. She has also written on Boethius in *Logos: A Journal of Catholic Thought and Culture*, and on pagan versus Christian spirituality in "Natural Mysticism—Gateway or Detour? Aquinas, Maritain, and the Core/Contextualist Debate" in John J. Conley, S.J., ed., *Redeeming Philosophy: From Metaphysics to Aesthetics* (2014).

DOUG FLIPPEN received a Licentiate in Mediaeval Studies from P.I.M.S. in Toronto, and received his Ph.D. from the University of Toronto in philosophy. Both these dealt with metaphysics and epistemology. He has taught at the University of St. Thomas in Houston, Carroll College in Montana and, since 1989, at Christendom College in Virginia. His publications include articles in epistemology and natural law theory.

HEIDI M. GIEBEL is Associate Professor of Philosophy at the University of St. Thomas in St. Paul, Minnesota. Her primary interests include Aristotelian-Thomistic and Confucian-Mencian virtue ethics, biomedical ethics, and moral education. She is presently gearing up for a collaborative, interdisciplinary project comparing the self-concepts and life narratives of moral exemplars to those of non-exemplars. She lives in beautiful Hudson, Wisconsin with her husband and ten fabulous children.

BENJAMIN I. HUFF is Associate Professor of Philosophy at Randolph-Macon College. He was educated at Brigham Young University (B.A.) and the University of Notre Dame (Ph.D.), and his interests include virtue ethics, Confucianism, ancient Greek philosophy, and philosophy of religion. His current book project is an analysis of early Confucian ethics as a form of eudaimonism.

JAMES M. JACOBS is Professor of Philosophy and Assistant Academic Dean at Notre Dame Seminary in New Orleans, Louisiana, , where he has taught since 2003. He holds a B.A. from Harvard University and a Ph.D. from Fordham University. His major area of research is Thomistic natural law theory, and more generally the need for a philosophical realism as a response to modern nominalism and skepticism. He served as editor for a previous volume in the American Maritain Association series, *A Piercing Light: Beauty, Faith, and Human Transcendence* (2014).

FLORIAN MICHEL is Associate Professor of Modern History at the University of Paris 1 Panthéon Sorbonne; vice-president of the "Cercle d'études Jacques et Raïssa Maritain" (France); author of *La pensée catholique en Amérique du Nord. Réseaux intellectuels et échanges culturels entre l'Europe, le Canada et les États-Unis (années 1920–1960)* (Paris, Desclée de Brouwer, 2010); editor of the integral Jacques Maritain—Yves Simon correspondance—800 letters, published in two volumes, by Éditions CLD, Paris in 2008 and 2012. Michel is now working on the publication of the complete works of Étienne Gilson.

MARK MOES completed an M.A. in philosophical theology at the Midwest Dominican House of Studies when it was located in Dubuque, Iowa. He received his doctorate in philosophy at the University of Notre Dame. He is currently Associate Professor of Philosophy at Grand Valley State University in Michigan, specializing in Ancient Philosophy and teaching the close reading of Platonic dialogues. He is the author of *Plato's Dialogue Form and the Care of the Soul* and articles on ancient philosophy and philosophy of medicine. He is currently doing research on two connected projects: (1) on the idea of philosophy as a (higer-order) *craft* in Plato and Aristotle and the revival of this idea by modern thinkers such as Jacques Maritain, Michael Polanyi, Charles Taylor, and Alasdair MacIntyre; (2) on the whole corpus of the published writings of Alasdair MacIntyre.

BRENNA MOORE is an Associate Professor of Theology at Fordham University, where she also serves as the Associate Chair for Undergraduate Studies. She is the author of *Sacred Dread: Raïssa Maritain, the Allure of Suffering, and the French Catholic Revival 1904–1944* (Notre Dame University Press, 2013) and researches and teaches broadly in the field of modern Catholicism in Europe.

BERNADETTE E. O'CONNOR is Professor of Philosophy Emerita at the University of the Incarnate Word in San Antonio, Texas. Her research interests are Thomistic metaphysics, the Maritainian concept of connatural knowledge, and Heideggerian *Seinsdenken*. She has five other publications in recent American Maritain Association volumes.

MATTHEW PUGH received his Ph.D. at Fordham and was Associate Professor of Philosophy at Providence College until his untimely death in October 2015. His central research areas were the mediaeval period, Neo-Thomism, and Asian philosophy.

JAMES V. SCHALL, S.J. is Professor Emeritus, Georgetown University. His books include *Jacques Maritain: A Philosopher in Society, At the Limits of Political Philosophy*, and *Revelation & Political Philosophy*.

JOSHUA SCHULZ is Associate Professor of Philosophy at DeSales University, where he teaches moral philosophy in the Catholic intellectual tradition. Often writing about humor, economics, and bioethics, his articles have been published in the *American Catholic Philosophical Quarterly, The*

New Atlantis: A Journal of Technology and Society, and *Logos: A Journal of Catholic Thought and Culture.*

DANIEL SHIELDS is Assistant Professor of Philosophy at the Pontifical College Josephinum, a Roman Catholic seminary in Columbus, Ohio. After receiving his doctorate from the School of Philosophy at The Catholic University of America in Washington, D.C., he spent two years teaching at Xavier University in Cincinnati, Ohio, before moving to Columbus. Having received a B.A. in Liberal Arts from Thomas Aquinas College in southern California, his interests and training are broad, but his main areas of teaching and research are ethics, philosophy of nature and science, and the history of philosophy. With ties to Cleveland and Steubenville, as well, he is firmly planted in the great state of Ohio.

MICHAEL D. TORRE is the President of the American Maritain Association (2012–2016), having previously served as Vice-President of the *Institut International Jacques Maritain*. He is currently a professor of philosophy at the University of San Francisco. He has published two books—*Do Not Resist the Spirit's Call: Francisco Marín-Sola on Sufficient Grace* (The Catholic University of America Press, 2013) and *God's Permission of Sin: Negative or Conditioned Decree?* (Fribourg University Press, 2009)—as well as edited the AMA volume *Freedom in the Modern World: Jacques Maritain, Yves R. Simon, Mortimer J. Adler* (1989; second printing, 1990). He has contributed numerous articles to the AMA series of books, of which he was the General Editor from 2009–2013, bringing to print eight of its volumes.

JASON WEST is currently President of Newman Theological College in Edmonton, Alberta, Canada where he previously taught philosophy since 2005. He is the author of *How to Become a Rational Animal* (Justin Press). His articles on Aquinas, Maritain, MacIntrye, and other subjects have appeared in journals such as *The Journal for the History of Philosophy, The Thomist,* and *Gregorianum.* He is the Past-President of the Canadian Society for Christian Philosophers and is currently writing a book on the thought of Jacques Maritain.

JOHN F. WIPPEL is the Theodore Basselin Professor of Philosophy in the School of Philosophy at The Catholic University of America. He has authored *The Metaphysical Thought of Godfrey of Fontaines* (1981), *Metaphysical*

Themes in Thomas Aquinas (1984), *Boethius of Dacia: 'On the Supreme Good,' On the Eternity of the World,' 'On Dreams'* (1987), *Mediaeval Reactions to the Encounter between Faith and Reason* (1995), *The Metaphysical Thought of Thomas Aquinas* (2000), and *Metaphysical Themes in Thomas Aquinas II* (2007). He has coauthored, edited, or coedited five other volumes including most recently his edition of *The Ultimate Why Question: Why Is There Anything at All Rather than Nothing Whatsoever?* (2011). He has also authored many articles and book-chapters dealing with thirteenth-century thinkers such as Thomas Aquinas, Siger of Brabant, Boethius of Dacia, Henry of Ghent, Giles of Rome, Godfrey of Fontaines, and others.

Index

The Wisdom of Youth: Essays Inspired by the Early Work of Jacques and Raïssa Maritain
was designed in Arno and composed by Kachergis Book Design of Pittsboro,
North Carolina. It was printed on 60-pound House Natural Smooth and
bound by Sheridan Books of Chelsea, Michigan.